W9-BDT-285

THE ART OF
PUBLIC
SPEAKING

THE ART OF PUBLIC SPEAKING

THIRD EDITION

STEPHEN E. LUCAS
University of Wisconsin–Madison

McGraw-Hill Publishing Company
New York   St. Louis   San Francisco   Auckland   Bogotá   Caracas
Hamburg   Lisbon   London   Madrid   Mexico   Milan   Montreal   New Delhi
Oklahoma City   Paris   San Juan   São Paulo   Singapore   Sydney
Tokyo   Toronto

Third Edition
  67890 DOH/DOH 9 9 8 7 6 5 4 3 2 1
Copyright © 1989, 1986, 1983, by Stephen E. Lucas

All rights reserved. Printed in the United States of America. Execpt as permitted
under the United States Copyright Act of 1976, no part of this publication may be
reproduced or distributed in any form or by any means, or stored in a data base or
retrievel system, without the prior written permission of the publisher.

Library of Congress Cataloging-in-Publication Data
Lucas, Stephen.
  The art of public speaking.

    Includes bibliographies and index.
    1. Public speaking.   I. Title.
PN4121.L72   1989   808.5'1   88-18343
ISBN 0-07-555134-9

Chapter Opening Photo Credits: Chapter 1 Gerald Fritz/Monkmeyer; Chapter 2
Ulrike Welsch; Chapter 3 Bohdan Hrynewych/Southern Light; Chapter 4 Sarah
Putnam/The Picture Cube; Chapter 5 Frank Siteman/The Picture Cube; Chapter
6 UPI/Bettmann Newsphotos; Chapter 7 Brent Jones; Chapter 8 Ulrike Welsch;
Chapter 9 Joel Gordon; Chapter 10 Susan Lapides/Design Conceptions; Chapter
11 UPI/Bettmann Newsphotos; Chapter 12 Ulrike Welsch; Chapter 13 Ida Wyman;
Chapter 14 Ulrike Welsch; Chapter 15 Ulrike Welsch; Chapter 16 Bohdan Hry-
newych/Southern Light

Cover: "The Senate Chamber as It May Be" (State Historical Society of Wisconsin)
Hand painted by Janie Paul

Text and cover design: Lorraine Hohman

R. R. Donnelley & Sons Company was printer and binder.

PREFACE

The *Art of Public Speaking* is written for college students enrolled in public speaking classes. This third edition, like its predecessors, seeks to be thorough without being tedious, clear without being mechanical, lively without being frivolous. It reflects my belief that a basic text can maintain the intellectual integrity of speechmaking while meeting the needs and abilities of undergraduate students.

In preparing the third edition, I have retained what professors and students have identified as the main strengths of the previous editions. The book continues to be informed by classical and contemporary theories of rhetoric but does not present theory for its own sake. Keeping a steady eye on the practical skills of public speaking, it offers full coverage of all major aspects of speech preparation and presentation.

Throughout *The Art of Public Speaking* I have followed David Hume's advice that "He who would teach eloquence must do it chiefly by examples." Whenever possible I have tried to *show* the principles of public speaking in addition to telling about them. Thus you will find in the book a large number of narratives and extracts from speeches—set off from the text in a contrasting typeface. There are also many speech outlines and sample speeches. All these are provided so students can *see* how to formulate specific purpose statements, how to analyze and adapt to audiences, how to organize ideas and construct outlines, how to assess evidence and reasoning, how to use language effectively, and so forth.

Because the immediate task facing students is to present speeches in the classroom, I have relied heavily on examples that relate directly to students' classroom needs and experiences. At the same time, however, the classroom is a training ground where students develop skills that will serve them throughout life. Therefore, I have also included a variety of illustrations drawn from the kinds of speaking situations students will face after they graduate— in their careers and in their communities.

FEATURES OF THE THIRD EDITION

Given the favorable response of teachers and students to the first two editions of *The Art of Public Speaking*, I have kept the basic structure of the book intact. At the same time, I have taken advantage of the opportunity afforded by a new edition to make a number of improvements in response to suggestions from readers. These improvements include:

- Greater emphasis on critical thinking, including a new section in Chapter 1 on the relationship between public speaking and critical thinking. The ability to think critically is vital to a world in which personality and image too often substitute for thought and substance. While helping students become capable, responsible speakers, *The Art of Public Speaking* also aims at helping them become capable, responsible thinkers.

- Expanded treatment of the importance of organization in Chapter 7.

- Improved coverage of introductions and conclusions in Chapter 8— including new sample introductions and conclusions (with commentary) and fuller explanation of the ways students can use delivery to enhance the impact of their opening and closing materials.

- A new section on after-dinner speeches in Chapter 15, including a full sample speech.

- Thorough reworking of examples throughout the book to keep the material as clear, stimulating, and up-to-date as possible.

- Six new sample speeches. In addition to the after-dinner speech in Chapter 15, these include fresh speeches with commentary at the ends of Chapter 6 and Chapter 14, as well as replacements for three speeches in the Appendix. As in previous editions, the sample speeches have been carefully selected both for their originality and their pedagogical value.

Besides these changes, I have tried in every chapter to make sure the footnote references reflect current theory and research. My aim has been to maintain the readability of the text while using the footnotes to help students understand that the principles of effective speechmaking have been confirmed by substantial contemporary scholarship as well as by centuries of practical experience.

PLAN OF THE BOOK

One of the biggest challenges in writing a textbook is deciding what to include and in what order to present it. I have tried to structure *The Art of Public Speaking* so its coverage of the material and its sequence of chapters will fit the introductory public speaking class as it is offered at most colleges and universities. Still, only rarely does a textbook line up exactly with an instructor's established syllabus. For this reason I have made each chapter as self-contained as possible. Instructors should have little difficulty adapting the book to their own emphases and teaching methods.

Part One, "Speaking and Listening," introduces the basic principles of speech communication and the respective responsibilities of speakers and listeners. Chapter 1 explains the value of a course in public speaking, examines the basic elements of the speech communication process, and discusses the ethical obligations of public speakers. A major purpose of this chapter is to instill a positive orientation toward speechmaking and toward the speech class. To this end, the chapter confronts what is nearly always uppermost in students' minds at the beginning of the class—stage fright. It also compares public speaking with conversation, stressing the fact that students can build upon many of the skills they already use in everyday communication.

Chapter 2 deals with listening. It shows the importance of good listening, identifies the basic causes of poor listening, and suggests ways to become a better listener. A special feature of this chapter is its explanation of methods for effective note taking.

Part Two, "Speech Preparation: Getting Started," takes up the initial steps of speech preparation. Chapter 3 sets forth criteria for workable speech topics. It offers several methods of finding a topic when one does not spring to mind—including a full discussion of brainstorming. Chapter 3 also uses a variety of examples to clarify how a speaker moves from choosing a topic to formulating a specific purpose and phrasing a sharp central idea.

Chapter 4 introduces the basic principles of audience analysis and explains how to adapt a speech to an audience. Two other features of this chapter are its emphasis on the classroom as an authentic speaking situation, and its explanation of how to use questionnaires as a method of audience analysis for classroom speeches.

Chapter 5 is devoted to gathering speech materials. Since many students do not know how to use the library efficiently, this chapter explains the basic resources and methods of library research. It also explains interviewing techniques—and follows a sample research interview through the entire interview process. Of course, instructors can assign only as much of this chapter as is necessary to meet the needs of their students.

Chapter 6 explains the basic types of supporting materials and presents guidelines for using them effectively. A full student speech, accompanied by a running commentary, illustrates how to work supporting materials into a speech.

Part Three, "Speech Preparation: Organization and Outlining," consists of three chapters. Chapter 7 shows students how to organize the body of a speech. The basic patterns of speech organization are illustrated by many examples, with special attention given to clarifying topical organization. The chapter also has a thorough section on transitions, internal previews, internal summaries, and signposts.

Chapter 8 is devoted to introductions and conclusions, again with many examples. Chapter 9 presents the principles of outlining and exemplifies them with a complete, annotated preparation outline. A sample speaking outline is also provided to show how a detailed preparation outline is transformed into a brief set of speaker's notes.

Part Four, "Presenting the Speech," focuses on language, delivery, and the use of visual aids. Chapter 10 discusses the importance of language and offers a number of practical guides for using language accurately, clearly, vividly, and appropriately. Chapter 11 deals with the basic methods of speech delivery, the use of the speaker's voice, and the role of nonverbal communication in speechmaking. Chapter 12 explains the advantages of visual aids, the kinds of visual aids, and the ways to use visual aids most effectively.

Part Five, "Varieties of Public Speaking," takes up different types of discourse. Chapter 13 focuses on speaking to inform. The first part of the chapter explains how to analyze and organize four basic kinds of informative speeches—speeches about objects, speeches about processes, speeches about events, and speeches about concepts. The second part of the chapter offers guidelines for constructing effective informative speeches. The chapter concludes with an annotated student speech.

In Chapter 14 the topic is persuasive speaking. Here I have tried to give students the information they most need to create effective persuasive speeches—without bogging them down in theoretical issues or excessive jargon. The first part of the chapter explains how to analyze and organize speeches on questions of fact, questions of value, and questions of policy. The second part deals with the special requirements of audience adaptation in persuasive speaking. The third part presents persuasive methods—building credibility, using evidence, reasoning, and appealing to emotions. A sample student speech with commentary shows how these methods work together. All in all, I believe you will find that this chapter offers an unusually clear and practical introduction to persuasive speaking.

Chapter 15 deals with speeches for special occasions; each section of the chapter includes at least one full sample speech. Chapter 16 is designed for instructors who include a unit on group discussion in their classes.

RESOURCES FOR INSTRUCTORS

The Art of Public Speaking has a number of instructional resources to help students learn and apply the principles of effective speechmaking. As noted earlier, Chapters 6, 13, and 14 contain sample speeches with commentary. Chapter 9 has a complete preparation outline and speaking outline, both with commentary. The Appendix consists of six additional speeches for discussion and analysis. These Apendix speeches have been chosen to illustrate particular aspects of speechmaking, and all of them are dealt with in the chapter exercises.

A set of application exercises accompanies each chapter. The exercises are written assignments that students can complete on their own, in conjunction with reading assignments. They can also be used as the basis for classroom activities and discussion. In keeping with the importance of critical thinking and the experiential nature of speechmaking, these exercises require that students *work with* (rather than simply memorize) the principles presented in the book. The wide range of exercises—in the text and in the *Instructor's Manual*—should give instructors maximum flexibility in choosing those best suited for their students.

The *Instructor's Manual* contains supplementary exercises, speeches, and classroom activities; offers suggested course outlines and speaking assignments; provides synopses of the Appendix speeches; and gives a bibliography of additional teaching and learning resources.

There are also two videotapes of sample speeches that accompany *The Art of Public Speaking.* One was developed in conjunction with the second edition; the other is new to this edition. Taken together, they provide over a dozen speeches—informative and persuasive—that allow students to see the principles of effective speechmaking in action. A guide to each videotape is also available for instructors.

ACKNOWLEDGMENTS

Ralph Waldo Emerson said, " 'Tis the good reader that makes the good book." I have been fortunate to have very good readers indeed, and I would like to thank the following reviewers for their comments and suggestions: Jerry L. Allen, University of Bridgeport; David E. Axon, Johnson County Community College; Carl R. Burgchardt, Colorado State University; Randall Bytwerk, Calvin College; Kathryn J. French, University of Southern California; Thurmon Garner, University of Georgia; Thomas B. Harte, Southeast Missouri State University; Anne Holmquest, University of Louisville; Christopher Johnstone, Pennsylvania State University; Lawrence J. Rifkind, Georgia State University; Michael R. Schliessmann, South Dakota State University; Leah Slessinger, Post College; Geneva Smitherman-Donaldson, Wayne State University; William M. Strickland, University of South Carolina; Jeffrey Stromer, Queensborough Community College; Aileen Sundstrom, Henry Ford Community College; Susan M. Thomas, University of Illinois at Urbana–Champaign; Paul Trent, Mercy College; and James L. Wolford, Joliet Junior College.

I would also like to thank members of the Communication Arts 101 teaching staff at the University of Wisconsin–Madison who have helped me by collecting sample speeches, by identifying rough spots in the second edition, and by testing new exercises and assignments in the classroom. Among the people who deserve special mention in this regard are Mary Giovagnoli, Cherri Roden, Kristin Vonnegut, Lisa Glueck, Ken Hardy, Susan Zickmund, Andrea Dolan, Andy Sachs, Laura Sells, Kathy D'alessandro, Chuck Benesh, Bonny Donzella, Janie Harden, Greg Boiarsky, and Maggie Censky.

In addition, I am grateful to the students in Communication Arts 101 whose speeches provided the material for so many of the examples in the book; to Amy Slagell, who assisted with the instructor's manual; to Professor Larry Schnoor, Executive Director of the Interstate Oratorical Association, for permission to reprint from *Winning Orations*, to professor Richard Street, who prepared the initial draft of the chapter on group discussion; and to Jeffrey Lucas, who tabulated the survey results reported in Chapter 13.

I am also indebted to the many talented people at McGraw-Hill who have contributed to this edition. They include Roth Wilkofsky, Bob Greiner, Lorraine Hohman, Della Mancuso, Suzanne Thibodeau, Safra Nimrod, Harold Vaughn, Chris Migdol, and, above all, Kathleen Domenig, who is, without question, the best speech editor in the business. As always, my wife, Patty, has been invaluable for her counsel and her support, while Ryan Lucas has been a constant source of good cheer.

Finally, I would like to dedicate this edition in memory of my mother, to whom I owe so much and from whom I first learned the value of a good book.

Stephen E. Lucas
Madison, Wisconsin

CONTENTS

PART TWO
SPEECH PREPARATION: GETTING STARTED   43

CHAPTER 6 ▪ SUPPORTING YOUR IDEAS   116

PART THREE
SPEECH PREPARATION:
ORGANIZING AND OUTLINING   143

CHAPTER 7 ▪ ORGANIZING THE BODY OF THE SPEECH   144

PART FOUR
PRESENTING THE SPEECH   205

PART FIVE
VARIETIES OF PUBLIC SPEAKING   271

PART ONE

SPEAKING
AND
LISTENING

Speaking in Public

An old English proverb says "talk is cheap." Whoever coined that phrase obviously did not anticipate the latter part of the twentieth century. Nowadays, talk—good talk—can be very expensive indeed. The burden of this expense falls heavily both on those who wish to hear accomplished speakers and on those who wish to become accomplished speakers.

Throughout our country's history there have been people who earned a living by working the lecture circuit—traveling from city to city, town to town, delivering speeches as a form of entertainment or information to paying audiences. Today, however, the pay for such speechmaking has reached new heights. A polished speaker with expertise in some area of interest may command thousands of dollars for a single speech. Top-ranked stars of the lecture circuit—such as Walter Cronkite, Henry Kissinger, and Barbara Walters—are paid $20,000 or more per speech.

How do such people learn the art of public speaking? A few are "naturals" who seem to be born with the talent. Some have had the benefit of public speaking courses in college, like the one you are taking now. Others do it the expensive way. They seek private instruction in speechmaking, which can cost as much as $3,500 for six hours of individual work. No, talk is *not* cheap!

We should not be surprised that people place such a high value on public speaking. Throughout the history of Western civilization, this art has been a vital means of communication. What the Greek statesman Pericles said nearly twenty-five centuries ago is just as true today: "One who forms a judgment on any point but cannot explain himself clearly . . . might as well never have thought at all on the subject." In modern times, many men and women have spread their ideas and influence largely by public speaking. The list would include Susan B. Anthony, Franklin Roosevelt, Winston Churchill, Billy Graham, Martin Luther King, Barbara Jordan, Ronald Reagan, and Jesse Jackson.

As you read these names, you may think to yourself, "That's fine. Good for them. But what does that have to do with me? I don't plan to be a president or a preacher, or a crusader for any cause." Nevertheless the need for effective public speaking will almost certainly touch you sometime in your life—maybe tomorrow, maybe not for five years.[1] Can you imagine yourself in any of these situations?

You are a management trainee in a large corporation. Altogether, there are seven trainees in the program. One of you will get the lower-management job that has just opened. There is to be a large staff meeting, at which each of the trainees will discuss the project he or she has been developing. One by one your colleagues make their presentations. They have no experience in public speaking and are intimidated by the higher-ranking managers present. Their speeches are stumbling and awkward. You, however, call upon all the skills you learned in your public speaking course. You deliver an informative talk that is clear, well-reasoned, and articulate. You get the job.

You are married and have three children. One of your children has a learning disability. You hear that your local school board has decided, for budget reasons, to eliminate the special teacher who has been helping your child. At an open meeting of the school board, you stand up and deliver a thoughtful, compelling speech on the necessity for keeping the special teacher. The school board changes its mind.

You are the assistant manager in a branch office of a national company. Your immediate superior, the branch manager, is about to retire, and there will be a retirement dinner. All the executives from the home office will attend. As his close working associate, you are asked to give a farewell toast at the party. You prepare and deliver a speech that is both witty and touching—a perfect tribute to your boss. After the speech, everyone applauds enthusiastically, and a few people have tears in their eyes. The following week you are named branch manager.

Fantasies? Of course they are. Although any one of them could actually happen, in real life we cannot expect such uniformly happy endings. Yet happy endings *do* occur in life, and sometimes they are brought about by public speaking. The point is that effective public speaking *can* make a difference in things you care about very much.

The key phrase here is "make a difference." That is what most of us want to do in life—to make a difference, to change the world in some small way, to leave a mark of ourselves. Public speaking offers you at least three possibilities for making a difference—by *persuading* people to do something you feel is right; by *informing* people about things they do not know; or by *entertaining* people and making them feel happy and good about themselves. Look back for a moment at our three hypothetical situations. The first involves informing (about your business project). The second involves persuading (to keep the special teacher). And the third involves entertaining (in a witty speech at the party). These are the three major goals of public speaking—to persuade, to inform, to entertain. They are also the three major goals of everyday conversation.

SIMILARITIES BETWEEN PUBLIC SPEAKING AND CONVERSATION

How much time do you spend each day in talking to other people? The average adult spends about 30 percent of his or her waking hours in conversation. As you will see, there are many similarities between daily conversation and public speaking.

Children learn the art of conversation by trial and error. A baby cries to inform his mother that the diaper needs changing. A toddler says "Cookie!" to persuade her father to give her a snack. A five-year-old tells a little story to entertain grandma and gain admiration. If none of these things works—the diaper stays wet, the cookie isn't forthcoming, grandma is not amused—well, back to the drawing board. Next time the child will try it a slightly different way.

By the time you read this book, you will have spent a minimum of seventeen years perfecting the art of conversation. You may not realize it, but you already employ a wide range of skills when talking to people. These skills include the following:

1. *Organizing your thoughts logically.* Suppose you were giving someone directions to get to your house. You wouldn't do it this way:

> When you turn off the highway, you'll see a big diner on the left. But before that, stay on the highway to Exit 67. Usually a couple of the neighbors' dogs are in the street, so go slow after you turn at the blinking light. Coming from your house you get on the highway through Maple Street. If you pass the taco stand, you've gone too far. The house is blue.

Instead, you would take your listener systematically, step by step, from his or her house to your house. You would organize your message.

2. *Tailoring your message to your audience.* You are a geology major. Two people ask you how pearls are formed. One is your roommate; the other is your nine-year-old niece. You answer as follows:

> *To your roommate:* "When any irritant, say a grain of sand, gets inside the oyster's shell, the oyster automatically secretes a substance called nacre, which is principally calcium carbonate and is the same material that lines the oyster's shell. The nacre accumulates in layers around the irritant core to form the pearl."

> *To your niece:* "Imagine you're an oyster on the ocean floor. A grain of sand gets inside your shell and makes you uncomfortable. So you decide to cover it up. You cover it with a material called mother-of-pearl. The covering builds up around the grain of sand to make a pearl."

3. *Telling a story for maximum impact.* Suppose you are telling a friend about a funny incident at last week's football game. You don't begin with the punch line ("Jenny fell out of the stands right onto the field. Here's how it started. . . ."). Instead, you carefully build up your story, adjusting your words and tone of voice to get the best effect.

4. *Adapting to listener feedback.* Whenever you talk with someone, you are aware of that person's reactions—verbal, facial, and physical. For example:

> You are explaining an interesting point that came up in biology class. Your listener begins to look confused, puts up a hand as though to stop you, and says "Huh?" You go back and explain more clearly.

> A friend has asked you to listen while she practices a speech. At the end you say, "There's just one part I really don't like—that quotation from the attorney general." Your friend looks very hurt and says, "That was my favorite part!" So you say, "But if you just worked the quotation in a little differently it would be wonderful."

Each day, in casual conversation, you do all these things many times without thinking about them. You already possess these communication skills.[2] And these are among the most important skills you will need for public speaking.

To illustrate, let's return briefly to one of the hypothetical situations at the beginning of this chapter. When addressing the school board about the need for a special teacher:

You *organize* your ideas to present them in the most persuasive manner. You steadily build up a case about how the teacher benefits the school.

You *tailor your message* to your audience. This is no time to launch an impassioned defense of special education in the United States. You must show how the issue is important to the people in that very room—to their children and to the school.

You tell your story for *maximum impact.* Perhaps you relate an anecdote to demonstrate how much your child has improved. You also have statistics to show how many other children have been helped.

You *adapt to listener feedback.* When you mention the cost of the special teacher, you notice sour looks on the faces of the school board members. So you patiently explain how small that cost is in relation to the overall school budget.

In many ways, then, public speaking requires the same skills used in ordinary conversation. Most people who communicate well in daily talk can learn to communicate just as well in public speaking. By the same token, training in public speaking can make you a more adept communicator in a variety of situations such as conversations, classroom discussions, business meetings, and interviews.

DIFFERENCES BETWEEN PUBLIC SPEAKING AND CONVERSATION

Despite their many similarities, public speaking and everyday conversation are not identical. Let's consider an example in which casual conversation expanded gradually into a true—and vital—public speaking situation. Here the speaker originally had no intention of becoming a *public* speaker and had not trained formally for that role. She was forced to learn by trial and error—in circumstances where her efforts could affect both life and death:

At one time, Sheila Petersen's world focused on the small town of North Salem, north of New York City, where she lives with her husband and children. Petersen taught first grade and served on the school board. She had always been involved with children, but her concern was private until tragedy struck another family. In 1978, a couple who were friends of the Petersens learned that their adopted daughter Karen, then aged 14, had La Fora's disease—a rare, genetically transmitted, and always fatal

Many skills used in conversation also apply to public speaking. As you learn to speak more effectively in public, you may also learn to communicate more effectively in other situations.
(Rae Russell)

illness. The family wanted to bring Karen home to die, but they could not afford the immense cost of home care. Then Sheila Petersen went into action.

She began talking to people—friends, neighbors, anyone who would listen. Her message was simple: We must do something to help. But conversations with a few people would not solve the problem. What was needed was money—a lot of money. Soon Petersen started the project called ''Friends of Karen'' as a means of raising donations. To support the fund-raising, Petersen found herself in many public speaking situations—service clubs, schools, church groups. As people started listening, Petersen learned to adapt her conversational style to larger audiences and more structured speaking situations. The spontaneous give-and-take of conversation evolved into speeches prepared in advance.

Then the media began to pay attention. Petersen was interviewed for newspaper articles, radio broadcasts, and local television newscasts. Again she had to adapt her speaking technique—this time, to meet the demands of a two- or three-minute on-the-air spot. Petersen met these challenges, and money began pouring in. Karen came home from the hospital, and in 1979 died peacefully in her own bed.

Although Sheila Petersen might have thought her brief career as a public speaker was over, it had barely started. Soon other families with sick children began appealing to her for help. Friends of Karen became a full-scale organization, and to date it has helped hundreds of families of terminally ill children. As the need for funds has increased, so have Petersen's speaking responsibilities. Today she delivers over 120 speeches a year—exclusive of radio, television, and newspaper interviews—to spread her message of caring. ''If you had told me ten years ago I'd be giving that many speeches,'' she remarks, ''I'd have said you were crazy. But when you have ideas you want to get across, and a program that must be supported, you find a way to do it.''

Sheila Petersen traveled quite a distance in ten years—from conversations with friends and neighbors to a regular schedule of speeches to audiences that often number in the hundreds. While the role of public speaker was far from her mind a decade ago, she discovered that when you *must* get people to listen, you *learn* how to make them listen. A major part of the learning process involved adapting her natural speaking style. In conversation with friends, Petersen's speech could be termed "volcanic." She erupts. She talks a mile a minute, interrupts herself, circles around and back, overflows with enthusiasm. For a more formal speaking situation, however, this would not be appropriate, so Petersen learned to temper and structure her normal style; eventually she transformed herself into an effective, compelling public speaker.

As her responsibilities expanded, Sheila Petersen had to adapt to three major differences between conversation and public speaking:

1. *Public speaking is more highly structured.* It usually imposes strict time limitations on the speaker. In most cases, the situation does not allow listeners to interrupt with questions or commentary. The speaker must accomplish his or her purpose *in the speech itself.* In preparing the speech, the speaker must anticipate questions that might arise in the minds of listeners and answer them. Consequently, public speaking demands much more detailed planning and preparation than ordinary conversation.

2. *Public speaking requires more formal language.* Slang, jargon, and bad grammar have little place in public speeches. Despite the increasing informality of many aspects of American life, listeners usually react negatively to speakers who do not elevate and polish their language when addressing an audience. A speech is supposed to be "special."

3. *Public speaking requires a different method of delivery.* When conversing informally, most people talk rather quietly, interject stock phrases such as "you know" and "I mean," adopt a casual posture, and use what are called vocalized pauses ("uh," "er," "um"). Effective public speakers, however, adjust their voices to be heard clearly throughout the audience. They assume a more erect posture. They avoid distracting mannerisms and verbal habits.

With study and practice, you will be able to master these differences and expand your conversational skills into speechmaking. Your speech class will provide the opportunity for this study and practice.

DEVELOPING CONFIDENCE: YOUR SPEECH CLASS

One of the major concerns of students in any speech class is stage fright. We may as well face the issue squarely. Many people who converse easily in all kinds of everyday situations become frightened at the idea of standing up before a group to make a speech. If you are worried about stage fright, you may feel better knowing you are not alone. A survey conducted in 1973 asked more than 2,500 Americans to list their greatest fears. To the surprise of the researchers, the largest number of people—41 percent—listed speaking before a group among their greatest fears. By contrast, only 18 percent included death as one of their greatest fears.[3] Amazing as it may seem, many Americans appear to consider public speaking a fate worse than death.

In a more recent study, conducted at the University of Tulsa and the University of Iowa College of Medicine, researchers concentrated on social situations and, again, asked their subjects to list their greatest fears. Here is how they responded:[4]

GREATEST FEAR	PERCENT NAMING
A party with strangers	74
Giving a speech	70
Asked personal questions in public	65
Meeting a date's parents	59
First day on a new job	59
Victim of a practical joke	56
Talking with someone in authority	53
Job interview	46
Formal dinner party	44
Blind date	42

Again, speechmaking ranks near the top in provoking anxiety.

Nervousness Is Normal

Actually, most people tend to be anxious about doing anything important in public. Actors are nervous before a play; politicians are nervous before a campaign speech; athletes are nervous before a big game. The ones who succeed have learned to use their nervousness to their advantage. Listen to tennis star Martina Navratilova, speaking after her match against Chris Evert Lloyd in the 1981 U.S. Open: "I was psyched up for today's match. I was *so* nervous! Had the butterflies in the stomach. I've never been that way for the Open." Putting her butterflies to good use, Navratilova beat Lloyd two sets to one.

Much the same thing happens in speechmaking. Surveys show that 76 percent of experienced speakers have stage fright before taking the floor.[5] But their nervousness is a healthy sign that they are getting "psyched up" for a good effort. Novelist and lecturer I. A. R. Wylie explains: "Now after many years of practice I am, I suppose, really a 'practiced speaker.' But I rarely rise to my feet without a throat constricted with terror and a furiously thumping heart. When, for some reason, I *am* cool and self-assured the speech is always a failure."[6]

In other words, it is perfectly normal—even desirable—to be nervous at the start of a speech. The question is: How can you control your nervousness and make it work for you rather than against you?

Dealing with Nervousness

You have already taken the first step. You are enrolled in a public speaking course, where you will learn about speechmaking and gain speaking experience. Think back to your first day at kindergarten, your first date, your first day at a new job. You were probably nervous in each situation because you were facing something new and unknown. Once you became accustomed to the situation, it was no longer threatening. So it is with public speaking. For most students, the biggest part of stage fright is fear of the unknown. The more you learn about public speaking and the more speeches you give, the less threatening speechmaking will become.[7]

Your speech class will provide knowledge and experience to help you speak with confidence. Of course, the road to confidence will sometimes be bumpy. Learning to give a speech is not much different from learning any other skill—it proceeds by trial and error. The purpose of your speech class is to shorten the process, to minimize the errors, to give you a nonthreatening arena—a sort of laboratory—in which to undertake the "trial." Your teacher recognizes that you are a novice and is trained to give the kind of guidance you need to get started. In your fellow students you have a highly sympathetic audience who will provide valuable feedback to help you improve your speaking skills. As the class goes on, your fears about public speaking will gradually recede until they are replaced by only a healthy nervousness before you rise to speak.[8]

Another key to gaining confidence is to pick speech topics you truly care about—and then to prepare your speeches so thoroughly you cannot help but be successful. Here is how one student combined enthusiasm for his topic with thorough preparation to score a triumph in speech class:*

Mike Roberts was a quiet fellow. He certainly didn't seem the type to be a strong public speaker. Even around his friends he was soft-spoken. Everyone wondered how he would survive his speech class. But when the time came for Mike's first speech, his friends got a surprise.

Mike's topic for the speech was the technique of cardiopulmonary resuscitation (CPR). Mike had spent his last three summers working as a lifeguard and had saved the lives of two people by using CPR. He believed strongly that everyone should learn the procedure. To communicate the various steps of CPR, he prepared a series of diagrams. Even better, he borrowed from the local Red Cross a life-size dummy of a human torso on which he could demonstrate the technique.

As Mike spoke, it became clear he was enthusiastic about his subject and

---

* Like most of the examples in the book, this one is based on a true story. Usually the names have been changed and the situations altered slightly to protect privacy.

genuinely wanted his classmates to share his enthusiasm. Because he was intent on communicating with his audience, he forgot to be nervous. He spoke clearly, fluently, and dynamically. Soon the entire class was engrossed in his speech.

Afterward, Mike admitted that he had surprised even himself. ''It was amazing,'' he said. ''Once I passed the first minute or so, all I thought about were those people out there listening. I could tell I was really getting through to them.''

A speech is much like a play. While the actual performance of a play may take no more than two hours, those two hours represent the final, polished product of hundreds of hours of work. Of course, you will not spend hundreds of hours preparing a speech. But like an actor who rehearses a role until it is just right, you will find that your confidence as a speaker increases when you work on a speech until it is just right.

If you follow the techniques suggested by your teacher and in the rest of this book, you will stand up for every speech fully prepared. Imagine that the day for your first speech has arrived. You have studied your audience and selected a topic you know will interest them. You have researched the speech thoroughly and practiced it several times until it feels absolutely comfortable. You have even tried it out before two or three trusted friends. The subject is one you feel strongly about. How can you help but be confident of success?

Besides stressing the importance of being fully prepared, your teacher will probably give you several tips for dealing with nervousness in your first speeches. They may include:[9]

- Think positively. Visualize yourself giving a strong, effective speech. Confidence is mostly the well-known power of positive thinking. If you think you can do it, you usually can do it.

- Be at your best physically and mentally. It is not a good idea to stay up until 4:00 A.M. partying with friends or cramming for an exam the night before your speech. A good night's sleep will serve you better.

- Concentrate on communicating with your audience rather than on worrying about your nervousness. If you get caught up in your speech, your audience will too.

- Take a couple of deep breaths before you start to speak. It really does help to get a healthy dose of oxygen into your system.

- Work especially hard on your introduction. The butterflies in your stomach will be most active at the start of a speech. A good introduction will help calm them down and build your confidence for the rest of your speech.

- Make eye contact with members of your audience. Remember they are individual people, not a blur of faces. And they are your friends.

- Use visual aids. They create interest, draw attention away from you, and make you feel less self-conscious.

It may also help you to know that your listeners probably won't realize how tense you are—especially if you do your best to act confident on the outside. Most of the time when students confess after a speech, "I was so nervous I thought I was going to die," their classmates are surprised. To them the speaker looked calm and self-assured.[10]

Even if you do make a mistake during a speech, that is no catastrophe. Consider the plight of Princess Diana of England. During her wedding to Prince Charles, faced by platoons of cameras and lights and microphones, with virtually the whole world listening, she managed to garble the names of her almost-husband. Nobody thought she had made a fool of herself. Instead, that one small error in an otherwise flawless performance only made her seem more human.

If you are like most students, you will find your speech class to be a very positive experience. As one student wrote on her course evaluation form at the end of the class:

> I was really dreading this class. The idea of giving all those speeches scared me half to death. But I'm glad now that I stuck with it. It's a small class, and I got to know a lot of the students. Besides that, this is one class in which I got to express *my* ideas, instead of spending the whole time listening to the teacher talk. I even came to enjoy giving the speeches. I could tell at times that the audience was really with me, and that's a great feeling.

Over the years thousands of students have developed confidence in their speechmaking abilities. As your confidence grows, you will be better able to stand before other people and tell them what you think and feel and know— and to make them think and feel and know those same things. The best part about confidence is that it nurtures itself. After you score your first triumph, you will be that much more confident the next time. And as you become a more confident public speaker, you will likely become more confident in other areas of your life as well.

PUBLIC SPEAKING AND CRITICAL THINKING

> That guy at the party last night really demolished me when we got into a discussion. I know my information is right, and I'm sure there was something wrong with his argument, but I can't put my finger on it.

> I need a word processor, and every television commercial says its brand is state-of-the-art. But which is really the best buy for me?

> I've worked hard on my term paper, but I'm not satisfied. It just doesn't seem to hang together, and I can't figure out what's wrong.

> Political speeches are so confusing. The candidates talk and talk, and they make everything sound rosy, but I still don't know whom to vote for.

Do any of these situations sound familiar? Have you ever found yourself in similar situations? If so, you may find help in your speech class.[11] Besides building confidence, a course in public speaking can develop your skills as a critical thinker. Those skills can make the difference between the articulate debater and the pushover, the careful consumer and the easy mark, the A student and the C student, the thoughtful voter and the coin-tosser.,

What is critical thinking? To some extent, it is a matter of logic—of being able to spot weaknesses in other people's arguments and to avoid them in your own. It also involves such related skills as distinguishing fact from opinion, judging the credibility of statements, and assessing the soundness of evidence. In the broadest sense, critical thinking is focused, organized thinking—the ability to see clearly the relationships among ideas. It has often been said that there are few new ideas in the world, only reorganized ideas. The greatest thinkers, scientists, and inventors have often taken information that was readily available and put it together differently to produce new insights. That, too, is critical thinking.

If you are wondering what this has to do with your public speaking class, the answer is quite a lot. As the class proceeds, for example, you will probably spend a good deal of time organizing your speeches. While this may seem like a purely mechanical exercise, it is closely interwoven with critical thinking. If the structure of your speech is disjointed and confused, odds are your thinking is also disjointed and confused. If, on the other hand, the structure is clear and cohesive, there is a good chance your thinking is too. Organizing a speech is not just a matter of arranging the ideas you already have. Rather, it is an important part of shaping the ideas themselves.

What is true of organization is true of many aspects of public speaking. The skills you learn in your speech class can help you become a more effective thinker in a number of ways. As you work on expressing your ideas in clear, accurate language, you will enhance your ability to think clearly and accurately. As you study the role of evidence and reasoning in speechmaking, you will see how they can be used in other forms of communication as well. As you learn to listen critically to speeches in class, you will be better able to assess the ideas of speakers (and writers) in a variety of situations.[12]

To return to the four examples at the beginning of this section:

That guy at the party last night—would sharpened critical thinking have helped you pounce on the flaws in his argument?

Buying a word processor—are television commercials a reliable source of information, or should you try to find out more about prices and the features you need?

The term paper—would better organization and a clear outline help pull it together?

The politicians—once you filter out the fluff, are they drawing valid conclusions from sound evidence?

The powers of analysis you develop in researching and organizing speeches are also vital to critical thinking and listening.
(Susan Lapides/Design Conceptions)

If you take full advantage of your speech class, you will be able to enhance your skills as a critical thinker in many circumstances. This is one reason public speaking has been regarded as a vital part of education since the days of ancient Greece.

THE SPEECH COMMUNICATION PROCESS

As you begin your first speeches, you may find it helpful to understand what goes on when one person talks to another. Regardless of the kind of speech communication involved, there are seven elements—speaker, message, channel, listener, feedback, interference, and situation. Here we shall focus on how these elements interact when a public speaker addresses an audience.[13]

Speaker

Speech communication begins with a speaker. If you pick up the telephone and call a friend, you are acting as a speaker. (Of course, you will also act as a listener when your friend is talking.) In public speaking, you will usually present your entire speech without interruption.

Your success as a speaker depends on *you*—on your personal credibility, your knowledge of the subject, your preparation of the speech, your manner of speaking, your sensitivity to the audience and the occasion. But successful speaking is more than a matter of technical skill. It also requires enthusiasm. You can't expect people to be interested in what you say unless you are interested yourself. If you are truly excited about your subject, your audience is almost sure to get excited along with you. You can learn all the techniques of effective speechmaking; but before they can be of much use, you must first have something to say—something that sparks your own enthusiasm.

Message

The message is whatever a speaker communicates to someone else. If you are calling a friend, you might say, "I'll be a little late picking you up tonight." That is the message. But it may not be the only message. Perhaps there is a certain tone in your voice that suggests reluctance, hesitation. The underlying message might be "I really don't want to go to that party. You talked me into it, but I'm going to put it off as long as I can."

Your goal in public speaking is to have your *intended* message be the message that is *actually* communicated. Achieving this depends both on what you say (the verbal message) and on how you say it (the nonverbal message).

Getting the verbal message just right requires work. You must narrow your topic down to something you can discuss adequately in the time allowed for the speech. You must do research and choose supporting details to make your ideas clear and convincing. You must organize your ideas so listeners can follow them without getting lost. And you must express your message in words that are accurate, clear, vivid, and appropriate.

Besides the message you send with words, you also send a message with your tone of voice, appearance, gestures, facial expression, and eye contact. Imagine that one of your classmates gets up to speak about student loans. Throughout her speech she slumps behind the lectern, takes long pauses to remember what she wants to say, stares at the ceiling, and fumbles with her visual aids. Her intended message is "We must make more money available for student loans." But the message she actually communicates is "I haven't prepared very well for this speech." One of your jobs as a speaker is to make sure your nonverbal message does not distract from your verbal message.

Channel

The channel is the means by which a message is communicated. When you pick up the phone to call a friend, the telephone is the channel. Public speakers may use one or more of several channels—each of which will affect the message received by the audience.

Consider a speech to Congress by the President of the United States. The speech is carried to the nation by the channels of radio and television. For the radio audience the message is conveyed entirely by the President's voice. They can hear him, but they can't see him. For the television audience the message is conveyed by both the President's voice and the televised image of the President and his surroundings. The people in Congress have a more direct channel. They hear the President's voice as amplified through a microphone, but they can see him and the setting at firsthand.

In a public speaking class your channel is the most direct of all. Your classmates will see you and hear you without any electronic intervention.

Listener

The listener is the person who receives the communicated message. Without a listener, there is no communication. When you talk to a friend on the phone, you have one listener. In public speaking you will have many listeners.

Everything a speaker says is filtered through a listener's *frame of reference*—the total of his or her knowledge, experience, goals, values, and attitudes. Because a speaker and a listener are different people, they can never have exactly the same frame of reference. And because a listener's frame of reference can never be exactly the same as a speaker's, the meaning of a message will never be exactly the same to a listener as to a speaker.

You can test the impact of different frames of reference quite easily. Ask each of your classmates to describe a chair. If you have fifteen classmates, you'll probably get fifteen different descriptions. One student might picture a large, overstuffed easy chair, another an elegant straight-backed chair, yet another an office chair, a fourth a rocking chair, and so on. Even if two or more envision the same general type—say a rocking chair—their mental images of the chair could still be different. One might be thinking of an early American rocker, another of a modern Scandinavian rocker—the possibilities are unlimited. And "chair" is a fairly simple concept. What about "patriotism" or "freedom"?

Because people have different frames of reference, a public speaker must take great care to adapt the message to the particular audience being addressed. To be an effective speaker, you must be *audience-centered*. You must do everything in your speech with your audience in mind. You cannot assume that listeners will be interested in what you have to say. You must understand their point of view as you prepare the speech, and you must work to get them involved. You will quickly lose your listeners' attention if your presentation is either too basic or too sophisticated. You will also lose your audience if you do not relate to *their* experience, interests, knowledge, and values. When you make a speech that causes listeners to say "That is important to *me*," you will almost always be successful.

Feedback

When the President addresses the nation on television, he is engaged in one-way communication. You can talk back to the television set, but the

President won't hear you. Most situations, however, involve *two-way* communication. Your listeners don't simply absorb your message like human sponges. They send back messages of their own. These messages are called feedback.

For example, when you phone your friend to say you will be late, you may hear, "Oh, no you don't! I don't care *what* your problem is, you get here on time!" That is feedback.

This kind of verbal give-and-take is unusual in public speaking. Still, there is always plenty of feedback to let you know how your message is being received. Do your listeners lean forward in their seats, as if paying close attention? Do they applaud in approval? Do they laugh at your jokes? Do they have quizzical looks on their faces? Do they shuffle their feet and gaze at the clock? The message sent by these reactions could be "I am fascinated," "I am bored," "I agree with you," "I don't agree with you," or any number of others. As a speaker, you need to be alert to these reactions and adjust your message accordingly.

Like any kind of communication, feedback is affected by one's frame of reference. How would you feel if, immediately after your speech, all your classmates started to rap their knuckles on the desks? Would you run out of the room in despair? Not if you were in a European university. In many parts of Europe, students rap their knuckles to show great admiration for a classroom lecture. You must understand the feedback to be able to deal with it.

We can now begin to draw a model of the speech communication process. Figure 1.1 illustrates the two-way—or, more accurately, circular—movement of ideas from speaker to listener and back.

There are still two more elements we must consider to understand fully what happens in speech communication.

Interference

Interference is anything that impedes the communication of a message. When you talk on the telephone, sometimes there is static and occasionally wires get

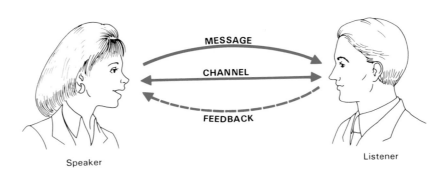

Speaker   Listener

FIGURE 1.1

crossed in such a way that two different conversations are going on at once. That is a kind of interference. Many classrooms are subject to interference—from traffic outside the building, the clatter of a radiator, students conversing in the hall. Any of these can distract your listeners from what you are saying.

There are also other sources of interference. Many of them come from *within* your audience, rather than from the outside. Perhaps one of your listeners has a bad mosquito bite or a patch of poison ivy. She may be so distracted by the itch that she doesn't pay attention to your speech. Another may be worrying about a test coming up in the next class period. Yet another could be brooding about a fight he had with his girlfriend.

As a speaker, you must try to hold your listeners' attention despite these various kinds of interference. In the chapters that follow you will find many ways to do this. Now we must add only one more element to complete the model.

Situation

The situation is the time and place in which speech communication occurs. Conversation always takes place in a certain situation. Sometimes the situation helps—as when you propose marriage over an intimate candlelight dinner. Other times it may hurt—as when you try to speak words of love in competition with a blaring jukebox. When you have to talk with someone about a touchy issue, you usually wait until the situation is just right.

Public speakers must also be alert to the situation. Certain occasions—funerals, church services, graduation ceremonies—require certain kinds of speeches. Physical setting is also important. It makes a great deal of difference whether a speech is presented indoors or out, in a small classroom or in a gymnasium, to a densely packed crowd or to a handful of scattered souls. When you adjust to the situation of a public speech, you are only doing on a larger scale what you do every day in conversation.

Now let us look at a complete model of the speech communication process, as shown in Figure 1.2.[14]

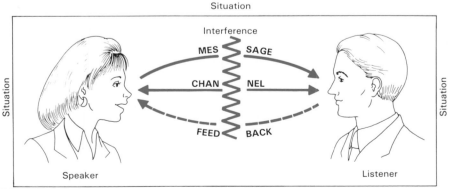

FIGURE 1.2

The Speech Communication Process: Example with Commentary

The following example shows how the various components of the speech communication process interact:

Situation	*It was the Fourth of July, and a large crowd had gathered for the annual town picnic.* Everyone was in a festive mood and looking forward to the fireworks that would come later in the evening. The mayor had made a speech, and so had the president of the historical society. Then
Speaker	it was time for *Michael Chen,* chairman of the town's Interfaith Council, to speak.
Listeners	As Michael walked toward the podium to address the *picnickers,* he knew he faced a difficult task. He hoped to persuade them *to*
Message	*organize and staff a food kitchen for poor people.* Most of those gathered for the Fourth of July celebration, Michael knew, led extremely busy lives, with jobs, family responsibilities, and other community work. They would not readily accept the added chore of running a food kitchen.
Channel	Michael stepped up to the *microphone* and began his speech. He told the gathering about the many homeless, ill-fed people who lived in their community, side by side with prosperity. He urged them to take an active part in feeding the hungry by starting a food kitchen.
Feedback	At first the townspeople reacted negatively. Michael could see them *frowning and shaking their heads,* no doubt thinking about their busy schedules. Also, Michael's speaking conditions were far from ideal. Many families had brought their babies and young children to the picnic.
Interference	Several *babies were crying,* and a number of *children were chasing each other* around the tables. But Michael had expected that, and he
Dealing with Interference	was ready. He stopped for a moment and smiled. Then he said, "*Your children are full of the holiday spirit* today. They've just had a wonderful picnic supper. They can cry and run and play because they are well cared for. But other children in our community don't have the energy to cry or play. They are too hungry. Won't you help to feed them?"
Feedback	The townspeople *stared.* Many had *rueful smiles* on their faces. Michael knew the tide had turned. He knew he would get volunteers for the food kitchen.

SPEAKING ETHICALLY

Speechmaking is a form of power and therefore carries with it heavy ethical responsibilities. When the power of speech is abused, the results can be disastrous. Adolf Hitler was unquestionably a persuasive speaker. With his speeches, he galvanized the German people into following one ideal and one leader. But his aims were horrifying and his tactics despicable. He remains today the ultimate example of why the power of the spoken word needs to be guided by a strong sense of integrity.

Questions of ethics in speechmaking usually focus on the speaker's goals and methods.[15] Your first responsibility is to make sure your *goal* is ethically sound. Hitler stirred the German people to condone war, invasion, genocide. There can be no question that these are not worthy goals. Similarly, a speaker who extols worthless products or incites mob violence or encourages political repression is on shaky ground ethically. But look back for a moment at the examples of speechmaking given in this chapter. What do the speakers hope to accomplish? Report on a business project. Improve the quality of education. Pay tribute to a fellow worker. Ease the suffering of dying children. Save lives with cardiopulmonary resuscitation. Few people would question that these goals are ethically sound.

What about the *methods?* Even if your goal is worthy, you are not ethical if you use shoddy methods to achieve it. In other words, the ends do not justify the means. Over the years, experts have set up four basic guidelines for ethical methods in speechmaking:

1. *Be well informed about your subject.* You have an obligation—to yourself and to your listeners—to explore your speech topic as fully as possible. Investigate the whole story, learn about both sides of an issue, seek out competing viewpoints, get the facts right.

2. *Be honest in what you say.* Beware of the temptation to distort the truth for your own purposes. Responsible speakers do not falsify facts, do not present a few facts as the whole story, do not present tentative findings as firm conclusions. Nor do they present other people's ideas as their own. They do not plagiarize their speeches.

3. *Use sound evidence.* Good speeches are not composed of hot air. You will need evidence to explain and support your ideas. When using evidence, be sure not to take quotations out of context, not to juggle statistics, not to present unusual cases as representative examples. Use sources of information that are objective and qualified.

4. *Employ valid reasoning.* In Chapter 14 we will look closely at reasoning in speechmaking. For now, it is enough to know that responsible speakers try to avoid such fallacies as making hasty generalizations, asserting causal connections where none exist, using invalid analogies, and pandering to passion and prejudice.

Your classroom speeches will offer a good testing ground for questions of ethical responsibility. Today, as for the past 2,000 years, the good person speaking well remains the ideal of commendable speechmaking.

feedback; (5) the strategic changes you would make in preparing for and carrying out the conversation if you had it to do over again.

2. Divide a sheet of paper into two columns. Label one column "Characteristics of an Effective Public Speaker." Label the other column "Characteristics of an Ineffective Public Speaker." In the columns, list and briefly explain what you believe to be the five most important characteristics of effective and ineffective speakers. Be prepared to discuss your ideas in class.

3. On the basis of the lists you developed for Exercise 2, candidly evaluate your own strengths and weaknesses as a speaker. Identify the three primary aspects of speechmaking you most want to improve.

NOTES

[1] A number of surveys have shown this to be true for people in all walks of life, and especially for people with college degrees. See Kathleen Edgerton Kendall, "Do Real People Ever Give Speeches?" *Central States Speech Journal,* 25 (1974), 233–235; Samuel L. Becker and Leah R. V. Ekdom, "That Forgotten Basic Skill: Oral Communication," *Association for Communication Administration Bulletin,* 33 (August 1980), 12–25.

[2] The extent to which everyday conversation employs many of the skills and strategies required for public speaking was first made apparent in Erving Goffman's *The Presentation of Self in Everyday Life* (New York: Doubleday, 1959), and has been corroborated by twenty-five years of research. For a useful review of that research see E. Tory Higgins, "The 'Communication Game': Implications for Social Cognition and Persuasion," in E. Tory Higgins, C. Peter Herman, and Mark P. Zanna (eds.), *Social Cognition: The Ontario Symposium,* Vol. I (Hillsdale, N.J.: Lawrence Erlbaum, 1981), pp. 343–392.

[3] "What Are Americans Afraid Of?" *The Bruskin Report,* 53 (July 1973).

[4] These figures are based on unpublished research by Warren Jones, University of Tulsa, and Dan Russell, University of Iowa. They were communicated to me by Professor Jones and were summarized in the *New York Times,* December 18, 1984. The *Times* incorrectly identified Professor Russell as being from "the University of Ohio."

[5] Jeffrey C. Hahner, Martin A. Sokoloff, Sandra Salisch, and Geoffrey D. Needler, *Speaking Clearly: Improving Voice and Diction* (New York: Random House, 1983), p. 12.

[6] A. R. Wylie, quoted in Bert E. Bradley, *Fundamentals of Speech Communication: The Credibility of Ideas,* 5th ed. (Dubuque, Iowa: Brown, 1988), p. 36.

[7] See, for example, Michael J. Beatty and Gregory S. Andriate, "Communication Apprehension and General Anxiety in the Prediction of Public Speaking Anxiety," *Communication Quarterly,* 33 (1985), 174–184.

[8] A number of studies have shown that taking a public speaking class is especially effective in reducing stage fright. Among the most recent are Don W. Stacks and John D. Stone, "An Examination of the Effect of Basic Speech Courses, Self-Concept, and Self-Disclosure on Communication Apprehension," *Communication Education,* 33 (1984), 317–332; Robert S. Littlefield and Timothy L. Sellnow, "The

Use of Self-Disclosure as a Means for Reducing Stage Fright in Beginning Speakers," *Communication Education,* 36 (1987), 62–64.

[9] For research on these and other approaches to dealing with stage fright see Susan R. Glaser, "Oral Communication Apprehension and Avoidance: The Current Status of Treatment Research," *Communication Education,* 30 (1981), 321–341; Joe Ayres and Theodore S. Hopf, "Visualization: A Means of Reducing Speech Anxiety," *Communication Education,* 34 (1985), 318–323.

[10] Kimberly McEwan and Gerald Devins, "Is Increased Arousal in Social Anxiety Noticed by Others?" *Journal of Abnormal Psychology,* 92 (1983), 417–421.

[11] See, for example, Rebecca B. Rubin and Elizabeth E. Graham, "Communication Correlates of College Success: An Exploratory Investigation," *Communication Education,* 37 (1988), 14–27.

[12] Virginia P. O'Keefe, *Affecting Critical Thinking Through Speech* (Urbana, Ill.: ERIC Clearinghouse on Reading and Communication Skills, 1986); Richard A. Katula and Celest A. Martin, "Teaching Critical Thinking in the Speech Communication Classroom," *Communication Education,* 33 (1984), 160–167; Paul A. Fritz and Richard L. Weaver II, "Teaching Critical Thinking Skills in the Basic Speaking Course: A Liberal Arts Perspective," *Communication Education,* 35 (1986), 174–182.

[13] For other perspectives on the basic process of speech communication, see Stewart L. Tubbs and Sylvia Moss, *Human Communication,* 4th ed. (New York: Random House, 1983), pp. 22–49.

[14] For other models of the speech communication process, see John T. Masterson, Steven A. Beebe, and Norman H. Watson, *Speech Communication: Theory and Practice* (New York: Holt, Rinehart and Winston, 1983), pp. 11–17; Brent D. Ruben, *Communication and Human Behavior* (New York: Macmillan, 1984), pp. 40–65.

[15] See Richard L. Johannesen, *Ethics in Human Communication,* 2nd ed. (Prospect Heights, Ill.: Waveland Press, 1983) for a comprehensive discussion.

CHAPTER 2

Listening

It was a hot afternoon in May. The professor of ancient history was lecturing on the fall of the Roman Empire. She began: "Yesterday we discussed the political and social conditions that weakened the empire from within. Today we will talk about the barbarian invasions that attacked the empire from the outside—the Visigoths from the northwest, the Ostrogoths from the northeast, the Vandals from the south, the Huns from the west, and Miss Piggy from the southeast."

Nobody batted an eye. Nobody looked up. The classroom was quiet, except for the scratch of pens as the students took notes—presumably recording Miss Piggy as a barbarian.

This story illustrates what one research study after another has revealed—most people are shockingly poor listeners. We fake paying attention. We can look right at someone, appear interested in what that person says, even nod our heads or smile at the appropriate moments—all without really listening.

Not listening doesn't mean we don't *hear.* Hearing is a physiological process, involving the vibration of sound waves on our eardrums and the firing of electrochemical impulses from the inner ear to the central auditory system of the brain.[1] But *listening* involves paying close attention to, and making sense of, what we hear. Even when we think we are listening carefully, we usually grasp only 50 percent of what we hear. After two days we can remember only half of that—or 25 percent of the original message.[2] It's little wonder that listening has been called a neglected art.[3]

Although most people listen poorly, there are exceptions. Top-flight business executives, successful politicians, brilliant teachers—nearly all are excellent listeners. So much of what they do depends on absorbing information that is given verbally—and absorbing it quickly and accurately. If you had an interview with the president of a major corporation, you might be shocked (and flattered) to see how closely that person listened to your words. One businessman admitted, "Frankly, I had never thought of listening as an important subject by itself. But now that I am aware of it, I think that perhaps 80 percent of my work depends upon my listening to someone, or upon someone listening to me."[4] A recent survey by Brigham Young University asked business managers to rank-order the skills most crucial to their jobs. They ranked listening number one.[5]

Skilled listeners weren't born that way. They have *worked* at learning how to listen effectively. Even if you don't plan to be president of a corporation, the art of listening can be helpful in almost every part of your life. This is not surprising when you realize that people spend more time listening than in any other communicative activity—more than reading, more than writing, more even than speaking.[6] Parents and children, husbands and wives, doctors and patients, teachers and students—all depend on the apparently simple skill of listening. No matter what your profession or walk of life, you never escape the need for a well-trained ear.

Listening is also important to you as a speaker. It is probably the way you get most of your ideas and information—from television, radio, conversation, and lectures. If you do not listen well, you will not understand what you hear and may pass along your misunderstanding to others.

Besides, in class—as in life—you will listen to many more speeches than you give. It is only fair to pay close attention to your classmates' speeches; after all, you want them to listen carefully to *your* speeches. An excellent way to improve your own speeches is to listen attentively to the speeches of other people. One student, reflecting on her speech class, said, "As I listened to the speeches, I discovered things that seemed to work—things I could try. I also learned what didn't work—what to avoid. That helped a lot in my own speeches." Over and over, teachers find that the best speakers are usually the best listeners.

A side benefit of your speech class is that it offers an ideal opportunity to work on the art of listening. During the 95 percent of the time when you are not speaking, you have nothing else to do but listen and learn. You can sit there like a stone—or you can use the time profitably to master a skill that will serve you in a thousand ways.

FOUR CAUSES OF POOR LISTENING

Not Concentrating

The brain is incredibly efficient. Although we talk at from 125 to 150 words a minute, the brain can process from 400 to 800 words a minute.[7] This would seem to make listening very easy, but actually it has the opposite effect. Because we can take in a speaker's words with ease and still have plenty of spare "brain time," we are tempted to interrupt our listening by thinking about other things. And thinking about other things is just what we do. Here's what happens:

Joel Nevins is the youngest member of the public relations team for a giant oil company. He is pleased to be included in the biweekly staff meetings. After two dozen or so meetings, however, he is beginning to find them rather tedious.

This time the vice president is droning on about executive speech writing—an area in which Joel is not directly concerned. The vice president says, "When the draft of a speech hits the president's desk . . ."

"Desk," thinks Joel. "That's my big problem. It's humiliating to have a metal desk when everyone else has wood. There must be some way to convince my boss that I need a new wooden desk." In his imagination, Joel sees himself behind a handsome walnut desk. He is conducting an interview, and his visitor is so impressed . . .

Sternly, Joel pulls his attention back to the meeting. The vice president has moved on to a public relations problem in Latin America. Joel listens carefully for a while, until he hears the words "especially in the Caribbean."

"Oh, if only I could get away for a winter vacation this year," he thinks. He is lost in a reverie featuring white beaches, tropical drinks, exotic dances, scuba-diving, sailboats, himself tanned and windblown . . .

". . . will definitely affect salary increases this year" brings him back to the meeting with a jolt. What did the vice president say about salary increases? Oh well, he can ask someone else after the meeting. But now the vice president is talking about budgets. All those dreary figures and percentages . . . And Joel is off again.

His date last night. Margie really seems to like him and yet . . . Was it something he did that made her say goodnight at the door and go inside alone? Could she have been *that* tired? The last time she invited him in for coffee. Of course, she really did have a rough day. Anybody can understand that, but still . . .

". . . an area that Joel has taken a special interest in. Maybe we should hear from him." Uh, oh! *What* area does the vice president mean? Everyone is looking at Joel, as he tries frantically to recall the last words said at the meeting.

It's not that Joel *meant* to lose track of the discussion. But there comes a point at which it's so easy to give in to physical and mental distractions— to let your thoughts wander rather than to concentrate on what is being said. After all, concentrating is hard work. Louis Nizer, the famous trial lawyer, says, "So complete is this concentration that at the end of a court day in which I have only listened, I find myself wringing wet despite a calm and casual manner."[8]

Later in this chapter, we will look at some things you can do to concentrate better on what you hear.

Listening Too Hard

Until now we have been talking about not paying close attention to what we hear. But sometimes we listen *too* hard. We turn into human sponges, soaking up a speaker's every word as if every word were equally important. We try to remember all the names, all the dates, all the places. In the process we often miss the speaker's point by submerging it in a morass of details. What is worse, we may end up confusing the facts as well.

The car with out-of-state plates and ski racks on the roof pulled up outside a Vermont farmhouse. The driver called out to the farmer, "Can you tell us how to get to Green Mountain Lodge?"

"Well," replied the farmer, "I guess you know it's not there anymore. Terrible thing. But if you want to know where it *used* to be, you go down the road two miles, take a left at the blinking light, make the next right at the cheese shop, and follow the mountain road for about eight miles until you get to the top. Really a sad thing it's all gone."

"Let me make sure I heard you right," said the driver. "Two miles down the road, and then a left at the light, a right at the cheese shop, and then up the mountain road for eight miles to the top?"

"That's it," answered the farmer. "But you won't find much when you get there."

"Thanks a lot," called the driver, as the car drove away.

When the car had pulled out of sight, the farmer turned to his son. "Do you suppose," he said, "they don't know the lodge burned down last summer?"

This is a typical example of losing the main message by concentrating on details. The driver of the car had set his mind to remember directions—

period. In so doing, he blocked out everything else—including the information that his destination no longer existed.

The same thing can happen when you listen to a speech. You pick up details but miss the point. It just isn't possible to remember everything a speaker says. Efficient listeners usually concentrate on main ideas and evidence. We'll discuss these things more thoroughly later in the chapter.

Jumping to Conclusions

Janice and David are married. One day they both come home from work exhausted. While Janice struggles to get dinner on the table, David pours a glass of wine for each of them and then falls down in front of the television set to watch the evening news. Over dinner, this conversation takes place:

JANICE: There's going to be a big change around here.

DAVID: I know, I know, I haven't been pulling my share of the cooking and cleaning, but I'm really going to try to be better about it.

JANICE: Well, that's certainly true, but it's not the only thing . . .

DAVID: Look, I *know* I didn't take out the garbage last night and you had to do it. I promise I won't forget the next time.

JANICE: No, you're not listening. I'm talking about a much more basic change, and . . .

DAVID: I hope you don't want to write up one of those contract things, like the one you read to me from *Ms.* magazine. All that stuff about who does what on which days. Because I think that's ridiculous. We can work this out sensibly.

JANICE: No, I don't mean that at all. You're not paying attention. I mean something a *lot* more basic, and . . .

DAVID: Janice, we're both reasonable, intelligent people. We can work this out if we just approach it rationally.

JANICE: Of course we can. If you would only *listen* for a minute. I'm trying to tell you I had a call from my sister today. She's lost her job and she doesn't have any money. I told her she could stay with us for a few months until she finds another one.

Why is there so much confusion here? Clearly, Janice is unhappy about the amount of household work David does and has mentioned it several times. Equally clearly, David feels guilty about it. So when Janice starts to talk about a "change," David jumps to a conclusion and assumes Janice is going to bring up household work again. This results in a breakdown of communication. The whole problem could have been avoided if when Janice said, "There's going to be a change . . . ," David had asked, "What change?"—and then *listened*.

This is one form of jumping to conclusions—putting words into a speaker's mouth. It is one reason why we sometimes communicate so poorly with people we are closest to. Because we are so sure we know what they mean, we don't listen to what they actually say. Sometimes we don't even hear them out.

Another way of jumping to conclusions is prematurely rejecting a speaker's ideas as boring or misguided. We may decide early on that a speaker has nothing valuable to say. Suppose you are passionately committed to the idea of seeking closer cooperation among nations and a speaker's announced topic is "The United Nations: Is It Time for Us to Leave?" You may decide in advance not to listen to anything the speaker has to say. This would be a mistake. You might pick up useful information that could either strengthen or modify your thinking. In another situation, you might jump to the conclusion that a speech will be boring. Let's say the announced topic is "Altered States of Consciousness." It sounds dull, so you tune out—and miss a fascinating discussion of hypnosis.

Nearly every speech has something to offer you—whether in information, point of view, or technique. You are cheating yourself if you prejudge and choose not to listen.

Focusing on Delivery and Personal Appearance

George Matthews had just received his engineering degree from a major university—magna cum laude and Phi Beta Kappa. Several good firms were interested in hiring him. At his first interview the company's personnel manager took him to meet the hiring executive, with whom George spent nearly an hour. At the end of the interview George felt he had made an excellent impression.

Later, the personnel manager called the executive and asked, "What did you think of Matthews?" The executive replied, "He won't do. He's a lightweight. Everything he said made me think he's not serious about a career in engineering."

"Funny," said the personnel manager, "he didn't seem like a lightweight to me. What exactly did he say?"

The executive hemmed and hawed. He couldn't remember the *precise* words, but the guy was definitely a lightweight. He would not be able to handle the work load or make a contribution to the firm. Still the personnel manager persisted. What was the problem? Finally, the executive was pinned down.

"The man wouldn't fit in," he said, "He had on a polyester double-knit suit, and we're a Brooks Brothers type of company. To tell you the truth, I didn't hear a word he said, because the minute he walked in I knew he wouldn't do. For crying out loud, he was wearing yellow socks!"

This story illustrates a very common problem. We tend to judge people by the way they look or speak and therefore don't listen to what they *say.*[9] Some people are so put off by personal appearance, regional accents, speech defects, or unusual vocal mannerisms that they can't be bothered to listen. This kind of emotional censorship is less severe in the United States now than it was a decade or two ago; but we need always to guard against it. Nothing is more deadly to communication.

HOW TO BECOME A BETTER LISTENER

Take Listening Seriously

The first step to improvement is always self-awareness. Analyze your short-comings as a listener and commit yourself to overcoming them. Good listening does not go hand in hand with intelligence, education, or social standing. Like any other skill, it comes from practice and self-discipline.

You should begin to think of listening as an *active* process. So many aspects of modern life encourage us to listen passively. We "listen" to the radio while studying or "listen" to the television while moving about from room to room. This type of passive listening is a habit—but so is active listening. We can learn to identify those situations in which active listening is important. If you work seriously at becoming a more efficient listener, you will reap the rewards in your schoolwork, in your personal and family relations, and in your career.

Resist Distractions

In an ideal world, we could eliminate all physical and mental distractions. In the real world, however, this is not possible. Because we think so much faster than a speaker can talk, it's easy to let our attention wander while we listen. Sometimes it's very easy—when the room is too hot, when construction machinery is operating right outside the window, when the speaker is tedious. But our attention can stray even in the best of circumstances—if for no other reason than a failure to stay alert and make ourselves concentrate.

Whenever you find this happening, make a conscious effort to pull your mind back to what the speaker is saying. Then force it to stay there. One way to do this is to think a little ahead of the speaker—try to anticipate what will come next. This is not the same as jumping to conclusions. When you jump to conclusions, you put words into the speaker's mouth and don't actually listen to what is said. In this case you *will* listen—and measure what the speaker says against what you had anticipated.

Another way to keep your mind on a speech is to review mentally what the speaker has already said and make sure you understand it. Yet another is to listen between the lines and assess what a speaker implies verbally or says nonverbally with body language. Suppose a politician is running for reelection. During a campaign speech to his constituents he makes this statement: "Just last week I had lunch with the President, and he assured me that he has a special concern for the people of our state." The careful listener would hear this implied message: "If you vote for me, there's a good chance more tax money will flow into the state."

To take another example, suppose a speaker is introducing someone to an audience. The speaker says, "It gives me great pleasure to present to you my very dear friend, Mrs. Smith." But the speaker doesn't shake hands with Mrs. Smith. He doesn't even look at her—just turns his back and leaves the podium. Is Mrs. Smith really his "very dear friend"? Certainly not.

Attentive listeners can pick up all kinds of clues to a speaker's real message. At first you may find it difficult to listen so intently. If you work at it, however, your concentration is bound to improve.

Don't Be Diverted by Appearance or Delivery

If you had attended Abraham Lincoln's momentous Cooper Union speech of 1860, this is what you would have seen:

> The long, ungainly figure upon which hung clothes that, while new for this trip, were evidently the work of an unskilled tailor; the large feet and clumsy hands, of which, at the outset, at least, the orator seemed to be unduly conscious; the long, gaunt head, capped by a shock of hair that seemed not to have been thoroughly brushed out, made a picture which did not fit in with New York's conception of a finished statesman.[10]

But although he seemed awkward and uncultivated, Lincoln had a powerful message about the moral evils of slavery. Fortunately, the audience at Cooper Union did not let his appearance stand in the way of his words.

Similarly, you must be willing to set aside preconceived judgments based on a person's looks or manner of speech. Einstein had frizzy, uncombed hair and wore sloppy clothes; Gandhi was a very unimpressive-looking man who often spoke dressed in a loincloth or wrapped in a blanket; Helen Keller—deaf and blind from earliest childhood—always had trouble articulating words distinctly. Yet imagine if no one had listened to them. Even though it may tax your tolerance, patience, and concentration, don't let negative feelings about a speaker's appearance or delivery keep you from listening to the message.

On the other hand, try not to be misled if the speaker has an unusually attractive appearance. It is all too easy to assume that because someone is good-looking and has a polished delivery he or she is speaking eloquently. Some of the most unscrupulous speakers in history have been handsome people with hypnotic delivery skills. Again, be sure you respond to the message, not to the package it comes in.

Suspend Judgment

Unless we listen only to people who think exactly as we do, we are going to hear things with which we disagree. When this happens, our natural inclination is to argue mentally with the speaker or to dismiss everything he or she says. But neither response is fair—to the speaker or to ourselves. In both cases we blot out any chance of learning or being persuaded.

Does this mean you must agree with everything you hear? Not at all. It means you should hear people out *before* reaching a final judgment. Try to understand their point of view. Listen to their ideas, examine their evidence, assess their reasoning. *Then* make up your mind. If you're sure of your beliefs, you need not fear listening to opposing views. If you're not sure, you have every reason to listen carefully. It has been said more than once that a closed mind is an empty mind.

Focus Your Listening

As we have seen, skilled listeners do not try to absorb a speaker's every word. Rather, they focus on specific things in a speech. Here are three suggestions to help you focus your listening.

Listen for Main Points   Most speeches contain from two to four main points. Here, for example, are the main points of a recent speech by John J. Coury, President of the American Medical Association:[11]

1. Astronomical malpractice awards and the spiraling cost of malpractice insurance are seriously jeopardizing the quality of health care in America.

2. A nationwide initiative is needed to meet the growing health crisis among teenagers and adolescents.

3. If a cure or immunization for AIDS is not found in the near future, it will unquestionably become the most deadly medical scourge in American history.

These main points are the heart of Dr. Coury's message. As with any speech, they are the most important things to listen for.

Unless a speaker is terribly scatterbrained, you should be able to detect his or her main points with little difficulty. Often a speaker will give some idea at the outset of the main points to be developed in the speech. For example, in his introduction Dr. Coury said, "What I want to talk to you about are three major problems that society and medicine are facing today and that apparently are going to get worse." Noticing this, a sharp listener would have been prepared for a speech with three main points, each dealing with one of the major problems facing society and medicine. Dr. Coury also gave a brief preview statement identifying each of the problems before he started the body of his speech. After this, only the most inattentive of listeners could have been in the dark about Coury's main points.

Listen for Evidence   Identifying a speaker's main points, however, is not enough. You must also listen for supporting evidence. By themselves, Dr. Coury's main points are only assertions. You may be inclined to believe them

Focusing your listening includes listening for main points and evidence. In addition, focusing on an effective speaker's techniques can help you improve your own speaking skills. (Richard Sobol/Stock, Boston)

just because they come from the president of the American Medical Association. Yet a careful listener will be concerned about evidence no matter who is speaking. Had you been listening to Coury's speech, you would have heard him support his claim about the health crisis among teenagers and adolescents with a mass of verifiable evidence. Here is an excerpt:

We've thought that those years from age eleven or twelve to eighteen, nineteen, or twenty were the healthy young days. . . . But we did a study recently and came up with some very terrible, horrifying figures. Since 1965 the incidence of gonorrhea in teenagers—particularly teenage girls—has gone up 400 percent. . . . We also found out that there are a million teenage pregnancies a year; 400,000 abortions a year; and 40,000 pregnancies a year in children under the age of fifteen. . . .

I'll bet you didn't know that there are 900,000 teenagers involved in prostitution throughout this country: 600,000 of them are females and about 300,000 are males. They're the runaways, the ignored, those on drugs.

You probably don't know that alcohol kills about 8,000 teenagers a year in auto accidents, and injures another 40,000 seriously.

There are four basic questions to ask about a speaker's evidence:

Is it *accurate?*

Is it taken from *objective* sources?

Is it *relevant* to the speaker's claim?

Is it *sufficient* to support the speaker's point?

In Dr. Coury's case the answer to each question is yes. His figures about teenage pregnancies, venereal disease, prostitution, and alcohol-related deaths come from AMA-sponsored research and can be verified by independent government and medical sources. They are clearly relevant to Dr. Coury's claim about the teenage health crisis, and they are sufficient to support that claim. If Coury's evidence were inaccurate, biased, irrelevant, or insufficient, you should be wary of accepting his claim.

We will discuss these—and other—tests of evidence in detail in Chapters 6 and 14. For now, it is enough to know that you should be on guard against unfounded assertions and sweeping generalizations. Keep an ear out for the speaker's evidence and for its accuracy, objectivity, relevance, and sufficiency.

Listen for Technique   We said earlier that you should not let a speaker's delivery distract you from the message, and this is true. However, if you want to become an effective speaker, you should study the methods other people use to speak effectively. When you listen to speeches—in class and out—focus above all on the content of a speaker's message; but also pay attention to the techniques the speaker uses to get the message across.

Analyze the introduction: What methods does the speaker use to gain attention, to relate to the audience, to establish credibility and goodwill? Assess the organization of the speech: Is it clear and easy to follow? Can you pick out the speaker's main points? Can you follow when the speaker moves from one point to another?

Study the speaker's language: Is it accurate, clear, vivid, appropriate? Does the speaker adapt well to the audience and occasion? Finally, diagnose the speaker's delivery: Is it fluent, dynamic, convincing? Does it strengthen or weaken the impact of the speaker's ideas? How well does the speaker use eye contact, gestures, and visual aids?

As you listen, focus on both the speaker's strengths and weaknesses. If the speaker is not effective, try to determine why. If he or she *is* effective, try to pick out techniques you can use in your own speeches. If you listen in this way, you will be surprised how much you can learn about successful speaking.

This is why many teachers require students to complete evaluation forms on their classmates' speeches. Figure 2.1 (page 38) is an example of such a form. To fill in the form conscientiously, you must listen carefully. But the effort is well worth the rewards. Not only will you provide valuable feedback to your classmates about their speeches, you will also find yourself becoming a much more efficient listener.

Speaker _____   Topic _____

Rate the speaker on each point by using this scale:

5	4	3	2	1
excellent	good	average	fair	poor

Introduction:

_____ Gained attention and interest

_____ Introduced topic clearly

_____ Related topic to audience

_____ Established speaker's credibility

_____ Previewed body of speech

Body:

_____ Main points clear

_____ Main points fully supported

_____ Organization well planned

_____ Language accurate

_____ Language clear

_____ Language appropriate

_____ Connectives effective

Conclusion:

_____ Prepared audience for ending

_____ Reinforced central idea of speech

_____ Vivid ending

Delivery:

_____ Began speech without rushing

_____ Maintained strong eye contact

_____ Avoided distracting mannerisms

_____ Articulated words clearly

_____ Used pauses effectively

_____ Used vocal variety to add impact

_____ Presented visual aids well

_____ Departed from lectern without rushing

Overall Evaluation:

_____ Topic challenging

_____ Specific purpose well chosen

_____ Message adapted to audience

_____ Speech completed within time limit

_____ Held interest of audience

What did the speaker do most effectively? _____

_____

What should the speaker pay special attention to next time? _____

_____

General comments: _____

_____

_____

FIGURE 2.1   Speech Evaluation Form

Develop Note-Taking Skills

Speech students are often amazed at how easily their teacher can pick out a speaker's main points, evidence, and techniques. Of course, the teacher knows what to listen for and has had plenty of practice. But the next time you get an opportunity, watch your teacher during a speech. Chances are he or she will be listening with pen and paper. When note taking is done properly, it is a sure-fire way to improve your concentration and keep track of a speaker's ideas.[12]

The key words here are *when done properly.* Unfortunately, many people don't take notes effectively. Some try to write down everything a speaker says. They view note taking as a race, pitting their penmanship agility against the speaker's rate of speech. As the speaker starts to talk, the note taker starts to write. But soon the speaker is winning the race. In a desperate effort to keep up, the note taker slips into a scribbled writing style with incomplete sentences and abbreviated words. Even this is not enough. The speaker pulls so far ahead that the note taker can never catch up. Finally, the note taker concedes defeat and spends the rest of the speech grumbling in frustration.[13]

Some people go to the opposite extreme. They arrive armed with pen, notebook, and the best of intentions. They know they can't write down everything, so they settle comfortably in their seats and wait for the speaker to say something that grabs their attention. Every once in a while the speaker rewards them with a joke, a dramatic story, or a startling fact. Then the note taker seizes pen, jots down a few words, and leans back dreamily to await the next fascinating tidbit. By the end of the lecture the note taker has a set of tidbits—and little or no record of the speaker's important ideas.

As these examples illustrate, most inefficient note takers suffer from one or both of two problems: they don't know *what* to listen for, and they don't know *how* to record what they do listen for. The solution to the first problem is to focus on a speaker's main points and evidence. But once you know what to listen for, you still need a sound method of note taking.

Although there are a number of systems, most students find the *key-word outline* best for listening to classroom lectures and formal speeches. As its name suggests, this method briefly notes a speaker's main points and supporting evidence in rough outline form. Suppose a speaker says:

Let us turn first to the problem of sexual harassment. At this point, we know that approximately 80 percent of all working women suffer some degree or some form of sexual harassment. An obvious question at this point is, why does it happen? A *Ms.* magazine article defined this problem as a "phenomenon more related to power than sex, . . . a symbol of superiority, ownership and dominance." I realize that this is not the only explanation for the problem. However, I think it provides a broad base for explaining why sexual harassment occurs. If a woman's job is being threatened, I would suggest that there is some degree of power-play in the interaction between employer and employee.

Another question you may be asking yourself is, "Who is usually harassed? Who is the typical victim?" United Working Women Institute of New York has found that the victim is the woman who is most economically vulnerable. What this translates into is the woman who can least afford to lose her job. This is a major reason why it is so difficult to persuade women to testify against their employers.[14]

A key-word outline note taker would record something like this:

> 80% working women sexually harassed.
> Why?
>   *Ms.* magazine: basic cause power, not sex.
>
> Who is typical victim?
>   Economically vulnerable: fears being fired.
>   Explains why women won't testify.

Notice how brief the notes are. They contain only 27 words (compared to the speaker's 190), yet they accurately summarize the speaker's ideas. Also notice how clear the notes are. By separating main points from subpoints and evidence, the outline format shows the relationships among the speaker's ideas.

Perfecting this—or any other—system of note taking requires practice.[15] But with a little effort you should see results soon. As you become a better note taker, you will become a better listener. There is also a good chance you will become a better student. Common sense and experience suggest that students who take effective notes usually get higher grades than those who do not.

SUMMARY

Most people are poor listeners. Even when we think we are listening carefully, we usually grasp only half of what we hear, and we retain even less. Improving your listening skills can be helpful in every part of your life—including speechmaking. The best speakers are often the best listeners. Your speech class gives you a perfect chance to work on your listening skills as well as your speaking skills.

The most important cause of poor listening is giving in to physical and mental distractions. Many times we let our thoughts wander rather than concentrating on what is being said. Sometimes, however, we listen *too* hard. We try to remember every word a speaker says, and we lose the main message by concentrating on details. In other situations, we may jump to conclusions and prejudge a speaker without hearing out the message. Finally, we often judge people by their appearance or speaking manner instead of listening to what they *say*.

You can overcome these poor listening habits by taking several steps. First, take listening seriously. Think of listening as an active process and commit yourself to becoming a better listener. Second, resist distractions. Make a conscious effort to keep your mind on what the speaker is saying.

Third, try not to be diverted by appearance or delivery. Set aside preconceived judgments based on a person's looks or manner of speech. Fourth, suspend judgment until you have heard the speaker's entire message—even if you think you are going to disagree. Fifth, focus your listening by paying attention to main points, to evidence, and to the speaker's techniques. Finally, develop your note-taking skills. When done properly, note taking is an excellent way to improve your concentration and to keep track of a speaker's ideas. It almost forces you to become a more attentive and creative listener.

REVIEW QUESTIONS

After reading this chapter, you should be able to answer the following questions:

1. What is the difference between hearing and listening?
2. Why is listening important to you as a public speaker?
3. What are the four main causes of poor listening?
4. What are six ways to become a better listener?

APPLICATION EXERCISES

1. Which of the four causes of poor listening do you consider the most important? Choose a specific case of poor listening in which you were involved. Explain what went wrong.
2. Write a candid evaluation of your major strengths and weaknesses as a listener. Explain what steps *you* need to take to become a better listener. Be specific.
3. Watch the lead story on *60 Minutes* this week. Using the key-word method of note taking, record the main ideas of the story.
4. Choose a lecture in one of your other classes. Analyze what the lecturer does most effectively. Identify three things the lecturer could do better to help students keep track of the lecture.

NOTES

[1] Raymond Daniloff, Gordon Schuckers, and Lawrence Feth, *The Physiology of Speech and Hearing* (Englewood Cliffs, N.J.: Prentice-Hall, 1980), pp. 368–434.
[2] Lyman K. Steil, Larry L. Barker, and Kittie W. Watson, *Effective Listening* (Reading, Mass.: Addison-Wesley, 1983), pp. 38, 51.

[3] Wendell Johnson, "Do You Know How to Listen?" in Sam Duker (ed.), *Listening: Readings* (New York: Scarecrow, 1966), p. 41.

[4] Ralph G. Nichols and Leonard A. Stevens, *Are You Listening?* (New York: McGraw-Hill, 1957), p. 141.

[5] Bruce E.Gronbeck, "Oral Communication Skills in a Technological Age," *Vital Speeches,* 47 (1981), 431.

[6] The classic study on this subject is Paul T. Rankin, "The Importance of Listening Ability," *English Journal,* 17 (1928), 623–630. For a recent review of the scholarly literature on listening see Kittie W. Watson and Larry L. Barker, "Listening Behavior: Definition and Measurement," in Robert N. Bostrom and Bruce Westley (eds.), *Communication Yearbook 8* (Beverly Hills, Calif.: Sage, 1984), pp. 178–197.

[7] Florence L. Wolff, Nadine C. Marsnik, William S. Tacey, and Ralph G. Nichols, *Perceptive Listening* (Englewood Cliffs, N.J.: Prentice-Hall, 1983), p. 154.

[8] Louis Nizer, *My Life in Court* (New York: Doubleday, 1961), pp. 297–298.

[9] Nichols and Stevens, *Are You Listening?,* pp. 109–110.

[10] George H. Putnam, *Abraham Lincoln* (New York: Putnam, 1909), pp. 44–45.

[11] John J. Coury, Jr., "Medicine Today and Tomorrow," *Vital Speeches,* 53 (1987), 621–624.

[12] See, for example, Andrea Weiland and Steven J. Kingsbury, "Immediate and Delayed Recall of Lecture Material as a Function of Note Taking," *Journal of Educational Research,* 72 (1979), 228–230; M. Maqsud, "Effects of Personal Lecture Notes and Teacher-Notes on Recall of University Students," *British Journal of Educational Psychology,* 50 (1980), 289–294.

[13] Nichols and Stevens, *Are You Listening?,* pp. 113–114.

[14] Dan Ramczyk, "A Harmless Game," *Winning Orations, 1980* (Mankato, Minn.: Interstate Oratorical Association, 1980), p. 70.

[15] See Wolff, Marsnik, Tacey, and Nichols, *Perceptive Listening,* pp. 88–97, for several alternative note-taking systems.

PART TWO

SPEECH PREPARATION: GETTING STARTED

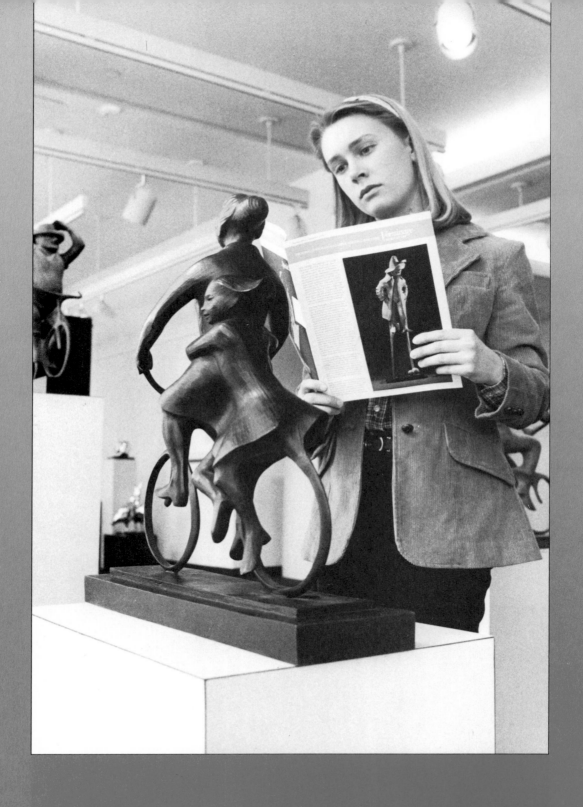

CHAPTER 3

Selecting a Topic and Purpose

A s you read through this book, you will find examples of hundreds of speeches that were delivered in classrooms, in the political arena, in community and business situations. Here is a very small sample of the topics they cover:

amnesia	nursing homes
bicycles	organ donation
capital punishment	Picasso
dinosaurs	quotas for imports
Egyptian burial tombs	rodeos
fireworks	Special Olympics
gun control	Titanic
hypnotism	UFOs
ice cream	violence in films
jogging	women's intercollegiate sports
kleptomania	x-rays
lasers	Yucatán peninsula
mail-order fraud	zoos

Undoubtedly you noticed that the list runs from A to Z. This array of topics wasn't planned. It happened naturally in the course of presenting many different kinds of speeches. The list is given here simply to show you that there are literally *endless* possibilities for speech topics—from A to Z.

CHOOSING A TOPIC

The first step in speechmaking is choosing a topic. For speeches outside the classroom this is seldom a problem. Usually the speech topic is determined by the occasion, the audience, and the speaker's qualifications. When Henry Kissinger lectures on a college campus, he is invited to speak about foreign affairs. Ted Koppel will discuss television news and current events. Geraldine Ferraro might share her views about women in politics and society. The same is true of ordinary citizens. The police officer is asked to tell junior-high-school students about the dangers of drug abuse. The banker discourses on investment procedures, the florist on how to grow thriving house plants.

In a public speaking class the situation is different. Most of your speech assignments will not come with a designated topic. Students generally have great leeway in selecting subjects for their speeches. This would appear to be an advantage, since it allows you to talk about matters of personal interest.

Yet there may be no facet of speech preparation that causes more gnashing of teeth than selecting a topic.

It is a constant source of amazement to teachers that students who regularly chat with their friends about almost any subject under the sun become mentally paralyzed when faced with the task of deciding what to talk about in their speech class. Fortunately, once you get over this initial paralysis, you should have little trouble choosing a good topic.

There are two broad categories of potential topics for your classroom speeches: (1) subjects you know a lot about and (2) subjects that interest you and that you would like to know more about. Let's start with the first.

Most people speak best about subjects with which they are most familiar. You can't go too far wrong by drawing on your own knowledge and experience. You may think to yourself, "That's impossible. I've never done anything fascinating. My life is too ordinary to interest other people." But that isn't true. Everyone knows things or has done things that can be used in a speech.

Think for a moment about unusual experiences you may have had. Think also about special knowledge or expertise you may have acquired. You are bound to come up with something. One student, who worked part-time as a bank teller, presented a fascinating speech on how to detect counterfeit currency. Another used her knowledge as an art major to prepare a speech about famous art forgers of the past. A third student, who had suffered his whole life from hemophilia, gave a deeply moving speech about that dreaded disease.

Too dramatic? You have nothing in your life that is so interesting? Yet another student, who described herself as "just a housewife," delivered a speech about the joyful experience of bringing her young baby, once a week, to visit an elderly neighbor who is both deaf and blind. This speaker talked eloquently about watching the old woman with the child, enjoying the senses that were left to her—the touch of a baby moving and kicking, the smell of a baby.

Here are a few more examples of speech topics based largely on the students' personal knowledge and experience:

Two Years in the Peace Corps

How to Win at Blackjack

Inside Your Friendly McDonald's

Diabetes: You Can Live with It

Running a Mink Farm

Scuba Diving: A New World Under Water

Working as a Circus Clown

The Ups and Downs of Sky Diving

Training Your Dog

Sign Language for the Deaf

Library resources can provide ideas for topics, as well as material for the speech itself.
(Christopher Morrow/Stock, Boston)

On the other hand, you may decide to make your speech a learning experience for yourself as well as for your audience. You may choose a subject about which you already have some knowledge or expertise but not enough to prepare a speech without doing additional research. You may even select a topic that hasn't touched you at all before but that you want to explore. Say, for example, you've always been interested in reincarnation but never knew much about it. This would be a perfect opportunity to research a fascinating subject—and turn it into a fascinating speech.

Still another possibility—especially for persuasive speeches—is to think of subjects about which you hold strong opinions and beliefs. Imagine you are at dinner with a friend and find yourself arguing that television broadcasters should not report the projected results of presidential elections until polls have closed throughout the country. Why not give a speech in class on the same topic? Or suppose you believe your school should set up a program to help students deal with alcohol abuse. Why not try to convince your classmates and get them to petition for such a program?

Like everyone else, you surely have issues about which you care deeply. They may include national or international concerns such as arms control, protection of the environment, or the spread of pornography. Or perhaps you are closely involved in a local issue, such as a teacher's strike, the campaign for mayor, or a proposal to increase tuition. Not all such topics must be "political." They can deal with anything from graduation requirements to helping the handicapped, from religious cults to preserving a nature sanctuary, from dormitory regulations to building a church recreation center.

After all this you may still be thinking, "I *don't* care about reincarnation, I *didn't* run a mink farm. I'm *not* active in politics. WHAT am I going to speak about?" If you are having trouble selecting a topic, there are a number of procedures you can follow to get you started. Here are three possibilities.

First, make a quick inventory of your experiences, interests, hobbies, skills, beliefs, and so forth. Jot down anything that comes to mind, no matter how silly or irrelevant it may seem. From this list may come a general subject area out of which you can fashion a specific topic. This method has worked for many students.

If the first method doesn't work, try the second. It is a technique called *brainstorming*. Take a sheet of paper and divide it into ten columns. Label the columns as follows: People, Places, Things, Events, Processes, Concepts, Natural Phenomena, Supernatural Phenomena, Problems, and Plans and Policies.[1] Then list in each column the first five or six items that come to mind. The result might look like this:

PEOPLE	PLACES	THINGS
Ronald Reagan	my home town	computers
George Washington	China	Shroud of Turin
Pancho Villa	Grand Canyon	surfboards
Willie Nelson	campus tavern	mushrooms
my grandmother	Hollywood	Great Pyramids
Sally Field		Bible

EVENTS	PROCESSES
midterm exams	how beer is made
World Series	what happens when people dream
rock concert	darkroom techniques in photography
my brother's wedding	handwriting analysis
bar mitzvah	being a college freshman
registration week	

CONCEPTS	NATURAL PHENOMENA	SUPERNATURAL PHENOMENA
free enterprise	earthquakes	UFOs
communism	volcanic explosions	ghosts
Christianity	blue skies	reincarnation
democracy	bird migration	prophecies
astrology	snow	ESP
	solar system	

PROBLEMS	PLANS AND POLICIES
ozone layer	combatting child abuse
grades	prayer in public schools
drunk drivers	maternity leave
cost of tuition	building a new dormitory
missing library books	stopping cheating in college athletics
drug abuse	revising the grading system

Very likely, several items on your lists will strike you as potential topics. If not, take the items you find most intriguing and compose sublists for each. Try to free-associate. Write down a word or idea. What does that trigger in your mind? Whatever it is, write that down next, and keep going until you have six or seven ideas on your list. For example, working from the brainstorming lists printed above, one student composed sublists for Willie Nelson, earthquakes, and UFOs:

WILLIE NELSON	EARTHQUAKES	UFOs
Waylon Jennings	San Francisco	Star Wars
cowboys	Nob Hill	missile systems
Indians	cable cars	arms control
horses	mass transportation	Soviet Union
pony express	traffic jams	Afghanistan
mail service	rush hour	freedom

Can you follow her trail of association? In the first column Willie Nelson made her think of Waylon Jennings. Jennings reminded her of cowboys. Cowboys suggest Indians. Indians ride horses. Horses reminded her of the pony express. The pony express was an early form of mail service. Suddenly, this student remembered a magazine article she had read comparing the U.S. postal service to mail service around the world. The idea clicked in her mind. After considerable research she developed an excellent speech entitled "The U.S. Postal Service: Not Perfect, but Still First Class."

That's a far cry from Willie Nelson! If you started out free-associating from Willie Nelson, you would doubtless end up somewhere completely different. This is what brainstorming is all about.

By brainstorming, most people are able to come up with a topic rather quickly. But if you are still stymied, don't despair. There is a third technique you can use as a last resort. Go to the reference room of the library and browse through an encyclopedia, the *Reader's Guide to Periodical Literature*, the *New York Times Index*, or some other reference work until you stumble across what might be a good speech topic. As an experiment, one student decided to try flipping through the dictionary and limiting herself to the letter "k." Within ten minutes she had come up with these potential topics:

karate	koala bears	kindergarten	Kentucky Derby
kibbutzim	kamikaze	kissing	Ku Klux Klan
kangaroos	Koran	kites	kleptomania
kidnapping	Kriss Kringle	knighthood	Kabuki
Khmer people	Kremlin	Kewpie dolls	kaleidoscopes

With proper research and development, any one of these could make an exciting speech.

Whatever means you use for selecting a topic, *start early.* The major reason students have difficulty choosing speech topics is that, like most people, they tend to procrastinate—to put off starting projects as long as possible. Since choosing a topic is your first step in the process of speech preparation, it is only natural to postpone facing up to it. But if you postpone it too long, you may dig yourself into a hole from which you cannot escape.

Start thinking about your topic as soon as each assignment is announced. Pay attention to interesting subjects in class and conversation, on the radio and television, in newspapers and magazines. Jot down in your notebook ideas for topics as they occur to you. Having an inventory of possible topics to choose from is much better than having to rack your brain for one at the last minute. If you get an early start on choosing a topic, you will have plenty of time to pick just the right one and prepare a first-rate speech.

DETERMINING THE GENERAL PURPOSE

Along with choosing a topic, you need to determine the *general purpose* of your speech. Usually it will fall into one of two overlapping categories—to inform or to persuade. (As noted in Chapter 1, there is a third possible category—the speech to entertain. But classroom speeches are rarely of this type.)

When your general purpose is to *inform,* you act as a teacher or lecturer. Your goal is to convey information—and to do so clearly, accurately, and interestingly. If you describe how to lift weights, narrate the events leading up to the bombing of Hiroshima, give an account of your trip to Europe, report on your sorority's financial position, or explain how a nuclear generator works, you are speaking to inform. Your aim is to enhance the knowledge and understanding of your listeners—to give them information they did not have before.

When your general purpose is to *persuade,* you act as an advocate or partisan. You go beyond giving information to espousing a cause. You want to *change* or *structure* the attitudes or actions of your audience. The difference between informing and persuading is the difference between "explaining" and "exhorting."[2] If you try to convince your listeners that they should start a regular program of weight lifting, that the United States should not have dropped the atomic bomb at Hiroshima, that more students should study foreign languages, that your sorority should start a fund-raising drive to balance its budget, or that the United States is falling dangerously behind other industrialized nations in developing nuclear power plants—then you are speaking to persuade. In doing so, you cannot help but give information; but your primary goal is to win over your listeners to your point of view—to get them to believe something or do something as a result of your speech.

In speech classes, the general purpose is usually specified as part of the speech assignment. For speeches outside the classroom, however, you have to make sure of your general purpose yourself. Usually this is quite easy to do. Are you going to explain, report, or demonstrate something? Then your general purpose is to inform. Are you going to sell, advocate, or defend something? Then your general purpose is to persuade. But no matter what the situation, you must be certain of exactly what you hope to achieve by speaking. Knowing your general purpose is the first step. The next step is determining your specific purpose.

DETERMINING THE SPECIFIC PURPOSE

Once you have chosen a topic and a general purpose, you must narrow your choices to determine the *specific purpose* of your speech. The specific purpose should focus on *one aspect* of a topic. You should be able to state your specific purpose in a single infinitive phrase (to inform my audience about . . .; to persuade my audience to . . .) that indicates *precisely* what you hope to accomplish with your speech. Perhaps an example will help to clarify the process of choosing a specific purpose.

Steve Perkins, a student at Penn State, decided to give his first classroom speech on a topic from his personal experience. Steve played defensive end on the Penn State football team, which at the time was ranked in the top five nationally and hadn't lost a game in two years. So he planned to speak about what it was like to be a member of a high-powered college football team. This gave him a topic and a general purpose, which were:

Topic: The Penn State football team

General Purpose: To inform

So far, so good. But what aspect of the team would Steve discuss? The coach? The players? The games? The pressures? The thrills? He had to choose something interesting that he could explain in five minutes. Finally, he settled on giving a behind-the-scenes view of how the coaches and players go about preparing for a game, from the time one game ends until the next begins. He stated his specific purpose this way:

Specific Purpose: To inform my audience how the football team prepares each week for its next game.

This turned out to be an excellent choice, and Steve's speech was among the best in the class.

Notice how clear and concise the specific purpose is. Notice also how it relates the topic directly to the audience. That is, it states not what the *speaker* wants to *say* but what the speaker wants the *audience* to *know* as a result of the speech. This is very important, for it helps keep the audience at the center of your attention as you prepare the speech.

Look what happens when the specific purpose statement does not include the audience:

Specific Purpose: To explain how the football team prepares each week for its next game.

Explain to whom? To visiting players from another team? To a group of art majors? To a delegation of exchange students from China? Those would be three different speeches. The visiting players know about preparing for a game. For them the speaker might concentrate on whatever is unique in the way Penn State prepares. The art majors will understand the basics of football but probably know little about how a team prepares for a game. So the speaker will focus on the general characteristics of preparation. The Chinese exchange students don't have the foggiest idea what football is all about. In this case the speaker must design a speech about game preparations that doesn't depend on a knowledge of football.

When the audience slips out of the specific purpose, it may slip out of the speaker's consciousness. You may begin to think your task is the general one of preparing "an informative speech," when in fact your task is the specific one of informing a particular group of people. This may seem like a small point right now, but as we shall see in the next chapter, it is almost impossible to prepare a good speech without keeping constantly in mind the *people* for whom it is intended.

Tips for Formulating the Specific Purpose Statement

Formulating a specific purpose is the most important early step in developing a successful speech. In writing your purpose statement, try to follow the general principles outlined below.

Write the Purpose Statement as a Full Infinitive Phrase, Not as a Fragment

Ineffective: The world of witchcraft.

More Effective: To inform my audience of the three major kinds of witchcraft practiced today.

Ineffective: Buying a personal computer.

More Effective: To inform my audience of the best way to select a personal computer suited to their individual needs.

The ineffective statements above are adequate as announcements of the speech topic, but they are not thought out fully enough to indicate the specific purpose.

Express Your Purpose as a Statement, Not as a Question

Ineffective: What really happened to Atlantis?

More Effective: To inform my audience of three leading scientific theories about the legendary lost city of Atlantis.

Ineffective: Is the U.S. space program necessary?

More Effective: To persuade my audience that the U.S. space program provides many important benefits to people here on earth.

The questions might make adequate titles, but they are not effective as purpose statements. They give no indication about what direction the speech will take or what the speaker hopes to accomplish.

Avoid Figurative Language in Your Purpose Statement

Ineffective: To persuade my audience that the university's plan to reduce the number of campus parking spaces assigned to students is a real bummer.

More Effective: To persuade my audience to petition against the university's plan to reduce the number of campus parking spaces assigned to students.

Ineffective: To persuade my audience that banning all fraternities because there have been hazing accidents at some colleges would be like throwing out the baby with the bath water.

More Effective: To persuade my audience that banning all fraternities because there have been hazing accidents at some colleges would punish the vast majority of fraternities for the irresponsible actions of a few.

Although the ineffective statements indicate something of the speaker's viewpoint, they do not state concisely what he or she hopes to achieve. Metaphors, analogies, and the like are effective devices for reinforcing ideas within a speech, but they are too ambiguous for specific purpose statements.

Limit Your Purpose Statement to One Distinct Idea

Ineffective: To persuade my audience that registration procedures should be simplified and that credits for remedial courses should not count toward graduation.

This purpose statement expresses two unrelated ideas. The easiest remedy is to select one or the other as a focus for your speech.

More Effective: To persuade my audience that registration procedures should be simplified.

More Effective: To persuade my audience that credits for remedial courses should not count toward graduation.

One way to avoid the double-idea purpose statement is to stay away from compound sentences. If your specific purpose statement contains the word "and" or "or," this may be a hint that it contains two distinct ideas and should be rephrased.

Make Sure Your Specific Purpose Is Not Too Vague or General

Ineffective: To inform my audience about handwriting analysis.

More Effective: To inform my audience about the three major methods of handwriting analysis.

The ineffective purpose statement above falls into one of the most common traps—it is too broad and ill-defined. It gives no clues about what aspect of handwriting analysis the speaker will cover. The more effective purpose statement is sharp and concise. It reveals clearly what the speaker plans to discuss.
      Here is another example, this time for a persuasive speech:

Ineffective: To persuade my audience that something should be done about the federal budget deficit.

More Effective: To persuade my audience that a national sales tax should be instituted to help reduce the federal budget deficit.

Again, the ineffective purpose statement is vague and indistinct. It gives no indication of the speaker's stance toward the topic. The "something" that "should be done" about the federal budget could include anything from raising income taxes to reducing spending for national defense or Social Security. The more effective purpose statement is crisp and clear. It does not leave us guessing about what the speaker hopes to accomplish.

The more precise your specific purpose, the easier it will be to prepare your speech. Consider this topic and specific purpose:

Topic: Acupuncture

Specific Purpose: To inform my audience about acupuncture.

With such a hazy purpose, you have no systematic way of limiting your research or of deciding what to include in the speech and what to exclude. The history of acupuncture, its use today in the Far East, its reputation in Western medical circles—all could be equally relevant to a speech designed to "inform my audience about acupuncture."

In contrast, look at this topic and specific purpose:

Topic: Acupuncture

Specific Purpose: To inform my audience about the two major theories of how acupuncture works to solve medical problems.

Now it is very easy to decide what is germane and what is not. The history of acupuncture, its use today in the Far East, its reputation in the West—all are interesting, but none is essential to the specific purpose of explaining "the two major theories of how acupuncture works." Thus you need not worry about researching these matters or about explaining them in the speech. You can spend your preparation time efficiently.

Questions to Ask About Your Specific Purpose

Sometimes you will arrive at your specific purpose almost immediately after choosing your topic. At other times you may do quite a bit of research before deciding on a specific purpose. Much will depend on how familiar you are with the topic, as well as on any special demands imposed by the assignment, the audience, or the occasion. But whenever you settle on your specific purpose, ask yourself the following questions about it.

Does My Purpose Meet the Assignment?   Students occasionally stumble over this question. Be sure you understand your assignment, and shape your specific purpose to meet it. If you have questions, check with your instructor.

Can I Accomplish My Purpose in the Time Allotted?   Most classroom speeches are quite short, ranging from four or five minutes up to ten minutes. That may seem like a lot of time if you have never given a speech before. But you will quickly find what generations of students have discovered, much to their surprise—time flies when you are giving a speech! Most people speak at an average rate of 120 to 150 words a minute. This means that a six-minute speech will consist of roughly 720-900 words. That is not long enough to develop a highly complex topic. Here are some specific purpose statements that would simply defy being handled well in the time normally allocated for classroom speeches:

> To inform my audience about the nature of humankind.

> To persuade my audience of the ten greatest people in history.

> To inform my audience about the rise and fall of the Roman Empire.

> To persuade my audience to convert to Buddhism.

You are much better off with a limited purpose that you have some reasonable hope of achieving in the short span of four to ten minutes.

Is the Purpose Relevant to My Audience?   The price of retirement homes in Sun City might be an engrossing topic for older citizens who are in the market for such dwellings. And the quality of hot lunches in the elementary schools is of great concern to the students who eat them and the parents who pay for them. But neither subject has much relevance for an audience of college students. No matter how well you construct your speeches, they are likely to fall flat unless you speak about matters of interest to your listeners.

This is not to say you must select only topics that pertain *directly* to the college student's daily experience—the grading system, dormitory conditions, parking spaces on campus, and the like. Most students have wide-ranging backgrounds, interests, ideas, and values. And most of them are intellectually curious. They can get involved in an astonishing variety of subjects. Follow your common sense, and make sure *you* are truly interested in the topic. Also, when speaking on a subject that is not obviously relevant to your listeners, take time in your speech to tie the subject in with their goals, values, interests, and well-being. We'll discuss how to do this in the next chapter.

Is the Purpose Too Trivial for My Audience?   Just as you need to avoid speech topics that are too broad or complicated, so you need to steer clear of topics that are too superficial. How to build a fire without matches might absorb a group of Cub Scouts, but your classmates would probably consider it frivolous. Unfortunately, there is no absolute rule for determining what is trivial to an audience and what is not. Here are some examples of specific purposes that are too trivial for classroom speeches:

> To inform my audience how to make popcorn.

> To persuade my audience to drink Dr. Pepper instead of Coca-Cola.

> To inform my audience how to tie a bow tie.

> To persuade my audience to send Mother's Day cards.

Is the Purpose Too Technical for My Audience?   Nothing puts an audience to sleep faster than a dry and technical speech. Beware of topics that are inherently technical, as well as of treating ordinary subjects in a technical fashion. Although you may be perfectly familiar with the principles and vocabulary of quantum physics, physical anthropology, generic criticism, molecular biology, clinical psychology, or constitutional law, most of your classmates probably are not. There are aspects of these and similar subjects that *can* be treated clearly, with a minimum of jargon. But if you find you can't fulfill your specific purpose without relying on technical words and concepts, you should reconsider your purpose. Here are some examples of specific purposes that are overly technical for most classroom speeches:

> To inform my audience about statistical models of regression analysis.
>
> To persuade my audience that Michell's theory of black holes is superior to that of Shklovskii.
>
> To inform my audience how to bid a slam in bridge.
>
> To inform my audience about the latest developments in mathematical modeling.

We shall discuss the details of audience analysis and adaptation in Chapter 4. For the moment, remember to make sure that your specific purpose is appropriate for your listeners. If you have doubts, ask your instructor, or circulate a questionnaire among your classmates (see pages 81–85).

PHRASING THE CENTRAL IDEA

The specific purpose of a speech is what you hope to accomplish. The *central idea* is a concise statement of what you *expect to say.* Sometimes it is called the thesis statement, the subject sentence, or the major thought. Whatever the term, the central idea is usually expressed as a simple, declarative sentence that refines and sharpens the specific purpose statement.

Imagine you run into a friend on your way to speech class. She says, "I have to dash to my history lecture, but I hear you're giving a speech today. Can you tell me the gist of it in one sentence?" "Sure," you reply. "America's prison system suffers from three major problems—overcrowding of inmates, lack of effective rehabilitation programs, and high expense to taxpayers."

Your answer is the central idea of your speech. It is more precise than your topic (America's prison system) or your specific purpose statement ("To inform my audience of the three major problems facing America's prison system"). By stating exactly what the three major problems are, the central idea "sums up" your speech in a single sentence.

Another way to think of the central idea is as your *residual message*— what you want your audience to remember after they have forgotten everything else in the speech. Most of the time the central idea will encapsulate the main points to be developed in the body of the speech. To show how this works, let's take a few of the examples we had earlier in this chapter and develop them from the topic, general purpose, and specific purpose to the central idea. We can start with the speech about intercollegiate football:

Topic:	Penn State football team
General Purpose:	To inform
Specific Purpose:	To inform my audience how the football team prepares each week for its next game.
Central Idea:	Preparing for each week's football game involves five major steps that begin almost as soon as the previous game is over.

Look carefully at this example. It shows how the speaker might start with a rather broad subject (Penn State football team) that gets narrower and narrower as the speaker moves from the general purpose to the specific purpose to the central idea. Notice also how much the central idea suggests about the content of the speech. From it we can expect the speaker to develop five main points in his speech—each corresponding to one of the five major steps in preparing for a college football game.

This sharpening of focus as one proceeds to the central idea is crucial. Here is another example:

Topic:	Witchcraft
General Purpose:	To inform
Specific Purpose:	To inform my audience of the three major kinds of witchcraft practiced today.
Central Idea:	The three major kinds of witchcraft practiced today are black magic, sorcery, and satanism.

This central idea is especially well-worded. We can assume from it that the body of the speech will contain three main points—on black magic, sorcery, and satanism.

Much the same is true of this example:

Topic:	Campus parking
General Purpose:	To persuade
Specific Purpose:	To persuade my audience to petition against the university's plan to reduce the number of campus parking spaces assigned to students.
Central Idea:	The university's plan to reduce student parking spaces is an infringement of student rights and will result in widespread illegal parking.

From this central idea we can deduce that the student will develop two main points in the speech: (1) students have a right to park on campus; and (2) if this right is limited, the students' only recourse is to park illegally.

There is something else important about these examples. Notice in each case how much more the central idea reveals about the content of the speech than does the specific purpose. This is not accidental. Often you can settle on your specific purpose statement rather early in preparing your speech. The central idea, however, usually emerges later—after you have done your research and have decided on the main points of the speech. The process may work like this:

Bob Sennhauser had become interested in the debate over national health insurance. He decided to give his informative speech on the subject of rapidly escalating doctors' fees. Tentatively, he adopted this specific purpose statement: "To inform my audience why doctors' fees in the United States have risen dramatically in recent years." Then Bob started his research.

An article in *Newsweek*, which Bob located through the *Readers' Guide to Periodical Literature*, spoke of the extremely high cost of a medical education. According to the article, a student graduating from medical school typically is saddled with a student-loan debt as high as $60,000. And the newly created M.D. has no immediate prospect of paying off the debt, since he or she faces some three to four years of residency with moderate income.

Next Bob found a newspaper story that discussed the cost of malpractice insurance, which every physician must carry. To his shock, Bob learned that the premiums for malpractice insurance run into thousands of dollars per year and can go well over $100,000 a year for an orthopedic surgeon.

Then Bob hit upon the idea of interviewing his own doctor. The doctor confirmed Bob's findings about the cost of medical education and malpractice insurance and also mentioned another area of concern. The expense of running an office today can be staggering, with staff, high rents, office insurance, and increasingly sophisticated equipment.

Bob digested all this information. Now he was ready to formulate his central idea: "Doctors' fees in the United States have risen rapidly in recent years because of the high costs of medical education, malpractice insurance, and maintaining an office."

What makes a well-worded central idea? Essentially the same things that make a well-worded specific purpose statement. The central idea should be expressed in a full sentence, should not be in the form of a question, should avoid figurative language, and should not be vague or overly general.

Here, for example, are four poorly written central ideas. See if you can identify the problem with each and figure out how each might be phrased more effectively:

Ineffective: Motorcycle helmet laws are a good idea.

Ineffective: Uses of the laser.

Ineffective: How can you protect your apartment against burglaries?

Ineffective: The Yucatán peninsula is a fantastic place for a vacation.

Number one, of course, is too general. To say motorcycle helmet laws are a "good idea" does not convey the speaker's viewpoint sharply and clearly. What does the speaker mean by a "good idea"? That motorcycle helmet laws reduce the rate of serious head injuries in accidents? That the speaker's state should pass a motorcycle helmet law? If so, the central idea should say as much. A revised central idea for this speech might be:

More Effective: Because motorcycle helmet laws have been proven to reduce the rate of serious head injuries in accidents, our state should pass a law requiring all motorcyclists to wear protective helmets.

The second ineffective central idea is also too general, but it suffers further from not being written as a complete sentence. "Uses of the laser" might work as a topic statement, but it does not reveal enough about the content of the speech to serve as the central idea. It should be rewritten as a full sentence that identifies the major uses of the laser to be discussed in the speech. For example:

More Effective: The laser is a highly versatile device with important uses in many areas, including medicine, industry, telecommunications, and art.

The third poorly written central idea is phrased as a question rather than as a full declarative sentence. Asking "How can you protect your apartment against burglaries?" would be a good way to catch the interest of your listeners, but it does not encapsulate the main points to be developed in the speech. A more effective central idea would be:

More Effective: You can help protect your apartment against burglaries by installing high-quality deadbolt locks, by knowing your neighbors, by using automatic timers on lights, and by marking your valuables through the Operation Identification Program.

The final ineffective central idea is flawed by its use of figurative language. To say that the Yucatán peninsula is a "fantastic" place for a vacation does not state the speaker's central idea clearly and concisely. It does not indicate what characteristics of the Yucatán peninsula the speaker intends to discuss. Moreover, "fantastic" could mean quite different things to different people. A better central idea might be:

More Effective: Mexico's Yucatán peninsula has many attractions for vacationers, including a warm climate, excellent food, and extensive Mayan ruins.

Notice that in all these examples the more effective central idea capsulizes or sums up the main points of the speech in a single sentence. If you are having trouble phrasing your central idea, the reason may be that you do not yet have a firm grasp on the main points of your speech. Do not worry too much about your central idea until after you have developed the body of your speech (see Chapter 7). If, at that point, you still cannot come up with a clear, concise central idea, it may be that your speech itself is not very clear or concise. Keep working on the speech until you can compose a central idea that fits the criteria just discussed. The result will be a sharper central idea and a tighter, more coherent speech.

SUMMARY

The first step in speechmaking is choosing a topic. For classroom speeches it is often best to choose a subject you know well or in which you have personal experience, but you can also succeed with a topic you research especially for the speech. If you have trouble picking a topic, you can follow at least three procedures. First, make a quick inventory of your hobbies, interests, skills, experiences, beliefs, and so forth. Second, use the technique of brainstorming and write down on a sheet of paper the first topics that come to mind in several categories. Third, if you are really stuck, browse through a reference book for ideas.

After you choose a topic, you need to settle on the general purpose of your speech. Usually it will be to inform or to persuade. When your general purpose is to inform, you act as a teacher. Your goal is to communicate information clearly, accurately, and interestingly. When your general purpose is to persuade, you act as an advocate. You go beyond giving information to espousing a cause. Your goal is to win listeners over to your point of view.

Once you know your topic and general purpose, you must narrow in on a specific purpose that you can express as a single infinitive phrase. The phrase should indicate precisely what your speech seeks to achieve; for example, "To inform my audience of the major kinds of witchcraft practiced today." The specific purpose statement should (1) be a full infinitive phrase, not a fragment; (2) be phrased as a statement, not a question; (3) avoid figurative language; (4) concentrate on one distinct idea; (5) not be too vague or general.

In addition, keep several questions in mind as you formulate your specific purpose statement: Does my purpose meet the assignment? Can I accomplish my purpose in the time allotted? Is the purpose relevant to my audience? Is the purpose too trivial or too technical for my audience?

The central idea refines and sharpens your specific purpose. It is a concise statement of what you will say in your speech, and it usually crystallizes in your thinking after you have done your research and have decided on the main points of your speech. An example of a central idea is "The three major kinds of witchcraft practiced today are black magic, sorcery, and satanism.'' As you can see, the central idea usually capsulizes the main points to be developed in the body of your speech.

REVIEW QUESTIONS

After reading this chapter, you should be able to answer the following questions:

1. What three procedures can you follow if you are having trouble choosing a topic for your speech?

2. What are the two general purposes of most classroom speeches? How do they differ?

3. Why is determining the specific purpose such an important early step in speech preparation? Why is it important to include the audience in the specific purpose statement?

4. What are five tips for formulating your specific purpose?

5. What are five questions to ask about your specific purpose?

6. What is the difference between the specific purpose and the central idea of a speech? What are four criteria for checking the effectiveness of your central idea?

APPLICATION EXERCISES

1. Using the method of brainstorming described in the chapter, come up with three topics you might like to deal with in your next classroom speech. For each topic, devise two possible specific purpose statements suitable for the speech assignment. Make sure the specific purpose statements fit the guidelines discussed in the chapter.

2. Below are six topics. Choose three, and for each of the three compose two specific purpose statements—one suitable for an informative speech and one suitable for a persuasive speech.

   Example:

   Topic: Ozone layer

   Informative: To inform my audience how the buildup of CFCs in the atmosphere is destroying the Earth's ozone layer.

Persuasive: To persuade my audience that the United Nations should develop a policy prohibiting all use of CFCs by the year 2000.

weight lifting	airline safety
electoral college	health care
television	education

3. Here are several specific purpose statements for classroom speeches. Identify the problem with each, and rewrite the statement to correct the problem.

   To inform my audience how to make a great submarine sandwich.

   To inform my audience about the growth of credit card fraud and the methods of sound financial planning.

   To persuade my audience that something has to be done about the problem of America's deteriorating bridges.

   To inform my audience about Disneyland.

   What is Lyme disease?

   To inform my audience why square grooves are superior to U-shaped grooves on golf clubs.

   Give blood.

   To persuade my audience that being a Big Brother or a Big Sister is an unreal experience.

4. Below are four central ideas for speeches. Which two are from informative speeches and which two are from persuasive speeches?

   The five major elements of art design are shape, space, color, line, and texture.

   The U.S. space program should put greater emphasis on unstaffed scientific missions because they are less costly and more beneficial than staffed programs such as the space shuttle.

   A program of equal pay for jobs of comparable worth should be instituted because it will help eliminate the gap between salaries paid to men and salaries paid to women.

   The three major types of sleep disorders are insomnia, narcolepsy, and apnea.

5. Below are three sets of main points for speeches. For each set supply the general purpose, specific purpose, and central idea.

   General Purpose:

   Specific Purpose:

   Central Idea:

Main Points: I. The first stage in dealing with the death of a loved one is denial.
II. The second stage in dealing with the death of a loved one is anger.
III. The third stage in dealing with the death of a loved one is depression.
IV. The fourth stage in dealing with the death of a loved one is acceptance.

General Purpose:

Specific Purpose:

Central Idea:

Main Points: I. Elizabeth Porter should be elected to the legislature because she will promote economic growth.
II. Elizabeth Porter should be elected to the legislature because she will vote to reduce property taxes.
III. Elizabeth Porter should be elected to the legislature because she will combat fraud in state government.

General Purpose:

Specific Purpose:

Central Idea:

Main Points: I. As a social worker, Jane Addams founded the settlement house movement in Chicago.
II. As a reformer, Jane Addams campaigned for child-labor laws, unemployment compensation, and better public sanitation.
III. As a suffragist, Jane Addams fought to give women the vote.
IV. As a writer, Jane Addams is best known for her autobiographical *Twenty Years at Hull House.*

NOTES

[1] Adapted from R. R. Allen and Ray E. McKerrow, *The Pragmatics of Public Communication,* 3rd ed. (Dubuque, Iowa: Kendall/Hunt, 1985), pp. 42–44.
[2] James C. Humes, *Roles Speakers Play* (New York: Harper & Row, 1976), p. 5.

CHAPTER 4

Analyzing the Audience

AUDIENCE-CENTEREDNESS

YOUR CLASSMATES AS AN AUDIENCE

THE PSYCHOLOGY OF AUDIENCES

DEMOGRAPHIC AUDIENCE ANALYSIS
  Age
  Sex
  Religion
  Racial, Ethnic, or Cultural Background
  Group Membership

SITUATIONAL AUDIENCE ANALYSIS
  Size
  Physical Setting
  Disposition Toward the Topic
  Disposition Toward the Speaker
  Disposition Toward the Occasion

GETTING INFORMATION ABOUT THE
  AUDIENCE
  Interviewing
  Questionnaires

ADAPTING TO THE AUDIENCE

Dr. Simmons was pleased. Just three months after moving to the small Midwestern town, he had been invited to address an evening meeting of the Chamber of Commerce. Here was the perfect opportunity to show his knowledge of modern medicine and to get his practice off to a flourishing start. With this in mind, the doctor prepared carefully.

On the night of his speech, Dr. Simmons was delighted to see that the meeting hall was full. After being introduced, he strode confidently to the lectern and announced his topic: "Recent Advances in Medicine." He began with a detailed discussion of Creutzfeldt-Jakob disease, a rare brain disorder that had recently been covered in the *New England Journal of Medicine.* Next he outlined the progress that had been made in studying immune system disorders.

Just about this time, halfway through his speech, Dr. Simmons began to notice a certain restlessness in his audience. People were murmuring and shuffling their feet. Someone in the fourth row seemed to be glancing at a newspaper. Nevertheless, Dr. Simmons plowed on. He had saved the best for last. He quoted extensively from an article in the *Lancet* about genetic research, feeling sure his audience would be impressed by his familiarity with this prestigious British medical journal.

Then the speech was over. Dr. Simmons had expected to be surrounded by enthusiastic people, congratulating him and asking questions. Instead he found himself standing alone. Finally the president of the Chamber of Commerce came up to him. "Something tells me," said Dr. Simmons, "that my speech was *not* an unqualified success! I can't understand it. I worked so hard to make it interesting!"

"Oh, it was a fine speech," replied the president. "But maybe it would have gone over better with a different audience. Creutzfeldt-Jakob disease is not exactly a factor in these people's everyday experience. You know, here we are in January. If you'd talked about ways to avoid getting the flu, you'd have had them on the edges of their seats!"

AUDIENCE-CENTEREDNESS

This story points up an important fact about public speaking: Good speakers are audience-centered. They know the primary purpose of speechmaking is not to display one's learning or demonstrate one's superiority or blow off steam. Rather, it is to gain a *desired response* from listeners. The key to successful communication is to "translate a truth into language perfectly intelligible to the person to whom you speak."[1] Dr. Simmons' desired response at the Chamber of Commerce meeting was to have his listeners see him as a competent physician. But he didn't make his message meaningful to them. If he had adapted to his listeners, he might well have gained their confidence; instead, he talked about medical problems far outside their experience.

Being audience-centered does not mean taking any means to an end. You need not prostitute your beliefs to get a favorable response from your audience. Nor should you use devious, unethical tactics to achieve your goals. You can remain perfectly true to yourself while at the same time adapting your message to the needs of a particular audience. When working on your speeches, you should keep several questions in mind:

To whom am I speaking?

What do I want them to know, believe, or do as a result of my speech?

What is the most effective way of composing and presenting my speech to accomplish that aim?

The answers to these questions will influence every decision you make along the way—selecting a topic, determining a specific purpose, settling on your main points and supporting materials, organizing the message, and, finally, delivering the speech.

It can be instructive to watch how political candidates deal with audience-centeredness. Suppose a person is running for Congress. To an audience of senior citizens he or she might talk about Social Security benefits; to a group of farmers the speech might emphasize agricultural price supports; to urban apartment dwellers the candidate might stress methods to counteract street crime. This strategy is perfectly legitimate, provided all the policies are part of the candidate's overall program. If the candidate were to concentrate on agricultural price supports before a group of white-collar workers, they simply wouldn't care. The speaker's aim is to adjust to the concerns of the audience, not to show how much he or she knows about a wide variety of issues.

This is not very different from what you do in your daily social contacts. A generation or two ago it was considered rude to bring up three topics in polite conversation—politics, religion, and sex. Nowadays we don't adhere to such strictures. But since these are among the most controversial topics of discussion, we are usually a bit careful about them. Very few people would walk into a party and announce, "What a jerk the President is!" Or, "Did you see those people praying in front of the Science Building? Silly bunch of fools!" Or, "You know, Lynn just moved in with her boyfriend. I don't care if times *have* changed, I still think it's immoral." If you made a statement like any of these, you would run the risk of having among your listeners: (a) an ardent supporter of the President; (b) someone who had participated in the prayer ceremony at the Science Building; (c) a woman who lives with her boyfriend; (d) all of the above. The resulting situation could be most embarrassing.

People usually prefer to open such topics with a fairly noncommittal position, to see how their listeners respond. You might say, "Did you hear what the President did today?" Or, "See the action in front of the Science Building?" Or, "How's Lynn doing?" Then when you have heard and processed your companion's response, you can tailor your statements accordingly. (You don't have to *agree* with a viewpoint different from your own; but neither do you have to hit your listeners over the head with your own opinion.)

When you make a speech, either in class or in some other forum, you can't just wait to see how your audience responds and then change the rest of the speech. But you can find out in advance as much as possible about your listeners' positions on various subjects. Unless you know what your listeners believe *now*, you cannot hope to change their beliefs.

At this point you may be nodding your head and saying, "Of course, everyone knows that. It's only common sense." But knowing a precept and putting it into practice are two different matters. The aim of this chapter is to introduce the basic principles necessary to understanding audiences. Chapters 13 and 14 will deal with those features of audience analysis and adaptation unique to informative and persuasive speaking.

YOUR CLASSMATES AS AN AUDIENCE

There is a tendency—among students and teachers alike—to view the classroom as an artificial speaking situation. In a way, it is. Your speech class is a testing ground where you can develop your communication skills before applying them outside the classroom. No elections, no verdicts, no business decisions, no promotions ride on your performance. The most serious measure of success or failure is your grade, and that is determined ultimately by your teacher.

Because of this, it is easy to lose sight of your fellow students as an authentic audience. But each of your classmates is a real person with real ideas, attitudes, and feelings. Your speech class offers an enormous opportunity to inform and persuade other people. As one student wrote on her evaluation form at the end of her speech class, "I thought the speeches would all be phony, but they weren't. Some of them really hit me hard. I've not only learned a lot about speaking—I've learned a lot about other things from listening to the speeches in class."

The best classroom speeches are those that take the classroom audience as seriously as a lawyer, a politician, a minister, or an advertiser takes an audience. Public speaking is not acting. The essence of speechmaking is not to learn a role that can be played over and over without variation, but to adapt one's ideas to particular audiences on particular occasions. If you regard your audience as artificial, you will probably give a speech that sounds artificial.

One key to successful speaking is to consider every audience—inside the classroom and out—as worthy of your best efforts to communicate your knowledge or convictions. At the least you show respect for your listeners. At the most you could make a real difference in their lives. The following story demonstrates the latter:

Julia Black gave an informative speech on the subject of preparing for a job interview. One of the points she made was this: "Of course you will expect to answer questions about yourself, your education, your experience. But you must also be ready to *ask* questions. Interviewers expect you to ask questions about the company, about your job responsibilities, about the prospects for growth, and so on. And if you are going to ask intelligent questions, you'll need to do a little research beforehand."

One of Julia's classmates, Phil Greene, paid close attention. Two weeks earlier Phil had had an important job interview. But the job had gone to someone else.

Good speakers are audience-centered. They work hard to find creative ways to evoke an enthusiastic response from their listeners. (Ulrike Welsch)

Listening to Julia, Phil saw himself back in the interviewer's office. When the interviewer had said, ''Do you have any questions?'' Phil had replied, ''No, I guess not. Everything seems pretty clear.'' As he replayed the conversation in his mind, Phil thought, ''Maybe that's why I didn't get the job.'' Then and there Phil resolved to be better prepared for his next interview. He would have ready a number of well-thought-out questions about the company and the job.

Did Phil really not get the first job because he didn't ask questions, or was it simply because he wasn't qualified? We can't know for sure. But certainly Phil will do much better in his next interview—thanks to his classmate's speech.

Most of your classroom speeches won't have this much immediate impact. Nevertheless, any topic that you handle conscientiously can influence your listeners—can enrich their experience, broaden their knowledge, perhaps change their views about something important.

THE PSYCHOLOGY OF AUDIENCES

What do you do when you listen to a speech? Sometimes you pay close attention; at other times you let your thoughts wander. People may be compelled to attend a speech, but no one can make them listen unless they want to. It's up to the speaker to make the audience *choose* to pay attention.

Even when people do pay attention, they don't process a speaker's message exactly as the speaker intended. Auditory perception is always *selective.* Every speech contains two messages—the one sent by the speaker and the one received by the listener. As we saw in Chapter 1, what a speaker says is filtered through a listener's frame of reference—the sum of his or her needs, interests, expectations, knowledge, and experience. As a result, we constantly listen and respond to speeches not as they are but as we are. Or as Paul Simon says in his classic song *The Boxer,* "A man hears what he wants to hear and disregards the rest."[2]

What do people want to hear? Very simply, they usually want to hear about things that are meaningful to them. People are *egocentric.* They pay closest attention to messages that affect their own values, their own beliefs, their own well-being. Listeners typically approach speeches with one question uppermost in mind: "Why is this important for *me?*"

What do these psychological principles mean to you as a speaker? First, they mean that your listeners will hear and judge what you say on the basis of what they already know and believe. Second, they mean that you must relate your message to your listeners—show how it pertains to them, explain why they should care about it as much as you do. Here's an example:

Marsha Stein was hired straight out of college to be marketing assistant for a major firm that manufactured greeting cards. After only a few months on the job, Marsha was assigned to present to the sales force of 150 people a brand-new line of cards. Marsha wrote a beautiful speech, pointing out the esthetic virtues of the artwork, the high quality of the verses, the excellence of the color reproduction. Luckily, Marsha's boss asked to hear the speech before the day of the sales meeting. Her boss said, "You really have learned a lot about the product, and that's fine. But now you have to learn about sales representatives. These people earn their living selling cards. Their commissions make the difference between steak and tuna fish on the dinner table. You have to reach them through their pocketbooks."

Marsha digested this and went back to work some more on her speech. On the day of the sales meeting, she stood up before her audience and began: "Here is a new line of cards that can increase your quarterly sales by 15 percent. Let me give you some tips on selling them that can push you over your quota." In a few moments she had everyone's attention, and her speech was off to a great start.

As Marsha's experience shows, you need some grasp of what your listeners know, believe, and care about. Saul Alinsky, the noted community organizer, advises: "People only understand things in terms of their experience," which means that to communicate with them, "you must get within their experience."[3]

Of course, you can't actually get inside another person's experience. But you can learn enough about your audience to know what you should do to make your ideas clear and meaningful. How you can do this is our next topic.

DEMOGRAPHIC AUDIENCE ANALYSIS

One of the ways speakers analyze audiences is by looking for observable traits such as age, sex, group membership, religious orientation, racial, ethnic, or cultural background, and the like. This is called *demographic* audience analysis.

It consists of two steps: (1) identifying the general demographic features of your audience; (2) gauging the importance of those features to a particular speaking situation. Here are a few of the major factors you will need to consider.

Age

Few things affect a person's outlook more than his or her age. Each generation has a more-or-less common set of values and experiences that sets it apart from other generations. No matter how hard they may try, for example, your grandparents will probably never be fully comfortable with men and women living together outside of marriage. To you, on the other hand, Babe Ruth, the Great Depression, Franklin Roosevelt, World War II, Joseph McCarthy—all are probably just people and events out of the past. Like your parents and grandparents, you are a product of your world, as your children will be products of their world.

You can see what this means for your speeches. Suppose you address an audience of older people. If you refer offhand to your "roommate"—making it clear that your roommate is someone of the opposite sex—your audience may be disturbed and simply tune out the rest of your speech. Similarly, if you speak to an audience of young adults and casually mention "Black Friday" (the stock market crash that began the Great Depression) or "Guadalcanal" (an important battle of World War II), they may not know what you are talking about. Even if younger listeners do recognize the names of the events, they will not have the emotional associations of older people who experienced the events—who lost their fortunes or lost their loved ones.

In your speech class, most of your listeners will probably be in their late teens or early twenties. If so, you can assume a common level of age experience. On the other hand, many college classrooms today include students in their thirties, forties, fifties, and beyond. You may then have to tackle two or three generations. This will give you good practice for speeches outside the classroom, where age is usually a major factor in audience analysis.

Sex

Shortly after graduation from college, Peter Harrington, who had been an art major, landed a dream job. He was hired as a guide-lecturer by a major museum, which meant he would conduct tours of people through the galleries and speak about the art. His first assignment was the contemporary art collection, and he prepared his talk carefully. At one point in it he said:

"The artist of today lives in a world that would have been incomprehensible to Rembrandt or Van Gogh. He can be a superstar by the time he is twenty-five. He might see his earning power increase overnight from $10 a painting to $10,000 a painting. He is lionized by the media and sought out by collectors. No longer need an artist fear he will achieve fame only after he dies."

When Peter had finished, he asked the tour group whether they had any questions. A woman raised her hand and said, "Your talk was very interesting, but I have one problem with it. You kept referring to the artist as 'he.' Right here in this gallery I see paintings by five women artists. Don't you think it's time we acknowledged that not all artists are men?"

This story illustrates a problem that continues to plague speakers in all fields. We think of our times as enlightened, but we still encounter people who automatically refer to artists or doctors as "he" and to grade-school teachers or nurses as "she." A speaker who makes such remarks is almost certain to offend some members of the audience.

In speechmaking you must be especially wary of making assumptions with respect to gender until you have tested those assumptions and found them to be correct. You must avoid false sex distinctions where they do not exist and acknowledge true sex distinctions where they do exist. This is not as difficult as it sounds. Mainly, you will need to strive for awareness and common sense.

Social distinctions between the sexes have been eroding for some years. Men now cook, keep house, take care of children, and do needlepoint. Women serve as umpires in professional baseball, work in construction trades, sit in the U.S. Congress, and enlist in the armed forces. The old stereotypes no longer apply.

Nonetheless, few adults today were raised in a sexually neutral environment. Until fairly recently it was assumed that boys should do certain kinds of things and girls other kinds of things. Therefore, if you have an all-male audience, you might expect a higher level of knowledge on such topics as auto mechanics or football. If you have an all-female audience, you might expect a higher level of knowledge on such topics as child care and fashion. Bear in mind, however, that these are generalizations. There are plenty of men who don't know the difference between a carburetor and a crankshaft, and plenty of women who don't know which end of the baby to burp.

In sum, women and men today share a much broader range of experiences, interests, and aspirations than they once did. Avoid outmoded gender stereotypes. At the same time, remember that men and women are still socialized differently. An astute speaker will be equally attuned to both the differences *and* the similarities between the sexes.

Religion

Charlie McKenna, a history major, decided to give his classroom speech on a subject that had long fascinated him—the Crusades of the Middle Ages. Part of his speech went like this:

"For nearly 200 years, beginning in 1096, they kept coming in waves—armies of Christians from northern Europe pouring south to do battle. Their journeys were arduous, and they died by the thousands, but the Crusaders never lost sight of their mission—to recapture the Holy Land of Jerusalem from control by the Muslims.

Nothing can match it as a sacred religious quest. Against all odds, the Crusaders set out to rescue the tomb of Christ from the hands of the infidels, to restore the Holy Land to the followers of Christ.''

Most of Charlie's classmates reacted positively to his speech, but finally one student raised his hand. He said, "I think I am one of the infidels you were talking about. I am a Muslim, and my parents came from the Middle East. The land you call holy is holy to other religions, not just Christianity. You think of the Crusades as a rescue mission, but I think of them as an invasion.''

This story illustrates a factor you must take into account in all your speechmaking. You cannot assume your views on religion—whatever they may be—are shared by your listeners. And religious views are among the most emotionally charged and passionately defended of all human concerns. Even your small speech class might include Baptists, Jews, atheists, Mormons, evangelical Christians, agnostics, Roman Catholics, Buddhists, Presbyterians, and Muslims. For speeches in the outside world, the probability of a religious mix is even greater. Whenever you speak on a topic with religious dimensions, be sure to consider the religious orientations of your listeners. At the very least, failure to do so can weaken your speech. At the most you will be seriously embarrassed.

Racial, Ethnic, or Cultural Background

Different racial, ethnic, and cultural groups have different customs and beliefs. This is particularly important to remember for speeches outside the classroom. But if your speech class includes international students, it will also be a factor in classroom speeches. Here's what happened to one student who forgot to allow for such differences:

Some years ago Mark Pantezzi, a student in a large California university, was addressing his class about the benefits of psychiatric counseling. His specific topic was crisis intervention, and he explained how he had been helped through a difficult period by short-term intensive counseling. As it happened, several students in the class were from Japan. Part of the way into the speech, they began to frown and look uncomfortable. By the end of the speech they were clearly disapproving.

After class, Mark sought out one of his friends among the Japanese students. "What was the matter with you?" he asked. "All through my speech you looked as though you'd swallowed a lemon!"

"You couldn't have known unless you had asked," replied his friend. "But in Japan, psychotherapy is not at all common. Most Japanese consider it an invasion of privacy, and to tell one's problems to a stranger would mean loss of face. In times of crisis we turn to our families.''

Even among students from the United States there is great diversity. Despite their similarities as Americans, people of European descent, blacks, Chicanos, Latinos, Chinese-Americans, and others may have special racial, ethnic, or cultural orientations bearing upon your speech topic. If so, be sure to find out about them and plan your speech accordingly.

Group Membership

"Tell me thy company," says Don Quixote, "and I'll tell thee what thou art." For all of our talk about rugged individualism, Americans are very group-oriented. Workers belong to unions, businesspeople to chambers of commerce. Hunters join the National Rifle Association, environmentalists the Sierra Club, feminists the National Organization for Women. Doctors enroll in the American Medical Association, lawyers in the American Bar Association. There are thousands of such voluntary organizations in the United States.

Similar groups abound on campus. Some of your classmates may belong to fraternities or sororities, some to Campus Crusade for Christ, some to the Young Republicans, some to the film society, some to the ski club, and so forth. For speeches in the classroom, as well as for those outside the classroom, the group affiliations of your audience may provide excellent clues about your listeners' interests and attitudes.

Age, sex, religion, group membership, racial, ethnic, or cultural background—these are just a few of the variables to consider in demographic audience analysis. Others include occupation, economic position, social standing, education, intelligence, and place of residence. Indeed, *anything* characteristic of a given audience is potentially important to a speaker addressing that audience. For your classroom speeches, you may want to learn about your classmates' academic majors, years in school, extracurricular activities, living arrangements, and job aspirations.

Perhaps the most important thing to keep in mind about demographic audience analysis is that it is not an end in itself. Your aim is not just to list the major traits of your listeners but to find in those traits clues about how your listeners will respond to your speech. Once you have done that, you are ready to move on to the second stage of audience analysis.

SITUATIONAL AUDIENCE ANALYSIS

Situational audience analysis usually builds on the demographic analysis. It identifies traits of the audience unique to the speaking situation at hand. These traits include the size of the audience, attitudes influenced by the physical setting, and the disposition of the audience toward the subject, the speaker, and the occasion.

Size

Outside the classroom, the size of an audience can, with the aid of television and radio, range in the millions. Most speech classes, however, consist of between fifteen and thirty people—a small to medium-size audience. This is a good size for beginning speakers, most of whom are horrified at the prospect of addressing a huge crowd. As you gain more experience, though, you may welcome the challenge of speaking to larger groups. Some speakers actually prefer a large audience to a small one.

No matter what size group you are addressing, bear in mind one basic principle: The larger the audience, the more formal your presentation must be. This will have the greatest impact on your delivery, but it may also affect your language, choice of appeals, and use of visual aids.

Physical Setting

The receptivity of listeners to your speech frequently will be influenced by factors beyond their control—and sometimes beyond your control. Which of the following would you rather address?

> An audience assembled immediately after lunch, crammed into an overheated room with inadequate seating

> An audience assembled at 10:00 in the morning, comfortably seated in an airy, well-lighted room

Undoubtedly you chose the second option. Any of the adverse conditions listed in the first could seriously impair your audience's willingness to accept your ideas or even listen to you at all.

When you face any speaking situation, it is important to know in advance if there will be any difficulties with the physical setting. For classroom speeches, of course, you already do know. But speeches outside the classroom can confront you with many unpleasant surprises unless you do your homework beforehand.

When you are invited to speak, don't be shy about asking questions of the person who arranged the speech. If possible, look over the room yourself a few days in advance, or else arrive early on the day of your speech to give the room a quick inspection. If it is too warm or too cold, see about adjusting the thermostat. Check the seating arrangements and the location of the lectern to be sure your audience can see you properly. In short, do everything you can to control the influence of physical setting on your audience.

But, you may wonder, what about circumstances you *can't* control? Your speech *is* scheduled directly after lunch or dinner. The room *is* too small for the audience expected, and the heat *cannot* be regulated. Then you are simply going to have to work harder to adapt to these aspects of your listeners' discomfort. When faced with an audience that is potentially hot, sleepy, and cross, do your best to make the speech as interesting and lively as you can. Above all, don't let *yourself* be influenced by the poor physical setting. If your audience sees that you are energetic, alert, and involved with your topic, chances are they will forget their discomfort and come right along with you.

Disposition Toward the Topic

As we saw in Chapter 3, you should keep your audience in mind when choosing a topic. Ideally, you will pick a topic that suits them as well as it suits you. Once you have your topic, however, you must consider in more detail how your listeners will react to it. In particular, you need to assess their interest in the topic, their knowledge about it, and their attitudes toward it.

Interest   Outside the classroom, people do not often expend the time and effort to attend a speech unless they are interested in the topic. But the members of your speech class are a captive audience. Sometimes they will be deeply interested in your topic, particularly if it relates directly to them. Most of the time they will range from fairly interested to mildly curious to downright indifferent.

One of your tasks will be to assess their interest in advance and to adjust your speech accordingly. Most important, if your topic is not likely to generate great interest, you must take special steps to get your classmates involved. Here are two brief examples of how to do this:

Richard planned to speak about small claims court, in which ordinary people can press law suits involving up to $2,000 without lawyers. At the beginning of his speech, he said: "It's two weeks after you have moved into a new apartment. A letter arrives from your old landlord. Expecting to get back your $250 security deposit, you joyfully tear open the envelope. Inside is a form letter explaining why your security deposit is not being returned. What can you do about it? Nothing, right? Wrong! You can file a claim in small claims court."

Anne's speech was about world hunger. Before she began to speak, she started a metronome that was set to tick at intervals of one-and-a-half seconds. Anne let the metronome tick for twenty-five seconds. Then she turned it off and said, "For each tick of this metronome, one person, somewhere in the world, has just died from starvation, malnutrition, or a malnutrition-caused disease."

In the chapters that follow, we will look closely at all the various ways you can develop interest in your topic—by an arresting introduction, provocative supporting details, vivid language, dynamic delivery, visual aids, and so forth.

Knowledge   There is often a strong correlation between interest in a topic and knowledge about it. People tend to be interested in what they know about. Likewise, they are inclined to learn about subjects that interest them. But there are exceptions. Few students know much about handwriting analysis, yet most would find it an absorbing topic. On the other hand, almost all know a lot about checking books out of the library, but few would find it a fascinating subject for a speech.

Why is it important to gauge your listeners' knowledge about your topic? Quite simply, because it will to a large extent determine what you can say in your speech. If your listeners know little about your topic—whether or not they find it interesting—you will have to talk at a more elementary level. If they are reasonably well informed, you can take a more technical and detailed approach.

Attitude   The attitude of your listeners toward your topic can be extremely important in determining how you handle the material. If you know in advance the prevailing attitude among your audience, you can adjust what you say to what your audience needs to hear. Consider the experiences of two students— one who did not account for listener attitude and one who did:

> Sandy Hollins spoke about vaccinating children against childhood diseases such as mumps and whooping cough. She believed such vaccinations were more dangerous than beneficial. Her topic was interesting but also highly controversial. Unfortunately, rather than acknowledging that her point of view was unusual, Sandy presented her material as though it were general knowledge.
>
> The speech was not well received. In fact, the class found Sandy's approach so inconsistent with everything they had heard about vaccination that they couldn't believe it. As one student told her after the speech, "I simply can't accept what you said—it sounded like something out of the *National Enquirer.* My whole life I have been told only good things about vaccination and have had many shots that helped me and none that have hurt me or anyone I know."

Had Sandy taken the skepticism of her audience into account, she could have established the scientific credibility of her material and thereby made her audience more receptive to it.

Compare the approach of Dan Robinson, who also espoused a minority viewpoint:

> Dan decided to give his persuasive speech in opposition to abortion. After circulating a questionnaire among his classmates, he found that almost all of them favored legalized abortion. They gave two reasons. They believed the fetus during the first trimester of pregnancy was not yet fully "human"; and they believed the right of a woman to control her own body was more important than the rights of an unborn child. Although Dan disagreed vehemently with these beliefs, he knew he could neither ignore them nor insult his classmates for holding them. He realized he would have to discuss these points logically and with hard evidence if he were to have any chance of persuading his audience.

As it turned out, Dan did convince some members of the class to reassess their beliefs. He could not have done so without first investigating what those beliefs were and then adapting his message to them.

Disposition Toward the Speaker

Let's return for a moment to Sandy's speech about vaccination. Sandy was a sophomore business major with no special medical or scientific background. It's not surprising that her classmates took her statements about vaccination with a large grain of salt. But suppose Sandy had been a recognized expert on childhood diseases and their control. Then her listeners would surely have found her much more believable. Why? Because an audience's response to a message is invariably colored by their perception of the speaker.

The more competent listeners believe a speaker to be, the more likely they are to accept what the speaker says. Likewise, the more listeners believe that a speaker has their best interests at heart, the more likely they are to respond positively to the speaker's message.

We will come back to this subject in detail when we deal with strategies for persuasive speaking in Chapter 14. For now, keep in mind that your listeners will always have *some* set of attitudes toward you as a speaker. Estimating what those attitudes are and how they will affect your speech is a crucial part of situational audience analysis.

Disposition Toward the Occasion

When Vanessa Redgrave won the Academy Award for Best Supporting Actress for her role in *Julia*, she began her acceptance speech by thanking the Academy and then turned to politics. She praised the film community for voting for her despite the opposition of the Jewish Defense League, "a small group of Zionist hoodlums whose behavior is an insult to Jews all over the world." At first the audience was stunned. Then boos and hisses began to fill the hall, even as Redgrave was speaking.

On most occasions Redgrave's comments would not have ignited such an angry response. But the Academy Awards presentation is not most occasions. The people who attend will tolerate even the most insipid of acceptance speeches, thanking everybody in some star's life from the hairdresser to the family cat. That is what they *expect* to hear. They do not expect to hear political rhetoric. What angered the audience was not just what Redgrave said, but that she exploited the occasion of the Academy Awards for political purposes.

No matter what the situation, listeners have fairly definite ideas about the speeches they consider appropriate. They expect to hear political speeches in Congress, sermons in church, after-dinner speeches after dinner, and so forth. Speakers who seriously violate these expectations can almost always count on infuriating the audience.

Perhaps most important, the occasion will dictate how long a speech should be. When you are invited to speak, the chairperson will usually say how much time you have for your talk. If not, be sure to ask. And once you know, pare down your speech so it fits easily within the allotted time. Do not exceed that time under any circumstances, for you are likely to see your audience dwindle as you drone on. (This is one reason why most teachers insist that classroom speeches be kept within the designated time limit. It provides crucial training for speeches you will give outside the classroom.)

There are other audience expectations that apply to your classroom situation. One is that speeches will conform to the assignment. Another is that speakers will observe appropriate standards of taste and decorum. Failure to adhere to these expectations may disturb your classmates and will almost certainly damage your grade.

GETTING INFORMATION ABOUT THE AUDIENCE

Now that you know *what* to learn about an audience, the next question is *how* do you learn it? A person running for high political office can rely on hired professional pollsters. If, as is more likely, you are invited sometime to address a particular group—say a meeting of the local Rotary club—the person who invites you can usually provide a good sketch of the audience. Ask your contact with the group where you can find out more about its history and purpose. Best of all, if you know someone else who has spoken to the same group, be sure to sound out that person.

What about your classmates as an audience? You can learn a lot about them just by observation and conversation. Still, you probably will need to know more about their backgrounds and opinions in relation to specific speech topics. Some teachers require students to do a formal audience analysis—either through interviews or through written questionnaires—for at least one of their speeches.

Interviewing

The face-to-face interview (see pages 93–98) is highly flexible and allows for in-depth questioning. When properly planned, structured, and conducted, it can be a superb way of learning about individual members of an audience. The great drawback, of course, is the cost in time and energy. Interviewing each member of a class before every speech may be the most thorough method of audience analysis, but it is seldom practical. Therefore, most teachers encourage their students to rely on questionnaires.

Questionnaires

Like interviewing, constructing a good questionnaire is an art you cannot be expected to master in a speech class. By following a few basic guidelines, however, you can learn to develop a questionnaire that will be more than adequate for analyzing your classroom audience.

There are three major types of questions to choose from: fixed-alternative questions, scale questions, and open-ended questions.[4]

Fixed-alternative questions, as their name implies, offer a fixed choice between two or more responses. For example:

Do you know what extrasensory perception is?

      Yes _____

      No _____

Not sure _____

If yes, do you believe extrasensory perception is a real phenomenon?

      Yes _____

      No _____

Not sure _____

By limiting the possible responses, such questions produce clear, unambiguous answers. They also tend to yield superficial answers. Other techniques are needed to get beneath the surface.

     Scale questions resemble fixed-alternative questions, but they allow more leeway in responding. For example:

How much of a role do you believe extrasensory perception plays in everyday life?

major |_____|_____|_____|_____ no
role   role

Do you agree or disagree with this statement: Every individual has the potential for extrasensory perception if he or she will develop it.

strongly agree	mildly agree	undecided	mildly disagree	strongly disagree

_____|_____|_____|_____|_____

Questions like these are particularly useful for getting at the strength of a respondent's attitudes or feelings.

     Open-ended questions give maximum latitude in responding. For example:

What is your opinion about extrasensory perception?

How would you respond if someone wanted to test *your* powers of extrasensory perception?

Although open-ended questions invite more detailed responses than the other two types, they also increase the likelihood of getting answers that do not give the kind of information you need.

     Because each type of question has its advantages and disadvantages,

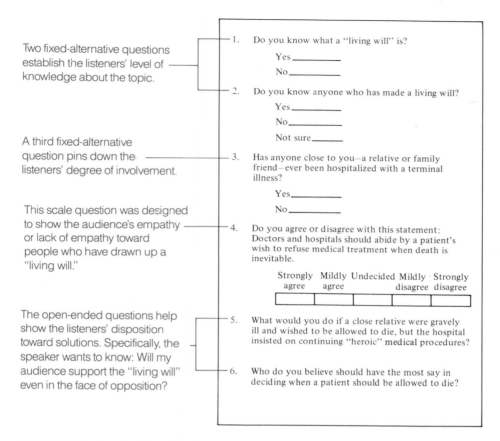

Two fixed-alternative questions establish the listeners' level of knowledge about the topic.

1. Do you know what a "living will" is?

   Yes _____

   No _____

2. Do you know anyone who has made a living will?

   Yes _____

   No _____

   Not sure _____

A third fixed-alternative question pins down the listeners' degree of involvement.

3. Has anyone close to you—a relative or family friend—ever been hospitalized with a terminal illness?

   Yes _____

   No _____

This scale question was designed to show the audience's empathy or lack of empathy toward people who have drawn up a "living will."

4. Do you agree or disagree with this statement: Doctors and hospitals should abide by a patient's wish to refuse medical treatment when death is inevitable.

Strongly agree	Mildly agree	Undecided	Mildly disagree	Strongly disagree

The open-ended questions help show the listeners' disposition toward solutions. Specifically, the speaker wants to know: Will my audience support the "living will" even in the face of opposition?

5. What would you do if a close relative were gravely ill and wished to be allowed to die, but the hospital insisted on continuing "heroic" medical procedures?

6. Who do you believe should have the most say in deciding when a patient should be allowed to die?

FIGURE 4.1   Sample Questionnaire

many questionnaires contain all three types. Figure 4.1 shows a questionnaire that was distributed before a classroom speech on "living wills"—documents written by people to indicate how much medical intervention they would want should they become terminally ill or incapacitated. By using all three types of questions, the student did two things—elicited specific information about the audience and probed more deeply into their attitudes toward the speech topic. The results of the questionnaire survey broke down like this:

1. Only half of the class knew what a living will is. Therefore, the speaker had to be sure to explain living wills clearly at the start of her speech.

2. Three students knew someone who had made a living will; most said they were not sure. Thus, the speaker could not depend on a high degree of personal involvement among the audience.

3. Five students reported that a relative—a grandparent or elderly uncle

Interviews and questionnaires can be useful methods for gathering information about an audience's knowledge, attitudes, and concerns. (Susan Lapides/Design Concepts)

or aunt—had been hospitalized with a terminal illness. One of these wrote movingly about a grandparent's pleas to "let me go."

4. More than 65 percent of the respondents either "strongly agreed" or "mildly agreed" that a patient's wishes should be paramount in refusing medical treatment. Another 20 percent were undecided. The speaker could therefore depend on an audience generally disposed toward the concept of a living will.

5. Responses to the fifth question—"What would you do if a close relative were gravely ill and wished to be allowed to die but the hospital insisted on continuing 'heroic' medical procedures?"—were quite varied. They ranged from "I guess I'd take the doctors' word; they know best" to "I'd pull the plug myself!" Obviously, this was a charged issue. The questionnaire showed the speaker would have to handle it very carefully.

6. Again, responses varied on the question of who should have the most say in deciding about a patient's death. Most students proposed a compromise— the patient *and* the family, or the family *and* the doctors. Only two thought lawyers and judges should be involved. In combination with the answers to question 4, these responses indicated that the audience could be classified as favorable to the speaker's views.

This questionnaire worked extremely well. It revealed a great deal about the listeners' knowledge, attitudes, and concerns. You should be able to put together an equally useful questionnaire. In doing so, keep the following principles in mind:

1. Plan the questionnaire carefully to elicit precisely the information you need.

2. Use all three types of questions—fixed-alternative, scale, and open-ended.

3. Make sure the questions are clear and unambiguous.

4. Keep the questionnaire relatively brief.

ADAPTING TO THE AUDIENCE

Once you have completed the audience analysis, you should have a pretty clear picture of your listeners. You should know their relevant demographic characteristics, their interest in and knowledge about the topic, their attitudes toward the topic and the speaker, and their expectations about the occasion. Knowing all this, however, does not guarantee a successful speech. The key is how well you *use* what you know in preparing the speech.

This point deserves special attention, because it poses one of the most serious problems facing novice speakers. Most people can identify the major characteristics of their audience, but many have difficulty *adapting* their ideas to the audience. If, for example, you plan to speak on a subject in which you are expert, you may have trouble putting yourself in the place of someone who knows nothing about it. To step outside your own frame of reference and see things from another person's point of view is a real achievement. Yet this is exactly what a successful speaker eventually learns to do. You must submerge your own views so completely that you can adopt, temporarily, those of your listeners. When you do this, you will begin to hear your speech through the ears of your audience and to adjust it accordingly.

You must keep your listeners constantly in mind as you prepare your speech. Try to imagine what they will like, what they will dislike, where they will have doubts or questions, whether they will need more details here or fewer there, what will interest them and what will not. At every point you must *anticipate* how your audience will respond. How will they react to your introduction and conclusion? Will they find your examples clear and convincing? Will your visual aids help them to grasp your ideas? How will they respond to your language and manner of delivery? As you answer these questions, consciously identify with your listeners. Put yourself in their places and respond to your speech as they would.

Here is how one student worked out his problems of audience adaptation:

Joe Ruiz, a junior geology major, decided to give an informative speech about how earthquakes occur. From his audience analysis he learned that only two or three of his classmates knew much of anything about geology. To most of them, a tectonic plate would be found on a dinner table rather than below the surface of the earth. Joe realized, then, that he must present his speech at an elementary level and with a minimum of scientific language.

As he prepared the speech, Joe kept asking himself, "How can I make this clear and meaningful to someone who knows nothing about earthquakes or geological principles?" Since he was speaking in the Midwest, he decided to begin by noting that the most severe earthquake in American history took place not in California or Alaska, but at New Madrid, Missouri, in 1811. If such an earthquake happened today, it would be felt from the Rocky Mountains to the Atlantic Ocean and would flatten most of the cities in the Mississippi Valley. That, he figured, should get his classmates' attention.

Throughout the body of the speech, Joe dealt only with the basic mechanics of earthquakes and carefully avoided technical terms such as "asthenosphere," "lithosphere," and "subduction zones." He also prepared visual aids diagramming fault lines so his classmates wouldn't get confused.

To be absolutely safe, Joe asked his roommate—who was not a geology major—to listen to the speech. "Stop me," he said, "any time I say something you don't understand." Joe's roommate stopped him four times—and at each spot Joe worked out a way to make his point more clearly. Finally, he had a speech that was interesting and perfectly understandable to his audience.

Like other aspects of speechmaking, adapting to your audience is easier said than done. But once you master it, you'll see that it pays dividends for your speeches. It may also help you in more personal facets of your life—when you adapt to an audience of one.

SUMMARY

Good speakers are audience-centered. They know the aim of speechmaking is to gain a desired response from listeners. When working on your speeches, keep three questions in mind: To whom am I speaking? What do I want them to know, believe, or do as a result of my speech? What is the best way to compose and present my speech to achieve that aim? Your classroom speeches will give you excellent practice in dealing with these questions, provided you always think of your classmates as a *real* audience.

To be an effective speaker, you should know something about the psychology of audiences. Auditory perception is selective. Even when people pay close attention, they don't process a speaker's message exactly as the speaker intended. People hear what they want to hear. People also are egocentric. They typically approach speeches with one question uppermost in mind: "Why is this important for *me?*" Therefore, you need to study your audience and adapt your speech directly to their beliefs and interests.

The first stage in learning about your audience is to undertake a demographic audience analysis. This involves identifying important demographic traits of your audience such as age, sex, religion, group membership, and racial, ethnic, or cultural background. The second stage in learning about your audience is to conduct a situational audience analysis. This involves identifying traits of the audience unique to the particular speaking situation at hand. These traits include the size of the audience, attitudes influenced by the physical setting, and your listeners' disposition toward the topic, toward you as a speaker, and toward the occasion.

For speeches outside the classroom, you can best get information about the audience by asking the person who invites you to speak. If possible, you should also sound out someone else who has spoken to the same group. For your classroom speeches, you can learn much about your audience by observation and conversation. You also can do a more formal audience analysis by interviewing or by circulating a questionnaire.

Once you complete the audience analysis, you must adapt your speech so it will be clear and convincing to your listeners. Keep them in mind constantly as you prepare the speech. Put yourself in their places. Try to hear the speech as they will. Anticipate their questions and objections, and try to answer them in advance. This may be difficult at first, but if you work at it you should soon see results.

REVIEW QUESTIONS

After reading this chapter, you should be able to answer the following questions:

1. Why must a public speaker be audience-centered?

2. What does it mean to say that people are egocentric? What implications does the egocentrism of audiences hold for you as a public speaker?

3. What are the five demographic traits of audiences discussed in this chapter? Why is each important to audience analysis?

4. What is situational audience analysis? What factors do you need to consider in situational audience analysis?

5. How can you get information about an audience?

6. What are the three kinds of questions used in questionnaires? Why is it a good idea to use all three in audience analysis?

7. What methods can you use to adapt your speech to your audience as you prepare the speech?

APPLICATION EXERCISES

1. Advertisers are usually very conscious of their audience. Choose an issue of a popular magazine such as *Time, Newsweek, Ms., Sports Illustrated, Cosmopolitan,* or the like. From that issue select five advertisements to analyze. Try to determine the audience being appealed to in each advertisement, and analyze the appeals (verbal and visual) used to persuade buyers. How might the appeals differ if the ads were designed to persuade a different audience?

2. Below are three general speech topics and, for each, two hypothetical audiences to which a speech might be delivered. For each topic, write a brief paragraph explaining how you might adjust your specific purpose and message according to the demographic characteristics of the audience.

   a. *Topic:* The Romantic style in painting, music, and literature
       Audience #1: 40% art majors, 40% English majors, 20% music majors
       Audience #2: 50% business majors, 30% engineering majors, 20% pre-law majors

   b. *Topic:* The War in Vietnam
       Audience #1: Day class, 90% age 18–22, 10% age 22 and over
       Audience #2: Evening class, 50% age 35 and over, 30% age 22–35, 20% age 18–22

   c. *Topic:* Nutrition in pregnancy
       Audience #1: 80% female, 20% male
       Audience #2: 80% male, 20% female

3. For your next speech, design and circulate among your classmates an audience analysis questionnaire like that discussed on pages 81–85. Use all three kinds of questions explained in the text—fixed-alternative questions, scale questions, and open-ended questions. After you have tabulated the results of the questionnaire, write an analysis explaining what the questionnaire reveals about your audience and what steps you must take to adapt your speech to the audience.

4. Analyze the speech in the Appendix by Alan Alda ("A Reel Doctor's Advice to Some Real Doctors," pages 388–392). Explain what special steps Alda

takes to fit his message to the audience. Be specific in your analysis, and be prepared to discuss your conclusions in class.

NOTES

[1] Ralph Waldo Emerson, quoted in Robert T. Oliver, *History of Public Speaking in America* (Boston: Allyn and Bacon, 1965), p. 122.

[2] *The Boxer,* © by Paul Simon, 1968.

[3] Saul Alinsky, *Rules for Radicals* (New York: Random House, 1971), p. 81.

[4] Fred N. Kerlinger, *Foundations of Behavioral Research,* 2nd ed. (New York: Holt, Rinehart and Winston, 1973), pp. 482–485.

CHAPTER 5

Gathering Materials

Suppose you want to build an audiovisual center for your home. You need to provide space for all the components (tape player, speakers, CD player, television, VCR, etc.), as well as storage for records, tapes, and discs. How do you go about it? You can talk to people who have built their own centers and ask them for details. You can write away to a magazine for plans. You can get books from the library and follow their instructions. On the other hand, if you've worked on an audiovisual center before, you can fall back on your experience and adapt it to your present needs. Since you want your center to be perfect, you gather as much information as you can before starting to build.

Gathering material for a speech is like gathering information for any project. Many resources are available to you if you take advantage of them. How do you get material for your speeches? There are several ways. You can interview people with specialized knowledge on a given topic. You can write to individuals or groups that collect information on your subject and are set up to provide it to the public. You can do research in the library. Sometimes you can use yourself as a resource—whenever you have personal experience or more-than-average knowledge about a subject. Let's turn first to the resource of your own experience.

USING YOUR OWN KNOWLEDGE AND EXPERIENCE

Everybody is an expert on something, whether it is auto mechanics or baking brownies or simply "Why I Failed Calculus." As we saw in Chapter 3, we usually speak best about subjects with which we are familiar. This is why teachers encourage students to capitalize on their own knowledge and experience in developing speech topics.

When you choose a topic from your own experience, you may be tempted to depersonalize it by relying solely on facts and figures from books. Such outside information is almost always necessary. But supplementing it with the personal touch can really bring your speeches to life.

One student, afflicted with diabetes, chose to explain how a person can live with the disease on a daily basis. He cited statistics on the incidence of diabetes in the United States, identified symptoms of the disease, and related how it is treated. Along the way he also illustrated his points by talking about his personal experiences. Here is part of what he said:

Being a diabetic presents a challenge one cannot afford to lose. On a personal note, I have tried not to let my diabetes affect my life style. Last year I spent nine months traveling in Central and South America. The trip was very memorable, but I had one particularly frightening experience that quickly makes you realize just how vulnerable a diabetic is. On the fifth day of a two-week excursion down the Amazon River in Brazil, our canoe tipped, dumping everything into the river.

Although I recovered my pack, part of its contents—including my insulin—were swallowed up by the river. Without insulin I could not eat any food, for if I did, my blood-sugar level would become too high and I could eventually go into convulsions, slip into a coma, and die. We returned back up the Amazon and traveled three days until we reached the first village and I could radio for more medicine. I was hot and hungry, but alive.

This speech has color and emotion. By drawing on his own experience, the speaker conveyed his point much more meaningfully than he could have in any other way.

Even if your life stories are not that dramatic, you can still put them to work for you. After all, you are the one who was there. You did, saw, felt, heard whatever it is you are speaking about. By thinking over your past experiences—gathering material from yourself—you can find many supporting details for your speeches.

INTERVIEWING

Most people think of interviewing in terms of job interviews or conversations with celebrities. But there is another kind of interview—the research (or investigative) interview. Among journalists it is a time-honored way to collect information. It is also an excellent way to gather materials for speeches.

A personal interview can be the most effective means of gathering material in at least four circumstances:

1. When you want up-to-the-minute information. Published sources, especially books, are always a little out of date.

2. When you need information about a fairly narrow subject that might not attract newspaper or other printed coverage. Some on-campus events fall into this category.

3. When you have access to a person who has specialized knowledge about a subject and is willing to share that knowledge.

4. When a particular person's viewpoint will add interest and force to your speech. This is why journalists covering the White House fight so hard to get a few words from the President—even when they can obtain the same information from his staff. They want to hear it "straight from the horse's mouth."

Suppose you are talking about everyday steps women can take to keep from being sexually assaulted. Why not contact your local police department as one source of information? Or suppose you are dealing with the problem of alcoholism among college students. Why not get in touch with the dean of students to find out the situation at your school? Once you begin to think about the possibilities, you will discover many people on your campus and in your community who can contribute to your speeches.

When done well, interviewing (like many things) looks deceptively easy.

In practice, it is a complex and demanding art. So before you dash off to conduct your interviews à la Mike Wallace or Barbara Walters, you should understand a few basic principles of effective interviewing. They fall into three groups—what to do before the interview, what to do during the interview, and what to do after the interview.

To illustrate, we'll follow the entire interview process for a hypothetical speech about women's collegiate athletics.

Before the Interview

Just as the outcome of most speeches is decided by how well the speaker prepares, so the outcome of most interviews is decided by how well the interviewer prepares. Here are five steps you should take ahead of time to help ensure a successful interview.

Define the Purpose of the Interview   You have done a fair amount of library research about women's athletics and have begun to grasp the issues fairly well. At this point you think it would be helpful to know the status of women's athletics at your school. You get some information from the newspaper, and some more from a handbook put out by the athletic department. But you still have many questions. You decide the only way to get answers is to interview someone associated with the athletic program. In that decision you have begun to formulate a purpose for the interview.

Decide Whom to Interview   There are a number of possibilities—players, coaches, administrators. You elect to start at the top—with the athletic director. Isn't that a bit presumptuous? Why not begin with someone a little further down the line—an assistant director or a coach, for instance? You could. But in dealing with administrative organizations it is usually best to go to the leaders first.[1] They are likely to have a broad understanding of the issues. And if you need more specific information than they have, they can get it for you or put you in touch with the right person.

Arrange the Interview   In this case, let's assume the athletic director is a man. The subject of women's athletics may be a delicate issue. Furthermore, he is a very busy person. So you work out a plan for getting him to agree to talk with you. Knowing that it is easier to brush someone off over the telephone than in person, you go to the athletic office to request the interview. You introduce yourself, identify your exact purpose, and explain why the interview is important. The athletic director agrees, and you set up the interview for three days later.

(You are astonished to get the interview, but you shouldn't be. Nearly everyone likes to be interviewed. If your purpose is a serious one and you conduct yourself well, the person you ask to interview is likely to cooperate.)

Decide Whether or Not to Use a Tape Recorder   If your subject does not want the interview tape-recorded, then the decision is made. Otherwise, you must choose. Here are some of the pros and cons:

ADVANTAGES OF THE TAPE RECORDER:

1. Your hands and brain are free of the chore of note taking, so you can concentrate on the interviewee's message and on formulating your next questions.

2. Your record of the interview will be exactly accurate. There is no possibility of misquoting or of forgetting important points.

DISADVANTAGES OF THE TAPE RECORDER:

1. Many interviewees are uncomfortable with having a recorder in the room. This may spoil the interview.

2. You will have to spend a lot of time after the interview playing the tape over and over to distill the recorded material. When you take notes, on the other hand, that distillation process takes place during the actual interview, because you write down only the important points.

Never try to tape-record an interview without the subject's knowledge or consent. Not only is it unethical, but the person being interviewed is bound to find out, and you will cause yourself more trouble than you had hoped to avoid.

Prepare Your Questions   You now face the most important of your preinterview tasks—working out the questions you will ask during the interview. Keep in mind the old adage, "Ask a stupid question, you'll get a stupid answer." You should devise questions that are sensible, intelligent, and meaningful. Here are some types of questions to *avoid:*

- Questions you can answer without the interview. (How long has the school had a women's athletic program? What sports does it include?) Queries like this just waste the subject's time and make you look foolish. Research this information yourself before the interview.

- Overly vague questions. (Do you think women's sports is a good idea? What is the future of women's athletics?)

- Leading questions. (You *do* think women should have as many athletic scholarships as men, *don't you?*)

- Hostile, loaded questions. (I think it's disgraceful that most of the women's athletic teams at this school are coached by men. Don't you think women can coach as well as men? Or maybe you just look at women's sports as another way to provide jobs for male coaches. What do you say to *that,* hmmm?)

You need not shy away from tough questions. Just phrase them as neutrally as possible and save them until near the end of the interview. That way, if your interviewee becomes irritated or uncooperative, you will still get most of the information you want.

When you are finished preparing, you should have a set of direct, specific, reasonable questions, such as the following:

- Our school now has seven intercollegiate sports for women. Are there plans to add others fairly soon?

- The budget for women's sports has grown tremendously in recent years, but it is still only one-fifth of the men's budget. Do you foresee that gap narrowing in the near future?

- A number of experts fear the growing pressure to win in women's athletics may soon produce the kinds of recruiting scandals that have plagued men's athletics. Do you agree? What are you doing to keep that problem from developing here?

- Last month the women's gymnastics team complained that while the athletic department spends a lot of money on women's basketball, it still does not provide adequate funds, facilities, or practice time for other sports. Is the complaint justified? If so, are steps being taken to deal with it?

- Some of your critics charge that you are not really committed to an equal athletics program for women. As evidence, they cite the gap between the budget for men's and women's sports, as well as the fact that you have hired men to coach almost all the women's teams. What is your response to the critics on that score? (Here is the toughest question—at the end of the interview.)

Although some experienced journalists prefer to go into interviews with only a few key-word notes on the areas to be covered (or even with all their questions in their heads), you want to be sure not to forget anything during the interview. So you arrange your questions in the order you want to ask them and take the list with you to the interview.

During the Interview

Every interview is unique. Just as a speaker adapts to the audience during a speech, so must an interviewer adapt to the person being interviewed. Because the session will seldom go exactly as you plan, you need to be alert and flexible. Here are several steps you can take to help make the interview proceed smoothly.

Dress Appropriately and Be on Time   The athletic director has a busy schedule and is doing you a favor by agreeing to an interview, so you make every effort to show up on time. Since the interview is a special occasion, you are careful to dress fittingly. This is one way of telling the athletic director that you regard the interview as serious business. In return, he is likely to take you more seriously.

Repeat the Purpose of the Interview   The athletic director invites you into his office. You exchange a few introductory remarks. Now, before you plunge into your questions, you take a minute or two to restate the purpose of the interview. This refreshes the athletic director's memory and gives the interview a sharper focus. You are more likely to get clear, helpful answers if your subject knows why you are following a certain line of questioning.

Set Up the Tape Recorder If You Are Using One   If your subject has agreed to the interview being recorded, keep one principle in mind: the tape-recording should be as casual and as inconspicuous as possible. Don't thrust the microphone into your subject's face. Don't fiddle endlessly with the tape or the machine. You should have practiced in advance, to make sure you understand the mechanism. Set up the recorder, start the tape, and then try to ignore it for the rest of the interview. With luck, your subject will ignore it too.

For this exercise, we'll assume the athletic director does not want the interview tape-recorded. You will be taking notes.

Keep the Interview on Track   You ask the athletic director the first question on your list. He answers it. You ask him the second question. He answers it, but in doing so he also answers question 4. What do you do now? Do you go on to question 5 or return to question 3?

Either approach is fine. As it turns out, you go back to question 3 (while also checking off question 4 from your list). Now, in answering question 3, the athletic director raises an important issue that is not covered anywhere in your list of questions. Do you pursue that issue or forge doggedly ahead with question 5?

You make the wise decision to veer slightly from your prearranged order of questioning to pursue the new issue. You pose a couple of questions about it, get helpful answers, then keep the interview on track by returning to your list of prepared questions.

This is more or less how things go for the rest of the interview. You pursue new leads when they appear, improvise probing follow-up questions when called for, then lead on again in an orderly fashion. The interview is freewheeling at times, but you never let it get out of control. When it is over, you have answers to all your prepared questions—and a lot more.

Listen Carefully   During the interview, you listen attentively while taking key-word notes (see pages 39–40). When you don't understand something, you ask for clarification. If you hear a statement you want to quote directly, you have the athletic director repeat it to make sure you get it exactly right. Chances are a prominent person like him will have been misquoted more than once in the press, so he'll be happy to oblige.

Don't Overstay Your Welcome   Try to keep within the stipulated time period for the interview, unless your subject clearly wants to prolong the session. When the interview is over, of course, you thank the athletic director for having given of his time and his insights.

After the Interview

Although the interview is over, the interviewing process is not. You must now review and transcribe your notes.

Review Your Notes as Soon as Possible   When you leave the athletic director's office, the interview is fresh in your mind. You know what the cryptic comments and scrawls in your notes mean. But as time passes, the details will become hazy. Don't let something like this true story happen to you:

Years ago, a prominent woman—writer and diplomat—was being interviewed by a young reporter. Among other things, the reporter asked about hobbies and leisure activities. The woman replied that she enjoyed skeet shooting and raised Siamese cats. The reporter scribbled in her notes ''shoots'' and ''cats''—but didn't bother to put a comma or a dash between the words. The interview was published. And ever since, that prominent woman has been trying to live down the reputation that she ''shoots cats.''

In reviewing your notes, try to concentrate on two things—discovering the main points that emerged during the interview, and pulling out specific information that might be useful in your speech.

The best way to locate the main points is to decide what you would answer if someone asked you to summarize the interview in one minute or less. As you look through your notes, you see three ideas that surface over and over in the athletic director's comments: (1) Funding a full slate of men's and women's teams is a continuing challenge for the athletic department. (2) Despite budgetary constraints, the quality of women's collegiate athletics will continue to improve. (3) The athletic director is planning to hire more women coaches in the future.

As you review the interview, you also seize on several specific items—figures, anecdotes, quotations—that look promising as supporting details for your speech. If any of them are unclear, call the athletic director to make sure you have the facts right.

Transcribe Your Notes   After reviewing the notes, you transcribe important ideas and information onto index cards. Since this will require filling in from memory various details of the interview, you do it as soon as possible. It's important to use index cards, because that is how you will record materials gathered in your library research (see pages 110–112). This way you will have all your research materials in the same format, so they can be arranged and rearranged easily when you begin to organize your speech.

WRITING AWAY FOR INFORMATION

If the subject of your speech is at all controversial, you can be pretty sure that somewhere there is an organization for it or against it—and probably both. Take the issue of exploring for oil in the national parks as an example. Companies like Exxon are for it; environmental groups like the Sierra Club are against it. Cigarette smoking? The American Tobacco Institute is for it; numerous organizations, including the American Cancer Society, are actively opposed to it.

There are thousands of special interest groups in this country, and most of them offer pamphlets and other literature related to their concerns—free for the asking. The *Encyclopedia of Associations,* available in the reference section of most libraries, will give you a list of these groups, along with their mailing addresses.

A bit of caution is needed in using material obtained from such groups, however. Since these organizations exist specifically to promote or oppose some cause, their information may be biased, slanted, even downright wrong. Whenever possible, check facts and statistics against a more impartial source.

Government agencies are another excellent source of information on a wide range of topics. Suppose you plan to speak on a subject related to farming. The Department of Agriculture publishes hundreds of bulletins, all available at little or no cost. A list of these can be obtained from the U.S. Government Printing Office, Washington, D.C. 20402.

If you are in doubt about which government agency is responsible for a particular subject, try calling or writing your congressional representative. His or her staff can point you in the right direction.

DOING LIBRARY RESEARCH

Some students regard the library as a sinner regards a church—as a place to be entered only in the most desperate circumstances. Then they take a speech class and discover that the library is not so forbidding after all. You will get most of the materials for your speeches from the library. Thus you need to know the basic techniques of doing library research. Of course, you may know them already, in which case you need only review this section of the book.

There are quick, easy, systematic ways to find whatever you need in the library. The first step is to learn your way around. Take the orientation tour offered by your library. While on the tour, you will probably receive a brief handbook or series of leaflets explaining what is in the library and how to find it. Keep this material with your class notes. It takes only a few minutes to read and will be helpful later.

Ultimately, the only way to become adept at library research is to do it— and to do it properly. You have four important resources for finding what you need in the library—the librarians, the card catalogue, the reference department, and computerized research services. We'll look at each in turn and then consider basic research techniques.[2]

The Librarians

Thanks to movies, comic strips, and television commercials, librarians have a bad image. They are typically portrayed as cold, stuffy, bespectacled people whose main goal in life is to keep people from talking above a whisper. In fact, most librarians are friendly men and women who can be of enormous help. Too often students waste their time wandering aimlessly in search of a source because they are afraid to ask for assistance. They don't want to appear stupid or to "bother" anyone. But would you be as sensitive about asking a doctor for help with a medical problem? Librarians are experts in their own field, trained in library use and research methods. If you have a question, don't hesitate to ask a librarian. He or she can help you find your way, locate sources, even track down a specific piece of information.

The Card Catalogue

The card catalogue is the key to locating material in the library. In it you will find listed alphabetically on 3 × 5 cards all the books and periodicals owned by the library. For each book there will be at least three cards—one listing it by the *author's last name,* one listing it by *title,* and one (or more) listing it by *subject.* If you know who wrote a book or know the book's title, your first step is to locate the catalogue card under author or title. When you do not know the author or title, or when you simply want to see what books are available on a given subject, check the catalogue under the appropriate subject.

Figure 5.1 (opposite) shows three sample catalogue cards that index the same book. As you can see, the catalogue cards give quite a bit of information about the book. The key to locating the book on the shelves is the *call number,* which is always found in the upper left-hand corner of the card. Once you have the call number, all you have to do is find the right section of the shelves (or stacks, as they are called in some libraries). Most libraries post charts indicating where books within a given range of call numbers can be found.

Periodicals are listed by title in the card catalogue. Figure 5.2 (opposite) shows a sample catalogue card for a periodical. Libraries usually have a special periodicals room in which they keep the latest issues of newspapers and magazines. Bound volumes of issues from past years are kept on the book shelves.

While it used to be that the only way to find items in the card catalogue was to search for them by hand, many libraries now are computerizing their catalogues. Depending on the situation at your school, you may be able to locate recent books and periodicals through the library's computer system. Be sure to check into this possibility before you begin your research, for it can save you a great deal of time.

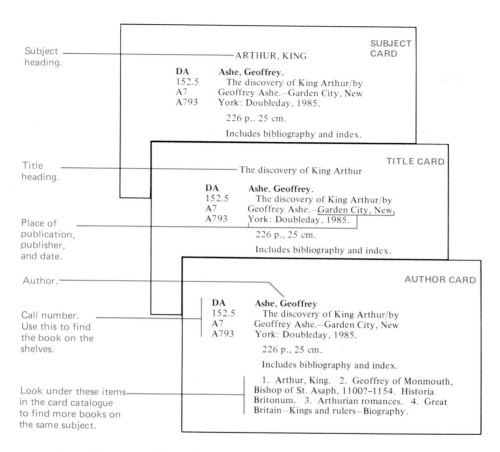

Subject heading.

Title heading.

Place of publication, publisher, and date.

Author.

Call number. Use this to find the book on the shelves.

Look under these items in the card catalogue to find more books on the same subject.

SUBJECT CARD

ARTHUR, KING

DA
152.5
A7
A793

Ashe, Geoffrey.
The discovery of King Arthur/by
Geoffrey Ashe.—Garden City, New
York: Doubleday, 1985.

226 p., 25 cm.

Includes bibliography and index.

TITLE CARD

The discovery of King Arthur

DA
152.5
A7
A793

Ashe, Geoffrey.
The discovery of King Arthur/by
Geoffrey Ashe.—Garden City, New
York: Doubleday, 1985.

226 p., 25 cm.

Includes bibliography and index.

AUTHOR CARD

DA
152.5
A7
A793

Ashe, Geoffrey
The discovery of King Arthur/by
Geoffrey Ashe.—Garden City, New
York: Doubleday, 1985.

226 p., 25 cm.

Includes bibliography and index.

1. Arthur, King. 2. Geoffrey of Monmouth,
Bishop of St. Asaph, 1100?–1154. Historia
Britonum. 3. Arthurian romances. 4. Great
Britain—Kings and rulers—Biography.

FIGURE 5.1   Three Catalogue Cards

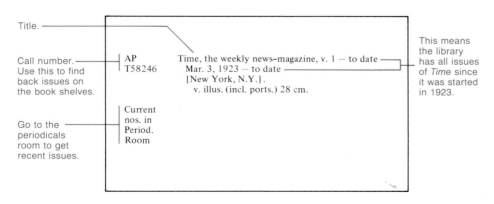

Title.

Call number. Use this to find back issues on the book shelves.

Go to the periodicals room to get recent issues.

AP
T58246

Current nos. in Period. Room

Time, the weekly news-magazine, v. 1 — to date
Mar. 3, 1923 — to date
[New York, N.Y.].
v. illus. (incl. ports.) 28 cm.

This means the library has all issues of *Time* since it was started in 1923.

FIGURE 5.2   Catalogue Card for a Periodical

The Reference Section

The card catalogue tells you what books and periodicals are in the library. But suppose you want to find a particular piece of factual information (such as the amount of French wine imported into the United States last year, the origins of the word "communism," or the distance from San Francisco to New Orleans). Or suppose you are trying to locate recent magazine articles on a given topic. You could rummage through a dozen books or thumb through a batch of magazines in hopes of stumbling across what you need. But the easy, efficient way to get the information is to go to the reference section.

The reference section puts a wealth of information at your fingertips. It contains encyclopedias, yearbooks, dictionaries, biographical aids, atlases, and indexes. Here are the ones you should find most useful in preparing your speeches.

Encyclopedias   We all are familiar with general encyclopedias such as the *Encyclopaedia Britannica* and the *Encyclopedia Americana.* They seek to provide accurate, objective information about all branches of human knowledge and are an excellent place to begin your research. Both *Britannica* and *Americana* are arranged alphabetically and publish annual supplements to update what is contained in the basic volumes.

In addition to the general encyclopedias, there are special encyclopedias devoted to particular subjects such as art, religion, science, and literature. They cover their fields in much more depth and detail than do the general encyclopedias. The most frequently used special encyclopedias are:

Encyclopedia of Philosophy

Encyclopedia of Psychology

International Encyclopedia of the Social Sciences

Encyclopedia of World Art

Encyclopedia of Education

Encyclopedia of Religion and Ethics

Grove's Dictionary of Music and Musicians

Grzimek's Animal Life Encyclopedia

McGraw-Hill Encyclopedia of Science and Technology

Yearbooks   As the name implies, yearbooks are published annually. They contain an amazing amount of concise information that would otherwise be all but impossible to track down. Here are three of the most valuable.

Statistical Abstract of the United States. Published since 1878 by the U.S. Bureau of the Census, the *Statistical Abstract* is the standard reference source for numerical information on the social, political, and economic aspects of American life. Among the incredible array of facts it contains are the U.S.

fertility rate, death rates from various diseases, labor union membership, median family income by state, and so on.

The World Almanac and Book of Facts.   Unlike the *Statistical Abstract,* the *World Almanac* is not limited to the United States or to numerical data. Among the things you can find out from it are all the Nobel Prize winners since 1901, the most-watched television shows of the previous year, records for professional and collegiate sports, the literacy rate in Afghanistan, and the natural resources of Peru.

Facts on File.   This is a weekly digest of national and foreign news events. It covers politics, sports, science, medicine, education, religion, crime, economics, and the arts. At the end of the year, all the weekly issues are published together as *Facts on File Yearbook.* This is an excellent place to check up quickly on something that happened in a given year.

Dictionaries   There are several excellent dictionaries of the English language, including *Webster's, Funk and Wagnalls,* and the *Random House Dictionary.* If you are interested more in the history of a word than in its present meaning, you should turn first to the *Oxford English Dictionary.* There are also several helpful popular accounts of how our language has developed. Among the best are *Safire's Political Dictionary,* by William Safire; *A Dictionary of Americanisms,* by Mitford Mathews; and *Dictionary of Word and Phrase Origins,* by William Morris and Mary Morris.

Biographical Aids   When you need information about people, living or dead, you should go first to the reference section, where you will find a number of excellent biographical guides. Here are the ones you are likely to find most useful:

Who's Who.   Published annually since 1849, *Who's Who* is the forerunner of the biographical guides to living persons. Its information is limited mostly to men and women who reside in the British Commonwealth of Nations, and it includes a full listing of the English Royal Family.

Who's Who in America.   Issued every other year since 1899, these volumes give brief life and career facts about 75,000 noteworthy contemporary Americans.

Who's Who of American Women.   Begun in 1958, this guide spotlights women who are making important contributions to American life.

International Who's Who.   Published annually since 1935, this reference work contains over 11,000 one-paragraph biographical sketches of people of international stature in almost every sphere of activity.

Current Biography.   Initiated in 1940, this exceedingly helpful magazine is published every month except December. During each year it offers some 400 independent and highly readable articles about newsworthy people all over the world. Each article is three to four pages long, and the fields covered include politics, science, the arts, labor, sports, and industry. At the end of the year, the articles are revised and collected alphabetically in a single volume entitled *Current Biography Yearbook*. An excellent cumulative index makes it easy to find the article you want from any year. If you are looking for information about someone now in the news, this is your best bet.

Dictionary of American Biography.   This monumental work contains first-rate biographies of more than 17,000 famous Americans—mostly men—who are no longer living.

Notable American Women.   This publication is modeled on the *Dictionary of American Biography* but is limited to American women.

Dictionary of National Biography.   This reference work is the British equivalent of the *Dictionary of American Biography.* It covers almost 32,000 historical figures who lived in England or its dominions.

Biography Index.   This source won't give you biographical information, but it will tell you where to find it. Published four times a year, the *Biography Index* provides references to biographical material appearing in selected books and some 2,600 periodicals. Although it includes information about recent articles on historical figures, it is especially useful for locating material about contemporary men and women the world over.

Atlases and Gazetteers   Atlases, of course, contain maps. But most modern atlases also contain a variety of charts, plates, and tables that furnish information about the geography of states, regions, and countries. Gazetteers are geographical dictionaries. They follow the same alphabetical format as regular dictionaries, but all the entries deal with geographical topics. In addition to helping you check the spelling and pronunciation of place names, a gazetteer will give you a wealth of information about the climate, elevation, population, economy, and natural resources of sites the world over. The best-known atlases and gazetteers are:

Rand McNally Cosmopolitan World Atlas.   This stunning work includes maps of the world by region as well as maps of each state of the United States. It also gives a wealth of information about the population, politics, and geography of the United States and other areas of the world.

Times Atlas of the World, Comprehensive Edition.   In addition to the usual maps, this book includes maps on the world's climate and its mineral, energy, and food resources. A special section on the universe and the solar system offers a map of the moon.

Webster's New Geographical Dictionary.   This volume lists more than 47,000 places around the world—countries, regions, states, cities, islands, lakes, mountains, rivers—and gives concise facts about each. It is where you should look to find such things as the height of Mount Everest, the state flower of Florida, and all the places in the world named Athens.

Periodical Indexes   Periodical indexes do for articles in magazines and journals what the card catalogue does for books. They include the well-known *Readers' Guide to Periodical Literature,* as well as a number of more specialized indexes.

Readers' Guide to Periodical Literature.   The *Readers' Guide* is the indispensable general-purpose index. It provides an up-to-date listing of more than 180 of the most widely read magazines in the United States. Included are *Time, Newsweek, Scientific American, Sports Illustrated, Aviation Week and Space Technology, Consumer Reports, Ebony, Ms., Vital Speeches, Rolling Stone,* and *Psychology Today.* Most libraries keep bound volumes of *Readers' Guide* going back to its start in 1900.

One of the virtues of the *Readers' Guide* is that it is very easy to use. Articles are indexed alphabetically by author and subject. Each entry gives all the necessary information for finding the articles in the magazines—title of article, author, name of magazine (abbreviated), volume number, page numbers, and date. If you were giving a speech about the growing use of robots, you would look in the *Readers' Guide* under "robots." Figure 5.3 shows what you would find.

Subject heading. ——————————————— **ROBOTS**
    See also
Look under this heading ——————————— Manipulators (Mechanism)
in the *Readers' Guide* to
find other articles on   Robots: the new helpmates? H. Boyer. il *Work*
the same topic.   *Woman* 9:134+ Ap '84
                           The smartest homebuilt robots. T. Carroll. il
                                Pop Mech 161:88–90 Ap '84
                           Spare parts [robot–builder C. Bailey] V. Haddock.
                                il por *Am Craft* 44:14–17 Ap/My '84—

————————————————————————— **Agricultural use**
                           Robots invade the farm. il *Sci Dig* 92:32 My '84
                           Will robots and electronics replace cowboys?
Subheadings to help you   *Success Farm* 82 no5:26AW Mr '84
find articles on
particular aspects of   —————————————————— **Exhibitions**
robots.   The robot exhibit. il *Am Craft* 44:12–13
                                Ap/My '84
                           Robots in revue [exhibit at the American Craft
                                Museum II] il *Americana* 12:112 Mr/Ap '84

————————————————————————— **Industrial use**
                           Death by robot [death of Bob Williams at Ford's
                                Michigan Casting Center] J. G. Fuller. il *Omni*
                                6:44–6+ Mr '84

                                        Military use
Single entry: includes   Birth of the killer robots. M. Rogers. il *Newsweek*
title of article, author, ——   103:51 Je 25 '84
name of magazine, volume,
page number, and date.

FIGURE 5.3   Sample *Readers' Guide* Entry

(*Readers' Guide to Periodical Literature* copyright © 1984 by the H. W. Wilson Company. Material reproduced by permission of the publisher.)

Special Indexes.   Sometimes you may need more specialized information than you can find in the general magazines covered by *Readers' Guide.* If so, check with your reference librarian, who will direct you to a special index. Examples are:

Applied Science and Technology Index

Art Index

Biological and Agricultural Index

Business Periodicals Index

Education Index

Humanities Index

Index to Legal Periodicals

Social Sciences Index

Index Medicus

Congressional Record Index

Public Affairs Information Service Bulletin

Newspaper Indexes   Newspapers are invaluable for research on many topics. Fortunately, back issues of several major U.S. newspapers are now indexed. Among them are:

New York Times (1913–present)

Wall Street Journal (1958–present)

Christian Science Monitor (1960–present)

Los Angeles Times (1972–present)

Washington Post (1972–present)

Chicago Tribune (1972–present)

New Orleans Times-Picayune (1972–present)

Detroit News (1976–present)

Of these papers, your library is most likely to carry back issues of the *New York Times* (usually on microfilm). To find what you are looking for in the *New York Times Index,* look under the subject. You will find listed all articles on that subject printed during the year. (See Figure 5.4 for a sample entry.)

Computerized Research Services

Many libraries now have computerized research services, and we can expect this type of service to expand greatly in the next few years. Even if you have no immediate need for the service, you should be aware of its potential.

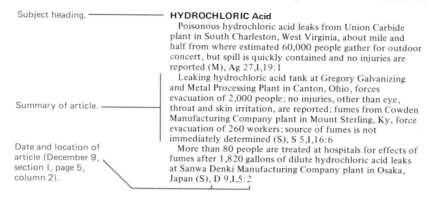

Subject heading.

HYDROCHLORIC Acid

    Poisonous hydrochloric acid leaks from Union Carbide plant in South Charleston, West Virginia, about mile and half from where estimated 60,000 people gather for outdoor concert, but spill is quickly contained and no injuries are reported (M), Ag 27,I,19:1

Summary of article.

    Leaking hydrochloric acid tank at Gregory Galvanizing and Metal Processing Plant in Canton, Ohio, forces evacuation of 2,000 people; no injuries, other than eye, throat and skin irritation, are reported; fumes from Cowden Manufacturing Company plant in Mount Sterling, Ky, force evacuation of 260 workers; source of fumes is not immediately determined (S), S 5,I,16:6

Date and location of article (December 9, section I, page 5, column 2).

    More than 80 people are treated at hospitals for effects of fumes after 1,820 gallons of dilute hydrochloric acid leaks at Sanwa Denki Manufacturing Company plant in Osaka, Japan (S), D 9,I,5:2

FIGURE 5.4   Sample *New York Times Index* Entry

Computerized research can save you hours of work—especially if your speech topic involves obscure or very specialized information. Suppose you need material on "bilingual education in the Southwest" or "conspiracy theories regarding the assassination of Abraham Lincoln." Instead of reading through a stack of periodical or newspaper indexes until you find the citations you need, you let the computer find them for you.

Various commercial organizations have developed computerized information retrieval services. The major systems are DIALOG (developed by Lockheed Corporation), ORBIT (developed by System Development Corporation), and BRS (Bibliographical Retrieval Service). If your library has facilities for computer-assisted research, it probably subscribes to one or more of these three services.

Each service contains a large set of indexes known as *databases.* Some of these databases are the same as printed periodical indexes, while others have been created just for use with computers and have no printed equivalent. Altogether there are hundreds of databases, covering every topic from agriculture to zoology. The specific databases you can use will depend on the retrieval systems available in your library. Here are a few of the major databases in the DIALOG, ORBIT, and BRS systems that you would be most likely to use in preparing one of your speeches:

Magazine Index.   Indexes some 400 popular American magazines since 1959. Includes all magazines covered by the *Readers' Guide to Periodical Literature.* Available through DIALOG.

National Newspaper Index.   Complete indexing of *The New York Times, Christian Science Monitor,* and *Wall Street Journal* from 1979 to the present. Also indexes the *Washington Post* and *Los Angeles Times* from 1983 onward. Available through DIALOG.

ERIC (Educational Resources Information Center).   Indexes books, articles, research findings, and unpublished materials on all aspects of education. Available through DIALOG, ORBIT, and BRS.

Social Science Citation Index.   Provides references on social science topics from more than 3,000 journals. Along with ERIC, perhaps the most frequently used database in college libraries. Available through DIALOG and BRS.

ASI (American Statistics Index).   Comprehensive guide to statistical data compiled by the United States government since 1973. Available through DIALOG and ORBIT.

You need not be a computer expert to take advantage of computer-assisted research. In most libraries, the first step is to make an appointment with a reference librarian. The librarian will help decide which databases are best for your topic. He or she will then direct the computer through its search. As a result of the search you will get a printout listing bibliographic citations for your topic. Depending on the database you have used, you may also be able to get a printout summarizing the articles on the list of citations. In some cases the printout will be available immediately; otherwise, it will be mailed to you.

Despite its many advantages, computer-assisted research has its drawbacks. Most computer databases cover only the past ten or fifteen years. If you are looking for materials published before the 1970s, you may be able to find them only through printed indexes. In addition, computerized research is expensive. Depending on the retrieval system, you can expect to spend about $10 to $20 for an "average" search. To get maximum value for your dollar, most librarians advise that you begin your research in the printed indexes and avoid using the computer until you have a clear idea of exactly what you are looking for.

As computer research services expand, all of these drawbacks will probably diminish. Some experts predict that within a few years you may be able to call up research citations—and perhaps even the complete text of newspaper and magazine articles—from a computer in your home or office.

TIPS FOR DOING RESEARCH

Few people regard doing research as one of life's great joys. There are, however, ways to make it less tedious and more productive. Learning how to use the library efficiently is one way. Here are some others.

Start Early

The biggest mistake students make when faced with a research project is waiting too long to begin. The longer you wait, the more problems you will encounter. You may find that a vital book has been checked out of the library, or that you no longer have time to arrange a crucial interview. Starting early also eases the tension of completing an assignment. Instead of sweating under intense time pressure, you can work at your convenience. No matter what kind of research you do, you can be sure of one thing. It will *always* take longer than you expect. So get started early and avoid the pitfalls that come from procrastinating.

Starting early also gives you plenty of time to think about what you find. In researching, you will collect much more material than you will actually use in the speech. Preparing a speech is a little like constructing a jigsaw puzzle. Once you gather the pieces, you have to decide how they fit together. The more time you give yourself, the more likely you are to get the pieces to fit just right.

Make a Preliminary Bibliography

As you go through the card catalogue and *Readers' Guide,* you will run across the titles of books and magazine articles that look as if they might contain helpful information about your speech topic. When this happens, prepare a preliminary bibliography card for the book or article. Fill out a separate 3 × 5 or 4 × 6 index card for each book or article. (It is important to use index cards because they can be put in alphabetical order quickly.)

For books, record the author, title, place of publication, publisher, date of publication, and call number. You may also want to include a brief comment indicating why the book may be valuable for your speech. Figure 5.5 (below) shows a sample bibliography card for a book.

For magazine articles, record the author (if identified), title of article, name of magazine, date of publication, and page numbers, as well as the call number. As with book entries, you may also want to include a brief comment to yourself about the article. Figure 5.6 (next page) shows a sample bibliography card for a magazine article.

One very important point needs to be stressed. You should fill out an index card for *each* book or article that looks as if it *could be* helpful in

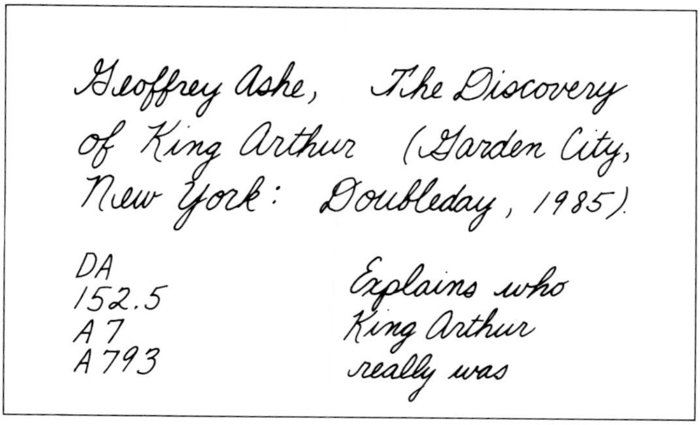
Geoffrey Ashe, The Discovery of King Arthur (Garden City, New York: Doubleday, 1985).

DA
152.5
A7
A793

Explains who King Arthur really was

FIGURE 5.5 Sample Bibliography Card for a Book

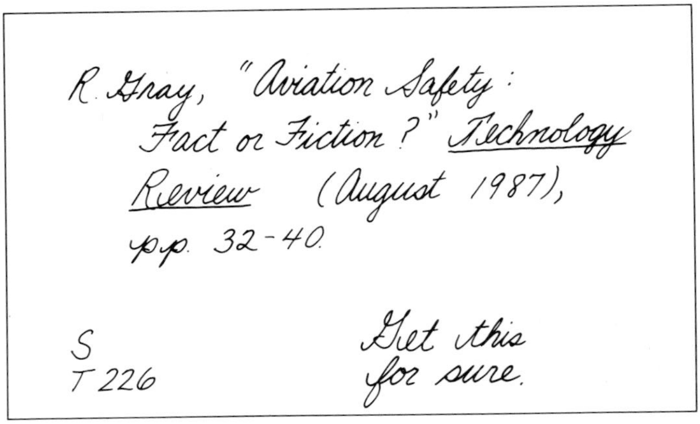
R. Gray, "Aviation Safety: Fact or Fiction?" *Technology Review* (August 1987), pp. 32-40.

S
T 226

Get this for sure.

FIGURE 5.6 Sample Bibliography Card for a Magazine Article

preparing your speech. As a result, you may well have fifteen or twenty preliminary bibliography cards. But remember that you have not yet seen the works listed on the cards. Of the fifteen or twenty preliminary sources, only seven or eight are likely to be of much use to you in drafting the speech. It is an inevitable fact of research that you must sift through many sources to find what you need. If you prepare a skimpy preliminary bibliography, you may well end up with a skimpy speech.

Take Notes Efficiently

Mike Simmons began his speech preparation with the best of intentions. His topic was a fascinating one—"Stone Age Peoples Today." Soon after receiving the assignment, he went to the library to start his research. Since he had no index cards with him, he took notes in the back of one of his notebooks. For two hours he industriously jotted down anything that seemed useful. Then he came upon a short book about an obscure tribe in the Philippines. The book was so engrossing that he read it straight through. He didn't bother taking notes, because he was sure he'd remember it all. The next day he returned to the library. When he got there, he saw he didn't have the same notebook with him but had one from another class. So he used that. He proceeded this way for two more days.

Then Mike remembered he had a test in another class. Somewhat panicked, he put aside his speech research to study for the test. When he got back to researching his speech, the deadline was only four days away. After a long search, he finally found the notes he had made. But what did they mean? He flipped back and forth through the pages several times, trying to make sense of them. One entry said, "Wilson—*important!!!!*" But who or what was Wilson? An author? An anthropologist? Or could it be a place? Another note was particularly frustrating. It said, "Unusual sexual customs—masks." Just the thing to spark up a speech! But where had he read it? He hadn't the faintest idea. With a sense of doom, Mike realized he would have to start all over—and finish in four days.

Sound familiar? This has happened to almost everyone at least once. But once is enough. There is a better way to take research notes. Here is a method that has worked well for many students:

1. Record notes on index cards. Many people prefer the 4 × 6 or 5 × 8 size. Both are large enough to hold quite a bit of information, yet they can be sorted easily when you start to organize the speech. The importance of using index cards cannot be overemphasized. It is the first step to more efficient note taking. Once you begin to use them, you'll be surprised at how much time and frustration they save.

2. On each card write the note, the source of the note, and a heading indicating the subject of the note (see Figure 5.7 below). The subject heading is particularly important, for it allows you to tell at a glance what the note is about. This simplifies the task of arranging your notes when you start to organize the speech. Use the same format for notes taken from an interview (see Figure 5.8, next page).

3. Use a separate card for each note. Many students try to write down all the information from one source on a single card. This defeats the purpose of index cards, because it makes your notes almost impossible to review and organize. You can avoid this problem by making a separate card for each quotation or piece of information you record. Although you may end up with several cards from the same book or article, you will find that this method allows you to keep better track of your research.

4. Take plenty of notes. Few things are more aggravating than trying to recall some bit of information you ran across in your research but neglected to record on a note card. You might have said to yourself, "That's sort of interesting, but I don't know whether it's important. I'll remember it if I need it." Now, of course, you don't remember it exactly. Worse yet, you don't

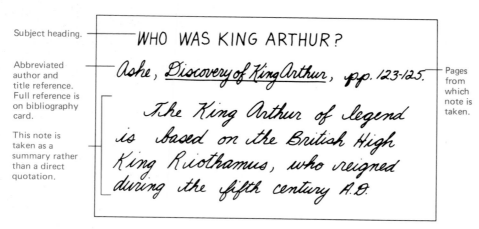

FIGURE 5.7   Sample Index Card for a Book

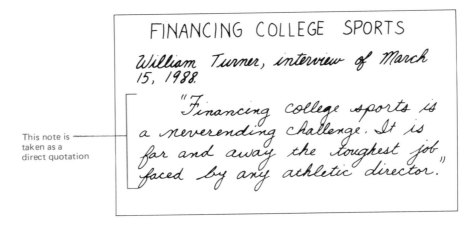

FIGURE 5.8   Sample Index Card for an Interview

remember where you read it. So you head back to the library hoping you can relocate the information. Even if you do find it, you have wasted a lot of time. The moral is clear: If there is even an outside chance you may need a piece of information, jot it down. This procedure will take a little extra time in the short run, but in the long run it can save you much grief.

Think About Your Materials as You Research

Students often approach the research process as a mechanical routine that involves simply gathering the materials to be used in a speech or paper. But when done properly, research can be extremely creative.

If you *think about* what you are finding in your research, you will see your topic just a little bit differently with each note you take. You will find new relationships, develop new questions, explore new angles. You will, in short, begin to write the speech in your head even as you do the research. As you learn more about the topic, you will formulate a central idea, begin to sketch out main points and supporting points, experiment with ways of organizing your thoughts. You may even change your point of view, as did this student:

Barbara Lopez began her speech preparation with this central idea in mind: "Wild animals make more interesting pets than dogs and cats." She went about her research conscientiously, spending many hours in the library. On her third day she came upon some disturbing information about the capture of wild animals. She read that young chimpanzees and other apes were literally snatched out of their mothers' arms, and that the mothers were afterward heard to cry almost like humans. Back in her room that night, Barbara couldn't get her mind off the baby chimpanzees. The next day at the library she found some more disturbing material. One source told about the extraordinarily high death rate of wild animals during shipment to the United States. Again that night, Barbara brooded about the young animals dying of fear and cold in the cargo holds of airplanes.

By the time she finished her research, Barbara's central idea was completely different. When she spoke, her central idea was ''The importation of wild animals for use as pets is inhumane.''

This is an example of creative research. Barbara kept her mind open, read everything she could find about her topic, and thought seriously about what she found. Because of this, she changed her mind.

Your own speech preparation may not cause you to reverse your position, but it should give you new insights into your topic. If you approach research in this way, you may well find that the time you spend researching is the most productive of all the time you devote to preparing your speech.[3]

SUMMARY

Gathering materials for a speech is like gathering information for any project. Many resources are available if you take advantage of them. When you have personal experience or more-than-average knowledge about a topic, you can use yourself as a resource. Most of the time, however, you will need outside information, which you can get in one or more of three ways. You can interview people with specialized knowledge about your topic. You can write away for information. You can do research in the library.

A personal interview takes place in three stages—before, during, and after the interview. Before the interview you should define its purpose, decide whom you are going to interview, and make an appointment with that person. You should also prepare the questions you will ask during the interview. Once the interview begins, be sure to keep it on track, to listen attentively, and to take accurate notes. Afterward, review and transcribe your notes as soon as possible, while they are still fresh in your mind.

Writing away for information is a good way to gather material if you have enough time before your speech. Government agencies, corporations, and special interest groups all offer free or very inexpensive publications.

The library will be the major source of material for most of your speeches. There are four important resources for finding what you need in the library—the librarians, the card catalogue, the reference department, and computerized research services. Librarians are trained to help you; never hesitate to ask their advice when you cannot find something. The card catalogue lists alphabetically all the books and periodicals owned by the library. The reference section contains encyclopedias, yearbooks, dictionaries, biographical aids, atlases, indexes, and the like. If your library has computerized research services, you may be able to locate even obscure sources quickly and efficiently.

No matter what kinds of facilities are available to you, your research will be more effective if you start early and make a preliminary bibliography to keep track of all the books and articles that look as if they might be helpful. By learning to take research notes efficiently, you will save yourself time and energy every step of the way. And if you think about your materials while you research, you may find that gathering materials is the most creative part of your speech preparation.

REVIEW QUESTIONS

After reading this chapter, you should be able to answer the following questions:

1. Why is it important to draw on your own knowledge and experience in gathering materials for your speeches?

2. What are the three stages of interviewing? What should you do as an interviewer in each stage to help ensure a successful interview?

3. What are four important resources for finding what you need in the library?

4. What kind of information will you find in each of the following:

general encyclopedias	biographical aids
special encyclopedias	atlases and gazetteers
yearbooks	periodical indexes
dictionaries	newspaper indexes

5. Why is it important to start your speech research early?

6. What is a preliminary bibliography? Why is it helpful to you in researching a speech?

7. What are four things you should do to take research notes efficiently?

APPLICATION EXERCISES

1. Plan to conduct an interview for one of your classroom speeches. Be sure to follow the guidelines for effective interviewing discussed in the chapter. Afterward, evaluate the interview. Did you prepare for it adequately? Did you get the information you wanted? What would you do differently if you could conduct the interview again?

2. Your library probably has the *Encyclopedia of Associations* in its reference section. Using the *Encyclopedia,* find the names and addresses of three organizations you might write to for information about one of your speech topics.

3. Using the card catalogue, locate three books on the subject of your next speech. Following the format explained on pages 109–110, prepare a preliminary bibliography card for each book.

4. In the *Readers' Guide to Periodical Literature,* find three articles on the subject of your next speech. Prepare a preliminary bibliography card for each article, and track down the articles in the stacks or in the periodicals section of the library.

5. This exercise is designed to give you firsthand acquaintance with some of the major reference works available to you. Your task is to answer each of the following questions. Some of the questions indicate where you will find the answer, and some do not. If necessary, recheck the chapter to see in which reference works you are most likely to find the answers. For each question, record both your answer and where you found it.

Example:

> *Question:* Who discovered the island of Grenada, and what did he name it?
> *Answer:* The island of Grenada was discovered in 1498 by Christopher Columbus, who named it Concepción. *Webster's New Geographical Dictionary,* page 466.

a. In what two years did Ella Fitzgerald receive Grammy awards as best female jazz vocalist?

b. According to the 1987 edition of *Current Biography,* how much does Chicago Bears football coach Mike Ditka earn for giving a speech?

c. Which issue of the *New York Times* in 1985 carried a story about an alert from the Food and Drug Administration telling parents not to use Nutra-Milk infant formula?

d. What was the severity on the Richter scale of the earthquake that struck Los Angeles on October 1, 1987?

e. According to the *McGraw-Hill Encyclopedia of Science and Technology,* who were two of the earliest writers on the subject of extraterrestrial intelligence?

f. What color is a new-born killer whale?

g. How many times was Israel Thorndike elected to the Massachusetts legislature during the years 1788–1814?

h. What is the first definition of "flip" in the *Oxford English Dictionary?*

i. According to Volume 13 of the *Social Science Index,* what journal published an article entitled "The Prevalence of Bulimia among College Students" in September 1986?

j. How many students received bachelor's degrees from American colleges in 1984?

NOTES

[1] Ken Metzler, *Creative Interviewing* (Englewood Cliffs, N.J.: Prentice-Hall, 1977), p. 54.

[2] I would like to thank the staff of Memorial Library, University of Wisconsin–Madison, for their assistance in providing materials for this section.

[3] For research on this subject, see Keith Jensen and David A. Carter, "Self-Persuasion: The Effects of Public Speaking on Speakers," *Southern Speech Communication Journal,* 46 (1981), 163–174.

CHAPTER 6

Supporting Your Ideas

Ashley Moore was a dedicated swimmer who did laps almost daily in the campus pool. When the time came for her classroom speech, she prepared a talk entitled "Swim Yourself Slim." Part of it went like this:

"If you want to have a slim, attractive body, swimming is the best exercise you can do. In fact, swimming is so efficient for burning calories, you can lose weight without ever having to diet. Look at me, for example. I eat anything I want—pizza, cookies, ice cream—and as long as I put in my half a day in the pool, I never gain an ounce. Swimming can do the same for you."

After the speech Ashley's listeners were interested but skeptical. Most of them wanted more information before they would accept her statement about weight loss. As a classmate remarked, "One thin swimmer doesn't prove anything. Maybe she's always been thin! I'd like to see a little scientific evidence before I believe you can lose weight just by swimming."

Good speeches are not composed of hot air and generalizations. They need strong supporting materials to bolster the speaker's point of view. In the case of Ashley's topic, much research has been published on the health implications of regular swimming. Had she done her homework, Ashley might have come across a study done in 1987 at the University of California at Irvine that directly contradicted her point of view.[1] It demonstrated that swimming alone, with no change in diet, may not reduce weight at all. So Ashley's classmates were right to be skeptical. She had made the mistake of generalizing from her own experience with nothing concrete to support her ideas.

The problem with generalizations is that they do not answer the three questions listeners always mentally ask of a speaker: "What do you mean?" "Why should I believe you?" "So what?" Consider, for example, the following sets of statements:

GENERAL	LESS GENERAL	SPECIFIC
Noise pollution is a serious problem in America.	Americans are subjected to noise pollution from a number of ordinary, everyday sources.	The cacophony of noise in our world takes many forms—the scream of jet engines at 142 decibels, the machine-gun pounding of jackhammers, the piercing rhythms of rivet guns, the shattering whine of motorcycles. In our homes, washing machines, hair dryers, food blenders, and vacuum cleaners add to the cumulative attacks on our sensitive hearing apparatus.[2]

Many people suffer from allergies.	Allergies are among the most common and costly health problems in the United States.	According to the National Institutes of Health, more than 35 million Americans—one of every seven—suffer from allergies. Allergic diseases cost the U.S. more than $1 billion a year for doctors' services, hospitals, medications, and other charges. Lost wages and other indirect costs add $800 million more to the annual allergy bill.[3]
Public schools have changed a lot since earlier times.	America's public schools face discipline problems today that were unheard of in previous generations.	A survey made in the 1940's listed the top seven discipline problems in public schools—talking, chewing gum, making noise, running in the halls, getting out of turn in line, wearing improper clothes, not putting paper in wastebaskets. A 1980's survey lists these top seven—drug abuse, alcohol abuse, pregnancy, suicide, rape, robbery, and assault.[4]

Which groups of statements do you find most interesting? Most convincing? Chances are you will prefer those in the right-hand column. They are sharp and specific, clear and credible—just the sort of thing a speech needs to come alive.

The skillful use of supporting materials often makes the difference between a poor speech and a good one. In Chapters 13 and 14, we shall look at special uses of supporting materials in informative and persuasive speeches. In this chapter, we focus on the basic types of supporting materials—examples, statistics, and testimony—and general principles for using them.

EXAMPLES

Norma Espinosa passes through the unpaved streets of Barrio Riguero in eastern Managua at midnight. Dogs bark, and an unusually chilly wind blows through this working-class neighborhood. Espinosa, who is making her rounds as a neighborhood defense coordinator, is not afraid. A Colt .38 is tucked inside her ample cotton blouse, and other night patrol volunteers in each block provide her with more realistic protection.[5]

These were the opening lines of an article in *Ms.* magazine about the women of war-torn Nicaragua. It illustrates a device well known to magazine writers—and speechmakers. Get the audience *involved.*

See how skillfully this example accomplishes the goal. It gives us a specific person to focus on (Norma Espinosa). It sets the stage with time, place, weather, even the sounds of dogs barking. It provides details about the woman's clothing and the weapon she carries. We almost feel ourselves walking alongside Norma Espinosa as she makes her rounds in the night. We would not be nearly as involved if the article had merely said, "Armed women have taken to patrolling the streets of Nicaragua's cities." The *example* touches something in us that no generalization can.

Research has shown that vivid, concrete examples have more impact on listeners' beliefs and actions than any other kind of supporting material.[6] Without examples, ideas often seem vague, impersonal, and lifeless. With examples, they become specific, personal, and lively. This is nowhere better illustrated than in the Bible, which uses all manner of stories, parables, and anecdotes to make abstract principles clear and compelling.[7] There are several kinds of examples you may want to try in your speeches.

Brief Examples

Brief examples—also called specific instances—may be referred to in passing to illustrate a point. The following excerpt uses a brief example to illustrate the often mysterious bonds between identical twins:

Sometimes there seems to be a kind of telepathic communication between identical twins. *In Virginia, for example, Ruth and Nancy Miller sat on opposite sides of the room for their college entrance exams. They had a choice of six topics for the essay question. Not only did both pick the same topic, but they wrote word for word the very same answer!*

A brief example may also be used to introduce a topic:

When archaeologists broke the seal on Tutankhamen's tomb in the autumn of 1922, they uncovered an amazing treasure—a storehouse of ancient Egyptian art of priceless beauty that had lain, untouched and unseen, for more than 3,000 years. Archaeology is a profession of endless drudgery, painstaking research, and the occasional—very rare—marvelous find.

Another way to use brief examples is to pile them one upon the other until you create the desired impression. Here is how one student used the technique to reinforce her point that ignorance of foreign languages and cultures is a serious problem for American business overseas:

Linguistic and cultural ignorance has embarrassed America abroad time and again. General Motors was having trouble selling its Chevy Nova in Spanish-speaking countries. Eventually the company found out that in Spanish "Nova" or "no va" means "It doesn't go." An Iranian construction crew was forced to stop work when they came to the words "wet sheep" in a building manual. It seems an American had somehow come up with that translation for "hydraulic ram." The slogan "Come alive with Pepsi" created a sensation in China when it was advertised as "Pepsi brings your ancestors back from the dead."

Extended Examples

Extended examples are often called illustrations, narratives, or anecdotes. They are longer and more detailed than brief examples. By telling a story vividly and dramatically, they pull listeners into the speech. Here is such an example, from a student speech about the serious problem of "latchkey" children:

> Laura, who is six years old, has just left school with a group of her friends. When they get to Laura's house, she asks her friends to come in and watch television or play games. None of them stays because they have to get home. Laura says goodbye, walks to her door, and pulls out the house key she wears on a chain around her neck. Her heart pounds hard against her chest as she unlocks the door and slowly pushes it open. No one is home; the house is quiet. Laura quickly slams the door and locks it. Dashing to the family room, she flicks on the television and turns the volume up loud. Then she goes to the kitchen and arranges her books on the table as if she were going to sit down and read.
>
> But she's not going to read. Instead, she returns to the hallway and grabs the phone. Setting the phone down next to her, she huddles in the hallway closet, where she will hide for the next two hours while she waits for her parents to get home from work.

This long example captures vividly the terror and helplessness young children may experience when they come home daily to an empty house because their parents are working. The speaker could merely have said "latchkey children are frightened," but the story makes the point far more vividly.

Hypothetical Examples

Whether brief or extended, examples can also be either factual or hypothetical. All of the examples presented so far are factual; the incidents they refer to really happened. Sometimes, however, speakers will use a hypothetical example—one that describes an imaginary situation. Usually such examples are brief stories that relate a general principle.

Here is how one student used a hypothetical example to illustrate the need for blood donors to help out accident victims:

> Imagine this: You are on your way home after classes and you are walking with your best friend. You begin to cross University Avenue. All of a sudden, out of the blue comes a car which doesn't stop for the red light. Your friend is hit. It happened so fast that all you know is your friend is down and can't move. The ambulance arrives

and takes your friend to the hospital. At the hospital you find out your friend has serious internal bleeding and desperately needs blood. One major problem—at this time there is no blood available in your friend's blood type. Your throat tightens up. You naturally thought there was always enough blood. Now you find out there isn't.

Even though this situation is hypothetical, it is far from impossible. A poster from the Red Cross sums this up well: "Blood is like a parachute. If it's not there when you need it, chances are you'll never need it again."

This hypothetical example is particularly effective. Not only does the speaker create a realistic scenario, he also relates it directly to his listeners and gets them involved in the speech.

Tips for Using Examples

Use Examples to Clarify Your Ideas   You probably use clarifying examples all the time in everyday conversation. If you were explaining to a friend about different body types, you might say, "Look at Professor Jones. He's a typical ectomorph—tall, thin, and bony." Examples are an excellent way to clarify unfamiliar or complex ideas. This is why so many teachers use examples in the classroom. Examples put abstract ideas into concrete terms that listeners can easily understand.

This principle works exceptionally well in speeches. Suppose, for instance, you are talking about suspension bridges. You could give a technical description:

The suspension bridge has a roadway suspended by vertical cables attached to two or more main cables. The main cables are hung on two towers and have their ends anchored in concrete or bedrock.

If your audience were made up of people familiar with structural systems, they might be able to visualize what a suspension bridge looks like. But for listeners lacking this background, you might want to add a simple example:

Two well-known suspension bridges are the Golden Gate Bridge in San Francisco and the Brooklyn Bridge in New York.

Because almost everyone has at least seen a picture of the Golden Gate Bridge or the Brooklyn Bridge, using them as examples clarifies your meaning quickly and effectively.

Use Examples to Reinforce Your Ideas   In a speech titled "Science's Internal Poison," Veda Blackman, a student at Ball State University, claimed that federal agencies have found widespread cases of scientists deliberately falsifying the results of their experiments. Because scientists have such high credibility, her listeners were understandably skeptical. To help prove her point, Veda gave several examples of scientific fraud, including the case of Industrial Bio-Test Laboratories, which was closed down for such abuses of scientific procedure as replacing dead rats with live rats to make a chemical appear safe when it

Vivid, dramatic examples can be very effective in drawing listeners into a speech, especially if they are delivered well. (Joseph Schuyler/Stock, Boston)

was actually dangerous. She also told the story of a university scientist working on tissue rejection "who was caught coloring his mice with a black felt-tip pen to make the transplanted patches look healthy when they were really being rejected."[8]

When you use such examples, make sure they are representative—that they do not deal with unusual or exceptional cases. Your listeners are sure to feel betrayed if they suspect you have chosen an atypical example to prove a general point.

Use Examples to Personalize Your Ideas   People are interested in people. As social psychologist Eliot Aronson explains, "Most people are more deeply influenced by one clear, vivid, personal example than by an abundance of statistical data."[9] Whenever you talk to a general audience (such as your speech class), you can include examples that will add human interest to your speech. So far in this section we have seen a number of such examples—Norma Espinosa, identical twins Ruth and Nancy Miller, and so on. The abstract becomes more meaningful when applied to a person. Which of the following would you be more likely to respond to:

There are many hungry families in our community who could benefit from food donations.

Or:

Let me tell you about Ralph. Ralph is four years old. He has big brown eyes and a mop of black hair and an empty belly. In all his four years on this earth, Ralph has never once enjoyed three square meals in a single day.

Try using examples with human interest in your speeches. You will soon discover why accomplished speakers consider them "the very life of the speech."[10]

Make Your Examples Vivid and Richly Textured   The richly textured example supplies everyday details that bring the example to life. Recall the example on page 121 of Laura, the latchkey child. The speaker provided us with many details about Laura's situation. Laura wears her house key on a chain around her neck. She tries to get her friends to come in and keep her company. She turns on the television for sound and arranges her books in the kitchen to make it appear as though she were reading. Her hiding place for two hours is the hall closet, where she keeps the telephone next to her.

How much less compelling the example would have been if the speaker had merely said:

One little girl actually hides in a closet after school until her parents come home.

Instead, the details make us *see* Laura as she goes through her after-school ritual against fear. She is much more likely to stay in our minds than a vague "little girl hiding in a closet." Remember, the more vivid your examples—brief or extended—the more impact they are likely to have on your audience.[11]

Practice Delivery to Enhance Your Extended Examples   An extended example is just like a story, and the impact of your story will depend as much on delivery as on content. Many students have discovered this the hard way. After spending much time and energy developing a splendid example, they have seen the example fall flat on the day of the speech because they did not take the extra step to make it vivid and gripping for listeners.

When you use an extended example, think of yourself as a storyteller. Don't race through the example as though you were reading a newspaper, but instead use your voice to get listeners involved. Speak faster here to create a sense of action, slower there to build suspense. Raise your voice in some places, lower it in others. Pause occasionally for dramatic effect. Most important, maintain eye contact with your audience. The easiest way to ruin a fine example is to read it dully from your notes. As you practice the speech, "talk through" your extended examples without relying on your notes. By the day of your speech, you should be able to deliver your extended examples as naturally as if you were telling a story to a group of friends.

STATISTICS

We live in an age of statistics. Day in and day out we are bombarded with a staggering array of numbers: Bruce Springsteen has sold 45 million albums; the suicide rate among teenagers has increased by 300 percent since 1965;

Saudi Arabia produces 233,000 barrels of oil every hour; Americans spend more than $9 billion annually on cosmetics.

What do all these numbers mean? Most of us would be hard-pressed to say. Yet we feel more secure in our knowledge when we can express it numerically. According to Lord Kelvin, the nineteenth-century physicist, "When you can measure what you are speaking about, and express it in numbers, you know something about it. But when you cannot measure it, when you cannot express it in numbers, your knowledge is . . . meager and unsatisfactory." It is this widely shared belief that makes statistics, when used properly, such an effective way to clarify and support ideas.

Like brief examples, statistics are often cited in passing to clarify or strengthen a speaker's points. The following examples show how three students used statistics in their speeches:

To document the need for reform in college athletics: "According to *Sports Illustrated*, only 37 percent of all scholarship athletes graduate from college—and the percentage is even lower in football and basketball."

To illustrate the explosion in America's pet population: "The Humane Society estimates that 90 million dogs and cats are born in the United States each year. Of these, 14 million will be destroyed at animal shelters across the country."

To show the amount of government aid to American farmers: "The *New York Times* reports that this year American taxpayers will give farmers $30 billion in subsidies—the equivalent of about $700 for every non-farm family in the country."

Statistics can also be used in combination—stacked up to show the magnitude or seriousness of an issue. We find a good instance of this technique in a speech by James Zumberge, President of the University of Southern California. To help demonstrate his point about the vast increase in cultural interchanges between the United States and Pacific Basin nations such as China and Japan, Zumberge cited the following figures:

China's television audience of 400 million will soon be watching Jane Fonda exercises, Cable News Network, "Knots Landing," and "Falcon Crest." In 1979 there were only 28 students from the People's Republic of China in American universities. Today at USC alone there are 180. Nationally, the number is up to 17,000. Conversely, the Modern Language Association reports that college enrollments in Japanese language courses have increased 40 percent in the last six years.[12]

This is a well-supported argument. But what if the speaker had merely said:

There is much more contact today between the United States and countries in the Pacific Basin.

The second statement is neither as clear nor as convincing as the one containing statistics. The statistics make the speaker's claim credible and specific. Of course, the audience didn't remember all the numbers, but that's perfectly all right. The purpose of presenting a series of figures is to register their *overall* impact on listeners. What the audience did recall is that an impressive array of statistics supported the speaker's position.

Understanding Statistics

In his classic book *How to Lie with Statistics,* Darrell Huff exploded the notion that numbers don't lie. Strictly speaking, of course, they don't. But they can be easily manipulated and distorted. For example, which of the following statements is true?

a. Enriched white bread is more nutritious than whole wheat bread, because it contains as much or more protein, calcium, niacin, thiamine, and riboflavin.

b. Whole wheat bread is more nutritious than white bread, because it contains seven times the amount of fiber, plus more iron, phosphorus, and potassium.

As you might expect, *both* statements are true. And you might hear either one of them—depending on who is trying to sell you the bread.

One can play with statistics in all kinds of areas. Which of these statements is true?

a. The cheetah, clocked at 70 mph, is the fastest animal in the world.

b. The pronghorn antelope, clocked at 61 mph, is the fastest animal in the world.

The cheetah, right? Not necessarily. It's true the cheetah can go faster, but only for short sprints. The antelope can maintain its high speed over a much greater distance. So which is faster? It depends on what you're measuring. Put in terms of human races, the cheetah would win the hundred-yard dash, but the antelope would win the marathon.

When you are dealing with money, statistics become even trickier. For instance, consider the following facts:

a. In 1947 President Harry Truman earned a salary of $75,000.

b. In 1967 President Lyndon B. Johnson earned a salary of $100,000.

c. In 1987 President Ronald Reagan earned a salary of $200,000.

Which President was paid the most money? It depends. In purely mathematical terms, of course, Reagan was the highest earner. But as we all know, a dollar today does not buy nearly as much as it did when Harry Truman was President. One measure of the inflation rate is the Consumer Price Index, which gauges the value of the dollar in any given year against its purchasing power in 1967.

If we apply the Consumer Price Index to the three Presidents' salaries, we can see how much each earned in 1967 dollars:

a. In 1947 President Harry Truman earned a salary of $104,000.

b. In 1967 President Lyndon B. Johnson earned a salary of $100,000.

c. In 1987 President Ronald Reagan earned a salary of $62,000.

In other words, while Reagan had the highest salary, the value of his $200,000 was considerably less than the value of Truman's $75,000.

The point is that there is usually more to statistics than meets the eye. When you track down statistics for your speeches, be sure to evaluate them in light of the following questions.

Are the Statistics Representative?   Say that on your way to class you choose ten students at random and ask them whether they favor or oppose government tax credits for students attending private schools. Say also that six approve of such funding and four do not. Would you then be accurate in claiming that 60 percent of the students on your campus favor spending government money for private schools?

Of course not. Ten students is not a big enough sample. But even if it were, other problems would arise. Do the ten students interviewed accurately reflect your school's proportion of freshmen, sophomores, juniors, and seniors? Do they mirror the proportion of men and women students? Are the various majors accurately represented? What about part-time and full-time students? Rich students and poor students? Ethnic minorities?

In short, make sure your statistics are representative of what they claim to measure.

Are Statistical Measures Used Correctly?   Here are two groups of numbers:

GROUP A	GROUP B
7,500	5,400
6,300	5,400
5,000	5,000
4,400	2,300
4,400	1,700

Let us apply to each group three basic statistical measures—the mean, the median, and the mode.

The *mean*—popularly called the average—is determined by summing all of the items in a group and dividing by the number of items. The mean for group A is 5,520. For group B it is 3,960.

The *median* is the middle figure in a group once the figures are put in order from highest to lowest. The median for both group A and group B is exactly the same—5,000.

The *mode* is the number that occurs most frequently in a group of numbers. The mode for group A is 4,400. For group B it is 5,400.

Notice the results:

	GROUP A	GROUP B
Mean	5,520	3,960
Median	5,000	5,000
Mode	4,400	5,400

All of these measures have the same goal—to indicate what is typical or characteristic of a certain group of numbers. Yet see how different the results are, depending on which measure you use.

The differences among the various measures can be striking. For instance, the *mean* salary of major-league baseball players is $412,000 a year. But most players don't earn anywhere near that much. The average is highly inflated by the astronomical salaries (some in the range of $2 million a year) paid to a few superstars. By contrast, the *median* salary of major-league players is $265,000—not a sum to scoff at, but still $147,000 less than the average salary. And the *mode* (the salary paid to more players than any other amount) is just $62,500—almost $350,000 less than the mean.

How might a speaker use these different measures? The owner of a baseball club would probably cite the mean ($412,000) to show he or she is being bankrupted by high salaries. The president of the players' union might emphasize the mode ($62,500) to demonstrate the low compensation for a short career full of injuries and stress. Both speakers would be telling the truth, but neither would be completely honest unless the audience understood the meaning of the statistics.

Are the Statistics from a Reliable Source?   Which is the more reliable estimate of the number of birth defects caused by the anti-acne drug Accutane—one from the U.S. Food and Drug Administration or one compiled by Hoffman-La Roche Inc., makers of the drug? Easy—the estimate by the F.D. A., which does not have a vested interest in what the figures look like. What about nutritional ratings for fast foods offered by Consumer's Union (a highly respected nonprofit organization) or by Burger King? That's easy too—Consumer's Union, whose claims are not manipulated by advertising executives.

But now things get tougher. What about the competing statistics offered by groups for and against welfare reform? Or the conflicting numbers tossed out by a corporation and the union striking against it? In these cases the answer is not so clear, since both sides would present the facts according to their own partisan motives.

As a speaker, you must be aware of possible bias in the use of numbers.

Since statistics can be interpreted so many ways and put to so many uses, you should seek figures gathered by objective, nonpartisan sources.

Tips for Using Statistics

Use Statistics to Quantify Your Ideas The main value of statistics is to give your ideas numerical precision. This can be especially important when you are trying to document the existence of a problem. Examples can bring the problem alive and dramatize it in personal terms. But your listeners may still wonder how many people the problem actually affects. In such a situation, you should turn to statistics.

Suppose you are speaking about the problem of adult illiteracy in the United States. You give an example, you personalize it, you provide many details, as follows:

> Most people believe illiteracy is a problem only for those directly affected. But this simply isn't true. For example, a 42-year-old mother from Syracuse who can't read or write unintentionally poisoned her young daughter because she confused pink dishwashing soap with Pepto-Bismol.[13]

Confronted with that example, a listener might think, "Yes, that's very interesting, quite tragic, but are there really that many people in America who can't read?" Anticipating just such a response, a sharp speaker would include figures to quantify the problem:

> According to statistics from the Department of Education, 72 million adults— possibly one-third of our population—are at or below a marginal level of literacy. Of these, 26 million are functionally illiterate. This means they cannot read maps, signs, or bus schedules written at a fifth-grade level. *Publishers Weekly* points out that this number is increasing by 2.3 million people each year.[14]

Now the audience is much more likely to agree that illiteracy is a serious and growing problem.

Use Statistics Sparingly As helpful as statistics can be, nothing puts an audience to sleep faster than a speech cluttered with numbers from beginning to end. Insert statistics only when they are needed, and then make sure they are easy to grasp. Even the most attentive listener would have trouble sorting out this barrage of figures:

> According to the Census Bureau, single parents now head 25.7 percent of families with children under age 18 in the United States. A staggering 54.3 percent of these families live below the poverty line—which is roughly $11,500 for a family of four—compared with 18.2 percent of all families with children. For families headed by females, the figure is 47.2 percent, compared with 19.7 percent of families headed

by males. The problem will become even more severe in the 1990's, says the Department of Health and Social Services, when 33 percent of families, possibly even 50 percent, will be headed by single parents.

Instead of drowning your audience in a sea of statistics, use only those that are most important. For example:

According to the Census Bureau, 25 percent—one in four—of all U.S. families with school-age children are headed by single parents. More than half of these families live below the poverty line, especially if the single parent is a woman. Even more distressing, the Department of Health and Social Services estimates that the problem will get worse during the 1990's.

This second statement makes the same point as the first, but now the ideas emerge more clearly because they are not lost in a torrent of numbers.

Identify the Sources of Your Statistics   As we have seen, figures are easy to manipulate. This is why careful listeners keep an ear out for the sources of a speaker's statistics. One student learned this by experience. In a speech entitled "The Price of Keeping America Free," he claimed that the United States spends only about one-half as much of the federal budget for national defense now as it did in 1960, when John F. Kennedy was elected President. In 1960, he said, 52 percent of the budget was devoted to defense spending, as opposed to 27 percent now. This is a startling statistic—especially in light of the huge sums spent on defense in recent years. But because the speaker did not say where he got the figure, many of his classmates were not willing to accept it. They were sure he must be wrong.

As it turned out, the figure was quite reliable. It had come from the latest edition of the *Statistical Abstract of the United States,* an annual digest of statistics covering almost every aspect of American life. If the speaker had only mentioned this in his speech, he would have been more persuasive.

Explain Your Statistics   Statistics don't speak for themselves. They need to be interpreted and related to your listeners. Notice how effectively one speaker did this:

According to the latest report of the United States Surgeon General, cigarette smoking is the single largest cause of preventable death in America. When you add up all the cigarette-caused deaths from cancer, heart disease, strokes, emphysema, and so forth, the total comes to 350,000 Americans each year. To get an idea of just how many that is, it is *seven* times the number of people who die in traffic accidents each year. It is almost as many Americans as were killed in World War II, the Korean War, and the war in Vietnam *combined.*

Explaining what statistics mean is particularly important when you deal with large numbers, since they are hard to visualize. How, for example, can we comprehend the $3 trillion of the U.S. national debt? We could explain that a trillion is a thousand billion and a billion is a thousand million. But that doesn't do much good, since millions and billions are almost as hard to visualize as trillions. Suppose, instead, we translate the huge numbers into terms a listener can relate to. Here is what one speaker came up with:

> How much money is a trillion dollars? Think of it this way. If you had $1 million and spent it at the rate of $1,000 a day, you would run out of money in less than three years. If you had $1 billion and spent it at the rate of $1,000 a day, you would not run out of money for almost three thousand years. And if you had $1 trillion dollars and spent it at the rate of $1,000 a day, you wouldn't run out of money for nearly three million years!

Whenever you use statistics in your speeches, think of how you can make them meaningful for your audience. Rather than simply reciting the fact that, say, McDonald's has sold 65 billion hamburgers, find a way to make your audience *see* how many hamburgers that is. You might say:

> Since each McDonald's burger (with the bun) is about 2 inches thick, 65 billion hamburgers stacked on top of one another would reach about 1.9 million miles—eight times as far as the moon.

Or suppose you want to show the high incidence of cancer in the United States. You could say, "According to the American Cancer Society, one of every four Americans will have cancer during their lifetimes." This is an alarming statistic, but it is likely to go in one ear and out the other unless you bring the statistic home to your audience—as did one student in her speech:

> Figures compiled by the American Cancer Society show that one of every four Americans will have cancer during their lifetimes. In other words, the odds are that six of us in this class can expect to have cancer. It could be Perry or Bill, Lisa or Julie, Beth or Letone—indeed, it could be any of us.

Be creative in thinking of ways to relate your statistics to your audience. This is probably the single most important step you can take to make statistics work in your speeches.

Round Off Complicated Statistics Mount Everest is 29,028 feet high; the official world land speed record is 622.287 miles per hour; the world's highest waterfall has a total drop of 3,212 feet; the greatest attendance at any boxing match was 135,132 people; the moon is 238,855 miles from Earth.

These are intriguing figures—but they are much too complicated to be readily understood by listeners. Unless there is an important reason to give exact numbers, you should round off most statistics. You might say that Mount Everest is 29,000 feet high; the world land speed record is more than 622 miles per hour; the world's highest waterfall has a drop of some 3,200 feet; the greatest attendance at any boxing match was 135,000; and the moon is 239,000 miles from Earth.

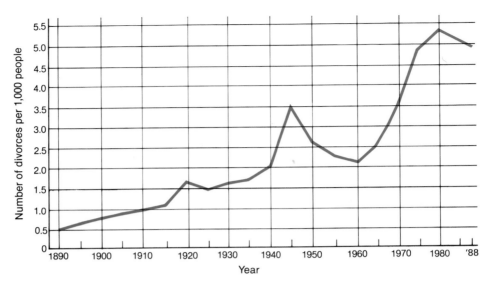

FIGURE 6.1   Divorce Rate, 1890–1988

Use Visual Aids to Clarify Statistical Trends   Visual aids can save you a lot of time, as well as make your statistics easier to comprehend. Suppose you are discussing the divorce rate in the United States and its relationship to social conditions. You could start by explaining that between 1890 and 1915 the divorce rate showed a very slow increase from 0.5 divorces per thousand people to 1.0 per thousand. Then in 1920, immediately following World War I, the rate took a slight jump to 1.5 per thousand. After this came a decline and leveling off until 1945, just after World War II, when the divorce rate increased sharply to 3.5 per thousand. Next the divorce rate declined once again, to a low of 2.2 per thousand in 1960. After 1960 the rate started climbing steadily, and it reached a peak of 5.3 per thousand in 1981—more than ten times the rate that existed ninety years earlier. Surprisingly, the divorce rate then leveled off and declined slightly, to 4.9 per thousand in 1988.

These happen to be quite interesting statistics, and you could build a good speech around them. But strung together in a few sentences they are hard to digest. Figure 6.1 shows how much more clearly the points can be made with a simple graph. We shall discuss visual aids in detail in Chapter 12. For the moment, keep in mind that they can be helpful in presenting statistical information.

Where to Find Statistics

Statistics can be found in any kind of reputable publication—books, magazines, newspapers, scholarly journals, government documents, business reports, and so forth. A world almanac (there are several established versions) can be a treasure house of interesting numbers. There are also some sources devoted solely to statistics. They include the *Statistical Abstract of the United States* (published annually since 1878) and the *Statistical Yearbook* (put out by the United Nations). These contain statistics on everything from the American economy to world population trends. The *Guinness Book of World Records* offers more esoteric information, such as the weight of the world's largest polished diamond, the internal temperature of the sun, and how many hours of television the average American child watches by age eighteen.

You will find these and other handy sources of statistics in the reference room of your library (see Chapter 5). Besides being easy to use, they can be fascinating to look through. This is why the *Guinness Book of World Records* remains a best-seller year after year.

TESTIMONY

When speakers quote or paraphrase the words of another person to support their ideas, they are using testimony. In most speeches you will probably rely mainly on *expert testimony*—testimony from people who are recognized authorities in their fields. Expert testimony is especially helpful for student speakers because they are seldom recognized as experts on their speech topics. Citing the views of people who are experts is a good way to lend credibility to your speeches. It shows that you are not just mouthing your own opinions but that your position is supported by people who are knowledgeable about the topic.

Expert testimony is even more important when a topic is controversial. The following story explains how one student enlisted expert testimony for his speech on the United States Joint Chiefs of Staff:

As John Quirk did his research for a speech on America's national defense system, he became convinced that the present structure of the Joint Chiefs of Staff should be changed to reduce waste in military spending and to allow the U.S. to act more quickly in case of a military emergency. Yet John was not an expert on the matter. Nor did he have any firsthand experience with the Joint Chiefs of Staff. How could he convince his audience to accept his ideas?

Statistics helped, and so did examples. But on such a controversial issue that was not enough. So to reinforce his credibility, John quoted a wide range of recognized experts who agreed with him—Admiral David C. Jones, Chairman of the Joint Chiefs of Staff from 1978 to 1982; John Collins, a senior defense analyst; General Edward Myer, Army Chief of Staff; and Harold Brown, former Secretary of Defense. By citing the views of these experts—many of whom might be expected to disagree with his point of view—John made his speech much more persuasive.[15]

Another type of testimony often used in speeches is *peer testimony*—opinions of people like ourselves, not prominent figures but ordinary citizens. One speaker, Christine Murphy, employed this technique most effectively in a speech urging the opening of sealed adoption papers so adoptees could locate their natural parents:

> "When I found my natural mother, I felt deep inside me that I had finally found myself. I could fill so many empty pockets: who I looked like; where my ancestors came from; where I got my interests, my talents, and even my allergies. Unless you are adopted, you cannot understand what this feels like."

Christine used this quotation—this bit of peer testimony—to begin her speech. Then, throughout the speech, she reinforced her point of view with quotations from other adoptees and adoptive parents, and with an especially moving statement from a natural mother who had given up her child: "I wish that it could have been different, but I had no choice but to give her away. That does not mean that I do not continue to love her and to want to know her. If she's out there looking, I hope she finds me."[16]

Although both John and Christine used direct quotation, testimony can also be presented by paraphrasing. Rather than quoting someone verbatim, you give the gist of their ideas in your own words—as did one student in her speech about Halley's comet:

> Writing in *Scientific American,* Robert Richardson, an astronomer at Palomar Observatory in California, estimated the possibility of a comet striking the earth as one chance in 80 million years. But, he added, if the comet struck a heavily populated city, the impact would be like all the atomic bombs in the world going off at one spot.

Paraphrasing is better than direct quotation in two situations: first, when the original wording of a quotation is obscure or cumbersome, as is often the case with scholarly works and government documents; second, when a quotation is longer than a sentence or two. Audiences often tune out partway through lengthy quotations, which tend to interrupt the flow of a speaker's ideas. Since the rest of the speech is in your own words, you should put longer quotations in your own words as well.

Tips for Using Testimony

Quote or Paraphrase Accurately   Accurate quotation involves three things: making sure you do not misquote someone; making sure you do not violate the meaning of statements you paraphrase; making sure you do not quote out of context. Of these, the last is the most subtle—and the most dangerous. By quoting out of context, you can twist someone's remarks so as to prove almost anything. Take movie advertisements. A critic pans a movie with these words:

> This movie is a colossal bore. From beginning to end it is a disaster. What is meant to be brilliant dialogue is about as fascinating as the stuff you clean out of your kitchen drain.

But when the movie is advertised in the newspapers, what appears in huge letters over the critic's name? "COLOSSAL! FROM BEGINNING TO END—BRILLIANT! FASCINATING!"

This is so flagrant as to be humorous. But quoting out of context can have serious consequences. In 1968 Michigan governor George Romney was a leading contender for the Republican presidential nomination until his famous "brainwashing" remark—a remark taken out of context—damaged his campaign beyond repair. Appearing on a Detroit talk show, Romney answered a question about his views on the war in Vietnam this way:

Well, you know, when I came back from Vietnam, I just had the greatest brainwashing that anybody can get when you go over to Vietnam. Not only by the generals, but also by the diplomatic corps over there, and they do a very thorough job. And since returning from Vietnam, I've gone into the history of Vietnam, all the way back into World War II and beyond. And, as a result, I have changed my mind. . . . I no longer believe that it was necessary for us to get involved in South Vietnam to stop communist aggression.

The "brainwashing" line was a throwaway. The main point of Romney's full statement was that Romney had changed his mind about the need for American military forces in Vietnam. But the day after the telecast, the *New York Times* carried a story with the headline: ROMNEY ASSERTS HE UNDERWENT "BRAINWASHING" ON VIETNAM TRIP. That evening the network news programs showed clips of Romney making his "brainwashing" remark, and the next day it was being quoted in newspapers and shown on television all over the nation—except that it was usually quoted and shown out of context, without the rest of Romney's original statement about his views on the war. For the next several weeks, Romney tried to clarify his remark and to explain why a man who had been "brainwashed" on Vietnam was competent to be President of the United States. That one remark—taken out of context—helped to destroy Romney's credibility as a presidential candidate.[17]

Clearly, quoting or paraphrasing accurately is an important ethical responsibility for speakers and writers alike.

Use Testimony from Qualified Sources   We have all become accustomed to the celebrity testimonial in television and magazine advertising. The tennis star endorses a particular brand of racket, the movie star praises a certain hair spray or shampoo, the marathon runner plugs a type of athletic shoe. So far, so good. These articles are the tools of the trade for the people who endorse them.

But what happens when a baseball player plugs a coffee machine? A comedian becomes spokesman for an oil company? A gymnast promotes some brand of cereal? Do they know more about these things than you or I? Probably not. They have been paid large sums of money to be photographed with the product, in hopes that their popularity will rub off on the product.

Being a celebrity or an authority in one area does not make someone competent in other areas. Listeners will find your speeches much more credible if you use testimony from sources qualified *on the subject at hand.* As we have seen, this may include either recognized experts or ordinary citizens with special experience on the speech topic.

Use Testimony from Unbiased Sources   In a speech about chocolate, one student made the following statement:

> Richard O'Connell, president of the Chocolate Manufacturers Association, claims that chocolate is not nearly as likely to cause cavities as some people think. In fact, he says, chocolate may actually contain chemical substances that slow down the bacterial action promoting cavities and dental plaque.

As you might suppose, the student's classmates were not persuaded. After all, what would you expect chocolate makers to say—that their product is a major cause of tooth decay? One listener reacted this way: "For all I know the statement by O'Connell may be true, but he is hardly an unbiased source. I wish you had cited an impartial expert instead."

Careful listeners are suspicious of opinion from biased or self-interested sources. Be sure to use testimony from credible, competent, objective authorities.

Identify the People You Quote or Paraphrase   The usual way to identify your source is to name the person and sketch his or her qualifications before presenting the testimony. The following excerpt is from a speech on the warming of the Earth known as the "greenhouse effect," which many experts predict will become a major problem in the 1990's:

> According to *John Hoffman, director of strategic studies for the Environmental Protection Agency,* the "greenhouse effect" is a major threat whose impact may be felt within a few years. Eventually, he says, "there could be big changes. New York City could have a climate like Daytona Beach, Florida, by 2100."

Had the speaker not identified John Hoffman, listeners would not have had the foggiest notion who he is or why his opinion should be heeded.

Examples, statistics, and testimony are all helpful devices for the speaker. Depending on your topic, you may want to use some of them, all, or none. Remember they are tools, and they all serve the same purpose—getting your message across to your listeners.

SAMPLE SPEECH WITH COMMENTARY

The following persuasive speech illustrates how to work supporting materials into a speech. As you read, study how the speaker uses a variety of examples, statistics, and quotations to make his ideas clear, credible, and convincing.[18]

TROUBLE IN THE SKIES

The speaker begins with an extended example to get the attention and interest of his audience. The example is specific and realistic in its details. We are told where the accident took place, the kind of plane involved, how many people were killed, and exactly why the plane crashed. These are the kinds of details that bring extended examples to life and get listeners involved in a speech.

In January 1985 a Galaxy Airlines Electra jet crashed shortly after takeoff from a Reno, Nevada, airport, killing 70 persons. During its investigation into the accident, the National Transportation Safety Board discovered that the crew, who had little experience flying Electra jets, had forgotten to run through a pre-departure safety checklist. As a result, the pilot did not notice that one of the access doors to the airplane was still open. The door caused a thumping noise during takeoff. Once the plane was airborne, the pilot tried to see if the noise was coming from one of the engines. Unfortunately, he did so by reducing the power to all four engines—at once. This dangerous maneuver caused the plane to stall and crash.

The speaker moves deftly into testimony suggesting that the opening story is representative of a major problem facing America's airlines. When you use an extended example, it is usually a good idea to precede or follow the example with statistics, testimony, or some other indication that the example is not unusual or exceptional.

This is only one of the more tragic examples of what Robert Reed Gray of the Flight Safety Foundation calls the "alarming shortage of well-trained pilots" facing America's commercial airlines. In researching this speech, I discovered that as the demand for commercial air travel has soared in the last decade, airlines have been forced to hire more and more pilots with fewer and fewer hours of training. The result, as we shall see, is a dangerous erosion in the safety of air travel.

In his first main point the speaker explains how the shortage of qualified pilots has come about. Supporting materials in this and the next two paragraphs back up the point.

To understand how the shortage of highly trained pilots came about, we have to go back to the 1978 Airline Deregulation Act. This act, which permitted true competition between the airlines, led to price wars that have saved travelers an estimated $6 billion a year. These price wars have made air travel more attractive—so much so, says *Newsweek*, that the number of airline passengers has doubled in the past ten years. At the same time, the number of airlines has tripled. According to *Technology Review*, there are now 124 certified air carriers in the United States, compared with just 39 in 1978.

Notice how the speaker identifies the sources of his supporting materials and integrates those sources smoothly into the text. There are many examples of this technique throughout the speech.

As in the previous paragraph, the speaker uses a series of statistics to support his claims. Rather than giving the exact numbers of new pilots, he rounds them off, making them easier to grasp and recall.

This huge growth in demand for air travel has created a shortage of skilled pilots. According to the *Christian Science Monitor*, airlines in the United States hired some 2,500 new pilots each year during the 1970's. During the last three years, however, they have taken on about 7,000 per year. Moreover, as *Aviation Week and Space Technology* reports, another 10,000 pilots may be hired this year.

Notice how the speaker handles his figures about the drop in the number of hours of jet flight training received by most new pilots. After presenting the figures, he first explains their meaning by noting that the average pilot today receives only one-third as much training as before. Then he uses the hypothetical example of a surgeon to relate the one-third fraction directly to his audience. This is an excellent technique and is something you should try to do when you use statistics in a speech.

The speaker begins his second main point—that poorly trained pilots are posing a danger to safe air travel. As we shall see, he supports the point with an excellent mix of examples, statistics, and testimony.

An extended example puts the statistics of the previous paragraph in human terms. This example, like that at the start of the speech, is filled with specific details that make it interesting and credible. Particularly effective is the speaker's statement, "Yes, you heard me correctly—30 feet, less than the distance from where I am standing to the last row of seats in our classroom." This is a fine case of how a speaker can emphasize ideas by translating facts and figures into visual images that relate directly to the experience of the audience.

This great hiring pressure has seriously reduced the qualifications of the typical airline pilot. According to an article in *Flying* magazine, some major carriers no longer require that pilots have a college degree, while others are reducing the age, vision, height, and experience requirements for new pilots. Elaborating on this fact, the *Washington Post Weekly* reports that the average number of jet flight training hours among new pilots has dropped from 2,400 in 1983 to only 900 in 1986. In other words, the average new pilot receives only about one-third as much training as would have been the case a few years ago. To put this figure in perspective, think how you would like to be operated on by a surgeon who received this little training. Yet when you fly on a commercial airline, your life is in the hands of the pilot no less than it is in the hands of a surgeon when you go into the operating room.

The effects of poorly trained pilots are plainly visible in deteriorating air safety statistics. The Federal Aviation Agency has recorded an alarming increase in the number of near collisions over the last few years. Whereas there were 311 near-misses in 1982, there were more than 1,000 last year—an increase of well over 300 percent. Some of this is due to the growing volume of air traffic, but *USA Today* reports that federal aviation officals attribute up to two-thirds of the near-misses to pilot error and inexperience.

One of the worst of those near-misses occurred last July 8 over the Atlantic Ocean, when a Delta Airlines jumbo jet strayed 60 miles off course and almost collided with a Continental Airlines plane. According to the official investigation by the Department of Transportation, as reported in *Time* magazine, the planes came within 30 feet of each other. Yes, you heard me correctly—30 feet, less than the distance from where I am standing to the last row of seats in our classroom." The Delta crew, inexperienced in transoceanic flight, had entered the wrong data in their computer navigation system and then had failed to verify their position by other means. Had the Continental crew not seen the Delta plane, the resulting collision would have taken almost 600 lives, making it the deadliest single disaster in the history of American aviation.

Although tragedy was avoided in this case, that is small comfort. Captain Hank Duffy, president of the Air Line Pilots Association, fears that the alarming increase of

The quotation from Captain Hank Duffy is a good instance of expert testimony, which the speaker uses well throughout the speech. Notice that this quotation, like others in the speech, is short and powerful. There is no reason to use a direct quotation unless it makes the point more clearly and forcefully than you could in your own words.

The speaker once again uses an effective combination of statistics and examples—this time to support his claim that pilot error and inexperience are indeed responsible for many airline crashes. Here, as elsewhere, the speaker cites the sources of his statistics and draws his examples clearly, vividly, and persuasively.

This is a very effective example. Brief and dramatic, it ends the body of the speech on a strong note.

The speaker begins his conclusion by summarizing the two main points he had made in the body of the speech. He then ends with a dramatic closing line. As we shall see in Chapter 8, this is a particularly effective way to pull a speech together and to reinforce its central idea.

near mid-air collisions is a grim warning of what is to come. Given the large numbers of inexperienced pilots and the continuing growth of air travel, "it's just a matter of time," he says, "until two planes slam together." As it is, the Department of Transportation reports there were more accidents—thirty-one—on scheduled United States airlines last year than in any year since 1974. Moreover, in contrast with 1986, when there were no fatal accidents, 231 people died in airline crashes in the United States last year.

Although many factors contribute to such crashes, the most important is pilot error. Indeed, the *New York Times Magazine* reports that 65 percent of all jet transport accidents worldwide from 1959 to 1986 have been traced to errors by flight crews. The January 1982 crash of an Air Florida Boeing-737 during a snow storm in Washington, D.C., is a case in point. That accident claimed 78 lives. The captain was fairly new to the kind of plane he was piloting that day, and he had logged almost no prior cold-weather flying hours. Yet due to the great demand for pilots, Air Florida had quickly promoted him to captain of the Boeing-737. The National Transportation Safety Board inquiry, which concluded that the accident was caused by the captain's inadequate response to the weather conditions, also found that he lacked the normal seasoning expected of a first officer, much less that expected of a captain.

Another incident demonstrates even more clearly the dangers of inexperienced pilots. Last November 15, a Continental Airlines DC-9 flipped over and crashed moments after liftoff from snowbound Stapleton Airport in Denver. Twenty-seven people were killed, including co-pilot Lee Bruecher. According to *U.S. News and World Report*, 26-year-old Bruecher was making only his second trip as a DC-9 co-pilot, and he had never flown in snow before. Yet he was flying the plane at takeoff!

So we have seen how the increased demand for air travel has produced a shortage of qualified pilots. And we have seen some of the tragic results produced by this shortage. Air travel is still statistically safer than all other forms of mass transportation, but that fact is of little consolation if yours is the plane that crashes due to the errors of an inexperienced or poorly trained pilot.

SUMMARY

Good speeches are not composed of hot air and unfounded assertions. They need strong supporting materials to bolster the speaker's point of view. In fact, the skillful use of supporting materials often makes the difference between a good speech and a poor one. The three basic types of supporting materials are examples, statistics, and testimony.

In the course of a speech you may use brief examples—specific instances referred to in passing—and sometimes you may want to give several brief examples in a row to create a stronger impression. Extended examples—often called illustrations, narratives, or anecdotes—are longer and more detailed. Hypothetical examples describe imaginary situations and can be quite effective for relating ideas to the audience. All three kinds of examples help to clarify ideas, to reinforce ideas, or to personalize ideas. To be most effective, though, they should be vivid and richly textured.

Statistics can be extremely helpful in conveying your message, as long as you use them sparingly and explain them so they are meaningful to your audience. Above all, you should understand your statistics and use them fairly. Numbers can easily be manipulated and distorted. Make sure your figures are representative of what they claim to measure, that you use statistical measures correctly, and that you take statistics only from reliable sources.

Testimony is especially helpful for student speakers, because they are seldom recognized as experts on their speech topics. Citing the views of people who are experts is a good way to make your ideas more credible. When you include testimony in a speech, you can either quote someone verbatim or paraphrase their words. As with statistics, there are guidelines for using testimony. Be sure to quote or paraphrase accurately and to cite qualified, unbiased sources. If the source is not generally known to your audience, be certain to establish his or her credentials.

REVIEW QUESTIONS

After reading this chapter, you should be able to answer the following questions:

1. Why do you need supporting materials in your speeches?

2. What are the three kinds of examples discussed in the chapter? How might you use each kind to support your ideas?

3. What are five tips for using examples in your speeches?

4. Why is it so easy to lie with statistics? What three questions should you ask to judge the reliability of statistics?

5. What are six tips for using statistics in your speeches?

6. What is testimony? Explain the difference between expert testimony and peer testimony.

7. What are four tips for using testimony in your speeches?

APPLICATION EXERCISES

1. Each of the following statements violates at least one of the criteria for effective supporting materials discussed in the chapter. Identify the flaw (or flaws) in each statement.

   a. According to a study conducted by General Motors, there is no significant difference in quality between American-made cars and foreign imports.
   b. A random poll of 45 people taken recently in Pittsburgh, Pennsylvania, showed that 83 percent of those interviewed favored a substantial increase in federal assistance for the steel industry. Clearly, the American people support such a policy.
   c. It's just not true that television has an influence on crimes by young people. All my friends watch television, and none of us has ever committed a major crime.
   d. In the words of one expert, "The escalating cost of malpractice insurance is nothing less than a national crisis. If it is not solved soon, the whole health-care system may be seriously damaged."
   e. Every day 15,000 people die of starvation. That's one person every 4.5 seconds. A half-billion people are chronically hungry. The U.S. Bureau of Labor states that over 900 million people are trying to subsist on less than $300 a year for a family of four. Of that 900 million, one-half are starving. Another million people suffer from malnutrition. An additional billion people in 40 nations try to live on 27¢ a day.
   f. As Robert Redford said in a recent interview, the Star Wars defense system should be abandoned permanently. It won't work, and it only serves to escalate the arms race.
   g. The total land and water mass of the United States is 3,623,420 square miles. The largest state is Alaska, with 591,004 square miles; the smallest state is Rhode Island, with 1,212 square miles.
   h. According to statistics compiled by the School Board, the annual median salary for teachers in our district is $29,850 a year. This shows that teachers average almost $30,000 a year.

2. Analyze the speech in the Appendix by Susan Zaeske, ("Warning: Household Chemicals," pages 000–000). Identify the main points of the speech and the supporting materials used for each. Evaluate the speaker's use of supporting materials in light of the criteria discussed in this chapter.

NOTES

1 Reported in William Stockton, "Exercise Gains Support as a Key Ingredient in a Weight-Loss Plan," *New York Times*, March 28, 1988, p. C10.

2 Larry Elwell, "Hearing: Safeguarding an Endangered Resource," *Vital Speeches*, 50 (1984), 716.

3 Adapted from Donald Robinson, "When Home Can Hurt You," *Parade Magazine* (November 24, 1985), p. 8.

4 George Will, "Three Balls, Two Strikes," *Newsweek* (January 5, 1987), p. 64.

5 June Carolyn Erlick, "Women of Nicaragua," *Ms.* (November 1984), p. 66.

6 Richard Nisbett and Lee Ross, *Human Inference: Strategies and Shortcomings of Social Judgment* (Englewood Cliffs, N.J.: Prentice-Hall, 1980), pp. 43–62.

7 For an interesting recent study see William G. Kirkwood, "Parables as Metaphors and Examples," *Quarterly Journal of Speech*, 71 (1985), 422–440.

8 Veda Blackman, "Science's Internal Poison," in *Winning Orations, 1984* (Mankato, Minn.: Interstate Oratorical Association, 1984), pp. 18–21.

9 Eliot Aronson, *The Social Animal*, 4th ed. (New York: W. H. Freeman, 1984), p. 87.

10 James A. Winans, *Speech-Making* (New York: Appleton-Century-Crofts, 1922), p. 141.

11 See Nisbett and Ross, *Human Inference*, pp. 43–62.

12 James H. Zumberge, "Education and Technology: The Pacific Century," *Vital Speeches*, 54 (1988), 367.

13 Joan Braaten, "It's English," *Winning Orations, 1984* (Mankato, Minn.: Interstate Oratorical Association, 1984), pp. 12–15.

14 *Ibid.*

15 John Quirk, "Defense Under Fire," *Winning Orations, 1984* (Mankato, Minn.: Interstate Oratorical Association, 1984), pp. 12–15.

16 Christine E. Murphy, "Adoption: The Adoptee's Search for Identity," *Winning Orations, 1980* (Mankato, Minn.: Interstate Oratorical Association, 1980), pp. 41–43.

17 Theodore White, *The Making of the President, 1968* (New York: Atheneum, 1969), pp. 66–69.

18 Reprinted with permission of Eric Nelson.

PART THREE

SPEECH PREPARATION: ORGANIZING AND OUTLINING

CHAPTER 7

Organizing the Body of the Speech

I f you thumb through any mail-order catalogue today, you will discover that a large portion of the items for sale are *organizers*—closet organizers, kitchen organizers, tape and disc organizers, office organizers. Read enough catalogues, and you must conclude that if something exists, it can be organized.

Why all this quest for organization? Obviously, when the objects you possess are well organized, they serve you better. These's little point in having multiple possessions if you can't find them when you need them. Organization allows you to see what you have and to put your hands immediately on the garment, the tool, the tape, the piece of paper you want without a frenzied search.

Much the same is true of your speeches. If they are well organized, they will serve you better. Organization allows you—and your listeners—to see what ideas you have and to put mental "hands" on the most important ones.

ORGANIZATION IS IMPORTANT

Several years ago a college professor took a well-organized speech and scrambled it by randomly changing the order of its sentences. He then had a speaker deliver the original version to one group of listeners and the scrambled version to another group. After the speeches, he gave a test to see how well each group understood what they had heard. Not surprisingly, the group that heard the original, unscrambled speech scored much higher.[1]

A few years later, two professors repeated the same experiment at another school. But instead of testing how well the listeners comprehended each speech, they tested to see what effects the speeches had on the listeners' attitudes toward the speakers. They found that people who heard the well-organized speech believed the speaker to be much more competent and trustworthy than did those who heard the scrambled speech.[2]

These are just two of many studies that show the importance of organization in effective speechmaking.[3] They confirm what most of us know from experience. How many times have you listened to someone who rambled aimlessly from one idea to another? You realize how difficult it is to pay attention to the speaker, much less to understand the message. In fact, when students explain what they hope to learn from their speech class, they almost always put "the ability to organize my ideas more effectively" near the top of the list.

This ability is especially vital for speechmaking. Listeners demand coherence. They have little patience with speakers who bounce wildly from idea to idea. Keep in mind that listeners—unlike readers—cannot flip back to a previous page if they have trouble grasping a speaker's ideas. In this respect a speech is much like a movie. Just as a director must be sure viewers can follow the plot of a film from beginning to end, so must a speaker be sure listeners can follow the progression of ideas in a speech from beginning to end. This requires that speeches be organized *strategically*. They should be put together in particular ways to achieve particular results with particular audiences.

Speech organization is important for other reasons as well. As we saw in Chapter 1, it is closely connected to critical thinking. When you work to organize your speeches, you gain practice in the general skill of establishing clear relationships among your ideas. Many studies have shown that this skill will serve you well throughout your college days and in almost any career you may choose.[4] There is also evidence that using a clear, specific method of speech organization can boost your confidence as a speaker and improve your ability to deliver a message fluently.[5]

The first step in developing a strong sense of speech organization is to gain command of the three basic parts of a speech—introduction, body, and conclusion—and the strategic role of each. In this chapter we deal with the body of the speech. The next chapter will take up the introduction and conclusion.

There are good reasons for talking first about the body of the speech. The body is the longest and most important part. Also, you will usually prepare the body first. It is much easier to create an effective introduction after you know exactly what you will say in the body.

The process of organizing the body of a speech begins when you determine the main points.

MAIN POINTS

The main points are the central features of your speech. You should select them carefully, phrase them precisely, and arrange them strategically. Here are the main points of a student speech about the medical uses of hypnosis:

Specific Purpose: To inform my audience of the major medical uses of hypnosis.

Central Idea: The major medical uses of hypnosis today are to control pain, to improve athletic performance, and to combat obesity.

Main Points:
   I.   Hypnosis is used to help reduce the pain of chronic physical ailments.
   II.   Hypnosis is used to help athletes improve their performance.
   III.   Hypnosis is used to combat obesity.

These three main points form the skeleton of the body of the speech. If there are three major *uses* of hypnosis for medical purposes, then logically there can be three *main points* in the speech.

How do you choose your main points? Sometimes they will be evident from your specific purpose statement. Suppose your specific purpose is "To inform my audience about the origins, events, and philosophy of the Special

Olympics." Obviously, your speech will have three main points. The first will deal with the origins of the Special Olympics, the second with the events of the Special Olympics, the third with the philosophy of the Special Olympics. Written in outline form, the main points might be:

Specific Purpose: To inform my audience about the origins, events, and philosophy of the Special Olympics.

Central Idea: The Special Olympics gives mentally retarded people an opportunity to experience athletic competition.

Main Points: I.   The Special Olympics was founded in 1968 to promote physical fitness for the mentally retarded.
II.   Held locally every year and internationally every four years, the Special Olympics has sports events similar to those in the Olympic Games.
III.   Although medals are awarded, the Special Olympics stresses effort and participation rather than winning.

Even if your main points are not stated expressly in your specific purpose, they may be easy to project from it. Let us say your specific purpose is "To inform my audience of the basic steps in making French red wine." You know each of your main points will correspond to a step in the wine-making process. They might look like this in outline form:

Specific Purpose: To inform my audience of the basic steps in making French red wine.

Central Idea: There are five basic steps used by French wine makers in making red wine.

Main Points: I.   The first step is harvesting the grapes.
II.   The second step is preparing the grapes.
III.   The third step is fermenting the grapes.
IV.   The fourth step is pressing the grapes.
V.   The fifth step is aging the wine.

You will not always settle on your main points quite so easily. Often they will emerge as you research the speech and evaluate your findings. Suppose your specific purpose is "To persuade my audience that natural foods are not necessarily better for you than processed foods with additives and preservatives." You know each main point in the speech will present a *reason* why natural foods are not necessarily superior to processed foods. But you don't know how many main points there will be or what they will be. As you research and study the topic, you decide there are two major reasons to support your view. Each of these reasons will become a main point in your speech. Written in outline form, they might be:

Specific Purpose: To persuade my audience that natural foods are not necessarily better for you than processed foods with additives and preservatives.

Central Idea: Natural foods are not necessarily more nutritious or safer than processed foods containing additives and preservatives.

Main Points:
   I. Natural foods are not necessarily more nutritious than processed foods containing additives and preservatives.
  II. Natural foods are not necessarily safer than processed foods containing additives and preservatives.

You now have two broad areas around which to organize your ideas.

Number of Main Points

You will not have time in your classroom speeches to develop more than four or five main points, and most speeches will contain only two or three. Regardless of how long a speech might run, if you have too many main points, the audience will have trouble sorting them out.[6] When everything is equally important, nothing is important. Imagine you have a particularly lenient professor who gives everyone in the class an A. Your A won't have much value for you. But if only three students in the class get an A and you are one of them, then you stand out from the crowd. That is what you must aim to do in your speeches—to make a few main points stand out and be remembered.

If, when you list your main points, you find you have too many, you may be able to condense them into categories. Here is a set of main points for a speech about lasers:

Specific Purpose: To inform my audience about the uses of lasers.

Central Idea: Lasers harness the power of light for a wide range of uses.

Main Points:
    I. Laser gravity-wave detectors allow astronomers to "see" deep into space.
   II. Automobile manufacturers use lasers for many purposes in making cars.
  III. Neurosurgeons use lasers to vaporize brain tumors.
  IV. Lasers help create billions of industrial goods every year.
   V. With lasers, scientists can chart the fastest of chemical reactions.
  VI. The telephone industry sends phone calls underseas to Europe with lasers.
 VII. Eye specialists routinely use lasers to "weld" loose retinas back in place.
VIII. Lasers allow doctors to make early diagnoses of certain kinds of cancer.

So you have eight main points—which is too many. But if you look at the list, you see that the eight points fall into three broad categories: lasers in science, lasers in industry, lasers in medicine. You might therefore restate your main points this way:

    I.   Lasers have many important uses in science.

    II.   Lasers have become indispensable to industry.

    III.   Lasers are revolutionizing the practice of medicine.

Strategic Order of Main Points

Once you establish your main points, you need to decide in what order you will present them in your speech. This is extremely important, for it will affect both the clarity and the persuasiveness of your ideas.

The most effective order depends on three things—your topic, your purpose, and your audience. Chapters 13 and 14 will deal with special aspects of organizing informative speeches and persuasive speeches. Here let us look briefly at the five basic patterns of organization used most often by public speakers.

Chronological Order   Speeches arranged chronologically follow a time pattern. They may narrate a series of events in the sequence in which they happened. For example:

Specific Purpose:	To inform my audience about the development of the American rodeo.
Central Idea:	The rodeo has developed in three major stages.
Main Points:	I. Rodeos began in the Old West as contests of skill among cowboys during cattle roundups.
	II. By 1920 rodeos had become a popular spectator sport for the general public.
	III. Today rodeos combine traditional western events with a circus-like atmosphere and the marketing techniques of big business.

Chronological order is also used in speeches explaining a process or demonstrating how to do something. For example:

Specific Purpose:	To inform my audience how commercial ice cream is made.
Central Idea:	There are five basic steps in making commercial ice cream.

Main Points:	I.	The first step is blending milk solids, sugar, and water to create the ice-cream mixture.
	II.	The second step is pasteurizing the mixture to destroy any harmful bacteria.
	III.	The third step is homogenizing the mixture to give it a smooth texture.
	IV.	The fourth step is adding color and flavor to the mixture.
	V.	The fifth step is freezing the mixture to create the final product.

As you can see, chronological order is especially useful for informative speeches.

Spatial Order   Speeches arranged spatially follow a directional pattern. That is, the main points proceed from top to bottom, left to right, front to back, inside to outside, East to West, or some other route. For example:

Specific Purpose:	To inform my audience about the components of a medieval suit of armor.
Central Idea:	The medieval suit of armor had specific pieces to protect various parts of the body.

Main Points:	I.	The head was protected by a helmet.
	II.	The torso was protected by shoulder pieces, pallettes, a breastplate, a skirt of tasses, and a tuille.
	III.	The arms and hands were protected by brassards, elbow pieces, and gauntlets.
	IV.	The legs and feet were protected by cuisses, knee pieces, jambeaux, and sollerets.

Or:

Specific Purpose:	To inform my audience about the interior design of an ancient Egyptian burial tomb.
Central Idea:	The ancient Egyptian burial tomb usually had four sections— the entrance passage, the antechamber, the treasury, and the burial chamber.

Main Points:	I.	The outermost section was the entrance passage.
	II.	The next section was the antechamber.
	III.	The third section was the treasury.
	IV.	The fourth—and most important—section was the burial chamber.

Spatial order, like chronological order, is used most often in informative speeches.

Effective speakers organize their ideas strategically to achieve the results they want with a particular audience.
(Ulrike Welsch)

Causal Order   Speeches arranged in causal order organize main points so as to show a cause-effect relationship. When you put your speech in causal order, you have two main points—one dealing with the causes of an event, the other dealing with its effects. Depending on your topic, you can either devote your first main point to the causes and the second to the effects, or you can deal first with the effects and then with the causes.

Suppose your specific purpose is "To persuade my audience that the extensive deforestation of South America is a serious problem." Then you would begin with the causes of deforestation and work toward its effects:

Specific Purpose: To persuade my audience that the extensive deforestation of South America is a serious problem.

Central Idea: The deforestation of South America will have damaging effects throughout the Western hemisphere.

Main Points: I. The rain forests of South America are being cut down at an alarming rate to make way for population growth and economic development.

II. If the process of deforestation continues, it will threaten the ecological balance of the entire hemisphere.

When the effects you are discussing have already occurred, you may want to reverse the order and talk first about the effects and then about their causes. For example:[7]

Specific Purpose: To inform my audience of the possible causes of the unusual occurrences in the Bermuda Triangle.

Central Idea: The causes of the unusual occurrences in the Bermuda Triangle have not yet been fully explained.

Main Points:
I.   Many unusual occurrences have taken place in the Bermuda Triangle.
II.   Experts have advanced three major explanations about the causes of these unusual occurrences.

Because of its versatility, causal order can be used both for persuasive speeches and informative speeches.

Problem-Solution Order   Speeches arranged in problem-solution order are divided into two main parts. The first shows the existence and seriousness of a problem. The second presents a workable solution to the problem. For example:

Specific Purpose: To persuade my audience that our state should require mandatory recertification of lawyers every ten years.

Central Idea: The growing problem of incompetent lawyers can be curtailed by requiring all lawyers to pass recertification standards every ten years.

Main Points:
I.   Many citizens are victimized every year by incompetent lawyers.
II.   A bill requiring lawyers to stand for recertification every ten years will do much to help solve the problem.

Or:

Specific Purpose: To persuade my audience that high-school, college, and professional football leaders should act now to reduce the incidence of serious injuries in their sport.

Central Idea: Serious football injuries are a growing problem which can be controlled by changes in rules, equipment, and playing surfaces.

Main Points:
I.   In the past ten years serious football injuries have risen dramatically among high-school, college, and professional players.
II.   The best way to control this problem is through changes in rules, equipment, and playing surfaces.

As these examples indicate, problem-solution order is most appropriate for persuasive speeches.

Topical Order   Speeches that are not in chronological, spatial, causal, or problem-solution order usually fall into topical order. Topical order results when you divide the speech topic into *subtopics,* each of which becomes a main point in the speech. The main points are not part of a chronological, spatial, causal, or problem-solution sequence, but are simply parts of the whole. If this sounds confusing, a few examples should help to make it clearer.

Suppose your specific purpose is "To inform my audience of the major kinds of fireworks." This topic does not lend itself to chronological, spatial, causal, or problem-solution order. Rather, you separate the subject—kinds of fireworks—into its constituent parts, so that each main point deals with a single kind of firework. Your central idea and main points might look like this:

Specific Purpose: To inform my audience of the major kinds of fireworks.

Central Idea: The major kinds of fireworks are skyrockets, Roman candles, pinwheels, and lances.

Main Points:

I.   Skyrockets explode high in the air, producing the most dramatic effects of all fireworks.

II.   Roman candles shoot out separate groups of sparks and colored flames with a series of booming noises.

III.   Pinwheels throw off sparks and flames as they whirl on the end of a stick.

IV.   Lances are thin, colorful fireworks used in ground displays.

To take another example, let's say your specific purpose is "To inform my audience about the artistic versatility of Pablo Picasso." You could organize your speech chronologically—perhaps by "period" (the Blue Period, the Rose Period, the Cubist Period) or even by the women in Picasso's life (the Olga years, the Dora Maar years, the Françoise years). On the other hand, you could arrange it topically—by dividing Picasso's accomplishments into categories. Then your central idea and main points might be:

Specific Purpose: To inform my audience about the artistic versatility of Pablo Picasso.

Central Idea: Picasso was equally versatile as a painter, sculptor, and printmaker.

Main Points:

I.   As a painter, Picasso tested the limits of abstraction.

II.   As a sculptor, Picasso often incorporated "found" objects.

III.   As a printmaker, Picasso gave vent to his whimsy and eroticism.

Notice that in both of the above examples the main points subdivide the speech topic logically and consistently. In the first example each main point deals with a single category of fireworks. In the second example each main point isolates one aspect of Picasso's genius as an artist. But suppose your main points look like this:

    I.   As a painter, Picasso tested the limits of abstraction.

    II.   As a sculptor, Picasso often incorporated ''found'' objects.

    III.   In his Blue Period, Picasso painted the forgotten souls of Montmartre.

This would *not* be a good topical order, since main point III is inconsistent with the rest of the main points. It deals with a *period* in Picasso's career, whereas main points I and II deal with *media* of expression.

All the examples so far refer to informative speeches. But topical order also works for persuasive speeches. Usually the topical subdivisions are the *reasons* why you believe in a certain point of view. For example:

Specific Purpose: To persuade my audience to oppose capital punishment.

Central Idea: Capital punishment is neither an effective deterrent to crime nor a morally justifiable punishment.

Main Points: I.   Capital punishment does not deter murder or other serious crimes.

           II.   Capital punishment is morally unjustifiable.

Because it is applicable to almost any subject and to any kind of speech, topical order is used more often than any other method of speech organization.

Tips for Preparing Main Points

Keep Main Points Separate   Each main point in a speech should be clearly independent of the other main points. Take care not to lump together what should be separate main points. Compare these two sets of main points for a speech about the criminal justice process:

INEFFECTIVE	MORE EFFECTIVE
I. The first step is charging the accused.	I. The first step is charging the accused.
II. The second step is plea bargaining.	II. The second step is plea bargaining.
III. The third step is convicting the accused and then sentencing the convicted.	III. The third step is convicting the accused.
	IV. The fourth step is sentencing the convicted.

The problem with the left-hand list is that point III contains two main points. It should be divided, as shown in the right-hand list.

Try to Use the Same Pattern of Wording for Main Points   Consider the following main points for an informative speech about the benefits of running.

INEFFECTIVE	MORE EFFECTIVE
I. Regular running increases your endurance.	I. Regular running increases your endurance.
II. Your sleeping pattern is improved by regular running.	II. Regular running improves your sleeping pattern.
III. It is possible to help control your weight by regular running.	III. Regular running helps control your weight.

The set of main points on the right follows a consistent pattern of wording throughout. Therefore, it is easier to understand and easier to remember than the set on the left.

You will find that it is not always possible to use this kind of parallel wording for your main points. Some speeches just don't lend themselves to such a tidy arrangement. But try to keep the wording parallel when you can, for it is a good way to make your main points stand out from the details surrounding them.

Balance the Amount of Time Devoted to Main Points   Because your main points are so important, you want to be sure they all receive enough emphasis to be clear and convincing. This means allowing sufficient time to develop each main point. Suppose you discover that the proportion of time devoted to your main points is something like this:

I.   85 percent

II. 10 percent

III. 5 percent

A breakdown of this sort indicates one of two things. Either points II and III aren't really *main* points, and you have only one main point; or else points II and III haven't been given the attention they need. If the latter, you should revise the body of the speech to bring the main points into better balance.

This is not to say that all main points must receive exactly equal emphasis, but only that they should be roughly balanced. For example, either of the following would be fine:

I. 30 percent	I. 20 percent
II. 40 percent	II. 30 percent
III. 30 percent	III. 50 percent

The amount of time spent on each main point depends on the amount and complexity of supporting materials for each point. Supporting materials are, in effect, the "flesh" that fills out the skeleton of your speech.

SUPPORTING MATERIALS

By themselves, main points are only assertions. As we saw in Chapter 6, listeners need supporting materials to accept what a speaker says. When the supporting materials are added, the body of a speech looks like this in outline form:

    I.   High-protein diets are high in protein and low in carbohydrates.
       A.   The best-known high-protein fad diets are the Atkins diet and the Scarsdale diet.
       B.   High-protein diets are unbalanced and often dangerous.
          1.   They can increase the amount of uric acid in the blood to dangerous levels.
            a.   Quotation from Elizabeth B. Spannhake of Loyola University.
            b.   Story of Nancy B., who died of a heart attack.
          2.   They can provide harmful excesses of protein.
            a.   Can lead to kidney disease.
            b.   Can promote calcium deficiency and bone loss.
   II.   High-carbohydrate diets are high in carbohydrates and low in protein.
       A.   The best-known high-carbohydrate fad diet is the Beverly Hills fruit diet.
       B.   Extreme high-carbohydrate diets are unbalanced and dangerous.
          1.   They can make a dieter severely deficient in calcium and iron.
          2.   They can cause the body to break down muscle tissue, not just fat.
            a.   Quotation from American Medical Association.
            b.   Story of George L.
  III.   Fasting diets involve total abstention from food for a long period of time.
       A.   Fasting diets may be recommended for extremely obese people.
       B.   Unless the person is under constant medical supervision, fasting diets are extremely dangerous.
          1.   They can induce severe depression.
          2.   They can increase the risk of sudden death due to heart-rhythm abnormalities.

In Chapter 6 we discussed the major kinds of supporting materials and how to use them. Here we need stress only the importance of *organizing* your supporting materials so they are directly relevant to the main points they are supposed to support. Misplaced supporting materials are confusing. Here's an example:

I.   There are several causes of headaches.
    A.   Millions of people suffer from headaches.
    B.   Most headaches are caused by tension.
    C.   Some headaches are caused by irregularities in the blood vessels.
    D.   Other headaches are caused by specific illnesses, such as colds and sinus infections.

The main point deals with the causes of headaches, as do supporting points B, C, and D. Supporting point A (millions of people suffer from headaches) does not. It is out of place and should not be included with this main point.

If you find such a situation in one of your own speeches, try to reorganize your supporting points under appropriate main points, like this:

I.   Millions of people suffer from headaches.
    A.   People have put up with headaches since the beginning of recorded history.
    B.   More than 20 percent of Americans have severe, recurring headaches.
II.   There are several causes of headaches.
    A.   Most headaches are caused by tension.
    B.   Some headaches are caused by irregularities in the blood vessels.
    C.   Other headaches are caused by specific illnesses, such as colds and sinus infections.

Now you have two supporting points to back up your "suffering" point and three supporting points to back up your "causes" point. Your speech is clearly organized—and so should be clear to your listeners.

Once you have organized your main points and supporting points, you must give attention to the third element in the body of a speech—connectives.

CONNECTIVES

Jane Ketcham was addressing her class about the need to ban smoking in public facilities. She had spent a lot of time preparing, had a well-defined central idea, three sharp main points, and strong supporting details. But when Jane delivered the speech, she said "Okay" every time she moved from one thought to the next. All in all, she said "Okay" twelve times in seven minutes. After a while, her classmates started counting. By the end of the speech most had stopped listening. They were too busy waiting for the next "Okay." Afterward, Jane said, "I didn't even realize I was saying 'Okay' at all."

This experience is not unusual. We all have stock phrases that we habitually use to fill the space between thoughts. In casual conversation they are seldom troublesome. But in speechmaking they create a problem—particularly when they call attention to themselves.

What Jane's speech lacked were strong *connectives*—words or phrases that join one thought to another and indicate the relationship between them. Connectives in the body of a speech are like ligaments and tendons in a human body. Without connectives, a speech is disjointed and uncoordinated—much as a person would be without ligaments and tendons to join the bones and hold the organs in place. Four types of speech connectives are transitions, internal previews, internal summaries, and signposts.

Transitions

Transitions are words or phrases that indicate when a speaker has completed one thought and is moving on to another. Technically, transitions state *both* the idea the speaker is leaving and the one he or she is coming up to. In the following examples the transitional phrases are underlined:

In addition to helping people in need, working as a hospital volunteer also provides you with valuable job experience.

Increasing the amount of money spent on education is only one part of the solution. The other part is to ensure that the money is spent wisely.

Now that we have explored the ancient origins of astrology, let us turn to its modern popularity.

So much for the present; what about the future?

We have spent a lot of time talking about the problem. It's time now to discuss the solution.

Notice how these phrases remind the listener of the thought just completed, as well as reveal the thought about to be developed.

Internal Previews

Internal previews let the audience know what the speaker will take up next, but they are more detailed than transitions. In effect, an internal preview works just like the preview statement in a speech introduction, except that it comes in the body of the speech—usually as the speaker is starting to discuss a main point. For example:

> In discussing the problem of America's deteriorating public works system, we shall deal first with our streets and highways, second with our bridges, and third with our water systems.

After hearing this, the audience knows exactly what to listen for as the speaker develops the "problem" main point.

Internal previews are often combined with transitions. For example:

> [*Transition*]: Now that we have seen how serious the problem of missing children is, let's look at some solutions. [*Internal preview*]: I will focus on three in particular—stronger legal custody laws to combat parental kidnapping, a national clearing house on missing children, and a local program to fingerprint all school-age children. Let's consider them in turn.

You will seldom need an internal preview for each main point in your speech, but be sure to use one whenever you think it will help listeners keep track of your ideas.

Internal Summaries

Internal summaries are the reverse of internal previews. Rather than letting listeners know what is coming up next, internal summaries remind listeners of what they have just heard. Such summaries are generally used when a speaker finishes a complicated or particularly important main point or set of main points. Rather than moving immediately to the next point, the speaker takes a moment to summarize the preceding point or points. For example:

> In short, palm reading is an ancient art. Developed in China more than five thousand years ago, it was practiced in classical Greece and Rome, flourished during the Middle Ages, survived the Industrial Revolution, and remains popular today

> I hope I've made clear the advantages of compact discs over conventional records and tapes. From the deepest bass to the highest treble, they produce almost perfect sound, with no distortion and without annoying scratches and hisses. They offer the closest thing possible to the sound of live music—and at a surprisingly reasonable price.

Such internal summaries are an excellent way to clarify and reinforce ideas. By combining them with transitions, you can also lead your audience smoothly into your next main point:

> [*Internal summary*]: In going back over the effects of exposing the body to extreme cold, we see that the first signs of hypothermia are excessive shivering or

numb hands and feet. More serious signs are exhaustion, falling body temperature, dizziness, impaired judgment, slurred speech, heart tremors, and unconsciousness. [*Transition*]: Now that you know the symptoms of hypothermia, I am going to tell you the first-aid measures to take when you see them.

[*Internal summary*]: Let's pause for a moment to recapitulate what we have found so far. First, we have seen that America's criminal justice system does not effectively deter crime. Second, we have seen that prison programs to rehabilitate criminals have failed miserably. [*Transition*]: We are now ready to explore solutions to these problems.

Signposts

Signposts are very brief statements that indicate exactly where you are in the speech. Frequently they are just numbers. Here is how one student used simple numerical signposts to help her audience keep track of the major causes for the growing problem of famine in Africa and Asia:

The first cause of this spreading problem is runaway population growth throughout Asia and Africa.

The second cause of continued famine is inefficient agricultural production.

The third cause is recurrent drought in the affected countries.

The final contributing cause for the persistence of famine is mismanagement of available food resources by local bureaucrats.

The signposts are underscored. Notice how they enumerate the introduction of each new point.

Another way to accomplish the same thing is to introduce your main points with a question, as did one student in his speech about mail-order fraud. His first main point dealt with the continuing growth of mail-order fraud. He introduced it this way:

What makes mail-order fraud such a persistent problem? Why do people keep falling for gimmicks that are obviously too good to be true?

His second main point dealt with ways to curb mail-order fraud. He introduced it like this:

How can we solve this problem? Is there a way to protect the rights of legitimate mail-order companies while attacking the fraudulent ones?

Questions are particularly effective as signposts, because they invite subliminal answers and thereby get the audience more involved with the speech.

Besides using signposts to indicate where you are in the speech, you can also use them to focus attention on key ideas. You can do this with a simple phrase, as in the following example:

The most important thing to remember about abstract art is that it is always based on forms in the natural world.

The underlined words alert the audience to the fact that an especially significant point is coming up. So do phrases such as these:

Be sure to keep this in mind . . .

This is crucial to understanding the rest of the speech . . .

Above all, you need to know . . .

Let me repeat that last statement . . .

Depending on the needs of your speech, you may want to use two, three, or even all four kinds of connectives in combination. You needn't worry too much about what they are called—whether this one is a signpost and that a transition. In fact, many people lump them all together as "transitions." The important thing is to be aware of their functions. Properly applied, connectives can make your speeches much more unified and coherent.[8]

SUMMARY

Clear organization is vital to speechmaking. Listeners demand coherence. They get only one chance to grasp a speaker's ideas, and they have little patience for speakers who ramble aimlessly from one idea to another. A well-organized speech will enhance your credibility and make it easier for the audience to understand your message.

Speeches should be organized strategically. They should be put together in particular ways to achieve particular results with particular audiences. The first step in organizing speeches is to gain command of the three basic parts of a speech—introduction, body, conclusion—and the strategic role of each. In this chapter we have dealt with the body of the speech.

The process of planning the body of a speech begins when you determine the main points. These are the central features of your speech. You should choose them carefully, phrase them precisely, and organize them strategically. Because listeners cannot keep track of a multitude of main points, most speeches should contain no more than two to five main points. Each main point should focus on a single idea, should be worded clearly, and should receive enough emphasis to be clear and convincing.

You can organize main points in various ways. The strategic order will be determined by your topic, your purpose, and your audience. Chronological order means that your speech follows a time pattern. Speeches arranged in spatial order follow a directional pattern. To put your speech in causal order, you organize main points according to their cause-effect relationship. Topical order results when you divide your main topic into subtopics, each of which covers one aspect of the main topic. For problem-solution order you break the body of your speech into two main parts—the first showing a problem, the second giving a solution.

Supporting materials are the backup ideas for your main points. When organizing supporting materials, make sure they are directly relevant to the main points they are supposed to support.

Once you have organized your main points and supporting materials, you are ready to work out the third element in the body of your speech—connectives. Connectives help tie a speech together. They are words or phrases that join one thought to another and indicate the relationship between them. The four major types of speech connectives are transitions, internal previews, internal summaries, and signposts. Using them effectively will make your speeches more unified and coherent.

REVIEW QUESTIONS

After reading this chapter, you should be able to answer the following questions:

1. Why is it important that speeches be organized clearly and coherently?

2. How many main points will your speeches usually contain? Why is it important to limit the number of main points in your speeches?

3. What are the five basic patterns of organizing main points in a speech? Which are appropriate for informative speeches? Which is used only in persuasive speeches? Which is used most often?

4. What are three tips for preparing your main points?

5. What is the most important thing to remember when organizing supporting materials in the body of your speech?

6. What are the four kinds of speech connectives? What role does each play in a speech?

APPLICATION EXERCISES

1. Identify the organizational method used in each of the following sets of main points.

   I. The top layer of the earth is a rocky "skin" called the crust.

   II. Beneath the crust is a thick layer of rock called the mantle.

   III. The next lower section is a mass of melted rock called the outer core.

   IV. At the center of the earth is a solid mass called the inner core.

   I. Genetic engineering is producing new plant hybrids that will vastly increase world agricultural production.

   II. Genetic engineering is producing breakthroughs in medicine that will allow people to live healthier lives.

   III. Genetic engineering is producing bacteria that will help clean up industrial pollutants.

   I. Gambling addiction is an increasingly serious problem throughout America.

   II. The problem of gambling addiction can best be solved by a combination of education and rehabilitation.

   I. Early people did not have money, but used a system of exchange based on the barter of goods and services.

   II. Coin money was invented in ancient Turkey, China, and India before the birth of Christ.

   III. Paper money began in China about 600 A.D. but did not become popular in the West until the 1600s.

   IV. Today almost every country has an official currency tied to the international rate of exchange.

   I. Sickle-cell anemia is a hereditary blood disease caused by abnormal blood cells.

   II. The effects of sickle-cell anemia include liver damage, blindness, paralysis, and early death.

2. What organizational method (or methods) might you use to arrange main points for speeches with the following specific purpose statements?

   To inform my audience of the major stages in the development of the American film industry.

   To inform my audience of the causes and effects of acid rain.

   To inform my audience about the major categories of dog breeds.

To persuade my audience that our state legislature should enact tougher legislation to deal with the continuing problem of child abuse.

To inform my audience about the major geographical regions of modern China.

3. Turn to the outline of main points and supporting materials for the speech about fad diets on page 157. Create appropriate transitions, internal previews, internal summaries, and signposts for the speech.

NOTES

[1] Ernest C. Thompson, "An Experimental Investigation of the Relative Effectiveness of Organizational Structure in Oral Communication," *Southern Speech Journal,* 26 (1960), 59–69.

[2] Harry Sharp, Jr., and Thomas McClung, "Effect of Organization on the Speaker's Ethos," *Speech Monographs,* 33 (1966), 182–183.

[3] See, for example, Tom D. Daniels and R. Samuel Mehrley, "The Effects of Message Introduction, Message Structure, and Verbal Organizing Ability upon Learning of Message Information," *Human Communication Research,* 7 (1981), 147–160; Margaret Fitch Hauser, "Message Structure, Inference Making, and Recall," in Robert N. Bostrom and Bruce Westley (eds.), *Communication Yearbook 8* (Beverly Hills, Calif.: Sage, 1984), pp. 278–292

[4] Paul A. Fritz and Richard L. Weaver II, "Teaching Critical Thinking Skills in the Basic Speaking Course: A Liberal Arts Perspective," *Communication Education,* 35 (1986), 177.

[5] John O. Greene, "Speech Preparation Processes and Verbal Fluency," *Human Communication Research,* 11 (1984), 61–84.

[6] John P. Houston, et al., *Essentials of Psychology,* 2nd ed. (New York: Academic Press, 1985), p. 185.

[7] This example was provided by Professor Richard G. Nitcavic of Ball State University.

[8] For research on the value of internal summaries and, by implication, other connectives, see John E. Baird, Jr., "A Comparison of Distributional and Sequential Structure in Cooperative and Competitive Group Discussions," *Speech Monographs,* 41 (1974), 226–232.

Get Attention and Interest

"Unless a speaker can interest his audience at once, his effort will be a failure." So said the great lawyer Clarence Darrow. If your topic is not one of extraordinary interest, your listeners are likely to say to themselves, "So what? Who cares?" No matter how famous the speaker or how vital the topic, the speaker can quickly lose an audience if he or she doesn't use the introduction to get their attention and quicken their interest.

Getting the initial attention of your audience is usually easy to do—even before you utter a single word. After you are introduced and step to the lectern, your audience will normally give you their attention. If they don't, merely wait patiently. Look directly at the audience without saying a word. In a few moments all talking and physical commotion will stop. Your listeners will be attentive. You will be ready to start speaking.

Keeping the attention of your audience once you start talking is more difficult. Here are the methods used most often. Employed individually or in combination, they will help get the audience caught up in your speech.

Relate the Topic to the Audience   People pay attention to things that affect them directly. If you can relate the topic to your listeners, they are much more likely to be interested in it.

Suppose, for example, one of your classmates begins her speech like this:

Today I am going to talk about collecting postcards—a hobby that is both fascinating and financially rewarding. I would like to explain the basic kinds of collectable postcards, why they are so valuable, and how collectors buy and sell their cards.

This is certainly a clear introduction, but it is not one to get you hooked on the speech. Now what if your classmate were to begin her speech this way— as one student actually did:

It's Saturday morning, and you are helping clean out your grandmother's attic. After working a while, you stumble upon a trunk, open it, and discover inside hundreds of old postcards. Thinking about getting to the football game on time, you start tossing the cards into the trash can. Congratulations! You have just thrown away a year's tuition.

This time the speaker has used just the right bait. Chances are you will be hooked.

Even when you use other interest-arousing lures, you should *always* relate your topic to the audience. At times this will test your ingenuity, but it pays dividends. Here are two excellent examples. The first is from a speech about the physical barriers faced by many handicapped people. Notice how the speaker gets her classmates to put themselves in the place of someone who is handicapped:

How would you feel if you could not join your family at dinner because you were unable to get through the door of the restaurant? Think what it would be like if you could not cross an intersection because the curbs were too high. Imagine not being able to attend the church of your choice because of the decorative stairs leading to the entrance.

Picture yourself frustrated and humiliated because of these and a hundred other barriers you cannot overcome. You are now seeing yourself as many of the 11.3 million handicapped people in America see themselves.

The second example is from a student speech about Social Security:

Many of you may think, "What does Social Security have to do with me? I'm young, healthy, and nowhere near retirement age." But Social Security has a lot to do with you. If you don't have a job today, you will in a couple of years. And when you do, you will pay Social Security taxes. How much will you pay? That depends on your income. If you earn $30,000, you will pay more than $2,000 *a year* in Social Security taxes. At present tax rates, that comes to more than $90,000 in the course of your working career.

Today I would like to explain where all your money goes and to see whether you will ever benefit from it.

By linking Social Security directly to her classmates' pocketbooks, the speaker made sure of an attentive audience.

State the Importance of Your Topic   Presumably, you think your speech topic is important. Tell your audience why they should think so too. Here is how John C. Lawn of the U.S. Drug Enforcement Administration began his speech entitled "Drugs in America":

As the Administrator of the Drug Enforcement Administration, I face the drug problem every day. It is my problem. It is your problem. It is our problem. . . .

We are the most drug abusing nation in the history of the industrialized world. We consume three tons of aspirin a day. Each year over 120 million prescriptions are written for psychoactive drugs in this country. Thirty million of us take sedatives. Twenty million of us take stimulants. Eight million of us are chronic abusers of tranquilizers. . . . About 100 million people are regular consumers of alcohol, and about 13 to 15 percent are abusers—they're alcoholics.[1]

These are shocking statistics. By citing them in the introduction, Lawn dramatically emphasized the importance of his topic and captured the attention of his audience.

Clearly, this technique is easy to use when discussing social and political issues such as drug abuse, world hunger, toxic waste, or drunk driving, but it is appropriate for other kinds of topics as well. Here is how one student handled it in a speech about starting a home aquarium:

It is very hard to cuddle a fish. Fish won't roll over or fetch the morning paper. You won't find them curling up on your lap, chasing a ball of string, or rescuing a child from a burning building.

Yet despite these shortcomings, 250 million tropical fish have found their way into 10 million American homes. Tropical fish make up 50 percent of all live animal sales in the United States, and they have earned a spot next to the all-American dog and the cuddly kitten in the hearts of millions of people. Today I would like to explain how you can start a home aquarium and discover the pleasures of owning tropical fish.

The first paragraph— with its clever opening line—grabs the listener's attention. But it is the second paragraph that keeps the attention. Indeed, whenever you discuss a topic whose importance may not be clear to the audience, you should think about ways to demonstrate its significance in the introduction.

Startle the Audience   One sure-fire way to arouse interest quickly is to startle your listeners with an arresting or intriguing statement. Everyone in the audience paid close attention after this speaker's introduction:

Ladies and gentlemen, there has been a change of plans. Instead of graduating from school, you are going to be doing something else—something very different. I am asking you right now to change your plans. I want you to put three simple words on your calendar in the near future. The words are . . . World War III.

Notice the gradual build-up to the arresting phrase "World War III." The effect would have been much less if the speaker had said, "The chances of nuclear war are increasing daily."

Sometimes you may want to startle your audience in the very first sentence of your speech. Here is how one student began a speech about salvaging sunken treasure:

You could become a millionaire in just one day!

And here is a slightly longer example of the same technique:

Last week a man whom you all have heard of beat an innocent human being senseless. Hundreds of people watched him do it, but no one tried to stop him. He didn't do it in self-defense, or out of hate or revenge. He did it for money. The man is a professional boxer.

This technique is highly effective and easy to use. Just be sure the startling introduction relates directly to the subject of your speech. The example cited above made a good beginning for a speech in opposition to professional boxing. It would not work for a general speech about intercollegiate sports. If you choose a strong opening simply for its shock effect and then go on to talk about something else, your audience will be confused and quite possibly annoyed.

Arouse the Curiosity of the Audience   People are curious. One way to draw them into your speech is with a series of statements that progressively whet their curiosity about the subject of the speech. For example:

> The doorbell rings. Instantly, Frances jumps up from where she has been sitting, spins around three times, and runs back and forth from the door to the sofa. Next she hops onto the sofa and begins bouncing up and down. Is Frances deranged? No, Frances is a "Hearing Ear" dog, and she has just alerted her deaf owner to the fact that a visitor is at the door.

As another example, consider this finely crafted introduction from a student speech entitled "The Silent Killer":

> It is the most common chronic disease in the United States. Controllable but incurable, it is a symptomless disease; you can have it for years and never know until it kills you. Some 40 million Americans have this disease, and 300,000 will die from it before the year is out. Odds are that five of us in this class have it.
> What am I talking about? Not cancer, not AIDS, not heart disease. I am talking about hypertension—high blood pressure.

Not only does the speaker relate the topic directly to his classmates, he gets them further involved by building suspense about what the disease is. When used appropriately, this is an excellent way to capture and hold your listeners' interest.

Question the Audience   Asking a rhetorical question is another way to get your listeners thinking about your speech. Sometimes a single question will do:

> Have you ever wished you could see into the future?

> How would you react if someone accused you of being a traitor to your country?

> Do you know what a hot dog is made of?

In other circumstances you may want to pose a series of questions, each of which draws the audience deeper into the speech. Here is how one student developed this method:

> Have you ever imagined yourself walking down the old cobblestone streets of Europe, touring castles hundreds of years old, or sipping wine in a small French café? Have you ever wanted to visit wonders like Stonehenge, the Pyramids, or the Great Wall of China? Can you see yourself skiing in the Swiss Alps or sunbathing on the French Riviera? If so, you are in good company with the ever-increasing number of college students who want to travel abroad.

Like beginning with a startling statement, opening with a question works best when the question is meaningful to the audience and firmly related to the content of the speech. It also works most effectively when you pause for just a moment after each question. This adds dramatic impact and gives the question time to sink in. The audience, of course, will answer mentally—not out loud.

Begin with a Quotation   Another way to arouse the interest of your audience is to start with an attention-getting quotation. You might choose your quotation from the words of a famous speaker or politician, from Shakespeare, from the Bible or Talmud, even from a poem or song. One student used the last of these to introduce a speech about nineteenth-century railroads:

> "Casey Jones mounted to the cabin, Casey Jones, his orders in his hand." These are the opening lines of an old folk song describing the last, fatal trip of the legendary nineteenth-century locomotive engineer John Luther Jones. Today I would like to take you back to the romantic era of steam-powered railroads, when every train had a personality, every trip was an adventure, and the engineer was the hero of every child's fantasy.

You need not use a well-known or famous quotation. The following made an effective introduction for a speech about bird watching:

> "Even to this day I cannot describe what happened without feeling the excitement of the moment. I glimpsed a flash of color in the thicket. I raised my binoculars to my eyes, and then I saw it—a Bachman's Warbler, one of the rarest birds in all of America. For me, this was the equivalent of a coin collector discovering a rare silver dollar, or of a football player scoring a touchdown in the Super Bowl."
> This statement was made by my father. He is just one of the millions of people who have discovered the joys and thrills of bird watching.

A humorous quotation can afford double impact, as in this speech by NASA official James Beggs about the future of the U.S. space program:

> Mark Twain once said, "Predictions are very difficult to make—especially when they deal with the future."[2]

By opening his speech with Twain's words, Beggs not only got the attention of his audience, he also foreshadowed the central idea of his speech. Notice, too, that he used a short quotation. Starting your speech with a lengthy quotation is a sure way to set your audience yawning.

Tell a Story   We all enjoy stories—especially if they are provocative, amusing, dramatic, or suspenseful. To work well as introductions, they should also be clearly relevant to the main point of the speech. Used in this way, stories are perhaps the most effective way to begin a speech.

Consider, for example, the tragic story one student told to open his speech about the problem of unsafe amusement park rides:

> It was another beautiful day at the amusement park. Warm sunshine, the smell of cotton candy, the kids. And the rides. The roller coaster's whooshing 60-miles-per-hour speed was accompanied by the familiar screams of delight from kids of all ages. Another ride, the comet, was flying gracefully through the heavens, when suddenly a chain broke, flinging one of the gondolas 75 feet into the air before it crashed, killing a man and seriously injuring his son.
>
> This accident, on May 26 in Pontiac, Illinois, was just one of many last year—one of the many that could have been avoided.[3]

Like many good introductions, this one does a double job—it arouses the interest of the audience and gets listeners emotionally involved in the subject of the speech.

You can also use stories based on your personal experience, or stories with a humorous twist. Here is how one student combined the two in her introduction of an informative speech on the topic of leprosy:

> It happened about a week ago. I was in the women's locker room getting ready for my aerobics class. As I changed clothes, I carried on a casual conversation with one of our classmates, Terri. Just as I turned to leave, she asked, "Hey, Kris, how's your leprosy?"
>
> Suddenly the chattering voices that had filled the room were replaced by silent stares. I quickly responded that my *speech* about leprosy was coming along fine. The noise resumed. All was well. And yet, for a single moment, I felt the sense of shame and alienation that has surrounded lepers since Old Testament days.

As you can imagine, such an introduction depends on effective delivery. By using pauses, eye contact, and changes in her tone of voice, this speaker heightened both the humor and the dramatic impact of her words. See if you can do the same in your speech introductions.

The seven methods listed above are the ones used most often by student speakers to gain attention and interest. Other methods include referring to the occasion, inviting audience participation, using audio equipment or visual aids, relating to a previous speaker, and beginning with humor. For any given speech try to choose the method that is most suitable for the topic, the audience, and the occasion.

Reveal the Topic

In the process of gaining attention, be sure to state clearly the topic of your speech. If you do not, your listeners will be confused. And once they are confused, your chances of getting them absorbed in the speech are almost nil. This is a basic point—so basic that it may hardly seem worth mentioning. Yet you would be surprised how many students need to be reminded of it. You may hear speeches in your own class in which the topic is not clear by the end of the introduction. So you will know what to avoid, here is such an introduction, presented in a public speaking class:

> "Oh, beautiful for spacious skies, for amber waves of grain; for purple mountain majesties above the fruited plain." Most of us are familiar with the song "America the Beautiful" and its description of our natural resources. Let's step back a minute, however, and consider what this picture might look like in the future. What if the amber waves of grain withered and died because the water table had been disrupted and the water contaminated? Or consider if the fruited plain was no more than a barren landscape because floods had washed away all the topsoil. What I want to talk about today is one of America's most precious resources and how it is being destroyed.

What is the topic of this speech? The contamination of America's water resources? No. The erosion of America's topsoil? No. The assault on America's magnificent national parks? No. This student was speaking about the decline of America's family farms and the relentless growth of agribusiness! In her view the family farm is as precious a resource as the Great Plains. But she did not make the connection clear to her audience. Listening to her introduction, they expected her to talk about some aspect of America's *natural* resources.

This student found a dramatic introduction but ignored the fact that it didn't relate properly to her speech. Certainly the words of "America the Beautiful" are stirring. But in this case they were wasted. Suppose, instead, the student had begun her speech with a quotation from a different song:

> "Old MacDonald had a farm" . . . but a giant corporation bought it away from him!

This opening would also have provided drama and a way to get the listeners' attention. But in addition, it would have related directly to the speech topic.

If you beat around the bush in your introduction, you may lose your listeners. Even if they already know your topic, you should restate it clearly and concisely at some point in the introduction.

Establish Credibility and Good Will

Besides getting attention and revealing the topic, there is a third objective you may need to accomplish in your introduction—establishing your credibility and good will.

Credibility is mostly a matter of being qualified to speak on a given topic—and of being *perceived* as qualified by your listeners. If, for instance, Bruce Springsteen got up before an audience to speak about nuclear physics, he would have to take drastic steps to establish his credibility on the subject.

Here is how one speaker demonstrated her credibility on the subject of tennis, without sounding like a braggart:

> Never in the history of sports has there been a leisure-time phenomenon more

striking than the recent American love affair with the game of tennis. It is estimated that over 35 million Americans play tennis and that the number is still growing.

I am one of those 35 million Americans. I have been playing tennis for almost ten years. While in high school I played competitive tennis. I also taught tennis and worked in a tennis club.

Through my experiences, I found that one of the biggest mistakes people make is buying the wrong kind of racket. Whether you are a touring professional or just an occasional player during the summer, the kind of racket you choose can make a big difference in your game—not to mention your budget.

Today I would like to share with you the four most important criteria in choosing a racket.

Whether or not you play tennis, you will probably be more interested in the speech when you realize the speaker knows what she is talking about.

Your credibility need not be based on firsthand knowledge and experience. It can come from reading, from classes, from interviews, from friends—as in these cases:

I have been interested in Atlantis for several years, and I have read many books and articles about it.

The information I'm going to discuss today comes mostly from my psychology class and from an interview with Dr. Duane Roberts of the counseling center on campus.

I have learned a lot about the care of large animals from my brother, who was an apprentice keeper at the Bronx Zoo all last summer.

Whatever the source of your expertise, be sure to let the audience know.

Establishing your good will is a slightly different problem. It is often crucial outside the classroom, where speakers have well-established reputations and may be identified with causes that arouse hostility among listeners. In such a situation, the speaker must try to defuse that hostility right at the start of the speech.

Occasionally you may have to do the same thing in your classroom speeches. Suppose you advocate a highly unpopular position. You will need to make a special effort at the outset to ensure that your classmates will at least consider your point of view. This is how one student tried to minimize his classmates' opposition at the start of a speech in favor of the military draft:

When the military draft was abolished in 1973, Congress created the volunteer army as a way of providing men and women for the armed services. Unfortunately, as *Time* magazine said just last month, "It seems time to conclude that the all-volunteer force is not a success."

That is why I am speaking today in favor of something almost everyone in this class opposes—reinstituting the military draft. I opposed the draft too—until I began researching this speech and discovered the serious problems of the volunteer army.

Today I would like to share with you some of the facts I have found. I don't ask that you all change your minds as a result of my speech—only that you listen with an open mind and consider the merit of my arguments.

What reasonable listener could ignore such a sincere, forthright plea?

Preview the Body of the Speech

As we saw in Chapter 2, most people are poor listeners. Even good listeners need all the help they can get in sorting out a speaker's ideas. One way to help your listeners is to tell them in the introduction what they should listen for in the rest of the speech. Here is an excellent example, from a student speech about the potential effects of birth order:

> Where do you fit in your family structure? Are you at the top of the totem pole, partway down, or at the bottom? And how might your place in the family structure influence who you are? This morning I would like to explore how personality development can be affected by each of the four major patterns of birth order—the only child, the first child followed by younger brothers or sisters, the second or middle child, and the youngest child.

After this introduction, there is no doubt about the speaker's topic, central idea, or main points.

In some types of persuasive speeches, you may not want to reveal your central idea until later in the speech. But even in such a situation you must be sure your audience is not left guessing about the main points they should listen for as the speech unfolds. Nearly always, you should include some preview statement similar to the following:

> This afternoon I would like to show the diversity in the huge country of Brazil by traveling to three areas—the Amazon, the city of Brasilia, and Rio de Janeiro.

> Today I would like to explain some of the scientific and logical reasons why we should no longer believe our planet is the sole support of intelligent life in the universe.

> So let's take a close look at diplomatic immunity. We shall examine some of the problems posed by present diplomatic immunity laws, identify the causes of those problems, and recommend some measures to deal with abuses of the current laws.

Preview statements such as these serve another purpose as well. Because they usually come at the very end of the introduction, they provide a smooth lead-in to the body of the speech. They signal that the body of the speech is about to begin.

There is one other aspect you may want to cover in previewing your speech. You can use your introduction to give specialized information—definitions or background—that your listeners will need if they are to understand the rest of the speech. Often you can do this very quickly, as in these examples:

"Dumping" is defined as the exportation of goods banned as hazardous by the United States.

"Amerasian" children are half-American, half-Asian. Their fathers typically are American soldiers who served in the Korean War or the Vietnam conflict.

In other circumstances, you may have to explain an important term in more detail. Here is how one student handled the problem in a speech about the psychiatric disorder of depression. Knowing that most people use the term "depression" loosely, she took time in her introduction to give a more precise definition:

In popular usage "depression" refers to those brief periods of sadness, grief, or loneliness that everyone goes through from time to time. Thus we might say we are "really depressed" over doing poorly on an exam or over not getting a class we wanted. In this speech, though, I will use "depression" in its psychiatric sense—a serious mental disorder in which a person suffers long periods of intense sadness and despair. The most common of all mental disorders, depression affects about 10 to 14 million Americans. People suffering from depression usually feel tired all the time, often break into tears, and lose interest in work, school, social life, and other normal activities. In the most severe cases, depression may lead a person to attempt suicide.

Sample Introduction with Commentary

So far we have seen many excerpts showing how to fulfill the various objectives of an introduction. Now here is a complete introduction from a student speech. The side comments indicate the principles used in developing the introduction.

COMMENTARY   INTRODUCTION

SHOPLIFTING: THE INVISIBLE CRIME

The speaker begins by relating to the audience. This works particularly well to gain attention, because we all have been in the situation described by the speaker.

Imagine yourself walking through a large department store. You admire the new fashions, gawk at the fine jewelry, fiddle briefly with the cameras, and check out the latest stereo equipment. Now imagine you can have any of those items for free—all you have to do is steal them.

Now the speaker reveals her topic and uses statistics to show why it is important. This helps to strengthen the audience's interest.

The temptation is great—so great that shoplifting has become one of the most frequent and expensive crimes in the United States. According to *Time* magazine, there are 150 million incidents of shoplifting in the United States each year, and the total value of goods stolen by shoplifters amounts to about $10 billion annually. Before the end of the year some 5 million Americans will be arrested for shoplifting.

Here the speaker tells the audience why they should care about the topic. This is important, because many people think shoplifting harms only the store owners.

And who pays for this? We all do. The value of stolen merchandise, the increased cost of store security, the time consumed in legal proceedings—all are passed on to us in higher prices and higher taxes. Indeed, the Retail Merchants Association estimates that honest shoppers pay as much as 10 percent more to offset the cost of shoplifting.

The speaker does an excellent job of establishing her credibility by referring to her personal experience and her research.

By previewing the main points of her speech, the speaker lets her audience know what to listen for. She also provides a good lead-in to the body of the speech.

Although shoplifting is sometimes called an invisible crime, I myself have learned to see it, working as a retail sales person at Sears. By doing library research and by talking with security personnel at Sears, I have come to realize how widespread and how complex a problem it is. Today I would like to discuss with you the kinds of shoplifters and the security procedures used to fight them.

Tips for Preparing the Introduction

1. Keep the introduction relatively brief. Under normal circumstances it should not constitute more than about 10 to 20 percent of your speech.

2. Be on the lookout for possible introductory materials as you do your research. File them with your notes, so they will be handy when you are ready for them.

3. Be creative in devising your introduction. Experiment with two or three different openings and choose the one that seems most likely to get the audience interested in your speech. (Don't hesitate to discard a ''great'' introduction that doesn't quite fit your speech. You'll think of another great one.)

4. Don't worry about the exact wording of your introduction until you have finished preparing the body of the speech. After you have determined your main points, it will be much easier to make final decisions about how to begin the speech.

5. Work out your introduction in detail. Some teachers recommend that you write it out word for word; others prefer that you outline it. Whichever method you use, practice the introduction over and over until you can deliver it smoothly, from a minimum of notes, and with strong eye contact. This will get your speech off to a good start and give you a big boost of confidence.

THE CONCLUSION

"Great is the art of beginning," said Longfellow, "but greater the art is of ending." Longfellow was thinking of poetry, but his insight is equally applicable to public speaking. Many a speaker has marred an otherwise fine speech by a long-winded, silly, or antagonistic conclusion. Your closing remarks are your last chance to drive home your ideas. Moreover, your final impression will probably linger in your listeners' minds. Thus you need to craft your conclusion with as much care as your introduction.

No matter what kind of speech you are giving, the conclusion has two major functions:

To let the audience know you are ending the speech.

To reinforce the audience's understanding of, or commitment to, the central idea.

Let us look at each.

Signal the End of the Speech

It may seem obvious that you should let your audience know you are going to stop soon. However, you will almost certainly hear speeches in your class in which the speaker concludes so abruptly that you are taken by surprise. Even in casual conversation you expect some signal that the talk is coming to an end. You are taken aback when the person you are talking with suddenly walks off without warning. The same is true of speechmaking. Too sudden an ending leaves the audience puzzled and unfulfilled.

How do you let an audience know your speech is ending? One way is through what you say. "In conclusion," "One last thought," "In closing," "My purpose has been," "Let me end by saying"—these are all brief cues that you are getting ready to stop.

You can also let your audience know the end is in sight by your manner of delivery. The conclusion is the climax of a speech. A speaker who has carefully built to a peak of interest and involvement will not need to say anything like "in conclusion." By use of the voice—by its tone, pacing, intonation, and rhythm—a speaker can build the momentum of a speech so there is no doubt when it is over.

One method of doing this has been likened to a musical crescendo. As in a symphony in which one instrument after another joins in until the entire orchestra is playing, the speech builds in force until it reaches a zenith of power and intensity.[4] (This does *not* mean simply getting louder and louder. It is a combination of many things, including vocal pitch, choice of words, dramatic content, gestures, pauses—and possibly loudness.) A superb example of this method is the memorable conclusion to Martin Luther King's "I Have a Dream" speech:

When we allow freedom to ring—when we let it ring from every village and every hamlet, from every state and every city—we will be able to speed up that day when all of God's children, black men and white men, Jews and Gentiles, Protestants and

One of the most famous speeches in American history, Martin Luther King's "I Have a Dream," illustrates the power of a dramatic conclusion. (UPI/ Bettmann Newsphotos)

Catholics, will be able to join hands and sing in the words of the old Negro spiritual, "Free at last! Free at last! Thank God almighty, we are free at last!"

Another effective method might be compared to the dissolve ending of a concert song that evokes deep emotions: "The song seems to fade away while the light on the singer shrinks gradually to a smaller and smaller circle until it lights only the face, then the eyes. Finally, it is a pinpoint, and disappears with the last note of the song."[5] Here is a speech ending that does much the same thing. It is from General Douglas MacArthur's moving farewell to the cadets at West Point in 1962:

In my dreams I hear again the crash of guns, the rattle of musketry, the strange, mournful mutter of the battlefield. But in the evening of my memory always I come back to West Point. Always there echoes and re-echoes: duty, honor, country.

Today marks my final roll call with you. But I want you to know that when I cross the river, my last conscious thoughts will be of the Corps, and the Corps, and the Corps.

I bid you farewell.

The final words fade like the spotlight, bringing the speech to an emotional close.

You may think that you couldn't possibly end a speech with that much pathos—and you'd be right. MacArthur was a masterful speaker addressing a sympathetic audience at an inherently poignant moment. This combination rarely occurs. But that doesn't mean you can't use the dissolve ending effectively. The speaker we cited earlier—who used the opening lines of the folk song

"Casey Jones" to introduce a speech about nineteenth-century railroads—worked the last lines of the same song into a moving dissolve ending:

> Yes, the era of steam-powered railroads was a time of great adventure and romance—the click-click of wheels on the track, the mournful wail of the steam whistle in the night, the anticipation of discovery lying just around the next curve in the rails. But for the locomotive engineer, the great hero of children's fantasies, what lay around that next curve could be disaster. As the old folk song ends, "Casey Jones mounted to the cabin . . . on a farewell trip to the Promised Land."

Both the crescendo and the dissolve endings must be worked out with great care. Practice until you get the words and the timing just right. The benefits will be well worth your time.

Reinforce the Central Idea

The second major function of a conclusion is to reinforce the audience's understanding of, or commitment to, the central idea. There are many ways to do this. Here are the ones you are most likely to use.

Summarize Your Speech   Restating the main points is the easiest way to end a speech. One student used this technique effectively in his informative speech about daydreams:

> As we have seen, daydreaming is a mental process that is not yet totally understood by researchers. What I have tried to do, through the information available from studies and experiments, is to give you a general idea of who daydreams about what, the typical patterns of daydreams, and some explanation of why people daydream. I hope the information I have given you will help to broaden your awareness of the peculiar thought processes called daydreams.

The value of a summary is that it explicitly restates the central idea and main points one last time. But as we shall see, there are more imaginative and compelling ways to end a speech. They can be used in combination with a summary or, at times, in place of it.

End with a Quotation   A quotation is one of the most common and effective devices to conclude a speech. Here is a fine example, from a speech on the harmful effects of runaway spending on political campaigns:

> We cannot ignore what is happening to our political process. Changes in congressional election campaign funding are absolutely essential. In the words of Representative Henry Reuss of Wisconsin, "Campaign contributions are out of hand. Unless we do something meaningful about them, they will corrupt and ruin the republic."

The closing quotation is particularly good, because its urgency is exactly suited to the speech. When you run across a *brief* quotation that so perfectly captures your central idea, keep it in mind as a possible conclusion.

Make a Dramatic Statement   Rather than using a quotation to give your conclusion force and vitality, you may want to devise your own dramatic statement. Some speeches have become famous because of their powerful closing lines. One is Patrick Henry's legendary "Liberty or Death" oration. It takes its name from the final sentences Henry uttered on March 23, 1775, as he exhorted his audience to resist British tyranny:

> Is life so dear, or peace so sweet, as to be purchased at the price of chains and slavery? Forbid it, Almighty God! I know not what course others may take; but as for me, give me liberty, or give me death.

Although your classroom speeches are not likely to become famous, you can still rivet your listeners—as Henry did—with a dramatic concluding statement. What follows is a particularly striking example, from a speech on suicide prevention. Throughout the speech, the student referred to a friend who had tried to commit suicide the previous year. Then, in the conclusion, she said:

> My friend is back in school, participating in activities she never did before—and enjoying it. I'm happy and proud to say she's still fighting for her life and even happier she failed to kill herself. Otherwise, I wouldn't be here today trying to help you. You see, *I* am my "friend," and I'm more than glad to say, I've made it.

As you can imagine, the audience was stunned. The closing lines brought the speech to a dramatic conclusion.

Here is another example of the same technique—this time from a less unusual situation:

> It is so easy to label the homeless as "bums" and "bag ladies." It is also easy to see them as people who are just looking for a handout—and often we give it to them and walk away. But as we have seen, most homeless people are not simply looking for a handout—they are reaching for a hand. Don't you think we should extend it to them?

This conclusion works because it takes the listener slightly by surprise and creates a lingering impression in the audience. Here the speaker made it even more effective by pausing for just a moment before the last sentence, and by using his voice to give the closing words extra emotional force.

Refer to the Introduction   An excellent way to give your speech psychological unity is to conclude by referring to ideas in the introduction. This is an easy technique to use, and it may give your speech an extra touch of class. Here is how one student used the method in her speech about amnesia:

Introduction: For nearly half a year newspapers all across the country ran her story, complete with her photograph and physical description, in hopes that someone would recognize her. The newspapers described her as a "woman in mid-thirties, five feet seven inches tall, light brown hair, blue-gray eyes, two moles on neck."

That's all they knew about her, because that's all Jane Doe, as she was called, knew about herself. She was found in a park in Florida, lying beneath a tree, unconscious and near starvation. Her belongings were piled neatly beside her. She had not been hurt or molested, but she couldn't tell anyone how she came to be lying under that tree. When asked how she got there or where she had been, Jane Doe repeated over and over, "I don't remember."

Jane drew sympathy from all across the country because she was suffering from a condition we all fear—amnesia.

In the body of her speech the speaker did not mention Jane Doe again. She discussed the types of amnesia, explored their causes, and explained how doctors treat amnesia victims. Then, in her conclusion, she returned to Jane Doe to tie the whole speech together:

Conclusion: Whether amnesia is due to organic or psychological causes, it is a frightening, lonely, frustrating experience. Fortunately, all the publicity in the case of Jane Doe in Florida eventually turned up someone who gave Jane back her true identity. She is Cheryl Ann Tomiczec of Illinois. Family and friends who had lost track of Cheryl years before welcomed her back, but Cheryl's memory of those intervening years remains murky. Even today, if you asked Cheryl how she ended up under that palm tree in Florida, she would say, "I don't remember."

Summarizing the speech, ending with a quotation, making a dramatic statement, referring to the introduction—all these techniques can be used separately. But you have probably noticed that speakers often combine two or more in their conclusions. Actually, all four techniques can be fused into one—for example, a dramatic quotation that summarizes the central idea while referring to the introduction.

One other concluding technique you should know about is making a direct appeal to your audience for action. This applies only to a particular type of persuasive speech, however, and will be discussed in Chapter 14. The four methods covered in this chapter are appropriate for all kinds of speeches and occasions.

Sample Conclusion with Commentary

How do you fit these methods together to make a conclusion? Here is an example, from the same speech about shoplifting whose introduction we looked at earlier (pages 178–179).

COMMENTARY

The speaker gives an excellent summary of her speech. This is particularly important when you are speaking to inform, because it gives you one last chance to make sure the audience remembers your main points.

Referring back to the introduction unifies the entire speech. The speaker again relates the topic to her audience. This is often a good thing to do in the conclusion.

The forceful closing line reinforces the central idea and ends the speech on a strong note.

CONCLUSION

We have seen, then, that most shoplifters are between the ages of 18 and 29 and can be divided into three major groups—amateurs, who steal on impulse or for kicks; professionals, who steal for a living; and compulsive shoplifters or kleptomaniacs, who cannot control their urge to steal. We have also seen that merchants use a variety of methods to combat shoplifting, including store detectives, employee training programs, hidden cameras, two-way mirrors, and electronic anti-theft devices.

So the next time you are in a store, admiring the clothing or cameras or stereo equipment, remember there is a never-ending unseen battle being waged between the store and the shoplifter. And when you get upset about how much things cost, remember the extra price we all pay for the crime of shoplifting. The crime itself is usually invisible, but its effects are not.

Tips for Preparing the Conclusion

1. As with the introduction, keep an eye out for possible concluding materials as you research and develop the speech.

2. Conclude with a bang, not a whimper. Be creative in devising a conclusion that hits the hearts and minds of your audience. Work on several possible endings, and select the one that seems likely to have the greatest impact.

3. Don't be long-winded. The conclusion will normally make up no more than about 5 to 10 percent of your speech. Nothing aggravates audiences more than a speaker who says "In conclusion"—and then drones on interminably.

4. Don't leave anything in your conclusion to chance. Work it out in detail, and give yourself plenty of time to practice delivering it. Many students like to write out the conclusion word for word to guarantee it is just right. If you do this, make sure you can present it smoothly, confidently, and with feeling—without relying on your notes or sounding wooden. Make your last impression as forceful and as favorable as you can.

SUMMARY

First impressions are important. So are final impressions. This is why speeches need strong introductions and conclusions.

In most speech situations you need to accomplish four objectives with your introduction—get the attention and interest of the audience, reveal the topic of your speech, establish your credibility and good will, and preview the body of the speech. Gaining attention and interest can be done in several ways. You can show the importance of your topic, especially as it relates to your audience. You can startle or question your audience or arouse their curiosity. You can begin with a quotation or a story.

Be sure to state the topic of your speech clearly in your introduction; otherwise, your audience may be confused and wonder where the speech is going. Establishing credibility means that you tell the audience why you are qualified to speak on the topic at hand; establishing good will, although less important for classroom speeches than for speeches outside the classroom, may be necessary if your point of view is unpopular. Previewing the body of the speech helps the audience listen effectively and provides a smooth lead-in to the body of the speech.

The conclusion of a speech is particularly important, because the final impression is often what will stick in your listeners' minds. The conclusion has two major objectives—to let the audience know you are ending the speech, and to reinforce their understanding of, or commitment to, your central idea. Too sudden an ending may leave your audience puzzled; it is always a good idea to alert them that you are finishing. You can do this either by your words or by your manner of delivery.

You can use a number of techniques to reinforce your central idea in the conclusion. They include summarizing the speech, ending with a pertinent quotation, making a dramatic statement, and referring to the introduction. Sometimes you may want to combine two or more of these techniques. Be creative in devising a vivid, forceful conclusion.

REVIEW QUESTIONS

After reading this chapter, you should be able to answer the following questions:

1. What are four objectives of a speech introduction?

2. What are seven methods you can use in the introduction to get the attention and interest of your audience?

3. Why is it important to establish your credibility at the beginning of your speech?

4. What is a preview statement? Why should you nearly always include a preview statement in the introduction of your speech?

5. What are five tips for preparing your introduction?

6. What are the major functions of a speech conclusion?

7. What are two ways you can signal the end of your speech?

8. What are four ways to reinforce the central idea when concluding your speech?

9. What are four tips for preparing your conclusion?

APPLICATION EXERCISES

1. Here are six speech topics. Explain how you might relate each to your classmates in the introduction of a speech.

organ donation	soap operas
Alzheimer's disease	phobias
vandalism	lightning

2. Think of a speech topic (preferably one for your next speech in class). Create an introduction for a speech dealing with any aspect of the topic you wish. In your introduction be sure to gain the attention of the audience, to reveal the topic and relate it to the audience, to establish your credibility, and to preview the body of the speech.

3. Using the same topic as in Exercise 2, create a speech conclusion. Be sure to let your audience know the speech is ending, to reinforce the central idea, and to make the conclusion vivid and memorable.

NOTES

[1] John C. Lawn, "Drugs in America," *Vital Speeches*, 52 (1986), 322.

[2] James Beggs, "Humans to Mars—Why? *Vital Speeches*, 52 (1985), 51.

[3] Robert Rager, "Amusement Park Safety," *Winning Orations, 1985* (Mankato, Minn.: Interstate Oratorical Association, 1985), p. 38.

[4] Dorothy Sarnoff, *Speech Can Change Your Life* (Garden City, N.Y.: Doubleday, 1970), p. 189.

[5] *Ibid.*, p. 190.

Outlining the Speech

Think what might happen if you tried to build a house without a floor plan or architect's blueprint. You build the kitchen next to the driveway to make it convenient for carrying in groceries. But the dining room turns up at the other end of the house. When you cook and serve a meal, you have to run with the plates to keep the food from getting cold. You put the bathroom at the head of the stairs to make it accessible to visitors. But the door opens in such a way that the unwary guest is catapulted down the steps. You think it's a wonderful idea to have almost no interior walls. After all, the modern living space is supposed to be free and open. But when the first snowfall comes, your (unsupported) roof collapses.

Plans and blueprints are essential to architecture. So, too, are outlines essential to effective speeches. An outline is like a blueprint for your speech. By outlining, you make sure that related items are together, that ideas flow from one another, that the structure of your speech will "stand up"—and not collapse.

Probably you will use two kinds of outlines for your speeches—one very detailed, for the planning stage, and one very brief, for the delivery of the speech.

THE PREPARATION OUTLINE

The preparation outline is just what its name implies—an outline that helps you prepare the speech. Writing a preparation outline means actually putting your speech together. It is the stage at which you decide what you will say in the introduction, how you will organize the main points and supporting materials in the body of the speech, and what you will say in the conclusion.

Guidelines for the Preparation Outline

Over the years, a relatively uniform system for preparation outlines has developed. It is explained below and exemplified in the sample outline on pages 195–197. You should check with your teacher to see exactly what format you are to follow.

State the Specific Purpose of Your Speech   The specific purpose statement should be a separate unit that comes before the text of the outline itself. Including the specific purpose with the outline makes it easier to assess how well you have constructed the speech to accomplish your purpose.

Identify the Central Idea   Some teachers prefer that the central idea be given immediately after the purpose statement. Others prefer that it be given and identified in the text of the outline itself. Check to see which your teacher wants.

Label the Introduction, Body, and Conclusion   If you label the parts of your speech, you will be sure that you indeed *have* an introduction and conclusion, and have accomplished the essential objectives of each. Usually the names of the speech parts are placed in the middle of the page or in the far left margin. They are technical labels only and are not included in the system of symbolization used to identify main points and supporting materials.

Use a Consistent Pattern of Symbolization and Indentation   In the most common system of outlining, main points are identified by Roman numerals and are indented equally so as to be aligned down the page. Subpoints (components of the main points) are identified by capital letters and are also indented equally so as to be aligned with each other. Beyond this, there may be sub-subpoints and even sub-sub-subpoints. For example:

   I. Main point
      A. Subpoint
      B. Subpoint
          1. Sub-subpoint
          2. Sub-subpoint
              a. Sub-sub-subpoint
              b. Sub-sub-subpoint
  II. Main point
      A. Subpoint
          1. Sub-subpoint
          2. Sub-subpoint
      B. Subpoint

The clear visual framework of this outline immediately shows the relationships among the ideas of the speech. The most important ideas (main points) are farthest to the left. Less important ideas (subpoints, sub-subpoints, and so on) are progressively farther to the right. This pattern reveals the structure of your entire speech.

Once you have organized the body of your speech (see Chapter 7), you should have identified the main points. You need only flesh out your outline with subpoints and sub-subpoints, as necessary, to support the main points. But suppose, as sometimes happens, you find yourself with a list of statements and are not sure which are main points, which are subpoints, and so forth. Such a list might look like this:

There were 13 people at the Last Supper—Jesus and his 12 disciples.

One of the most common sources of superstitions is numbers.

In the United States, the 13 is usually omitted in the floor numbering of hotels and skyscrapers.

The number 13 has meant bad luck as long as anyone can remember.

Which statement is the main point? The second statement ("One of the most common sources of superstitions is numbers"), which is broader in scope than any of the other statements. This would be one of the main ideas of your speech. The fourth statement is the subpoint; it immediately supports the main point. The other two statements are sub-subpoints; they illustrate the subpoint. Rearranged properly, they look like this:

I.   One of the most common forms of superstition is numbers.
   A.   The number 13 has meant bad luck as long as anyone can remember.
      1.   There were 13 people at the Last Supper—Jesus and his 12 disciples.
      2.   In the United States, 13 is usually omitted in the floor numbering of hotels and skyscrapers.

Above all, remember that all points at the same level should immediately support the point that is just above and one notch to the left in your outline. If this sounds confusing, think of it as a business organization chart:

I.   President
   A.   Vice president—Operations
      1.   Manager—Domestic Operations
         a.   Assistant manager—East
         b.   Assistant manager—West
      2.   Manager—Foreign Operations
         a.   Assistant manager—Europe and Asia
         b.   Assistant manager—Africa
         c.   Assistant manager—Americas
   B.   Vice president—Administration
      1.   Manager—Finance
      2.   Manager—Personnel

As you can see, every person on this chart reports to the person who is above and one notch to the left—except, of course, the President, who is the "main point."

State Main Points and Subpoints in Full Sentences   Below are two sets of main points and subpoints for the same speech. The speaker's topic was one of the most notorious crimes in American history—the ax murders of Mr. and Mrs. Andrew Borden in 1892. Although their daughter, Lizzie, was acquitted, the speaker hoped to show she actually was guilty.

INEFFECTIVE	MORE EFFECTIVE
I. Motive	I. Lizzie Borden had the strongest motive.
A. Will	A. She was a major heir in her father's will.
B. Stepmother	B. She hated her stepmother.
1. Meals	1. Lizzie refused to eat meals with her stepmother.
2. Mrs. Borden	2. Lizzie addressed her stepmother as "Mrs. Borden."
II. Opportunity	II. Lizzie had the only opportunity to commit the murders.
A. Alone	A. Lizzie was alone in the house.
B. Front door	B. The front door was triple-locked.
C. Back door	C. No one could have come in the back door without being seen by the maid.
III. Alibi	III. Lizzie did not have an alibi for her whereabouts at the time of the murders.

The sample at left might serve adequately as a speaking outline, but it is virtually useless as a preparation outline. It gives only vague labels rather than distinct ideas. It does not indicate clearly the content of the main points and subpoints. Nor does it reveal whether the speaker has thought out his or her ideas. But there is no concern about any of these matters with the outline on the right.

In sum, a skimpy preparation outline is of little value. Stating your main points and subpoints in full sentences will ensure that you develop your ideas fully.

Label Transitions, Internal Summaries, and Internal Previews   One way to make sure you have strong transitions, internal summaries, and internal previews is to include them in the preparation outline. Usually they are not incorporated into the system of symbolization and indentation, but are labeled separately and inserted in the outline where they will appear in the speech.

Attach a Bibliography   You should include with the outline a list of the sources you consulted in preparing the speech. The bibliography will show all the books, magazines, and newspapers you read in preparing the speech, as well as any interviews or field research you conducted. You may use any one of a number of bibliographical formats; or your teacher may have a preference. No matter which format you adopt, make your statement of sources clear, accurate, and consistent.

Give Your Speech a Title, if One Is Desired   In the classroom you probably do not need a title for your speech unless your teacher requires one. In some other situations, however, a speech title is necessary—as when the speech is publicized in advance, when the group inviting you to speak requests a title, or when the speech is going to be published. Whatever the reason, if you do decide to use a title, it should (1) be brief; (2) attract the attention of your audience; and (3) encapsulate the main thrust of your speech.[1]

A good title need not have what Madison Avenue would call "sex appeal"— lots of glitter and pizazz. By the same token, there is certainly nothing wrong with a catchy title—as long as it is germane to the speech. Here are two groups of titles. Those on the left are straightforward and descriptive. Those on the right are figurative alternatives to the ones on the left.

GROUP I	GROUP II
Choosing a Personal Computer	The Apple of Your Eye
Funeral Home Reform	Making a Killing Off the Dead
Problems of the Social Security System	The Big Fraud
The Pleasures of Chocolate	Food of the Gods
Dangers of High Blood Pressure	The Silent Killer

Which group do you prefer? Neither is perfect. There are advantages and disadvantages to both. Those in the first group clearly reveal the topic of the speech, but they are not as provocative as those in the second group. Those in the second group are sure to arouse interest, but they do not give as clear an idea of what the speeches are about.

There is one other kind of title you should consider—the question. Phrasing your title as a question can be both descriptive and provocative. By this method we can construct a third set of titles combining the virtues of Groups I and II:

GROUP III

Can You Find Happiness with the Right Personal Computer?

Funeral Home Reform: Why Can't the Living Rest in Peace?

How Secure Is Social Security?

Why Was Chocolate Called "The Food of the Gods"?

High Blood Pressure: Can It Be Controlled?

Sometimes you will choose a title for your speech very early. At other times you may not find one you like until the last minute. Either way, try to be resourceful about creating titles for your speeches. Experiment with several and choose the one that seems most appropriate for the topic, the audience, and the occasion.

Sample Preparation Outline with Commentary

The following outline for a six- to eight-minute informative speech illustrates the guidelines just discussed. The commentary explains the procedures used in organizing the speech and writing the outline.[2] (Check with your teacher to see if he or she wants you to include a title with your outline.)

COMMENTARY

OUTLINE

THE COMMON COLD

Stating your specific purpose and central idea as separate units before the text of the outline makes it easier to judge how well you have constructed the outline to achieve your purpose and communicate your central idea.

Specific purpose: To inform my audience of the characteristics and treatment of the common cold.

Central idea: The common cold is a highly contagious virus that is best treated by the traditional remedy of rest, aspirin, and plenty of fluids.

Labeling the introduction marks it as a distinct section that plays a special role in the speech.

Introduction

Opening with a question helps to arouse interest.

I. What is the most common human ailment in the world?

II. If you answer, "the common cold," you are right.

Here the speaker shows the importance of the topic and relates it to the audience.

III. According to the U.S. Public Health Service, most adults average two to three colds each year.

Previewing the main points lets the audience know what to listen for in the body of the speech.

IV. Today I would like to answer two questions:
A. What exactly is a cold?
B. What is the best thing to do when you get one?

Including transitions ensures that the speaker has worked out how to connect one idea to the next. Notice that the transition is not included in the system of symbolization and indentation used for the rest of the outline.

(Transition: Let's start with the first question—what exactly is a cold?)

Labeling the body marks it as a distinct part of the speech.

Body

Main point I is phrased as a full sentence. As the outline progresses, notice that each main point contains only one idea and that the main points are arranged in topical order.

I. The common cold is a viral infection of the upper respiratory system.
A. It is important to stress that the cold is a viral infection.
1. Can be caused by over 100 different viruses.
2. Not caused by chill or dampness.
B. The symptoms of a cold are distressingly familiar.

The three subpoints are shown by the capital letters A, B, and C, and are

1. Dry, scratchy, tingling sensation in nose or

written in complete sentences to ensure that the speaker has thought them out fully.

Points below the level of subpoint are indicated by Arabic numerals and lower-case letters. Often they are not written in full sentences. Check to see what your teacher prefers.

The progressive indentation shows visually the relationships among main points, subpoints, sub-subpoints, etc.

throat—first sign that mucous membranes are starting to swell with viral growth.

2. Body temperature drops—sometimes causing chills.
3. Nasal discharge becomes thick—clogging the nostrils.
4. Clogged nostrils cut off air to the sinuses—producing a dull headache.

C. One reason we catch so many colds is that the cold virus is highly communicable.
   1. Usually spread by sneezing or coughing.
   2. Also spread by contact with the skin.
      a. Dr. J. O. Hendly, University of Virginia Medical School, says a cold virus can survive on the skin for 6 hours.
      b. If a cold sufferer coughs behind his or her hand and then touches a doorknob or water faucet, the virus is deposited there. The next person who touches that spot wipes off the virus and becomes infected through rubbing the eyes or nose.

The transition shows how the speaker will move from main point I to main point II.

Main point II, like main point I, is phrased as a full sentence.

The unusual historical information included under subpoint A adds interest, variety, and color.

(Transition: So you are bound to catch a cold. What is the best thing to do when you catch one?)

II. Over the years people have tried many remedies to combat the common cold.
    A. In previous centuries, people used all sorts of bizarre—and sometimes dangerous—remedies.
       1. "Bleeding" the patient by taking out a pint or two of blood—supposedly to remove the infection.
       2. Saturating a piece of flannel with foul-smelling salve and wrapping it around the patient's neck.
       3. Dousing the patient with huge quantities of baking soda mixed in water—to counteract "acidity," which was thought to be a cause of colds.

Note the pattern of subordination in this section. Rest, aspirin, and liquids are all parts of the traditional therapy announced in subpoint B, so they are arranged under that subpoint. Hot liquids and alcohol are particular types of liquids, so they are subordinated to item 3, about liquids. Items i and ii expand on the use of alcohol, so they come under item b, about alcohol.

    B. The traditional modern therapy—get plenty of rest, take aspirin, and drink lots of liquid—is still the best.
       1. Rest gives your body a chance to fight the virus.
       2. Aspirin reduces fever and combats the minor aches and pains of a cold.
       3. Liquids help loosen thickness in the chest and prevent internal shock.
          a. Hot liquids are especially useful.

        b. So are moderate doses of alcohol.
           i. Gives comfort and helps you sleep.
          ii. Old English adage for patients with a cold: "Hang one's hat on the bedpost, drink from a bottle of good whiskey until two hats appear, then get into bed and stay there."
  C. Many people believe that taking large amounts of vitamin C can cure a cold.
    1. Most research studies deny this.
    2. Some studies do suggest that small regular doses of vitamin C can help prevent colds by strengthening the body's resistance to viruses.

Internal summaries, like transitions, should be labeled and inserted in parentheses where they will appear in the speech.

(Internal summary: In short, there is no magic cure for the common cold. The best remedy is still rest, aspirin, and plenty of fluids.)

Labeling the conclusion marks it as a distinct part of the speech.

Conclusion

Here the speaker restates the importance of the topic.

I. People have been putting up with colds ever since Adam and Eve were thrown out of their virus-free paradise.

Summarizing the main points is usually standard procedure in concluding an informative speech.
The closing line is somewhat dramatic and provides unity by relating back to the introduction.

II. I hope you now have a better idea just what a cold is and what you should do when you get one—when you are stricken with the most common human ailment in the world.

This is the final bibliography. It lists the sources actually used in writing the speech and is shorter than the preliminary bibliography compiled in the early stages of research. (See Chapter 5 for a discussion of the preliminary bibliography.)

Bibliography
Josh Hammer, "The Cure for the Common Cold: In Search of a Better Chicken Soup," *Esquire*, December 1986, pp. 214–216.
Pat Ohlendorf, "The Relentless Cold," *Macleans*, November 5, 1984, pp. 53–56.
Lowell Ponte, "The Bugs That Bug Us: What We Should Know About Colds," *Reader's Digest*, October 1987, pp. 85–89.
Cory SerVaas, "Vitamin C and the Immune System," *Saturday Evening Post,* May 1978, pp. 131–132.
Richard L. Williams, "For the All-Too-Common Cold We Are Perfect, If Unwilling, Hosts," *Smithsonian*, December 1983, pp. 46–55.

THE SPEAKING OUTLINE

"I was never so excited by public speaking before in my life," wrote one publisher in 1820 after listening to Daniel Webster. "Three or four times I thought my temples would burst with the gush of blood. . . . I was beside myself, and am so still."[3]

Such reactions were not unusual among Webster's audiences. He thrilled two generations of Americans with his masterful orations. Incredible as it seems today, he did so while speaking for three, four, even five hours at a time. Equally incredible, he often spoke without using any notes! A reporter once asked how he managed this. "It is my memory," Webster said. "I can prepare a speech, revise and correct it in my memory, then deliver the corrected speech exactly as finished."[4]

Few people have Webster's remarkable powers of memory. Fortunately, it is no longer customary to speak from memory. Today most people speak extemporaneously—which means the speech is thoroughly prepared and carefully practiced in advance, but much of the exact wording is selected while the speech is being delivered (see Chapter 11). Your speeches will probably be of this type. You should know, then, about the speaking outline—the most widely recommended form of notes for extemporaneous speeches.

The aim of a speaking outline is to help you remember what you want to say. In some ways it is a condensed version of your preparation outline. It should contain key words or phrases to jog your memory, as well as essential statistics and quotations that you do not want to risk forgetting. But it should also include material *not* in your preparation outline—especially cues to direct and sharpen your delivery.

Most speakers develop their own variations on the speaking outline. As you acquire more experience, you too should feel free to experiment. But for now, you cannot go wrong by following the basic guidelines below and by imitating the sample speaking outline on pages 200–202.

Guidelines for the Speaking Outline

Follow the Visual Framework Used in the Preparation Outline   Your speaking outline should use the same visual framework—the same symbols and the same pattern of indentation—as in your preparation outline. This will make it much easier to prepare the speaking outline. More important, it will allow you to see instantly where you are in the speech at any given moment while you are speaking. You will find this a great advantage. As you speak, you will look down at your outline periodically to make sure you are covering the right ideas in the right order. It will be of little help if you have to hunt around to find where you are every time you look down.

Compare the following two versions of a partial speaking outline. They are from an informative speech about the development of psychoanalysis:

INEFFECTIVE	MORE EFFECTIVE
I. Sigmund Freud	I. Sigmund Freud
A. The early years	A. The early years
1. Medical background	1. Medical background
2. Self-analysis	2. Self-analysis
3. *The Interpretation of Dreams*	3. *The Interpretation of Dreams*
B. Mature work	B. Mature work
1. International recognition	1. International recognition
2. Defection of students	2. Defection of students
II. Freud's disciples	II. Freud's disciples
A. Carl Jung	A. Carl Jung
B. Alfred Adler	B. Alfred Adler
III. The American generation	III. The American generation
A. Erich Fromm	A. Erich Fromm
B. Karen Horney	B. Karen Horney
C. Harry Stack Sullivan	C. Harry Stack Sullivan

The wording of both versions is exactly the same. But the visual framework of the one on the right makes it easier to take in at a glance and reduces the odds of the speaker losing his or her place.

Make Sure the Outline Is Plainly Legible   You would be surprised how many students try to speak from messy, scribbled notes that would be hard to decipher at leisure, much less under the pressures of a speech situation. Your speaking outline is all but worthless unless it is instantly readable at a distance. When you make your outline, use dark ink and large lettering, leave extra space between lines, provide ample margins, and write or type on one side of the paper only. (People who speak a great deal have their outlines made on a typewriter with an extra-large typeface; if one is available, that is ideal.)

Some speakers put their notes on index cards. Most find the 3 × 5 size too cramped and prefer the 4 × 6 or 5 × 8 sizes instead. Other people write their speaking outlines on regular paper. Either practice is fine, as long as your notes are immediately legible to you while you are speaking.

Keep the Outline as Brief as Possible   If your notes are too detailed, you will have difficulty maintaining eye contact with your audience. A detailed outline will tempt you to look at it far too often, as one student discovered:

Susan Flexner was speaking about the joys of cross-country skiing. She had prepared her speech thoroughly and practiced it until it was nearly perfect. But when she delivered the speech in class, she referred constantly to her detailed notes. As a result, her delivery was choppy and strained. After the speech, her classmates remarked on how often Susan had consulted her notes, and she was amazed. "I didn't even know I was doing it," she said. "Most of the time I wasn't even paying attention to the outline. I knew the speech cold."

Many students have had the same experience. Having lots of notes is a psychological security blanket against the possibility that something will go terribly wrong. The feeling seems to be, "As long as I have plenty of notes, disaster will not strike." In fact, most beginning speakers use far too many notes. Like Susan, they find they don't need all of them to remember the speech. They also discover that too many notes can actually interfere with good communication.

To guard against having too many notes, keep your speaking outline as brief as possible. It should contain key words or phrases to help you remember major points, subpoints, and connectives. If you are citing statistics, you will probably want to include them in your notes. Unless you are good at memorizing quotations, write them out fully as well. Finally, there may be two, three, or four key ideas whose wording is so important that you want to state them in simple complete sentences. The best rule of thumb is that your notes should be the *minimum* you need to jog your memory and keep you on track. At first you may find it risky to speak from a brief outline, but you will soon become more comfortable with it.

Give Yourself Cues for Delivering the Speech   A good speaking outline reminds you not only of *what* you want to say, but also of *how* you want to say it. As you practice the speech, you will decide that certain ideas and phrases need special emphasis—that they should be spoken more loudly, softly, slowly, or rapidly than other parts of the speech. You will also determine how you want to pace the speech—how you will control its timing, rhythm, and momentum. But no matter how carefully you work these things out ahead of time, no matter how often you practice, it is easy to forget them once you get up in front of an audience.

The solution is to include in your speaking outline directions for delivering the speech. One way to do this is by underlining or otherwise highlighting key ideas that you want to be sure to emphasize. Then, when you reach them in the outline, you will be reminded to stress them. Another way is to jot down on the outline explicit cues such as "pause," "repeat," "slow down," "louder," and so forth. Both techniques are good aids for beginning speakers, but they are also used by most experienced speakers.

Sample Speaking Outline with Commentary

Below is a sample speaking outline for a six- to eight-minute informative talk on the common cold. By comparing it with the preparation outline for the same speech on pages 195–197, you can see how a detailed preparation outline is transformed into a concise speaking outline.

COMMENTARY	OUTLINE

These comments remind the speaker to establish eye contact and not to race through the speech.

EYE CONTACT !!
SLOW DOWN

I. Most common human ailment?

— PAUSE —

The word "pause" reminds the speaker to pause after the opening question.

II.   Common cold universal.
III. U.S. Health Service: 2–3/yr.
IV.   Today—"What is . . .?"
                "What to do . . .?"
(Let's start with 1st)

It's usually a good idea to pause briefly before launching into the first main point. This is another way of signaling that you are moving from the introduction to the body.

—PAUSE—

Most speakers find it helpful to demarcate the body of the speech in the speaking outline as well as in the preparation outline.

Note how the body of the speech follows the same visual framework as the preparation outline. This makes the outline easy to read at a glance.

Body
I. Viral infection of upper respiratory system
  A. Stress viral infection
  B. Symptoms:

    1. Dry nose or throat
    2. Temperature—chills
    3. Clogged nostrils
    4. Headache
  C. Highly contagious
    1. Sneeze or cough
    2. Skin

Identifying the source in the outline helps the speaker remember the source's qualifications.

      a. J. O. Hendly, U of Va, 6 HRS.
      b. Example—faucet or doorknob

Inserting transitions makes sure the speaker doesn't forget them.

(So BOUND to catch. What then?)

II. Many remedies over the years
  A.   Olden times
    1. Bleeding
    2. Salve
    3. Baking soda

Throughout the outline, key words are used to jog the speaker's memory. Because the final wording of an extemporaneous speech is chosen at the moment of delivery, it will not be exactly the same as that in the preparation outline.

  B.   Traditional modern therapy best
    1. Rest
    2. Aspirin
    3. Liquids
      a. Hot

COMMENTARY	OUTLINE
Quotations are usually written out in full in the speaking outline.	b. Alcohol: "Hang one's hat on the bedpost, drink from a bottle of good whiskey until TWO hats appear, then get into bed and STAY there."
	C. Vitamin C
	1. NOT a cure
Underlining reminds the speaker to stress key words or ideas.	2. May help PREVENT
A brief note makes sure the speaker includes an internal summary at the end of main point II.	(In short . . .)
It's usually a good idea to pause briefly before entering the conclusion.	— PAUSE —
Most speakers label the conclusion in the speaking outline as well as in the preparation outline.	*Conclusion*
Including the opening and closing lines of the last sentence jogs the speaker's memory and ensures that the speech will end as planned.	I. Adam and Eve
	II. I hope you have better idea . . . most common human ailment in the world.

SUMMARY

Outlines are essential to effective speeches. By outlining, you make sure that related ideas are together, that your thoughts flow from one to another, and that the structure of your speech is coherent. You will probably use two kinds of outlines for your speeches—the detailed preparation outline and the brief speaking outline.

The preparation outline helps you prepare your speech. In this outline you state your specific purpose and central idea, label the introduction, body, and conclusion, and designate transitions, internal summaries, and internal previews. You should identify main points, subpoints, and sub-subpoints by a consistent pattern of symbolization and indentation. It is usually advisable to state at least main points and subpoints in full sentences. Your teacher may require that you include a bibliography with your preparation outline.

The speaking outline consists of brief notes to help you while you deliver the speech. It should contain key words or phrases to jog your memory, as well as essential statistics and quotations. In making up your speaking outline, follow the same visual framework used in your preparation outline. Keep the speaking outline as brief as possible, and be sure it is plainly legible. You can also give yourself cues for delivering the speech—when to speak more softly or more slowly, when to pause, and so forth.

REVIEW QUESTIONS

After reading this chapter, you should be able to answer the following questions:

1. Why is it important to outline your speeches?

2. What is a preparation outline? What are the eight guidelines discussed in the chapter for writing a preparation outline?

3. What is a speaking outline? What are four guidelines for your speaking outline?

APPLICATION EXERCISES

1. In the left-hand column below is a partially blank outline from a speech about parachuting. In the right-hand column, arranged in random order, are the subpoints to fill in the outline. Choose the appropriate subpoint for each blank in the outline.

OUTLINE	SUBPOINTS
I. The history of parachuting goes back almost one thousand years.	Their rate of descent is 18–22 feet per second.
A.	The first successful parachute jump was in 1797 by Frenchman André-Jacques Garnerin.
B.	Even with the necessary training, 5 percent of military parachutists will be injured on impact during any given jump.
C.	Their slow rate of descent and ability to "brake" make parafoils ideal for skydivers and other civilian parachutists.
D.	
E.	In the twentieth century parachuting has been used mainly for fire fighting, troop deployment, and recreation.
II. The two major types of parachutes employed today are the traditional military style and the more modern parafoil.	Landing safely at this force requires considerable training.
A.	Parafoils are markedly slower and safer than military parachutes.

OUTLINE	SUBPOINTS
1.	At this rate of descent a military parachutist lands with a force equivalent to jumping off a one-story building.
2.	
a.	In 1147 a Turk leaped to his death trying to parachute off a tall building.
b.	Military parachutes are designed to descend quickly.
B.	In addition to descending more slowly than military parachutes, parafoils can be "braked" before impact.
1.	By 1830 parachutists were jumping in front of large crowds as a form of entertainment.
2.	They descend at a rate of 12–15 feet per second.
3.	In 1485 Leonardo Da Vinci sketched a parachute design that modern engineers say would have worked.

2. Following the format used in the sample preparation outline on pages 195–197, outline the speech in the Appendix by Kathy Weisensel ("David—and a Lot of Other Neat People," pages 396–399). Be sure to include a specific purpose statement, to identify the central idea, to label the introduction, body, and conclusion, to use a consistent pattern of symbolization and indentation, to state the main points and subpoints in full sentences, and to label transitions and internal summaries.

3. From the preparation outline you constructed in Exercise 2, create a speaking outline that you might use in delivering the speech. Follow the guidelines for a speaking outline discussed in this chapter.

NOTES

[1] There is indirect evidence to suggest that a speech title may help listeners remember a speaker's ideas. See D. James Dooling and Roy Lachman, "Effects of Comprehension on Retention of Prose," *Journal of Experimental Psychology*, 88 (1971), 216–222.

[2] Reprinted with permission of Mary Augsburger.

[3] Robert T. Oliver, *History of Public Speaking in America* (Boston: Allyn and Bacon, 1965), p. 143.

[4] *Ibid.*, p. 145.

PART FOUR

PRESENTING THE SPEECH

CHAPTER 10

Using Language

Have you ever played charades? The point of the game, of course, is to act out words or phrases so people watching you can guess them. Some words are easy—words like "me" and "walk" and "stomach" and "baseball." You can point or move your body in such a way that observers catch on immediately. But other types of words pose a real challenge for pantomime. Adjectives and adverbs can be especially difficult. Try acting out "very" or "appropriate" or "significant." The more abstract the word, the more difficult it is to mime. How would you act out "technology" or "loyalty"?

This is why language has evolved. Human beings need to communicate at a level far above what can be shown by body movements. But for language to work there must be a common understanding of what words mean. In effect, we've all made a pact that a certain collection of letters and sounds will mean the same thing to everybody. If you say "book," everybody who speaks English will picture something like what you're holding right now. On the other hand, when you don't use words properly, you "break the pact" and communication breaks down. Suppose you say to a friend, "Betsy, you're so pedestrian." You may mean she walks a lot; but Betsy is likely to get angry because you actually called her boring and ordinary.

LANGUAGE IS IMPORTANT

Good speakers have respect for language and how it works. How well do you use language? Do you say Michael Jordan plays basketball *good,* when you mean he plays *well?* Do you say *in the eventuality of* when *if* will do? Do you describe an earthquake as a *terrible disaster,* as if there were such a thing as a *good disaster?* Do you litter your speech with such meaningless words as *you know, like, I mean,* and *really?*

If you do these things, you are bound to be less effective as a speaker. And, unfortunately, you are not alone. Much American speech is turning into the linguistic equivalent of junk food.[1] For example:

Sportscaster Merlin Olson, discussing football strategy: "Coaches don't want to play inexperienced quarterbacks in pressurized games." (No doubt. Do pressurized football games bounce as high as pressurized tennis balls?)

Sign in an eyeglass shop: "Eyes examined while you wait." (Definitely more comfortable than the alternative.)

An aviation official, addressing reporters: "The craft departed the runway at the midfield barrier and suffered a catastrophic degradation of airframe integrity." (In plain English, "The airplane crashed.")

Letter to an insurance company explaining an automobile accident: "The telephone pole was approaching fast. I was attempting to swerve out of its path when it struck my front end." (Those rampaging telephone poles are a menace to drivers everywhere!)

The problem with these statements is not that they violate elitist standards of "good English." Americans have always talked casually. Our language has grown with as much vigor and variety as our population. We have borrowed words from other languages. We have coined new words and dropped old ones. But there is a big difference between the natural evolution of a living language and the misuse of that language.[2]

To misuse our language is much more than a matter of mere words. Contrary to popular belief, language does not mirror reality. It does not simply describe the world as it is. Instead, language helps create our sense of reality by giving meaning to events. Language is not neutral. The words we use to label an event determine to a great extent how we respond to it.[3]

Consider the political situation in El Salvador. If you see the government as a "democracy" that is defending "freedom" against a group of "communist insurgents" seeking to establish a "brutal dictatorship," you will likely support efforts to aid the government in its battle against the "insurgents." But if you see the government itself as a "brutal dictatorship" and the forces opposing it as "patriotic freedom fighters" trying to bring "justice" to an "oppressed" people, you will probably oppose efforts to aid the government.

What separates these two viewpoints? Not the events in El Salvador. Those events are the same for both sides. The difference is in the *meaning* given to the events by the words that label them. This is why, as one writer has said, a choice of words is also a choice of worlds.[4]

Words are vital to thinking itself. Thought and language are closely linked. We do not get an idea and then come up with words to express it. Rather, we usually think *in* words. How often have you said, "I know what I want to say, but I just don't know how to say it." In fact, if you truly knew what you wanted to say, you probably would be able to say it. On most occasions when we are looking for "just the right word," what we are really looking for is just the right *idea.*[5]

As a speaker, once you get the right idea you must decide how best to *communicate* it to listeners. To do this, you need to be especially conscious of what language can do. Unless you use language accurately and clearly, no one will understand your ideas. You might as well speak in a foreign tongue.

Words are the tools of a speaker's craft. They have special uses, just like the tools of any other profession. Have you ever watched a carpenter at work? The job that would take you or me a couple of hours is done by the carpenter in ten minutes—with the right tools. You can't drive a nail with a screwdriver or turn a screw with a hammer. It is the same with public speaking. You must choose the right words for the job you want to do.

As you select the wording for your speeches, keep these questions in mind: How do I want my audience to react? What do I want them to think or feel? Which words can best evoke these responses?

Good speakers are aware of the meanings of words—both their obvious and their subtle meanings. They also know how to use language accurately, clearly, vividly, and appropriately. The balance of this chapter will explore each of these aspects of language use.

MEANINGS OF WORDS

Words have two kinds of meanings—denotative and connotative. *Denotative* meaning is precise, literal, and objective. It carries no emotional overtones, no sentimental attachments, no moral judgments. It simply describes the object, person, place, idea, or event to which the word refers. One way to think of a word's denotative meaning is as its dictionary definition. For example, denotatively, the noun "school" means "a place, institution, or building where instruction is given."

Connotative meaning is more variable, figurative, and subjective. Put simply, the connotative meaning of a word is what the word suggests or implies. For instance, the connotative meaning of the word "school" includes all the feelings, associations, and emotions that the word touches off in different people. For one person, "school" might connote personal growth, childhood friends, and a special teacher. For another, it might connote frustration, discipline, and boring homework assignments.

Connotative meaning gives words their intensity and emotional power. It arouses in listeners feelings of anger, pity, love, fear, friendship, nostalgia, greed, guilt, and the like. Speakers, like poets, often use connotation to enrich their meaning. For example:

> The <u>terrorist</u> neither <u>listens to reason</u> nor engages in <u>reasoning</u> with others. His aim is to <u>generate</u> <u>fear</u>—to <u>frighten</u> people into <u>submission</u>. He measures success by the magnitude of the <u>fear</u> he generates through <u>brutal, savage acts of violence</u>. <u>Terrorists</u> like these are prepared to <u>kill</u> to further whatever cause they claim to be pursuing. And the <u>heinousness</u> of these <u>murders</u> is accented by the fact that they <u>murder without passion</u>. They <u>murder with cool deliberation and careful planning</u>. They are <u>utterly amoral</u>.[6]

The underlined words in this passage have powerful connotations that are almost certain to produce a strong emotional revulsion to terrorism.

Here, in contrast, is another version of the same statement—this time stripped of most of its connotative power:

> The terrorist does not seek to negotiate with his opponents. He seeks victory by using political and psychological pressure—including acts of violence that may endanger the lives of some people. To the terrorist, ultimate objectives are more important than the means used to achieve them.

Rather than using connotative words to evoke an emotional response, this statement is as neutral and objective as possible.

Which statement is preferable? That depends on the audience, the occasion, and the speaker's purpose. Do you want to stir up your listeners' emotions, rally them to some cause? Then select more connotative words. Or are you addressing a controversial issue and trying to seem completely

Good speakers use words accurately and correctly. They also use language that will be clear, vivid, and appropriate for their listeners. (Ellis Herwig/ Stock, Boston)

impartial? Then stick with more denotative words. Choosing words skillfully for their denotative and connotative meanings is a crucial part of the speaker's craft.

USING LANGUAGE ACCURATELY

Using language accurately is as vital to a speaker as using numbers accurately is to an accountant. One student found this out the hard way. In a speech about America's criminal justice system, he referred several times to "criminal *persecution.*" What he meant, of course, was "criminal *prosecution.*" This one error virtually ruined his speech. As one of his classmates said, "How can I believe what you say about our courts when you don't even know the difference between prosecution and persecution?"

Sometimes inaccuracy results from a misguided attempt to be elegant. This happened to the business manager of a magazine.

Mary Jo Hundt had a special fondness for adding "istic" to the end of a word. Addressing the magazine's editorial staff one day, she said, "We are going to streamline our paperwork to make it more *simplistic.* That's the *modernistic* way to do things. With less paperwork, we'll have more time to devote to the magazine, and that will be *impressionistic* to management."

Mary Jo clearly did not realize that "simplistic" doesn't mean simple or easy but instead refers to *over*simplification on shaky grounds. And "modernistic" refers to a particular style of design, not the general condition of being modern. "Impressionistic," of course, has nothing to do with making an impression on someone; it describes a certain type of art or music. But the editorial staff knew all these things, and they were embarrassed for Mary Jo.

The moral of this story is obvious. Don't use a word unless you are sure of its meaning. If you are not sure, look up the word in a dictionary.

Fortunately, such outright blunders are relatively rare among college students. However, we all commit more subtle errors—especially using one word when another will capture our ideas more precisely. Every word has shades of meaning that distinguish it from every other word. As Mark Twain said, "The difference between the right word and the almost right word is the difference between lightning and the lightning bug."

If you look in a thesaurus, you'll find the following words given as synonyms for "untruth":

lie	fib	falsification
story	myth	

All mean roughly the same thing—that the subject in question is not the absolute truth. But all these words have different shades of meaning. See if you can fill in the best word to complete each of the sentences below:

1. Icarus didn't really fly near the sun on wings made of wax. That's just a _____.

2. When I telephoned Professor Rodriguez at home, his little boy said "Daddy's in the shower," but I think that was a _____.

3. The worst thing that can happen to a scientist is for others to discover a _____ in laboratory records.

4. Even criminals sometimes find it hard to tell an outright _____ under oath in court.

5. George told me he was late for our date because his car broke down. Does he think I'm going to believe that tired old _____?

The best answers for the five statements are:

1.	myth	4.	lie
2.	fib	5.	story
3.	falsification		

Each of the words is a little different from the others, and each says something special to listeners.

As you prepare your speeches, ask yourself constantly, "What do I *really* want to say? What do I *really* mean?" Choose words that are precise, exact, accurate. When in doubt, consult the dictionary or thesaurus to make sure you have the best words to express your ideas.

If you have serious aspirations as a speaker, you should work out a systematic plan to improve your vocabulary. Years ago Malcolm X, the famous Black Muslim minister, did this by copying the dictionary, word by word! This method is extreme, and few people would take the time for it. A less arduous plan might be to try using one new word every day—and using the word correctly. The purpose of this is not to learn a lot of big words, but to "learn when certain words should be used, . . . to use the proper word at the proper time."[7]

USING LANGUAGE CLEARLY

Suppose you are on a ship, and you see someone go over the rail. Do you say, "It would appear from available empirical evidence that person or persons have been catapulted inadvertently into the surrounding liquid environment"? Of course not. You yell, "Man overboard!"

As many people have discovered, much to their dismay, it is possible to use language accurately without using it clearly. Here is a well-known story that shows how much trouble can be caused by not communicating clearly. A plumber wrote to a government agency to ask whether there was any harm in using hydrochloric acid to clean out drain pipes. The agency replied:

The efficacy of hydrochloric acid is indisputable, but the corrosive effect is incompatible with metallic permanence.

The plumber thanked the agency for approving the use of hydrochloric acid. The agency wrote back, saying:

We cannot assume responsibility for the production of toxic and noxious residue with hydrochloric acid and suggest you use an alternative procedure.

Once more the plumber thanked the agency for its approval. Finally, the agency—alarmed at the prospect of hundreds of ruined drain pipes—called in another scientist. He wrote:

Don't use hydrochloric acid. It eats holes in the pipes!

Remember, people are different. What makes perfect sense to some may be gobbledygook to others. You cannot assume that what is clear to you is clear to your audience. This is particularly true in speechmaking. Listeners, unlike readers, cannot turn to a dictionary or reread an author's words to discover their meaning. It is much more difficult for listeners to digest complex words and ideas.[8] A speaker's meaning must be *immediately* comprehensible; it must be so clear there is virtually no chance of misunderstanding. You can ensure this by using familiar words, by choosing concrete words over abstract words, and by eliminating verbal clutter.

Use Familiar Words

It may seem obvious that familiar words are better than unfamiliar ones. But you would be amazed how many students persist in bombarding listeners with complicated words—usually out of the mistaken belief that such words sound impressive. In truth, filling a speech with long, multisyllabic words only marks the speaker as stuffy and pretentious. Worse, it usually destroys understanding. One of the greatest barriers to clear speech is using big, bloated words where short, sharp ones will do the job better.[9]

Here, for example, are two passages expressing much the same idea. Which is easier to understand?

The supreme deity maintains custodial supervision over quadrupeds exhibiting ovine characteristics. Consequently, unfulfilled requirements are counterindicated. Under this jurisdiction it becomes mandatory to assume a recumbent posture in areas designated for agricultural endeavor. Controlled excursions in the vicinity of phlegmatic aquatic activity are undertaken. The aforementioned deity actuates reinstatement of nonverifiable metaphysical phenomena. In consideration of this appellation, there devolves an obligatory perambulation along approved thoroughfares.

Or,

The Lord is my shepherd; I shall not want. He maketh me to lie down in green pastures; he leadeth me beside the still waters. He restoreth my soul; he leadeth me in the paths of righteousness for his name's sake.

The second passage is, of course, the beginning of the Twenty-Third Psalm. It consists of short, simple, familiar words that are easy to comprehend. Its meaning comes across without forcing you to perform complex mental gymnastics. The first passage was written as it might be if a modern bureaucrat were writing the Bible. If you think it is hard to decipher in reading, imagine trying to make sense of it in listening. Better yet—since psalms were meant to be sung—try setting it to music!

When speaking about technical subjects, you may not be able to avoid unfamiliar words. If this happens, keep the technical terms to a minimum and define clearly those your audience may not understand. If you work at it, you will almost always be able to translate even the most specialized topic into clear, familiar language.

Here, for instance, are three passages explaining the potentially devastating effects of a pregnant woman's drinking on her unborn child. The first passage is in medical jargon, and it defies comprehension by ordinary listeners:

> Alcohol consumption by the pregnant woman seriously influences the intrauterine milieu and therefore contributes to the morbidity and mortality of children born to these mothers. In regard to the pathophysiology of this syndrome, genetic polymorphism of enzymes for ethanol metabolism may alter fetal susceptibility. There may also be poor microsomal or mitochondrial function or decreased ATP activity.

Even an educated person without a medical background would have trouble with "pathophysiology" and "polymorphism" and "mitochondrial," much less be able to put them all together.

The second passage represents an attempt to adapt to a nonmedical audience. It is in more familiar language but retains enough obscure words to be difficult:

> The deleterious effects of alcohol on the unborn child are very serious. When a pregnant mother consumes alcohol, the ethanol in the bloodstream easily crosses the placenta from mother to child and invades the amniotic fluid. This can produce a number of abnormal birth syndromes, including central-nervous-system dysfunctions, growth deficiencies, a cluster of facial aberrations, and variable major and minor malformations.

Well-informed listeners could probably figure out "deleterious effects," "central-nervous-system dysfunctions," and "facial aberrations." But these terms don't create a sharp mental image of what the speaker is trying to say. We still need to go one step further away from medical jargon toward ordinary language.

So we come to the third passage, which is utterly clear. It is from a speech by Annmarie Mungo, a student at Eastern Michigan University, and shows what can be done with work, imagination, and a healthy respect for everyday words:

> When the expectant mother drinks, alcohol is absorbed into her bloodstream and distributed throughout her entire body. After a few beers or a couple of martinis, she begins to feel tipsy and decides to sober up. She grabs a cup of coffee, two aspirin, and takes a little nap. After a while she'll be fine.
>
> But while she sleeps, the fetus is surrounded by the same alcoholic content as its mother had. After being drowned in alcohol, the fetus begins to feel the effect. But it can't sober up. It can't grab a cup of coffee. It can't grab a couple of aspirin. For the fetus's liver, the key organ in removing alcohol from the blood, is just not developed. The fetus is literally pickled in alcohol.[10]

This kind of plain talk is what listeners want. You cannot go wrong by following the advice of Winston Churchill to speak in "short, homely words of common usage." If you think big words (or a lot of words) are needed to impress listeners, bear in mind that the Gettysburg Address—considered the finest speech in the English language—contains 271 words, of which 251 have only one or two syllables.[11]

Choose Concrete Words

Concrete words refer to tangible objects—people, places, and things. They differ from abstract words, which refer to general concepts, qualities, or attributes. "Carrot," "pencil," "nose," and "door" are concrete words. "Humility," "science," "progress," and "philosophy" are abstract words.

Of course, few words are completely abstract or concrete. Abstractness and concreteness are relative. "Apple pie" is concrete, but the phrase also has abstract values of patriotism and conventional morals. Usually, the more specific a word, the more concrete it is. Let us say you are talking about baseball. Here are several words and phrases you might use:

physical activity	abstract/general
sports	
baseball	
American League	
New York Yankees	
Babe Ruth	concrete/specific

As you move down the list, the words become less abstract and more concrete. You begin with a general concept (physical activity), descend to one type of activity (sports), to a particular sport (baseball), to a division of that sport (American League), to one team in the American League (New York Yankees), to a specific player on that team (Babe Ruth).

The more abstract a word, the more ambiguous it will be. Although abstract words are necessary to express certain kinds of ideas, they are much easier to misinterpret than are concrete words. Also, concrete words are much more likely to claim your listeners' attention. Suppose you make a speech about litter in our cities. Here are two ways you could approach the subject— one featuring abstract words, the other concrete words.

ABSTRACT WORDS:

When someone tosses litter into the street, it becomes a problem for the municipal authorities. Weather conditions make the situation worse. Because of economic pressure, civic payrolls have declined. Litter may remain uncollected for long periods of time. Littering is a concern for everyone.

CONCRETE WORDS:

Every time one of us throws a McDonald's wrapper, a used paper cup, or a cigarette butt into the street, a sanitation worker has to come along and pick it up. If it rains before the cleanup truck gets to that street, the McDonald's wrapper becomes a soggy mess. Our city has 15 percent fewer sanitation workers than it did three years ago, because of the mayor's budget-trimming measures. So your McDonald's wrapper may lie in the street for two or three weeks, until it turns green—and you step in it! If you or I hadn't thrown the wrapper there to begin with, the city would have no mess to clean up.

Notice how much more persuasive the second version is. A speech dominated by concrete words will almost always be clearer, more interesting, and easier to recall than one dominated by abstract words.[12]

Eliminate Clutter

Cluttered speech has become a national epidemic. Whatever happened to such simple words as "before," "if," and "now"? When last seen they were being routed by their cluttered counterparts—"prior to," "in the eventuality of," and "at this point in time." By the same token, why can't weather forecasters say "It's raining," instead of saying "It appears as if we are currently experiencing precipitation activity"? And why can't politicians say "We have a crisis," instead of saying "We are facing a difficult crisis situation that will be troublesome to successfully resolve"?

This type of clutter is deadly to clear, compelling speech. It forces listeners to hack through a tangle of words to discover the meaning. When you make a speech, keep your language lean and lively. Beware of using several words where one or two will do. Avoid flabby phrases. Let your ideas emerge sharply and firmly. Above all, watch out for redundant adjectives and adverbs. Inexperienced speakers (and writers) tend to string together two or three synonymous adjectives, such as "a learned and educated man," or "a hot, steamy, torrid day."

Here is part of a student speech that has been revised to eliminate clutter.

Rock music is such a big ~~and important~~ part ~~of all~~ of our lives ~~today~~ that it is *hard* ~~extremely difficult~~ to imagine a time ~~in which~~ *when* people lived without it. But there was ~~once~~ such a time. ~~It was only 25 to 30 years ago.~~ The early 1950s were a time of bubble gum and soda pop—a pure and simple age. Then a new kind of music ~~started~~ *emerged* ~~coming on the scene~~ like a ~~huge~~ tidal wave ~~pouring onto~~ *engulfing* a ~~calm and~~ quiet beach. ~~A~~ ~~whole lot of~~ *Many* young performers ~~were appearing who~~ were revolutionizing ~~the shape of~~ American popular music. Bill Haley, Chuck Berry, Elvis Presley, Fats Domino, Little Richard, Jerry Lee Lewis—the list ~~is a long one that~~ goes on and on. But one ~~rock and roll~~ performer stands out ~~above the rest~~ as the most ~~original and~~ innovative of ~~them~~ all. His name? Buddy Holly.

Notice how much cleaner and easier to follow the revised version is. No longer are the speaker's ideas hidden in a thicket of wasted words.

This kind of pruning is easy once you get the knack of it. The hardest part—and it is often very hard—is recognizing clutter for what it is and then forcing yourself to throw away the unnecessary words. Watch for clutter when you write your speech outlines. Be prepared to revise the outline until your ideas emerge as clearly and crisply as possible. As with revising an essay or a term paper, this will take extra time. But if you keep at it, you will become a much more effective speaker—and writer.

You can also help eliminate clutter by practicing your speeches with one or more reliable friends. Ask your friends to keep an ear out not just for flabby phrases but for verbal fillers such as "you know," "like," and "really." (If you are a habitual "you-know"-er, you will find this exasperating at first, but try to stay with it. You will discover that people listen to you much more seriously when you conquer this verbal tic.)

After your friends have helped you trim the clutter, practice delivering the speech again. At first you may feel awkward and unnatural because you are forcing yourself to break old habits. But if you practice regularly and concentrate on trimming your speeches of wasted words, you will gradually develop a new habit of speaking naturally without all that clutter. This will not only make you a better public speaker, but it will help you present ideas more effectively in meetings, conversations, and group discussions.

USING LANGUAGE VIVIDLY

Just as you can be accurate without being clear, so you can be both accurate and clear without being interesting. Here, for example, is how Martin Luther King *might have* phrased part of his great "I Have a Dream" speech:

> Turning back is something we cannot do. We must continue to work against police brutality, segregated housing, disfranchisement, and alienation. Only when these problems are solved will we be satisfied.

Here is what King *actually* said:

> We cannot turn back. There are those who ask the devotees of civil rights, "When will you be satisfied?" We can never be satisfied as long as the Negro is the victim of the unspeakable horrors of police brutality. We can never be satisfied as long as our bodies, heavy with the fatigue of travel, cannot gain lodging in the motels of the highways and the hotels of the cities. We cannot be satisfied as long as a Negro in Mississippi cannot vote and a Negro in New York believes he has nothing for which

to vote. No, no, we are not satisfied, and we will not be satisfied until justice rolls down like waters and righteousness like a mighty stream.

Much more stirring isn't it? If you want to move people with your speeches, use moving language. Dull, dreary words make for dull, dreary speeches. Bring your speeches to life by using vivid, animated language. Although there are several ways to do this, here are two of the most important—imagery and rhythm.

Imagery

One sign of a good novelist is the ability to create word pictures that get you totally involved with a story. These word pictures let you "see" the haunted house, or "feel" the bite of the snow against your face, or "hear" the birds chirping on a warm spring morning, or "smell" the bacon cooking over an open campfire, or "taste" the hot enchiladas at a Mexican restaurant.

Speakers can use imagery in much the same way to make their ideas come alive. Consider the following description of the tragedy at Bhopal, India, in 1984:

The cloud of death seemed to come from nowhere. Workers at the Union Carbide plant in Bhopal did not take the gas leak seriously. On the night of December 2, 1984, they noticed the leak of methyl isocyanate at 11:30, but they decided to take a tea break before dealing with it. By the time their tea break was over an hour later, the town was doomed.

The cloud seeped out of the plant, slowly at first, then gaining strength, assuming a life of its own. It rose on the wind, formed itself, and swept through the city like an evil spell, leaving agony in its path. Wakened from sleep, the citizens of Bhopal poured from their homes, coughing, gasping for air, gagging, rubbing their streaming eyes. Many dropped in the streets, overcome by the choking stench. Many were blinded and tried to grope their way, sightless, to find help, any help. Before it finished its grisly work, the cloud of death had taken the lives of 2,000 people.

As this example indicates, *concrete words* are the key to effective imagery. They call up mental impressions of sights, sounds, touch, smell, and taste. In the speech just quoted, we do not merely learn that Bhopal experienced a devastating leak of poison gas. We visualize the "cloud of death" sweeping malevolently through the city, see it as an evil presence poised to kill. We identify with the helpless citizens who were "coughing, gasping for air, gagging, rubbing their streaming eyes." Because most listeners have some points of reference for these sights and sensations, the concrete words lead them to recall these references and to connect them with the speaker's ideas.

Besides the use of concrete words, two other devices for developing imagery are simile and metaphor. *Simile* is an explicit comparison between things that are essentially different yet have something in common. It always contains the words "like" or "as." Here are examples from student speeches:

The Philippine islands lie like pieces of broken emerald that were dropped into the South China Sea by some giant.

At John Kennedy's funeral procession, the American flag was draped over his coffin like a mother's arm wrapped around her child.

These are bright, fresh similes that clarify and vitalize ideas. Some similes, however, have become stale through overuse. Here are a few:

fresh as a daisy	hungry as a bear
fit as a fiddle	busy as a bee
strong as an ox	big as a mountain
stubborn as a mule	happy as a lark
blind as a bat	light as a feather

Such clichés are fine in everyday conversation, but you should avoid them in speechmaking. Otherwise, you are likely to be "dull as dishwater" and to find your audience "sleeping like a log"!

Metaphor is an implicit comparison between things that are essentially different yet have something in common. Unlike simile, metaphor does not contain the words "like" or "as." These examples are also from student speeches:

Walt Disney became a stock item in our cupboards. He was the spoonful of sugar that sweetened life's bitter medicine.

Mae West was not the cause of America's change in attitudes about women and sex. She wasn't the engine of the train, she was the oil on the wheels. She made the trip smoother and easier.

Metaphor, like simile, is an excellent way to turn a phrase. Sometimes, however, metaphors get out of control. The result is a *mixed metaphor,* in which two or more incongruous comparisons are run together—sometimes with comic results. Here is a classic example:

Communism is the snake in the grass which is gnawing at the foundations of our ship of state.

The speaker begins by comparing communism to a snake in the grass. Having done so, he then needs to make it behave like a snake. Instead, he has it gnawing at foundations—which would be fine for a rat or a termite, but not for a snake. To make matters worse, the foundations at which the snake is gnawing are the foundations of our ship of state. But ships, unlike buildings, do not have foundations. They have keels, bottoms, or hulls. Most ludicrous of all, the obviously talented snake who is gnawing at the ship's foundations is a snake in the *grass*—which can only mean that our ship of state is already beached or is sailing boldly on a meadow![13]

Needless to say, such a metaphor does more harm than good. When used effectively, however, metaphor—like simile—is an excellent way to bring color to a speech, to make abstract ideas concrete, to clarify the unknown, and to express feelings and emotions.

Rhythm

Language has a rhythm created by the choice and arrangement of words. Sometimes the appeal of a statement depends almost entirely on its rhythm—as in this children's verse:

> Pease porridge hot,
> Pease porridge cold,
> Pease porridge in the pot,
> Nine days old.

There is little meaning here. The appeal comes from the combination of sounds, which gives the passage an almost musical cadence.[14]

Speakers, like poets, sometimes seek to exploit the rhythm of language. By catching up their listeners in an arresting string of sounds, speakers can enhance the impact of their words—and therefore of their ideas. Winston Churchill was a master at this. Here is a passage from one of his famous speeches during World War II. To emphasize its cadence, the passage has been printed as if it were poetry rather than prose:

> We shall not flag or fail.
> We shall go on to the end.
> Even though large tracts of Europe
> and many old and famous states
> May fall into the grip of the Gestapo
> and all the odious apparatus of Nazi rule,
> We shall fight with growing confidence
> and strength in the air.
> We shall defend our island
> whatever the cost may be.
> We shall fight on the beaches.
> We shall fight on the landing grounds.
> We shall fight in the fields
> and in the streets.
> We shall fight in the hills.
> We shall never surrender.

The impact of the passage was heightened by Churchill's superb delivery; but even by themselves the words take on an emphatic rhythm that reinforces the message. You can see why John Kennedy said later that Churchill "mobilized the English language and sent it into battle."

Of course, a speech is not a poem. You should never emphasize sound and rhythm at the expense of meaning. And you may never have paid much conscious attention to the rhythm and flow of language. But you can develop an ear for vocal rhythms by study and practice. What's more, you can easily begin now to use four basic stylistic devices employed by Churchill and other fine speakers to enhance the rhythm of their prose.[15]

The first device is *parallelism*—the similar arrangement of a pair or series of related words, phrases, or sentences. For example:

> The denial of human rights *anywhere is a threat to* human rights *everywhere.* Injustice *anywhere is a threat to* justice *everywhere.* (Jesse Jackson)

> We will do that not so much *with speeches that* sound good as *with speeches that* are good and sound. Not so much *with speeches that* bring people to their feet as *with speeches that* bring people to their senses. (Mario Cuomo)

The effects of parallelism are perhaps best illustrated by seeing what happens when it is absent. For instance, compare this statement:

> Our mission is at once the oldest and most basic of this country—to right wrong, to do justice, to serve man. (Lyndon Johnson)

with this one:

> Our mission is at once the oldest and most basic of this country—to right wrong, to do justice, and serving man.

The first sentence is clear, consistent, and compelling. The second is not. By violating the principle of parallel structure, its final phrase ("and serving man") destroys the progression begun by the two preceding phrases ("to right wrong, to do justice"). It thereby turns a strong, lucid, harmonious sentence into one that is fuzzy and jarring.

The second device you can use to lend rhythm to your speeches is *repetition.* This means repeating the same word or set of words at the beginning or end of successive clauses or sentences. For example:

> *We left America* safe, *we left America* secure, *we left America* free—*still a* beacon of hope to mankind, *still a* light unto the nations. (Ronald Reagan)

> *Now is the time* to make real the promises of democracy. *Now is the time* to rise from the dark and desolate valley of segregation to the sunlit path of racial justice. *Now is the time* to lift our nation from the quicksand of racial injustice to the solid rock of brotherhood. (Martin Luther King)

As you can see, repetition inevitably results in parallelism. In addition to building a strong cadence, it also unifies a sequence of ideas, emphasizes an idea by stating it more than once, and helps create a strong emotional effect.

Alliteration is a third device you can use to enhance the rhythm of your speeches. The most common method of alliteration is repeating the initial consonant sound of close or adjoining words. For example:

> We will be *c*andid, *c*onsistent, and *c*onfident. (Gerald Ford)

> The *t*ask is heavy, the *t*oil is long, and the *t*rials will be severe. (Winston Churchill)

By highlighting the sounds of words, alliteration catches the attention of listeners and can make ideas easier to remember. Used sparingly, it is a marvelous way to spruce up your speeches. Used to excess, however, it can be laughable and draw too much attention, so that listeners get more involved in waiting for the next alliteration than in absorbing the content of the speech.

Finally, you might try using *antithesis*—the juxtaposition of contrasting ideas, usually in parallel structure. For example:

> Let us never negotiate out of fear. But let us never fear to negotiate. (John F. Kennedy)

> Ask not what your country can do for you; ask what you can do for your country. (John F. Kennedy)

It is no accident that both of these examples are from speeches by President Kennedy. Antithesis was one of his favorite figures of speech, and the one used in his most memorable phrases. Because antithesis nearly always produces a neatly turned phrase, it is a fine way to give your ideas extra impact as well as a special touch of class.[16]

You may be thinking that imagery and rhythm are fine for famous people like King and Kennedy, but are too fancy for ordinary speeches like yours. This is not true. Imagery and rhythm are easy to use and can enliven even the most routine of speeches. As an example, take a look at the following excerpt from a student speech about Mother Teresa, the famed nun who has spent much of her life working among the poor people of Calcutta, India, and who received the Nobel Peace Prize in 1979:

> Faced with the same position, could we survive? Could we survive the stench and stink of the wretched Calcutta shanty towns? Mother Teresa survives.
> Could we survive the sickness and disease which slowly rot these poor people to the skin and bones of half-existence? Mother Teresa survives.
> Could we survive the cries of hunger which squeal, then groan, then stop— eternally extinguished? Mother Teresa survives.
> Could we survive the sight of emaciated bodies, thin shrouds of skin stretched tightly over brittle, bulging bones? Mother Teresa survives—because she touches the

sick, she touches the homeless, she touches the underclothed and undernourished, she touches the helpless and the hopeless and the dying.

This is vivid, moving language. The imagery is sharp and poignant; the rhythm strong and insistent. Think of how you can do similar things to enliven your own speeches.

USING LANGUAGE APPROPRIATELY

Here is part of a famous oration given by John Hancock in 1774, during the American Revolution. Speaking of the British soldiers who killed five Americans in the Boston massacre, Hancock exclaimed:

Ye dark designing knaves, ye murderers, parricides! How dare you tread upon the earth, which has drank in the blood of slaughtered innocents shed by your wicked hands? How dare you breathe that air which wafted to the ear of heaven the groans of those who fell a sacrifice to your accursed ambition? . . . Tell me, ye bloody butchers, ye villains high and low, ye wretches . . . do you not feel the goads and stings of conscious guilt pierce through your savage bosoms?

This is certainly vivid language—and Hancock's audience loved it. But can you imagine speaking the same way today? In addition to being accurate, clear, and vivid, language should also be appropriate—to the occasion, to the audience, to the topic, and to the speaker.

Language that is appropriate for some occasions may not be appropriate for others. "There is a time for dialect, a place for slang, an occasion for literary form. What is correct on the sports page is out of place on the op-ed page; what is with-it on the street may well be without it in the classroom."[17] As a simple example, a coach might address the football team as "you guys" (or worse!), whereas the speaker in a more formal situation would begin with "ladies and gentlemen" or "distinguished guests." Try reversing these two situations, and see how ridiculous it becomes. It's only common sense to adjust your language to different occasions.

Appropriateness also depends on the audience. If you keep this in mind, it will help you greatly when dealing with technical or scientific subjects. When addressing an audience of physicians, for example, you might choose the word "paratosis" to refer to a viral disease marked by the swelling of the parotid glands. Your audience would know just what you meant. But when talking to a nonmedical audience, such as your classmates, a word like "paratosis" would not be appropriate. Your listeners would not understand it and might find you stuffy and pretentious. The appropriate word in this case would be "mumps."

You should be especially careful to avoid language that might offend your audience. If you were a stand-up comic, off-color humor or obscenity might be appropriate in a night club routine, but most listeners would find it offensive in a formal public speech. The same is true of language that might be perceived as racist or sexist. Many people, for instance, take offense at statements that refer to all members of occupational groups as "he." Suppose you want to say:

Each time a surgeon walks into the operating room, *he* risks a malpractice suit.

But not all surgeons are men. You can say instead:

Each time a surgeon walks into the operating room, *he or she* risks a malpractice suit.

Often, a more graceful way to solve this problem is to pluralize. For example:

Whenever surgeons walk into the operating room, *they* risk being sued for malpractice.

Using "he or she" or changing your pronoun to "they" may seem like a minor matter to you, but it may be very important to some members of your audience.[18]

Of course, you cannot always know for sure how listeners will respond to what you say. As a general rule, bend over backward to avoid language that may confuse or annoy your listeners. When it comes to appropriateness, you will seldom go wrong by erring on the side of caution. (Simply put, "erring on the side of caution" means: When in doubt—don't.)

Language should also be appropriate to the topic. You would not use metaphor, antithesis, and alliteration when explaining how to change a bicycle tire or how to perform routine maintenance on a car. But you might use all three in a speech celebrating the genius of Leonardo da Vinci or honoring the American soldiers who died in Vietnam. The first two topics call for straight-forward description and explanation. The latter two call for special language skills to evoke emotion, admiration, and appreciation.

No matter what the occasion, audience, or topic, language should also be appropriate to the speaker. Imagine the effect if George Bush tried to adopt the religious imagery and rhythmical cadence of Jesse Jackson. The results would be absurd. Every public speaker develops his or her own language style. Mario Cuomo seeks to create striking phrases through imagery, antithesis, and metaphor; Lee Iacocca seldom uses such devices. Yet both are among the most successful speakers in America.

"Terrific," you may be thinking. "I have my own style too. I feel more comfortable using abstract words, slang, and technical jargon. That's just me. It's *my* way of speaking." But to say language should be appropriate to the speaker does not justify ignoring the other needs for appropriateness. There is a difference between one's everyday personal style and one's *developed* style as a public speaker. Cuomo, Iacocca, and other accomplished speakers have developed their speaking styles over many years of trial, error, and practice. They have *worked* at using language effectively.

You can do the same if you become language conscious. Analyze your strengths and weaknesses. Work to increase your vocabulary and command of the language. Read and listen to the speeches of people like Cuomo, Iacocca, Churchill, and King. Study their techniques for achieving accuracy, clarity, and vividness, and try to adapt those techniques to your own speeches. But do not try to "become" someone else when you speak. Learn from other speakers, blend what you learn into your own language style, and seek to become the best possible you.

SUMMARY

Of all human creations, language may be the most remarkable. Through language we share experiences, formulate values, exchange ideas, transmit knowledge, and sustain culture. Indeed, language is vital to thinking itself. Contrary to popular belief, language does not simply mirror reality but helps to create our sense of reality by giving meaning to events.

Good speakers have respect for language and how it works. Words are the tools of a speaker's craft. They have special uses, just like the tools of any other profession. As a speaker, you should be aware of the meanings of words and know how to use language accurately, clearly, vividly, and appropriately.

Words have two kinds of meanings—denotative and connotative. Denotative meaning is precise, literal, and objective. It simply describes whatever a word refers to. One way to think of a word's denotative meaning is as its dictionary definition. Connotative meaning is more variable, figurative, and subjective. It is whatever the word suggests or implies. Connotative meaning includes all the feelings, associations, and emotions that a word touches off in different people.

Using language accurately is as vital to a speaker as using numbers accurately is to an accountant. Never use a word unless you are sure of its meaning. If you are not sure, look up the word in a dictionary. As you prepare your speeches, ask yourself constantly, "What do I *really* want to say? What do I *really* mean?" Choose words that are precise and accurate.

Using language clearly allows listeners to grasp your meaning immediately. You can assure this by using familiar words that are known to the average person and require no specialized background; by choosing concrete words in preference to more abstract ones; and by eliminating verbal clutter.

Using language vividly helps bring your speech to life. One way to make your language more vivid is through imagery, or the creation of word pictures. You can develop imagery by using concrete language, simile, and metaphor. Simile is an *explicit* comparison between things that are essentially different yet have something in common; it always contains the words "like" or "as." Metaphor is an *implicit* comparison between things that are different yet have something in common; it does not contain the words "like" or "as."

Another way to make your speeches vivid is by exploiting the rhythm of language. Four devices for creating rhythm are parallelism, repetition, alliteration, and antithesis. Parallelism is the similar arrangement of a pair or series of related words, phrases, or sentences. Repetition is the use of the same word or set of words at the beginning or end of successive clauses or sentences. Alliteration comes from repeating the initial consonant sounds of close or adjoining words. Antithesis is the juxtaposition of contrasting ideas, usually in parallel structure.

Using language appropriately means adapting to the particular occasion, audience, and topic at hand. It also means developing your own language style instead of trying to copy someone else's. If your language is appropriate in all respects, your speech is much more likely to succeed.

REVIEW QUESTIONS

After reading this chapter you should be able to answer the following questions:

1. How does language help to shape our sense of reality?

2. What is the difference between denotative and connotative meaning? How might you use each to convey your message most effectively?

3. What are the four criteria for using language effectively in your speeches?

4. What are the two aspects of accurate language you should pay attention to in preparing your speeches?

5. What are three things you should do to use language clearly in your speeches?

6. What are two ways to bring your speeches to life with vivid, animated language?

7. What does it mean to say you should use language appropriately in your speeches?

APPLICATION EXERCISES

1. Arrange each of the sequences below in order, from the most abstract word to the most concrete word.

   a. broccoli, greens, plant, vegetable
   b. elected official, Franklin Roosevelt, politician, President
   c. novel, book, publication, *Moby Dick*
   d. weapon, .38 revolver, firearms, handguns, guns

2. In each of the following sentences, select the most appropriate word to complete the statement.

   a.   walk, trudge, stroll, march

   On spring afternoons we like to _____ through the botanical gardens.

   I was too tired to do anything but _____ home.

   The best part about parades is watching the bands _____ by.

   If you _____ instead of driving, you'll improve your cardiovascular fitness.

   b.   madness, eccentricity, obsession, infatuation

   Professor Schwartz never wears an overcoat, even on the coldest days. That's his personal _____.

   My friend Jean has every Elvis Presley record ever made. She's gone beyond collecting to the point of _____.

   Cynthia's love for Tom Selleck isn't real love. It's just _____.

   My public speaking instructor thinks I'm going to deliver five speeches this semester. That's _____.

3. Rewrite each of the following sentences using clear, familiar words.

   a.   To pay for his crimes he will be incarcerated in a penal institution.
   b.   Subsequent to next Wednesday's meeting, we will implement the newly enacted guidelines.
   c.   I cannot conceive of any situation in which such an outcome could eventuate.
   d.   If we find the reasonable probability of repayment is slipping away from us, then we will have to respond in terms of nonextension of credit.
   e.   The citizenry were stirred to indignation by the recent action of their elected legislative representatives in Congress for increasing the burden of taxation.

4. Analyze Martin Luther King's "I Have a Dream" (Appendix, pages 399–402). Identify the methods King uses to make his language clear, vivid, and appropriate. Look particularly at King's use of familiar words, concrete words, imagery, and rhythm.

NOTES

[1] *New Yorker,* review of Edwin Newman, *A Civil Tongue* (New York: Warner, 1975).
[2] For two excellent and highly readable studies of changes in the English language over the years, see Robert Claiborne, *Our Marvelous Native Tongue: The Life and Times of the English Language* (New York: New York Times Books, 1983); Robert

McCrum, William Cran, and Robert MacNeil, *The Story of English* (New York: Viking, 1986).

[3] See, for example, Murray Edelman, *Political Language: Words That Succeed and Policies That Fail* (New York: Academic Press, 1977); Richard B. Gregg, *Symbolic Inducement and Knowing: A Study in the Foundations of Rhetoric* (Columbia: University of South Carolina Press, 1984).

[4] James R. Andrews, *A Choice of Worlds: The Practice and Criticism of Public Discourse* (New York: Harper & Row, 1973).

[5] This has been understood for many years by teachers of rhetoric. See the comment of Hugh Blair, in his *Lectures on Rhetoric and Belles Lettres* (London: W. Strahan, 1783), I, 245: "We may rest assured, that whenever we express ourselves ill, there is, besides the mismanagement of language, for the most part, some mistake in conceiving the subject. Embarrassed, obscure, and feeble sentences are generally, if not always, the result of embarrassed, obscure, and feeble thought. Thought and language act and react upon each other mutually. . . . He that is learning to arrange his sentences with accuracy and order is learning, at the same time, to think with accuracy and order."

[6] Clarence M. Kelley, quoted in Robert C. Jeffrey and Owen Peterson, *Speech: A Text with Adapted Readings,* 3rd ed. (New York: Harper & Row, 1980), pp. 386–387.

[7] Cited in Edward P. J. Corbett, *Classical Rhetoric for the Modern Student* (New York: Oxford University Press, 1971), p. 453.

[8] See, for example, Shelly Chaiken and Alice H. Eagly, "Communication Modality as a Determinant of Message Persuasiveness and Message Comprehensibility," *Journal of Personality and Social Psychology,* 34 (1976), 605–614.

[9] Dorothy Sarnoff, *Speech Can Change Your Life* (New York: Doubleday, 1970), p. 71.

[10] Annmarie Mungo, "A Child Is Born," in *Winning Orations, 1980* (Mankato, Minn.: Interstate Oratorical Association, 1980), pp. 49–50.

[11] These numbers are based on the text of the Gettysburg Address in Roy P. Basler (ed.), *The Collected Works of Abraham Lincoln* (New Brunswick, N.J.: Rutgers University Press, 1953), VII, 23.

[12] This has been confirmed by a number of studies, including Ian Begg and Allan Paivio, "Concreteness and Imagery in Sentence Meaning," *Journal of Verbal Learning and Verbal Behavior,* 8 (1969), 821–837; C. C. Jorgensen and W. Kintsch, "The Role of Imagery in the Evaluation of Sentences," *Cognitive Psychology,* 4 (1973), 110–116.

[13] Richard M. Weaver, *A Rhetoric and Composition Handbook* (New York: William Morrow, 1974), p. 251.

[14] Lawrence Perrine, *Literature: Structure, Sound, and Sense* (New York: Harcourt, Brace and World, 1956), p. 728.

[15] For an interesting discussion of rhythm in speechmaking, see Jerry Tarver, "Words in Time: Some Reflections on the Language of Speech," *Vital Speeches,* 54 (1988), 410–412.

[16] For fuller discussion of these and other stylistic devices, see Arthur Quinn, *Figures of Speech: Sixty Ways to Turn a Phrase* (Salt Lake City: Gibbs M. Smith, 1982).

[17] William Safire, *On Language* (New York: Times Books, 1980), p. xiv.

[18] The best guide on this subject is Casey Miller and Kate Swift, *The Handbook of Nonsexist Writing for Writers, Editors, and Speakers* (New York: Lippincott and Crowell, 1980).

CHAPTER 11

Delivery

I f you were to tape-record one of Johnny Carson's monologues, memorize it word for word, and stand up before your friends to recite it, would you get the same response Carson does? Not very likely. And why not? Because you would not *deliver* the jokes as Carson does. Of course, the jokes are basically funny. They should be, given Carson's team of highly paid writers. But Johnny Carson brings something extra to the jokes—his manner of presentation, his vocal inflections, his perfectly calculated pauses, his facial expressions, his gestures. All these are part of a masterful delivery. It would take you years of practice—as it took Carson—to duplicate his results.

No one expects your speech class to transform you into a multimillion-dollar talk show host. Still, this example demonstrates how important delivery can be to any public speaking situation. Even a mediocre speech will be more effective if it is presented well, whereas a wonderfully written speech can be ruined by poor delivery.

This does not mean dazzling delivery will turn a mindless string of nonsense into a triumphant oration. You cannot make a good speech without having something to say. But having something to say is not enough. You must also know *how* to say it.

WHAT IS GOOD DELIVERY?

Wendell Phillips was a leader in the movement to abolish slavery in the United States during the 1800s. Some people considered him the greatest speaker of his time. The following story suggests one reason why:

Shortly before the Civil War an Andover student, learning that Phillips was to lecture in Boston, made a twenty-two mile pilgrimage on foot to hear him. At first the trip seemed hardly worthwhile, for the student discovered that Phillips was not an orator in the grand manner, but spoke in an almost conversational style. He stood on the platform, one hand lightly resting on a table, talked for what seemed to be about twenty minutes, concluded, and sat down. When the student looked at his watch, he found to his astonishment that he had been listening for an hour and a half![1]

Good delivery does not call attention to itself. It conveys the speaker's ideas clearly, interestingly, and without distracting the audience. If you mumble your words, shuffle your feet, gaze out the window, or talk in a monotone, you will not get your message across. Nor will you be effective if you show off, strike a dramatic pose, or shout in ringing tones. Most audiences prefer delivery that combines a certain degree of formality with the best attributes of good conversation—directness, spontaneity, animation, emphasis, and a lively sense of communication.[2]

When you begin speaking in public, you will probably have many questions about delivery: "Should I be strong and aggressive or low-key?" "Where should

I stand?" "How should I gesture?" "How should I handle my notes?" "How fast should I speak?" "When should I pause?" "Where should I look?" "What do I do if I make a mistake?"

There are no hard-and-fast answers to these questions. Speech delivery is an art, not a science. What works for one speaker may fail for another. And what succeeds with today's audience may not with tomorrow's. You cannot become a skilled speaker just by following a set of rules in a textbook. In the long run, there is no substitute for experience. But take heart! A textbook *can* give you basic pointers to get you started in the right direction.

When you plan your first speech (or second or third), you should concentrate on such basics as speaking intelligibly, avoiding distracting mannerisms, and establishing eye contact with your listeners. Once you get these elements under control and begin to feel fairly comfortable in front of an audience, you can work on polishing your delivery to enhance the impact of your ideas. Eventually, you may find yourself able to control the timing, rhythm, and momentum of a speech as skillfully as a conductor controls an orchestra.

METHODS OF DELIVERY

There are four basic methods of delivering a speech: (1) reading verbatim from a manuscript; (2) reciting a memorized text; (3) speaking impromptu; and (4) speaking extemporaneously. Let us look at each.

Reading from a Manuscript

Certain speeches *must* be delivered word for word, according to a meticulously prepared manuscript. Examples include a Pope's religious proclamations, an engineer's report to a professional meeting, or a President's message to Congress. In such situations, absolute accuracy is essential. Every word of the speech will be analyzed by the press, by colleagues, perhaps by enemies. In the case of the President, a misstated phrase could cause an international incident.

Timing may also be a factor in manuscript speeches. Much of today's political campaigning is done on radio and television. If the candidate buys a one-minute spot and pays a great deal of money for it, that one minute of speech must be just right.

Although it looks easy, delivering a speech from a manuscript requires great skill. Some people do it well. Their words "come alive as if coined on the spot."[3] Others seem to ruin it every time. Instead of sounding vibrant and conversational, they come across as wooden and artificial. They falter over words, pause in the wrong places, read too quickly or too slowly, speak in a monotone, and march through the speech without even glancing at their audience. In short, they come across as *reading to* their listeners, not *talking with* them.

If you are in a situation where you must speak from a manuscript, do your best to avoid these problems. Practice aloud to make sure the speech sounds natural. Work on establishing eye contact with your listeners. Be certain the final manuscript is legible at a glance. Above all, reach out to your audience with the same directness and sincerity that you would if speaking extemporaneously.[4]

Reciting from Memory

Among the feats of the legendary orators, none leaves us more in awe than their practice of presenting even the longest and most complex speeches entirely from memory. Nowadays it is no longer customary to memorize any but the shortest of speeches—toasts, congratulatory remarks, acceptance speeches, introductions, and the like. If you are giving a speech of this kind and want to memorize it, by all means do so. However, be sure to memorize it so thoroughly that you will be able to concentrate on communicating with the audience, not on trying to remember the words. Speakers who gaze at the ceiling or stare out the window trying to recall what they have memorized are no better off than those who read dully from a manuscript.

Speaking Impromptu

An impromptu speech is delivered without any immediate preparation whatever. Few people choose to speak impromptu, but sometimes it cannot be avoided. In fact, many of the speeches you give in life will be impromptu. You might be called on suddenly to "say a few words" or, in the course of a class discussion, business meeting, or committee report, want to respond to a previous speaker.

When such situations arise, don't panic. No one expects you to deliver a perfect speech on the spur of the moment. If you are in a meeting or discussion, pay close attention to what the other speakers say. Take notes of major points you agree with or disagree with. In the process, you will automatically begin to formulate what you will say when it is your turn to speak.

In many cases you will be able to speak informally without rising from your chair. But if the situation calls for you to speak from a lectern, walk to it calmly, take a deep breath or two (not a visible gasp), establish eye contact with your audience, and begin speaking. No matter how nervous you are inside, do your best to look calm and assured on the outside.

Whenever you are responding to a previous speaker, try to present your speech in four simple steps: First, state the point you are answering. Second, state the point you wish to make. Third, support your point with appropriate statistics, examples, or testimony. Fourth, summarize and restate your point. This four-step method will help you organize your thoughts quickly and clearly.[5]

Whether you realize it or not, you have given thousands of impromptu "speeches" in daily conversation—as when you informed a new student how to register for classes, or explained to your boss why you were late for work, or answered questions in a job interview, or tried to persuade your roommate to loan you ten dollars until next week. There is no reason to fall apart when you are asked to speak impromptu in a more formal situation. If you keep cool, organize your thoughts, and limit yourself to a few remarks, you should do just fine.

Speaking Extemporaneously

In popular usage, "extemporaneous" means the same as "impromptu." But technically the two are different. Unlike an impromptu speech, which is totally off the cuff, an extemporaneous speech is carefully prepared and practiced in advance. In presenting the speech, the extemporaneous speaker uses only a set of brief notes or a speaking outline to jog the memory (see pages 198–202). The exact wording is chosen at the moment of delivery.

This is not as hard as it sounds. Once you have your outline (or notes) and know what topics you are going to cover and in what order, you can begin to practice the speech. Every time you run through it, the wording will be slightly different. As you practice the speech over and over, the best way to present each part will emerge and stick in your mind.

The extemporaneous method has several advantages. It gives more precise control over thought and language than does impromptu speaking; it offers greater spontaneity and directness than does speaking from memory or from a full manuscript; and it is adaptable to a wide range of situations. It also encourages the conversational quality audiences look for in speech delivery. "Conversational quality" means that no matter how many times a speech has been rehearsed, it still *sounds* spontaneous to the audience. When you speak extemporaneously—and have prepared properly—you have full control over your ideas, yet you are not tied to a manuscript. You are free to establish strong eye contact, to gesture naturally, and to concentrate on talking *with* the audience rather than declaiming *to* them.

Most experienced speakers prefer the extemporaneous method, and most teachers emphasize it. At the end of this chapter, we'll look at a step-by-step program for practicing your extemporaneous delivery.

THE SPEAKER'S VOICE

What kind of voice do you have? Is it rich and resonant like Kris Kristofferson's? Husky and alluring like Debra Winger's? Thin and nasal like Vin Scully's?

Squeaky and irritating like Pee Wee Herman's? Deep and powerful like Barbara Jordan's?

Whatever the characteristics of your voice, you can be sure it is unique. Because no two people are exactly the same physically, no two people have identical voices. This is why voiceprints are sometimes used in criminal trials as guides to personal identity. The human voice is produced by a complex series of steps that starts with the exhalation of air from the lungs. (Try talking intelligibly while inhaling and see what happens.) As air is exhaled, it passes through the larynx (or voice box), where it is vibrated to generate sound. This sound is then amplified and modified as it resonates through the throat, mouth, and nasal passages. Finally, the resonated sound is shaped into specific vowel and consonant sounds by the movement of the tongue, lips, teeth, and roof of the mouth. The resulting sounds are combined to form words and sentences.

The voice produced by this physical process will greatly affect the success of your speeches. A golden voice is certainly an asset, but you can manage without. Some of the most famous speakers in history had undistinguished voices. Abraham Lincoln had a harsh and penetrating voice; Winston Churchill suffered from a slight lisp and an awkward stammer; Will Rogers spoke with a nasal twang. Like them, you can overcome natural disadvantages and use your voice to the best effect. If you speak too softly to be heard, constantly stumble over words, spit out your ideas at machine-gun speed, or plod along as if you were reading a grocery list, your speeches will fail. Lincoln, Churchill, and Rogers learned to *control* their voices. You can do the same thing.

The aspects of voice you should work to control are volume, pitch, rate, pauses, variety, pronunciation, and articulation.

Volume

At one time a powerful voice was all but essential for an orator. Today, electronic amplification allows even the most feeble of speakers to be heard in any setting. But in the classroom you will speak without a microphone. When you do, be sure to adjust your voice to the acoustics of the room, the size of the audience, and the level of background noise. If you speak too loudly, your listeners will think you boorish. If you speak too softly, they will not understand you. Remember that your own voice always sounds louder to you than to a listener. Soon after beginning your speech, glance at the people farthest away from you. If they look puzzled, are leaning forward in their seats, or are otherwise straining to hear, you need to talk louder.

Pitch

Pitch is the highness or lowness of the speaker's voice. The faster sound waves vibrate, the higher their pitch; the slower they vibrate, the lower their pitch. Pitch distinguishes the sound produced by the keys at one end of a piano from that produced by the keys at the other end. In speech, pitch can affect the meaning of words or sounds. Pitch is what makes the difference between the "Aha!" triumphantly exclaimed by Sherlock Holmes upon discovering a seemingly decisive clue and the "Aha" he mutters when he learns the clue is not decisive after all. If you were to read the preceding sentence aloud, your voice would probably go up in pitch on the first "Aha" and down in pitch on the second.

Changes in pitch are known as *inflections.* They give your voice luster, warmth, and vitality. It is the inflection of your voice that reveals whether you are asking a question or making a statement; whether you are being sincere or sarcastic. Your inflections can also make you sound happy or sad, angry or pleased, dynamic or listless, tense or relaxed, interested or bored.

In ordinary conversation we instinctively use inflections to convey meaning and emotion. People who do not are said to speak in a *monotone*—a trait whose only known benefit is to cure insomnia in one's listeners. Few people speak in an absolute monotone, with no variation whatever in pitch, but many fall into repetitious pitch patterns that are just as hypnotic as a monotone. You can guard against this problem by tape-recording your speeches as you practice them. If all your sentences end on the same inflection—either upward or downward—work on varying your pitch patterns to fit the meaning of your words. As with breaking any other habit, this may seem awkward at first, but it is guaranteed to make you a better speaker.[6]

Rate

Rate refers to the speed at which a person speaks. Americans usually speak at a rate between 120 and 150 words per minute, but there is no uniform rate for effective speechmaking. Daniel Webster spoke at roughly 90 words per minute, Franklin Roosevelt at 110, John Kennedy at 180. Martin Luther King opened his "I Have a Dream" speech at a pace of 92 words per minute and finished it at 145. The best rate of speech depends on several things—the vocal attributes of the speaker, the mood he or she is trying to create, the composition of the audience, and the nature of the occasion.[7]

For example, if you wanted to convey the excitement of the Indianapolis 500 car race, you would probably speak rather quickly, but a slower rate would be more appropriate to describe the serenity of the Alaskan wilderness. A fast rate helps to create feelings of happiness, fear, anger, and surprise, while a slow rate is better for expressing sadness or disgust. A slower tempo is called for when you explain complex information, a faster tempo when the information is already familiar to the audience. Finally, research suggests that in most situations listeners will find a speaker with a somewhat faster rate than normal to be more competent and more persuasive than a speaker with a slower rate.[8]

Two obvious faults to avoid are speaking so slowly that your listeners get bored or so quickly that they lose track of your ideas. Novice speakers are particularly prone to racing through their speeches at a frantic rate. Fortunately, once a speaker begins to work on it, this is usually an easy habit to break, as is the less common one of crawling through one's speech at a snail's pace.

The key in both cases is becoming aware of the problem and concentrating on solving it. Use a tape recorder to check how fast you speak. Pay special attention to rate when practicing your speech. Finally, be sure to include reminders about delivery on your speaking outline, so you won't forget to make the adjustments when you give your speech in class.

Pauses

Learning when and how to pause is a major challenge for most beginning speakers. Even a moment of silence can seem like an eternity. As you gain more poise and confidence, however, you will discover how useful the pause can be. It can signal the end of a thought unit, give an idea time to sink in, and lend dramatic impact to a statement. "The right word may be effective," said Mark Twain, "but no word was ever as effective as a rightly timed pause."[9]

As Twain knew, the crucial factor is timing. "For one audience," he cautioned, "the pause will be short, for another a little longer, for another a shade longer still." Looking back on his own career as a speaker, he recalled: "When the pause was right the effect was sure; when the pause was wrong . . . the laughter was only mild, never a crash."[10]

Developing a keen sense of timing is partly a matter of common sense, partly a matter of experience. You will not always get your pauses just right at first, but keep trying. Listen to accomplished speakers to see how they use pauses to modulate the rate and rhythm of their messages. Work on pauses when you practice your speeches.

When you do pause, make sure you pause at the end of thought units and not in the middle. Otherwise, you may distract listeners from your ideas. Most important, do not fill the silence with "uh," "er," or "um." These *vocalized pauses,* as they are called, are always annoying, and they can be devastating. Not only do they create negative perceptions about a speaker's intelligence, but they often make a speaker appear deceptive.[11]

A classic example of this occurred in 1979, when Senator Edward Kennedy was battling for the Democratic presidential nomination. Two controversial issues about Kennedy were uppermost in the public's mind—his strained relationship with his wife and his accident at Chappaquiddick Island, in which a young woman drowned when a car driven by Kennedy plunged off a bridge. Kennedy had a perfect opportunity to defuse both issues in a television interview with newscaster Roger Mudd. The interview was aired nationally in prime time and drew a huge audience. Unfortunately for Kennedy, his delivery all but destroyed his credibility. When questioned, Kennedy seemed tentative and ill-at-ease. He looked down into his lap or off into the distance. Worst of all, he followed nearly every word with "uh" or "er." All of this made him seem evasive, even untruthful. After the interview, his standing in the public opinion polls dropped sharply. In the view of many experts, his campaign never fully recovered.

Vocal Variety

Just as variety is the spice of life, so is it the spice of public speaking. A flat, listless, unchanging voice is just as deadly to speechmaking as a flat, listless, unchanging routine is to daily life.

Try reading this limerick aloud:

I sat next to the Duchess at tea.
It was just as I feared it would be:
    Her rumblings abdominal
    Were simply abominable
And everyone thought it was me!

Now recite this passage from James Joyce's "All Day I Hear the Noise of Waters":

The grey winds, the cold winds are blowing
    Where I go.
I hear the noise of many waters
    Far below.
All day, all night, I hear them flowing
    To and fro.[12]

Certainly you did not utter both passages the same way. You instinctively varied the rate, pitch, volume, and pauses to distinguish the light-hearted limerick from the solemn melancholy of Joyce's poem. When giving a speech, you should modulate your voice in just this way to communicate your ideas and feelings.

How can you develop a lively, expressive voice? Above all, by approaching every speech as an opportunity to share with your listeners ideas that are important to you. Your sense of conviction and your desire to communicate will help give your voice the same spark it has in spontaneous conversation.

Diagnose your present speaking voice to decide which aspects need improvement. Tape record your speeches to hear how they sound. Try them out on members of your family, a friend, or a roommate. Check with your teacher for suggestions. Practice the vocal variety exercise at the end of this chapter. Vocal variety is a natural feature of ordinary conversation. There is no reason why it should not be as natural a feature of your speeches.

Pronunciation

We all mispronounce words now and again. Here, for example, are six words with which you are probably familiar. Say each one aloud:

genuine	err
schism	nuclear
theater	February

Very likely you made a mistake on at least one, for they are among the most frequently mispronounced words in our language. Let's see:

WORD	COMMON ERROR	CORRECT PRONUNCIATION
genuine	gen-u-wine	gen-u-win
schism	ski-zem	si-zem
theater	theé-até-er	theé-a-ter
err	air	ur
nuclear	nu-cu-lar	nu-cle-ar
February	Feb-u-ary	Feb-ru-ary

Every word leads a triple life: it is read, written, and spoken. Most people recognize and understand many more words in reading than they use in ordinary writing, and about three times as many as occur in spontaneous speech.[13] This is why we occasionally stumble when speaking words that are part of our reading or writing vocabularies. At other times, we may mispronounce the most commonplace words out of habit.

The problem is that we usually don't *know* when we are mispronouncing a word; otherwise we would say it correctly. If we are lucky, we learn the right pronunciation by hearing someone else say the word properly or by having someone gently correct us in private. If we are unlucky, we mispronounce the word in front of a roomful of people, who may raise their eyebrows, groan, or laugh. Even experienced speakers sometimes fall into this trap. In reporting about the 1984 presidential election, a local TV news anchorman referred several times to the number of votes needed to capture a majority in the e-lec-tóf-*e*-al college. When he had finished, his coanchor said (on the air!), "And it also takes 270 votes to win a majority in the e-leć-tor-al college." The first announcer tried to shrug it off, but he was noticeably embarrassed.

All of this argues for practicing your speech in front of as many trusted friends and relatives as you can corner. If you have any doubts about the proper pronunciation of certain words, be sure to check a dictionary.

There are, of course, regional and ethnic dialects that affect pronunciation. Some nonstandard pronunciations are perfectly acceptable to some audiences. In New York people may get "idears" about "dee-ah" friends. In Alabama mothers tell their children to clean up their rooms "rat now." In Utah people praise the "lard" and put the "lord" in the refrigerator. Such dialects are fine as long as your audience does not find them objectionable or confusing. Otherwise, you should try to avoid them, for they may cause listeners to make negative judgments about your personality, intelligence, competence, and integrity.[14]

Articulation

Articulation and pronunciation are not identical. Sloppy articulation is the failure to form particular speech sounds crisply and distinctly. It is one of several causes of mispronunciation; but not all errors in pronunciation stem from poor articulation.[15] You can articulate a word sharply and still mispronounce it. For example, if you say the "s" in "Illinois" or the "p" in "pneumonia," you are making a mistake in pronunciation, regardless of how precisely you articulate the sounds.

Errors in articulation can be caused by a cleft palate, by an overly large tongue, by a misaligned jaw, even by a poorly fitted dental plate or braces on the teeth. Serious problems require the aid of a certified speech therapist. But most of the time poor articulation is caused by laziness—by failing to manipulate the lips, tongue, jaw, and soft palate so as to produce speech sounds clearly and precisely. Whether or not Americans have "the worst articulation in the Western world,"[16] as one scholar claims, many of us are unquestionably sloppy speakers. We habitually chop, slur, and mumble our words rather than enunciating them plainly.

Among college students, poor articulation is more common than ignorance of correct pronunciation. We know that "let me" is not "lemme," that "going to" is not "gonna," that "did you" is not "didja," yet we persist in articulating these words improperly. Here are some other common errors in articulation you should work to avoid:

WORD	MISARTICULATION
ought to	otta
didn't	dint
coming	comin
don't know	dunno
have to	hafta
them	em
want to	wanna
will you	wilya

If you have sloppy articulation, work on identifying and eliminating your most common errors. Practice the articulation exercise at the end of this chapter. Like other bad habits, careless articulation can be broken only by persistent effort—but the results are well worth it. Not only will your speeches be more intelligible, but employers will be more likely to hire you, to place you in positions of responsibility, and to promote you. As Shakespeare advised, "Mend your speech a little, lest you may mar your fortunes."

NONVERBAL COMMUNICATION

Imagine you are at a party. During the evening you form impressions about the people around you. Alan seems relaxed and even-tempered, Margaret tense and irritable. Karen seems open and straightforward, Amy hostile and evasive. Eric seems happy to see you; Mark definitely is not.

How do you reach these conclusions? To a surprising extent, you reach them not on the basis of what people say with words, but because of what they say *nonverbally*—with their postures, gestures, eyes, and facial expressions. Suppose you are sitting next to Mark, and he says, "This is a great party. I'm really glad to be here with you." However, his body is turned slightly away from you, and he keeps looking at someone across the room. Despite what he says, you know he is *not* glad to be there with you.

Much the same thing happens in speechmaking. Here is the story of one student's first two classroom speeches and the effect created by his nonverbal actions on each occasion:

Dan O'Connor's first speech did not go very well. Even though he had chosen an interesting topic, researched the speech with care, and practiced it faithfully, he did not take into account the importance of nonverbal communication. When the time came for him to speak, a stricken look crossed his face. He got up from his chair like a condemned man and plodded to the lectern as though going to the guillotine. His vocal delivery was good enough, but all the while his hands were living a life of their own. They fidgeted with his notes, played with the buttons of his shirt, and drummed on the lectern. Throughout the speech Dan kept his head down, and he looked at his watch repeatedly. Regardless of what his *words* were saying, his *body* was saying, "I don't want to be here!"

Finally it was over. Dan rushed to his seat and collapsed into it, looking enormously relieved. Needless to say, his speech was not a great success.

Fortunately, when Dan's problem with nonverbal communication was pointed out to him, he worked hard to correct it. His next speech was quite a different story. This time he got up from his chair and strode to the lectern confidently. He kept his hands under control and concentrated on making eye contact with his listeners. This was truly an achievement, because Dan was just as nervous as the first time. However, he found that the more he made himself *look* confident, the more confident he became. After the speech his classmates were enthusiastic. "Great speech," they said. "You really seemed to care about the subject, and you brought this caring to the audience."

In fact, the wording of Dan's second speech wasn't much better than that of the first. It was his nonverbal signals that made all the difference. From the time he left his seat until he returned, his actions said, "I am confident and in control of the situation. I have something worthwhile to say, and I want you to think so too."

Posture, facial expression, gestures, eye contact—all affect the way listeners respond to a speaker. How we use these and other body motions to communicate is the subject of a fascinating area of study called kinesics. One of its founders, Ray Birdwhistell, estimates that more than 700,000 possible physical signals can be sent through bodily movement.[17] Clinical studies have demonstrated that in some situations these signals account for much of the meaning communicated by speakers. Modern research has also confirmed what the Greek historian Herodotus observed more than 2,400 years ago: "Men trust their ears less than their eyes." When a speaker's body language is inconsistent with his or her words, listeners tend to believe the body language rather than the words.[18]

Here are the major aspects of nonverbal communication that will affect the outcome of your speeches.

Personal Appearance

If you were Cher, you could show up to make an Academy Award presentation speech wearing a bizarre creation that had more headdress than dress. If you were Albert Einstein, you could show up to address an international science conference wearing wrinkled trousers, a sweater, and tennis shoes. While the members of your audience would certainly comment on your attire, your reputation would not be harmed. In fact, it might be enhanced. You would be one of the few, the very few, who live outside the rules, who are expected to be unusual.

Now imagine what would happen if the president of a corporation showed up to address a stockholders' meeting attired like Cher, or if the President of the United States spoke on national television wearing wrinkled clothes and tennis shoes. Both presidents would soon be looking for work. Barring the occasional eccentric, every speaker is expected by his or her audience to exhibit a personal appearance in keeping with the occasion of the speech.

The President of the United States can be photographed in golfing clothes or riding clothes for a quick weekend interview at Camp David, but that same President will don a conservative suit and tie to address a joint session of Congress. Similarly, a business executive speaking at a winter sales conference in Acapulco would probably wear slacks and a casual shirt, because a business suit, in this atmosphere, would seem much too formal. But back home in San Francisco, Chicago, or New York, the same executive will be immaculately dressed in a well-tailored suit.

A number of studies have confirmed that personal appearance plays an important role in speechmaking.[19] Listeners always see you before they hear you. Just as you adapt your language to the audience and the occasion, so should you dress and groom appropriately. Although the force of your speech can sometimes overcome a poor impression created by personal appearance, the odds are against it. (In a survey of top business executives, 84 percent revealed that their companies simply do not hire people who appear at job interviews improperly attired.)[20] No matter what the speaking situation, you should try to evoke favorable first impressions—impressions that are likely to make listeners more receptive to what you say.

Bodily Action

Novice speakers are often unsure what to do with their bodies while giving a speech. Some pace nonstop back and forth across the podium, fearing that if they stop, they will forget everything. Others are perpetual-motion machines, constantly shifting their weight from one foot to the other, bobbing their shoulders, fidgeting with their notes, or jingling coins in their pockets. Still others turn into statues, standing rigid and expressionless from beginning to end.

Such quirks usually stem from nervousness. If you are prone to distracting mannerisms, your teacher will identify them so you can work on controlling them in later speeches. With a little concentration, these mannerisms should disappear as you become more comfortable speaking in front of an audience.

As important as how you act during the speech is what you do just *before* you begin and *after* you finish. As you rise to speak, try to appear calm, poised, and confident, despite the butterflies in your stomach. When you reach the lectern, don't lean on it, and don't rush into your speech. Give yourself time to get set. Arrange your notes just the way you want them. Stand quietly as you wait to make sure the audience is paying attention. Establish eye contact with your listeners. Then—and only then—should you start to talk.

When you reach the end of your speech, maintain eye contact for a few moments after you stop talking. This will give your closing line time to sink in. Unless you are staying at the lectern to answer questions, collect your notes and return to your seat. As you do so, maintain your cool, collected demeanor. Whatever you do, don't start to gather your notes before you have finished talking; and don't cap off your speech with a huge sigh of relief or some remark like "Whew! Am I glad that's over!"

All of this advice is common sense, yet you would be surprised how many people need it. When practicing your speeches, spend a little time rehearsing how you will behave at the beginning and at the end. It is probably the easiest—and one of the most effective—things you can do to improve your image with an audience.

Gestures

Few aspects of delivery seem to cause students more anguish than deciding what to do with their hands. "Should I clasp them behind my back? Let them hang at my sides? Put them in my pockets? Rest them on the lectern? And what about gesturing? When should I do that—and how?" Even people who normally use their hands expressively in everyday conversation seem to regard them as awkward appendages when speaking before an audience.

Over the years, more nonsense has been written about gesturing than about any other aspect of speech delivery. Adroit gestures *can* add to the impact of a speech; but there is nothing to the popular notion that public speakers must have a vast repertoire of graceful gestures. Some accomplished

Some accomplished speakers use gestures to help emphasize their ideas; others do not. For inexperienced speakers, it is more important to concentrate on communicating with the audience than on using gestures. (Bob Daemmrich/Stock, Boston)

speakers gesture frequently; others hardly at all. The primary rule is this: Whatever gestures you make should not draw attention to themselves and distract from your message. They should *appear* natural and spontaneous, help to clarify or reinforce your ideas, and be suited to the audience and occasion.

At this stage of your speaking career, you have many more important things to concentrate on than how to gesture. Gesturing tends to work itself out as you acquire experience and confidence. In the meantime, make sure your hands do not upstage your ideas. Avoid flailing them about, wringing them together, cracking your knuckles, or toying with your rings. Once you have eliminated these distractions, forget about your hands. Think about communicating with your listeners, and your gestures will probably take care of themselves—just as they do in conversation.

Eye Contact

The eyeball itself expresses no emotion. Yet by manipulating the eyeball and the areas of the face around it—especially the upper eyelids and the eyebrow— we are able to convey an intricate array of nonverbal messages. So revealing are these messages that we think of the eyes as "the windows of the soul." We look to them to help gauge the truthfulness, intelligence, attitudes, and feelings of a speaker.

The quickest way to establish a communicative bond with your listeners is to look them in the eye, personally and pleasantly. Avoiding their gaze is one of the surest ways to lose them. At best, speakers who refuse to establish eye contact are perceived as tentative and ill-at-ease. At worst, they are perceived as insincere or dishonest.[21] No wonder teachers urge students to look at the audience 80 to 90 percent of the time they are talking.

You may find this disconcerting at first. But after one or two speeches, you should be able to meet the gaze of your listeners as comfortably as you do in casual conversation. As you look at your listeners, be alert for their reactions. Can they hear you? Do they understand you? Are they awake? Your eyes will help you answer these questions.

It isn't enough just to look at your listeners; *how* you look at them also counts. A blank stare is almost as bad as no eye contact at all. So is a fierce, hostile glower or a series of frightened, bewildered glances. Also beware of the tendency to gaze intently at one part of the audience while ignoring the rest. In speech class some students look only at the section of the room where the teacher is sitting. Others avoid looking anywhere near the teacher and focus on one or two sympathetic friends. You should try to establish eye contact with your whole audience. When addressing a small group (such as your class), you can usually look briefly from one person to another. For a larger group, you will probably scan the audience rather than trying to engage the eyes of each person individually. No matter what the size of your audience, you want your eyes to convey confidence, sincerity, and conviction. They should say, "I am pleased to be able to talk with you. I believe deeply in what I am saying, and I want you to believe in it too."

PRACTICING DELIVERY

Popular wisdom promises that practice makes perfect. This is true, but only if we practice properly. No matter how long and hard you practice playing the piano, you will never make beautiful music if you don't know the difference between a sharp and a flat. By the same token, you will do little to improve your speech delivery unless you practice the right things in the right ways. Here is a five-step method that has worked well for many students:

1. Go through your preparation outline *aloud* to check how what you have written translates into spoken discourse. Is it too long? Too short? Are the main points clear when you speak them? Are the supporting materials distinct, convincing, interesting? Do the introduction and conclusion come across well? As you answer these questions, revise the speech as needed.

2. Prepare your speaking outline. In doing so, be sure to follow the guidelines discussed in Chapter 9. Use the same visual framework as in the preparation outline. Make sure the speaking outline is easy to read at a glance. Keep the outline as brief as possible. Give yourself cues on the outline for delivering the speech.

3. Practice the speech aloud several times using only the speaking outline.

Be sure to "talk through" all examples and to recite in full all quotations and statistics. If your speech includes visual aids, use them as you practice. The first couple of times you will probably forget something or make a mistake, but don't worry about that. Keep going and complete the speech as well as you can. Concentrate on gaining control of the *ideas;* don't try to learn the speech word for word. After a few tries you should be able to get through the speech extemporaneously with surprising ease.

4. Now begin to polish and refine your delivery. Practice the speech in front of a mirror to check for eye contact and distracting mannerisms. Tape-record the speech to gauge volume, pitch, rate, pauses, and vocal variety. Most important, try it out on friends, roommates, family members—anyone who will listen and give you an honest appraisal. Don't be shy about asking. Most people love to give their opinion about something. Since your speech is designed for people rather than for mirrors or tape recorders, you need to find out ahead of time how it goes over with people.

5. Finally, give your speech a dress rehearsal under conditions as close as possible to those you will face in class. Some students like to try the speech a couple of times in an empty classroom the day before the speech is due. No matter where you hold your last practice session, you should leave it feeling confident and looking forward to speaking in your class.

If this or any practice method is to work, you must start early. Don't wait until the day of your speech, or even the night before, to begin working on delivery. A single practice session—no matter how long—is rarely enough. Allow yourself *at least* a couple of days, preferably more, to gain command of the speech and its presentation. No matter how brilliant your preparation outline, what counts is how the speech comes across when you deliver it. Give yourself plenty of time to make sure it comes across well.

SUMMARY

The impact of a speech is strongly affected by how the speech is delivered. You cannot make a good speech without having something to say. But having something to say is not enough. You must also know *how* to say it.

Good delivery does not call attention to itself. It conveys the speaker's ideas clearly, interestingly, and without distracting the audience. In your earliest speeches you should concentrate on speaking intelligibly, avoiding distracting mannerisms, and establishing eye contact with your listeners. Once you get these elements under control, you can work on refining your delivery so it adds to the impact of your ideas.

There are four basic methods of delivering a speech: reading verbatim from a manuscript, reciting a memorized text, speaking impromptu, and speaking extemporaneously. The last of these—speaking extemporaneously—

is the method you probably will use for classroom speeches and for most speeches outside the classroom. When speaking extemporaneously, you will have only a brief set of notes or a speaking outline. You will choose the exact wording of your speech at the moment of delivery.

A primary factor in delivery is the speaker's voice. In using your voice effectively you should work to control your volume, pitch, rate, pauses, vocal variety, pronunciation, and articulation. Volume is the relative loudness of your voice, and pitch is the relative highness or lowness. Rate refers to the speed at which you talk. Pauses, when carefully timed, can add great impact to your speech, but you should avoid vocalized pauses ("er," "um," and the like). Vocal variety refers to changes in volume, pitch, rate, and pauses, and is crucial to making your voice lively and animated. Most of us speak rather casually in everyday conversation, but for public speaking you should be sure to pronounce words correctly and to articulate them distinctly.

Nonverbal communication is another vital factor in delivery. Posture, personal appearance, facial expression, bodily movement, gestures, and eye contact all affect the way listeners respond to speakers. You can do little to change your face or body, but you can dress and groom appropriately for the situation at hand. You can also learn to control gestures and bodily movements so they enhance your message, rather than distract from it. Making eye contact with listeners is the quickest way to establish a communicative bond with them.

You should practice all these aspects of delivery along with the words of your speech. Start your practice sessions early, so you will have plenty of time to gain command of the speech and its presentation.

REVIEW QUESTIONS

After reading this chapter, you should be able to answer the following questions:

1. What is good speech delivery? Why is good delivery important to successful speaking?

2. What are the four methods of speech delivery?

3. Why is every person's voice unique?

4. What are the seven aspects of voice usage you should concentrate on in your speeches?

5. Why is nonverbal communication important to a public speaker?

6. What are the four aspects of nonverbal communication you should concentrate on in your speeches?

7. What are the five steps you should follow in practicing your speech delivery?

APPLICATION EXERCISES

1. Radio and television announcers must have outstanding articulation. One way they develop it is by practicing tongue twisters. Try these. Start by saying them slowly and firmly so that each sound is clearly formed. Gradually increase to your normal rate of speech.

   a. Which wily wizard wished wicked wishes for Willy?
   b. The sixth sick Sheik's sheep is sick.
   c. Fetch me the finest French-fried freshest fish that Finney fries.
   d. Shy Sarah saw six Swiss wrist watches.
   e. One year we had a Christmas brunch with Merry Christmas mush to munch. But I don't think you'd care for such. We didn't like to munch mush much.

2. An excellent way to improve your vocal variety is to read aloud selections from poetry that require emphasis and feeling. Choose one of your favorite poems that falls into this category, or else find one by leafing through a poetry anthology. Practice reading the selection aloud. As you read, use your voice to make the poem come alive. Vary your volume, rate, and pitch. Find the appropriate places for pauses. Underline the key words or phrases you think should be stressed. Modulate your tone of voice; use inflections for emphasis and meaning.

   For this to work, you must overcome your fear of sounding affected or "dramatic." Most beginning speakers do better if they exaggerate changes in volume, rate, pitch, and expression. This will make you more aware of the many ways you can use your voice to express a wide range of moods and meanings. Besides, what sounds overly "dramatic" to you usually does not sound that way to an audience. By adding luster, warmth, and enthusiasm to your voice, you will go a long way toward capturing and keeping the interest of your listeners.

   If possible, practice reading the selection into a tape recorder. Listen to the playback. If you are not satisfied with what you hear, practice the selection some more and record it again.

3. Watch a ten-minute segment of a television drama with the sound turned off. What do the characters say with their dress, gestures, facial expressions, and the like? Do the same with a television comedy. How do the nonverbal messages in the two shows differ? Be prepared to report your observations in class.

4. Attend a speech on campus. You may choose either a presentation by a guest speaker from outside the college or a class session by a professor who has a reputation as a good lecturer. Prepare a brief report on the speaker's vocal and nonverbal communication. In your report, first analyze the speaker's volume, pitch, rate, pauses, vocal variety, pronunciation, and articulation. Then evaluate the speaker's personal appearance, bodily action,

gestures, and eye contact. Explain how the speaker's delivery added to or detracted from what the speaker said. Finally, note at least two techniques of delivery used by the speaker that you might want to try in your next speech.

NOTES

[1] Irving Bartlett, "Wendell Phillips and the Eloquence of Abuse," *American Quarterly,* 11 (1959), 512–513.

[2] The stress on "conversational quality" as a hallmark of good delivery was pioneered by James A. Winans in his classic text, *Speech-Making* (New York: Appleton-Century-Crofts, 1938). That listeners do in fact prefer a conversational speaking style is indicated by W. Barnett Pearce and Bernard J. Brommel, "Vocalic Communication in Persuasion," *Quarterly Journal of Speech,* 58 (1972), 298–306.

[3] A. Craig Baird, *Rhetoric: A Philosophical Inquiry* (New York: Ronald Press, 1965), p. 207.

[4] Two excellent guides to speaking from a manuscript are James C. Humes, "Read a Speech Like a Pro," in *Talk Your Way to the Top* (New York: McGraw-Hill, 1980), pp. 125–135; Jack Valenti, *Speak Up with Confidence: How to Prepare, Learn, and Deliver Effective Speeches* (New York: Morrow, 1982), pp. 23–36.

[5] Adapted from Eugene E. White, *Practical Public Speaking,* 4th ed. (New York: Macmillan, 1982), pp. 353–355.

[6] For research on the tie between effective pitch patterns and successful speaking see Judith A. Hall, "Voice Tone and Persuasion," *Journal of Personality and Social Psychology,* 38 (1980), 924–934.; David B. Buller and Judee K. Burgoon, "The Effects of Vocalics and Nonverbal Sensitivity on Compliance: A Replication and Extension," *Human Communication Research,* 13 (1986), 126–144.

[7] Richard L. Street, Jr., and Robert M. Brady, "Speech Rate Acceptance Ranges as a Function of Evaluative Domain, Listener Speech Rate, and Communication Context," *Communication Monographs,* 49 (1982), 290–308.

[8] George B. Ray, "Vocally Cued Personality Prototypes: An Implicit Personality Theory Approach," *Communication Monographs,* 53 (1986), 266–276.

[9] Mark Twain, *Mark Twain's Speeches* (New York: Harper and Brothers, 1923), p. xv.

[10] Mark Twain, *Autobiography,* ed. Charles Neider (New York: Harper & Row, 1959), pp. 181–182.

[11] M. Zuckerman, B. M. DePaulo, and R. Rosenthal, "Verbal and Nonverbal Communication of Deception," in Leonard Berkowitz (ed.), *Advances in Experimental and Social Psychology* (New York: Academic Press, 1981), pp. 2–59; Anthony Mulac, Torborg Louisa Lundell, and James J. Bradac, "Male/Female Language Differences and Attributional Consequences in a Public Speaking Situation: Toward an Explanation of the Gender-Linked Language Effect," *Communication Monographs,* 53 (1986), 115–129.

[12] James Joyce, "Chamber Music," stanza XXXV, from *The Portable James Joyce,* ed. Harry Levin (New York: Viking, 1946–47). Copyright renewed 1974, 1975. Reprinted by permission of Viking Penguin Inc.

[13] Dorothy Sarnoff, *Speech Can Change Your Life* (Garden City, N.Y.: Doubleday, 1970), p. 73.

[14] Mark L. Knapp, *Nonverbal Communication and Human Interaction* (New York: Holt, Rinehart and Winston, 1978), pp. 330–336.

[15] The relationship between articulation and pronunciation is a matter of some dispute among experts and is far from clear even in such widely used textbooks as Hilda B. Fisher's *Improving Voice and Articulation* (Boston: Houghton Mifflin, 1978). I would like to thank Professor Raymond D. Kent, Chairman of the Department of Communicative Disorders, University of Wisconsin, Madison, for helping me sort out the distinctions.

[16] William Norwood Brigance, *Speech: Its Techniques and Disciplines in a Free Society*, 2nd ed. (New York: Appleton-Century-Crofts, 1961), p. 349.

[17] Ray L. Birdwhistell, *Introduction to Kinesics* (Louisville, Ky.: University of Louisville Press, 1952).

[18] See, for example, James B. Stiff and Gerald R. Miller, " 'Come to Think of It . . . ': Interrogative Probes, Deceptive Communication, and Deception Detection," *Human Communication Research*, 12 (1986), 339–357.

[19] Shelly Chaiken, "Communicator Physical Attractiveness and Persuasion," *Journal of Personality and Social Psychology*, 37 (1979), 1387–1397.

[20] John T. Malloy, *Dress for Success* (New York: Warner, 1975), p. 36.

[21] Judee K. Burgoon, Valerie Manusov, Paul Mineo, and Jerold L. Hale, "Effects of Eye Gaze on Hiring Credibility, Attraction, and Relational Message Interpretation," *Journal of Nonverbal Behavior*, 9 (1985), 133–146; Judee K. Burgoon, Deborah A. Coker, and Ray A. Coker, "Communicative Effects of Gaze Behavior: A Test of Two Contrasting Explanations," *Human Communication Research*, 12 (1986), 495–524.

CHAPTER 12

Using Visual Aids

Sarah Gans is a distant relative of Christian Frederick Martin, the master guitar maker who founded the Martin Guitar Company 150 years ago. Being proud of this heritage and interested in guitars, Sarah decided to give an informative speech explaining the differences between ordinary guitars and guitars of exceptional quality. But how could she do this for an audience who had limited knowledge about guitars? She did it by using a visual aid.

On the day of her speech Sarah brought two classical guitars—one a typical mid-quality instrument, the other a top-of-the-line Martin concert guitar. It was then easy for her to clarify the variations in construction between ordinary and extraordinary guitars by pointing to the different parts of the instruments. Sarah also played both guitars briefly, to show the quality of sound produced by each. In other words, she combined an audio aid with a visual aid. By *showing* the differences between the guitars, rather than just telling about them, Sarah made her speech more interesting and communicated her ideas more effectively.

As the old saying tells us, one picture is worth a thousand words. People find a speaker's message more interesting, grasp it more easily, and retain it longer when it is presented visually as well as verbally. After all, we live in a visual age. We are accustomed to seeing images. When the Japanese bombed Pearl Harbor in December 1941, bringing the United States into World War II, the whole nation sat glued to their radios listening to reports of the devastation. Had the attack occurred twenty-five years later, there would have been on-the-spot coverage by all three television networks. Television has conditioned us to expect a visual image.

ADVANTAGES OF VISUAL AIDS

Visual aids offer a speaker several advantages.[1] The primary advantage, of course, is *clarity.* If, like Sarah Gans, you are discussing an object, you can make your message clearer by showing the object or some representation of it. If you are citing statistics, showing how something works, or demonstrating a technique, a visual aid will make your information more vivid to your audience. Here is how one speaker used an imaginative visual aid to clarify his points about salt in the American diet:

On the day of his speech Tom Hexter brought to class a large box, which he set up on the table next to the lectern. This immediately caught the attention of Tom's listeners by arousing their curiosity. Tom took from the box a container of Morton's salt, a measuring cup, a teaspoon, and two plates. Then he began his speech.

First he explained how much salt is required by the body over the course of a month. To illustrate, he measured out 3 teaspoons of salt onto one plate and showed it to the audience. Next Tom gave statistics about how much salt the average American consumes in a month. Again, as he spoke, he measured. When he was finished measuring, the second plate had 1¼ pounds of salt. Finally Tom said, 'Now let's multiply that amount by twelve and see how much salt we eat over the course of a year." And he began taking out of the box one container of Morton's salt after another, until he had piled up a pyramid of 9 containers, or nearly 15 pounds of salt!

Visual aids help to make the abstract concrete. Can you picture a pound and a quarter of salt? Or 15 pounds of salt? You could if you had watched Tom measure out the salt and stack up the Morton's containers. This dramatic visual evidence brought home Tom's point more forcefully than any recitation of facts could have done.

Another advantage of visual aids is *interest.* Surely the people who heard Tom's speech about salt were more interested watching the visual display than they would have been listening to Tom reel off a string of numbers. In fact, the interest generated by visual images is so strong that visual aids are now used routinely in many areas, not just speechmaking. A generation or so ago, most college textbooks were rather dry—page after page of words. Today they are enlivened with photographs, drawings, and other visual aids that both clarify the material and make it more interesting. Encyclopedias have blossomed with photographs and maps; even dictionaries contain small drawings to highlight word definitions. You can do the same thing with your speeches.

Still another advantage of visual aids is *retention.* Visual images often stay with us longer than verbal ones. The audience who heard Tom's speech about salt may not remember exactly how much salt is in the typical American diet. But they probably will remember what the second plate looked like, spilling over with a mountain of salt. And perhaps they will envision that plateful of salt and the pyramid of salt containers the next time they hold a salt shaker over their French fries. We've all heard that words can "go in one ear and out the other." Visual images tend to stick.

For all these reasons, you will find visual aids of great value to you in your speeches. In this chapter we shall concentrate primarily on visual aids suitable for classroom speeches. However, the principles outlined here are true for all circumstances. For speeches outside the classroom—in business or community situations, for instance—you may use sophisticated, professionally prepared visual aids such as flip charts, overhead slides, or film clips. In these situations you should have no difficulty applying the general suggestions given here.[2]

Let us look first at the kinds of visual aids you are likely to use, and then at some tips for using them effectively.

KINDS OF VISUAL AIDS

Objects

As in Sarah Gans' speech about guitars, bringing the object of your talk to class can be an excellent way to clarify your ideas and give them dramatic impact. If you talk about scuba diving, why not bring diving equipment to show your listeners? If you plan to explain the different kinds of kites, what could be better than showing a sample of each kind? Or suppose you want to inform your audience how to make homemade pizza. You could bring the ingredients to class and show your classmates how to put together a pizza from scratch—for much less than a commercial pizza would cost.

In certain situations you might use living objects as visual aids. This worked well for a high school wrestling coach who returned to college to take a night class in public speaking. Not surprisingly, the coach gave one of his speeches about wrestling. On the night of his speech he brought along two of his high school students, who demonstrated each of the basic holds as the coach discussed them.

Many objects, however, cannot be used effectively in classroom speeches. Some are too big to be hauled into a classroom. Others are too small to be seen clearly by the audience. Still others may not be available to you. If you were speaking about a rare suit of armor in the local museum, you could, theoretically, transport it to class, but it is most unlikely that the museum would let you borrow it. You would have to look for another kind of visual aid.

Models

If the item you want to discuss is too large, too small, or unavailable, you may be able to work with a model. One kind is a small-scale model of a large object. A speaker used such a model to help explain the events connected with the sinking of the ocean liner *Titanic.* Another speaker brought to class a scaled-down model of a hang glider to demonstrate the equipment and techniques of hang gliding.

A second kind of model is a large-scale representation of a small object. Science teachers use such models to help students visualize minuscule structures like molecules. A good example of this type of model came in a speech about watches. Since the workings of a real watch would be too small for everyone to see, the speaker brought a large-scale model showing the interior mechanisms of a Swiss-movement watch.

Finally, models can be life-size. To demonstrate the techniques of cardiopulmonary resuscitation, one speaker borrowed a life-size dummy of a human torso from the Red Cross. Another speaker, an anthropology major, illustrated his speech with a full-scale model of a human skull, to show how archaeologists use bone fragments to reconstruct the forms of early humans.

Photographs

In the absence of an object or a model, you may be able to use photographs. A famous instance of such use came in a speech by Adlai Stevenson to the United Nations during the Cuban missile crisis of 1962. Stevenson showed enlargements of aerial photographs to prove beyond doubt that the Soviet Union had installed medium- and long-range ballistic missiles in Cuba.

Unfortunately, photographs will not work in a classroom speech unless you have access to oversize enlargements, which are very expensive. Normal-size photos are not big enough to be seen clearly without being passed around—which only diverts the audience from what you are saying. But if you do have a source for large-scale photos, by all means take advantage of it. One student, who had his own darkroom, used 2- by 3-foot enlargements to show the differences between professional and amateur photography. If you can't get photographs this large, however, you will be better off with another type of visual aid.

Drawings

Diagrams, sketches, and other kinds of drawings are superb alternatives to photographs. They are inexpensive to make. Moreover, since they are drawn specifically for one speech, they can be designed to illustrate your points exactly. This more than compensates for what they may lack in realism.

"But I'm not an artist," you may say. "I can hardly draw a straight line with a ruler." This is not a problem. The kinds of drawings used in classroom speeches are usually so simple that almost anyone can prepare them. For example, Figure 12.1 is a diagram used in a speech about palm reading. The student who gave the speech had no artistic experience. Nor did she need any, for her aim was not to draw a life-like hand. The diagram simply shows the basic lines used by palm readers to analyze a subject's personality and life

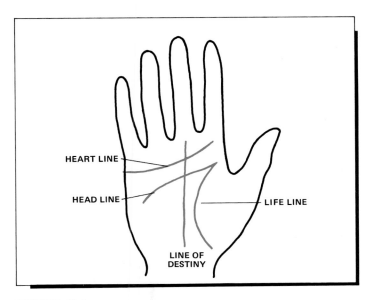

FIGURE 12.1

cycles. As you can imagine, it would have been almost impossible for the speaker to make her points clearly without some kind of visual aid.

To give another example, Figure 12.2 is a drawing used by a speaker to illustrate the three sails of a racing sailboat—jib, mainsail, and spinnaker.

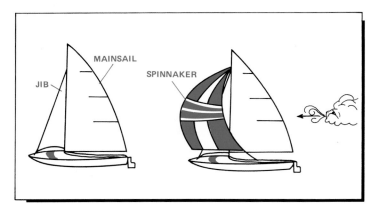

FIGURE 12.2

Figure 12.3 shows a drawing used to illustrate a speech about the kinds of problems faced by people who suffer from the learning disability known as dyslexia. This aid was particularly effective because it allowed the speaker to translate complex ideas into visual terms the audience could grasp almost immediately.

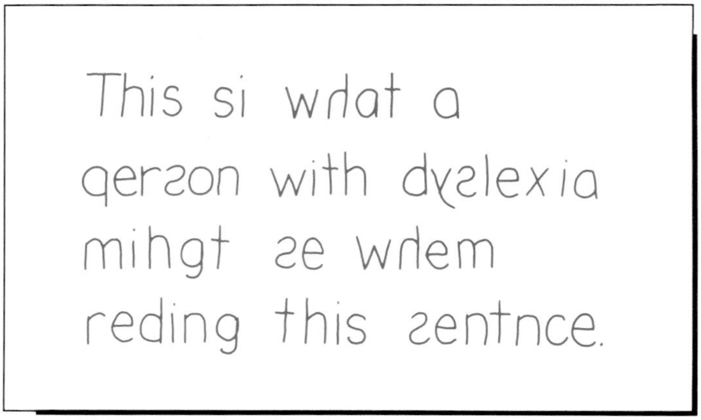

This si wɹat a qerƨon with dyƨlexia mihgt ƨe wɹem reding this ƨentnce.

FIGURE 12.3

Maps are another kind of drawing that is easy to prepare. You can trace the basic outlines from an atlas and then enlarge the scale to make your visual aid. Figure 12.4 is a map showing the location of the seven wonders of the ancient world—the Statue of Zeus at Olympia, the Temple of Artemis at Ephesus, the Mausoleum at Halicarnassus, the Colossus of Rhodes, the Lighthouse of Alexandria, the Pyramids of Egypt at Giza, and the Hanging Gardens of Babylon. Each site on the map illustrated a different point in the speech.

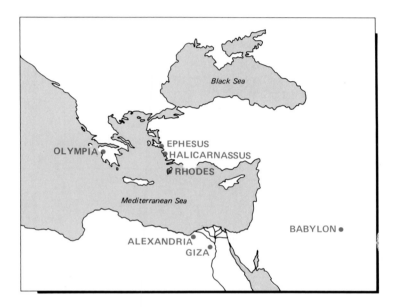

FIGURE 12.4

Graphs

Graphs are a good way to simplify and clarify statistics. Audiences often have trouble grasping a complex series of numbers. You can ease their difficulty by using graphs to clarify statistical trends and patterns.

The most common type is the *line graph.* Figure 12.5 (next page) shows such a graph, used in a speech about the problems of the elderly. The speaker explained the graph by saying:

As you can see from this graph based on figures released by the U.S. Census Bureau, the proportion of elderly people as a part of American society will continue to grow dramatically into the next century. Whereas in 1900 only 4 percent of Americans were 65 years of age or older, by 1980 the same age group made up almost 11 percent of the population. By the year 2030 they will comprise almost 20 percent— one-fifth—of all Americans.

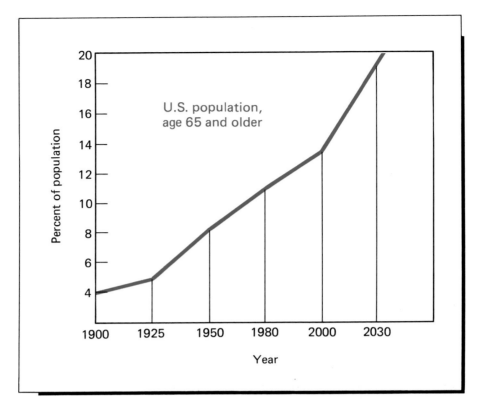

FIGURE 12.5

The *pie graph* is best suited for illustrating simple distribution patterns. You will see such a graph in your newspaper each year to show the division of the national budget. Figure 12.6 (opposite) shows how one speaker used pie graphs to help listeners visualize changes in the American work force during the twentieth century. The graph on the left shows the percent of American workers in major occupation groups in 1900. The graph on the right shows percentages for the same groups in 1980.

These pie graphs helped the speaker make three important points: (1) The percent of blue-collar workers and of service workers in the total labor force has remained relatively stable since 1900; (2) The percent of white-collar workers has almost tripled since the turn of the century; (3) The percent of farmworkers has declined to a tiny fraction of the entire work force.

Other distributions easily shown by a pie graph might include the proportional breakdown of the world's major religions; the ratio of registered Democrats, Republicans, and Independents; the nutritional constituents of a particular food; or the amount of money spent annually on admission tickets to various professional sports.

Because a pie graph is used to dramatize relationships among the parts

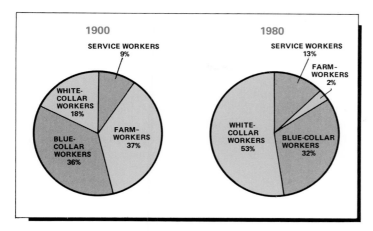

FIGURE 12.6

of a whole, you should keep the number of different segments in the graph as small as possible. A pie graph should ideally have from two to five segments, and under no circumstances should it have more than eight.[3]

The *bar graph* is a particularly good way to show comparisons between two or more items. It also has the advantage of being easy to understand, even by people who have no background in reading graphs. Figure 12.7 is an example of a bar graph from a speech entitled "The Pacific Century: Asia's Challenge to the West." It shows visually that while the United States still has

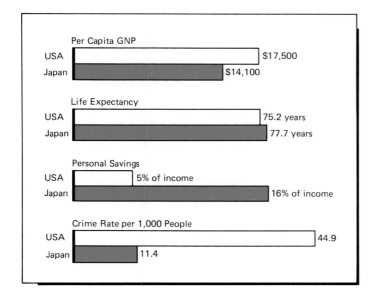

FIGURE 12.7

a larger per capita Gross National Product than does Japan, the U.S. lags behind in such crucial areas as life expectancy, the percentage of income devoted to savings, and controlling crime. As the graph shows, the average person in Japan can expect to live almost 78 years, while the average American will live only a little past 75. It also shows that the Japanese save 16 percent of their personal income—more than three times as much as Americans—a figure that helps explain why Japan has so much money available for investment. Finally, the graph indicates that the crime rate in Japan is only one-fourth of America's crime rate. The speaker could simply have recited all these statistics, but the bar graph presents them more clearly and impressively.

Charts

Charts are particularly useful for summarizing large blocks of information. One student, in a speech about the recording industry, used a chart to summarize the major categories of records sold annually in the United States (Figure 12.8). These are too many categories to be presented effectively in a pie graph or bar graph. By listing them on a chart, the speaker made it much easier for listeners to keep the information straight.

TYPE OF MUSIC	PERCENT OF TOTAL RECORD SALES
1. ROCK AND POP	52
2. COUNTRY	14
3. SOUL	11
4. EASY LISTENING	6
5. CHILDREN'S	6
6. JAZZ	4
7. CLASSICAL	4
8. OTHER	3

FIGURE 12.8

Charts are also valuable for presenting the steps of a process. One speaker used several charts in a speech about survival techniques in the wilderness, including one outlining the steps in emergency treatment of snakebites (Figure 12.9, opposite).

You can also use charts to present information your audience may want

EMERGENCY TREATMENT FOR POISONOUS SNAKEBITES

1. TIE A CONSTRICTING BAND 2 TO 4 INCHES ABOVE THE WOUND.

2. CLEAN THE WOUND WITH ALCOHOL.

3. MAKE TWO SHALLOW VERTICAL INCISIONS AT THE PUNCTURE POINTS.

4. DRAW THE VENOM FROM THE WOUND.

5. WASH THE AREA THOROUGHLY WITH SOAP AND WATER.

6. APPLY COLD COMPRESSES.

FIGURE 12.9

to write down. In a speech about consumer protection organizations, for example, a student might use a chart to let her audience know exactly where to write or phone for consumer services.

Slides and Movies

Slides and movies are a lot like photographs. In theory they make great visual aids. But in practice they are usually more trouble than they are worth for classroom speeches. They require darkened rooms, are difficult to coordinate with what you say, and involve cumbersome equipment that is prone to mechanical breakdowns. If you are considering using movies or slides, think whether you might be able to use another kind of visual aid instead. If you finally decide that you must have slides or movies, be sure to practice frequently with the equipment ahead of time so you can use it flawlessly during the speech.

The Speaker

Sometimes you can use your own body as a visual aid—by showing how to perform sign language for the deaf, by demonstrating the skills of modern dance, by doing magic tricks, and so forth. One student gave an informative speech on the art of mime. Throughout the speech she illustrated her points by performing mime routines. In addition to clarifying her ideas, this kept her classmates deeply engrossed in the speech. Many students have also found that doing some kind of demonstration reduces their nervousness during a speech by providing an outlet for their extra adrenalin.

Visual aids such as flip charts are common in business and community presentations. To be effective, they must be large enough to be read by the whole audience. (Elizabeth Crews)

Doing a demonstration well requires special practice to coordinate your actions with your words and to control the timing of your speech. Be especially cautious when attempting to demonstrate a process that takes longer to complete than the time allocated for your speech. If you plan to show a long process, you might borrow the techniques of television cooks. They work through most of the steps in making a perfect soufflé, but they have a second, finished soufflé ready to show you at the last minute.

TIPS FOR USING VISUAL AIDS

Avoid Using the Chalkboard for Visual Aids

At first thought, using the chalkboard in your classroom to present visual aids seems like a splendid idea. Usually, however, it is not. You have too much to do during a speech to worry about drawing or writing legibly on the board. Many students have marred an otherwise fine speech by turning their backs on the audience to use the chalkboard. Even if your visual aid is put on the chalkboard ahead of time, it seldom is as vivid or as neat as one composed on poster board.

Of course there are some speaking situations in which use of the chalkboard is essential. A teacher giving a lecture or a coach explaining a new play will write on the board while speaking. If you ever need to do this, make sure your writing is clear and large enough for all to read.

Prepare Visual Aids in Advance

No matter what visual aids you plan to use, prepare them well ahead of time. This has two advantages. First, it means you can make your visual aid at leisure, while you are not so nervous that you can barely draw a straight line or write legibly. You will have the time and resources to devise a creative, attractive visual aid that will truly enhance your speech. Audiences respond much more favorably to speakers who have obviously put a great deal of thought and effort into their visual aids.

Second, preparing your visual aids well ahead of time means you can use them while practicing your speech. Visual aids are effective only if they are integrated smoothly with the rest of the speech. If you lose your place, drop your aids, or otherwise stumble around when presenting them, you will distract your audience and shatter your concentration. You can avoid such disasters by preparing your visual aids far enough in advance.

Make Sure Visual Aids Are Large Enough

A visual aid is useless if nobody can see it. This is another of those points that would seem so obvious as to need no comment. But as many speakers have discovered, it is one thing to nod your head in agreement and another to prepare a visual aid properly. Beginning speakers in particular tend to use visual aids that are too small.

When you choose or make a visual aid, keep in mind the size of your classroom. Be sure the aid is big enough to be seen easily by everyone in the room. If you make a diagram, a chart, or a graph, guard against the tendency to write and draw too small. You probably will need a piece of poster board at least 2 by 3 feet in size. Use dark ink and an extra-wide marker, so that whatever you write or draw can be seen from the back of the room. Any lettering should be at least 2 to 3 inches tall. As you prepare the aid, check its visibility by getting as far away from it as your most distant listener will be sitting. If you have trouble making out the words or drawings, your audience will too. By making sure your visual aid is large enough, you will avoid having to introduce it with the lame comment, "I know some of you can't see this, but. . . ."

Display Visual Aids Where All Listeners Can See Them

Check the classroom ahead of time to decide exactly where you will display your visual aid. Keep in mind that inexpensive poster board is too flimsy to stand by itself in front of a lectern or on the edge of a chalkboard. Unless you use heavyweight poster board, or unless your classroom has an easel, you will need to hang your charts, graphs, and drawings in some fashion. Decide in advance what will work best, and on the day of the speech bring your own tape or thumbtacks in case none are available in the classroom.

Once you have set up the aid in the best location, don't undo all your preparation by standing where your audience can't see the aid without wrenching their necks. Stand to one side of the aid, and point with the arm nearest it. If possible, use a pencil, a ruler, or some other pointer. This will allow you to stand farther away from the visual aid, thereby reducing the likelihood that you will obstruct the view of people sitting on the same side of the room as you are standing.

Avoid Passing Visual Aids Among the Audience

Once visual aids get into the hands of your listeners, you are in trouble. At least three people will be paying more attention to the aid than to you—the person who has just had it, the person who has it now, and the person waiting to get it next.[4] By the time the visual aid moves on, all three may have lost track of what you are saying.

Nor do you solve this problem by preparing a handout for every member of the audience. There is no guarantee they will pay attention to it only when you want them to. In fact, they are likely to spend a good part of the speech looking over the handout at their own pace, rather than listening to you. Although handouts can be valuable, they usually just create competition for beginning speakers.

Every once in a while, of course, you will want listeners to have copies of some material to take home. When such a situation arises, keep the copies until after you've finished talking and can distribute them without creating a distraction. Keeping control of your visual aids is essential to keeping control of your speech.

Display Visual Aids Only While Discussing Them

Just as circulating visual aids distracts attention, so does displaying them throughout a speech. Whenever an aid is visible, at least some people will spend their time looking at it rather than listening to you. If possible, keep each visual aid covered or out of sight until you are ready to discuss it. When you finish using an aid, cover it or place it where it will not divert the attention of your listeners.

Talk to Your Audience, Not to Your Visual Aid

When explaining a visual aid, it is very easy to break eye contact with your audience and speak to the aid. Of course, your listeners are looking primarily at the aid, and you will need to glance at it periodically as you talk. But if you keep your eyes fixed on your visual aid, you may lose your audience. By keeping eye contact with your listeners, you will also pick up feedback about how the visual aid and your explanation of it are coming across.

Explain Visual Aids Clearly and Concisely

Visual aids don't explain themselves. Like statistics, they need to be translated and related to the audience. Figure 12.10, for example, is an excellent diagram,

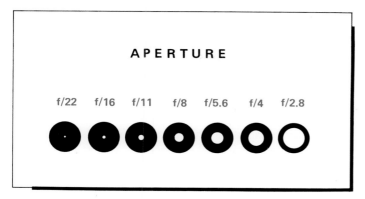

FIGURE 12.10

but do you know what it means? You do if you are a photography buff. You will see at once that it shows the different lens openings of a 35-millimeter camera. But if you are not versed in photography, you will have no idea what the different numbers and circles mean until they are explained to you.

Beginning speakers often rush over their visual aids without explaining them clearly and concisely. A visual aid can be of enormous benefit—but only if the viewer knows what to look for and why. Be sure to adapt your visual aid to your audience. Don't just say, "as you can see . . ." and then pass quickly over the aid. Tell listeners what the aid means. Describe its major features. Spell out the meaning of charts and graphs. Interpret statistics and percentages. Remember, a visual aid is only as useful as the explanation that goes with it.

Practice with Your Visual Aids

Mention has been made several times in this chapter of the need to practice with visual aids, but the point bears repeating. You do not want to suffer through an experience like the one that follows:

This is the story of a young man who was a brilliant designer and a good inventor, but who failed to realize that to complete his work he had to be able to explain it and to convince his supervisors that his invention was a worthwhile investment.

He had designed a machine that used several new and patentable ideas. The stage was set for him not only to show off his invention but to show himself to the managers, who would help him shape his ideas and give him additional opportunities. This was the part of the test he flunked.

He knew who his audience would be. He had been told to compose his talk thoughtfully, to prepare slides and other visual aids, and to practice in the conference room, using its rather complex lectern and public address system. At the lectern he could control the lights, show his slides in any sequence he chose, and have his choice of microphones and other visual and speaking aids.

Unfortunately, although he had done a brilliant job on the engineering project, he neglected to plan his presentation with similar care. His worst mistake was not practicing with the equipment he was now called on to operate. When he dimmed the lights, he could not read his text. When the first slide came on, it was not his but belonged to a former speaker. When the first correct slide was reached, the type was too small for anyone but the people in the first row to see. He could not turn on the light arrow indicator to point out the line he was talking about, so he walked away from the lectern to point things out directly on the screen. But he left the microphone behind, so people in the back rows could neither see nor hear.

When a picture of his machine appeared, he was too close to see the critical parts. Since he could not read his text because of the darkness, he lost track of what he was supposed to say. Reaching for a steel-tipped pointer because he could not operate the optical one, he managed to punch a hole through the screen.

In desperation, he abandoned the slides, turned up the lights, and in utter consternation raced through the rest of his talk so fast and with such poor enunciation that he was almost completely unintelligible. Finally, in embarrassment both for himself and for the audience, he sat down.[5]

This sounds like a routine from *Saturday Night Live,* but it is a true story. What makes the story especially sad is that it didn't have to happen. With some effort, thought, and preparation, the young inventor could have made a success of his presentation instead of turning it into a fiasco.

You can avoid following in his footsteps if you practice with the visual aids you have chosen. Rehearse with your equipment to be sure you can set up the visual aid with a minimum of fuss. Run through the entire speech several times, practicing the handling of the aids, the gestures you will make, the timing of each move. If necessary, practice removing the visual aid when you are finished with it. In using visual aids, as in other aspects of speechmaking, there is no substitute for the Boy Scout motto: Be Prepared.

SUMMARY

Visual aids can be of great help to you as a speaker. Listeners find a speaker's message more interesting, grasp it more easily, and retain it longer when it is presented visually as well as verbally.

There are many kinds of visual aids. Most obvious is the object about which you are speaking—or a model of it. Photographs can be useful if generous-size enlargements are available; but for classroom speeches, drawings may be more practical. One kind of drawing—a map—is especially useful for a speech topic involving physical terrain. Graphs can illustrate any subject dealing with numbers, while charts can help you summarize large blocks of information. Slides and movies are sometimes excellent visual aids, but they may pose too many problems for classroom speeches. Finally, you can act as your own visual aid by performing actions that demonstrate ideas or processes.

No matter what kind of visual aid you choose, it will be effective only if you prepare it carefully and present it skillfully. Try to avoid writing or drawing visual aids on the chalkboard. Work them up in advance, and make sure they are large enough to be seen easily by all your listeners. It is usually not advisable to pass visual aids among your audience. Instead, display each visual aid only while you are talking about it, and be sure to display it where everyone can see it without straining. When presenting a visual aid, maintain eye contact with your listeners. Talk to the audience, not to the aid, and explain the aid clearly and concisely. Above all, practice with your visual aids, so they fit into your speech smoothly and expertly.

REVIEW QUESTIONS

After reading this chapter, you should be able to answer the following questions:

1. What are the three major advantages of using visual aids in your speeches?

2. What are the kinds of visual aids you might use?

3. What tips for using visual aids are given in the chapter?

APPLICATION EXERCISES

1. Watch a "how-to" type of television program (a cooking or gardening show, for example) or the weather portion of a local newscast. Notice how the speaker uses visual aids to help communicate the message. What kind or kinds of visual aids are used? How do they enhance the clarity, interest, and retainability of the speaker's message? What would the speaker have to do to communicate the message effectively without visual aids?

2. Consider how you might use visual aids to explain each of the following:
    a. The increase in world population since 1790.
    b. The location of the major attractions in Yosemite National Park.
    c. How football helmets, as currently designed and used, contribute to the high rate of injuries in high school, college, and professional football.
    d. The basic equipment and techniques of scuba diving.
    e. How beer is made.
    f. Where to write for information about student loans.

g.   The proportion of the electorate that votes in major national elections in the United States, France, Germany, England, and Japan, respectively.
h.   How to build a brick patio.
i.   The anatomy of the human ear.
j.   How General Custer was outmaneuvered at the Battle of Little Big Horn.

3. Plan to use visual aids in at least one of your classroom speeches. Be creative in devising your aids, and be sure to follow the guidelines discussed in the chapter for using them. After the speech, analyze how effectively you employed your visual aids, what you learned about the use of visual aids from your experience, and what changes you would make in using visual aids if you were to deliver the speech again.

NOTES

[1] The advantages of visual aids are well documented. See, for example, Joel R. Levin and Alan M. Lesgold, "On Pictures in Prose," *Educational Communication and Technology Journal,* 26 (1978), 233–244; Emil Bohn and David Jabusch, "The Effect of Four Methods of Instruction on the Use of Visual Aids in Speeches," *Western Journal of Speech Communication,* 46 (1982), 253–265.

[2] For more detailed guides to the presentation of visual materials see Peter H. Selby, *Using Graphs and Tables: A Self-Teaching Guide* (New York: Wiley, 1979); Edward R. Tufts, *The Visual Display of Quantitative Information* (Cheshire, Conn.: Graphics Press, 1983).

[3] Robert Lefferts, *Elements of Graphics: How to Prepare Charts and Graphs for Effective Reports* (New York: Harper & Row, 1981), p. 65.

[4] Bert E. Bradley, *Fundamentals of Speech Communication: The Credibility of Ideas,* 5th ed. (Dubuque, Iowa: Brown, 1988), p. 266.

[5] Adapted from Eric A. Walker, "About the 'Death' of an Engineer," *Centre Daily Times,* April 25, 1972.

PART FIVE

VARIETIES OF PUBLIC SPEAKING

CHAPTER 13

Speaking To Inform

The scene is part of American folklore. It is Christmas Eve. The children are nestled all snug in their beds. But Mama and Papa? They have not settled down for a long winter's nap. Instead, they are in the living room, trying desperately to assemble the expensive toys they have bought for their children, following instructions that might as well have been written in Sanskrit. Why are they having a difficult time? Because the toy manufacturers, with all the resources available to them, have failed to provide information that any reasonable person could understand.

Although this situation makes good material for cartoons and television shows, it happens all too often in real life. We may be surprised that anyone could bungle the simple job of telling somebody else how to do something. But the job is not as simple as it seems. Giving information is an exacting task. Have you ever tried to teach someone how to use a stick shift? Or rewire a lamp? Or develop film in the darkroom? If so, you know you must go very slowly and make sure your listener understands each step before you go on to the next one. If you don't, you're likely to see your listener's eyes begin to glaze over.

Public speaking to inform occurs in a wide range of everyday situations. What kinds of people make informative speeches? The business manager explaining next year's budget. The military officer briefing subordinates. The teacher in a classroom. The church worker outlining plans for a fund drive. The union leader informing members about details in the new contract. There are endless situations in which people need to inform others. Competence in this type of communication should prove most valuable to you throughout your life.

One of your first classroom assignments probably will be to deliver an informative speech, in which you will act as a lecturer or teacher. You may describe an object, show how something works, report on an event, explain a concept. Your aim will be to convey knowledge and understanding—not to advocate a cause. Your speech will be judged in light of three general criteria:

Is the information communicated *accurately?*

Is the information communicated *clearly?*

Is the information made *meaningful* and *interesting* to the audience?

In this chapter, we shall look at four types of informative speeches and the basic principles of informative speaking. Along the way, we shall apply various general principles discussed in previous chapters.

TYPES OF INFORMATIVE SPEECHES: ANALYSIS AND ORGANIZATION

There are many ways to classify informative speeches. Here we focus on the four kinds of informative speeches you are most likely to give in your speech class: (1) speeches about objects; (2) speeches about processes; (3) speeches about events; and (4) speeches about concepts. These are not hard-and-fast categories, but they provide an effective method of analyzing and organizing informative speeches.[1]

Speeches About Objects

As the word is used here, "objects" include anything that is visible, tangible, and stable in form. Objects may have moving parts or be alive; they may include places, structures, animals, even people. Here are examples of subjects for speeches about objects:

Australia	compact disc players
hot-air balloons	Taj Mahal
Macbeth	mushrooms
the human eye	King Arthur
Martin Luther King	whales
peanuts	Mount Rushmore
gold	artificial sweeteners

You will not have time to tell your classmates everything about any of these subjects. Instead, you will choose a specific purpose that focuses on one aspect of your subject. The following are examples of good specific purpose statements for informative speeches about objects:

To inform my audience of the major achievements of Martin Luther King.

To inform my audience about the geographical regions of Australia.

To inform my audience who King Arthur really was.

To inform my audience about the anatomy of the human eye.

To inform my audience about what to look for when buying a compact disc player.

To inform my audience about the curse of *Macbeth*.

Notice how precise these statements are. As we saw in Chapter 3, you should select a specific purpose that is not too broad to achieve in the allotted time. "To inform my audience about the Mafia" is far too general for a classroom speech. "To inform my audience about *the origins of* the Mafia" is more exact and is a purpose you could reasonably hope to achieve in a brief talk.

If your specific purpose is to explain the history or evolution of your subject, you will put your speech in *chronological* order. For example:

Specific Purpose:	To inform my audience how the megaliths at Stonehenge were built.
Central Idea:	The megaliths at Stonehenge were built in three major stages.
Main Points:	I. The first stage of building was from 2000 to 1800 B.C., when the outer ring and pits were constructed.
	II. The second stage of building was from 1800 to 1600 B.C., when the main structure was erected.
	III. The third stage of building was from 1600 to 1400 B.C., when Stonehenge was in use—possibly as a giant calendar.

If your specific purpose is to describe the main features of your subject, you may organize your speech in *spatial* order:

Specific Purpose:	To inform my audience of the different routes followed by the famed railroad train, the Orient Express.
Central Idea:	Most people think there was only one Orient Express route across Europe, but actually there were four.
Main Points:	I. The northernmost route started at Warsaw, Poland, and crossed Czechoslovakia and Germany to Belgium.
	II. The next-lowest route began at Constanta in Rumania, traveled through Hungary, Austria, and Germany, and terminated in Paris.
	III. The next route began at Bucharest, Rumania, and crossed Hungary, Austria, and Switzerland before ending in Paris.
	IV. The southernmost route, made famous by Agatha Christie, began at two points—Constantinople and Athens—and traveled across Yugoslavia and Italy on its way to Paris.

As often as not, you will find that speeches about objects fall into *topical* order. Here is an example:

Specific Purpose:	To inform my audience about the achievements of Benjamin Franklin.
Central Idea:	Benjamin Franklin was an amazingly talented man who achieved distinction as a publisher, author, politician, diplomat, and scientist.
Main Points:	I. As a publisher, Franklin was involved in several periodicals, including the *Pennsylvania Gazette.*
	II. As an author, Franklin is best known for *Poor Richard's Almanac* and his *Autobiography.*

III. As a politician, Franklin contributed to both the Declaration of Independence and the Constitution.
IV. As a diplomat, Franklin helped frame the treaty of peace with England and served as first minister to France.
V. As a scientist, Franklin invented the Franklin stove and conducted important experiments with electricity.

No matter which of these organizational methods you use—chronological, spatial, or topical—be sure to follow the guidelines discussed in Chapter 7: (1) limit your speech to between two and five main points; (2) keep main points separate; (3) try to use the same pattern of wording for all main points; (4) balance the amount of time devoted to each main point.

Speeches About Processes

A process is a systematic series of actions that leads to a specific result or product. Speeches about processes explain how something is made, how something is done, or how something works. Here are examples of good specific purpose statements for speeches about processes:

To inform my audience how to save people from drowning.

To inform my audience how perfume is made.

To inform my audience how to buy a good used car.

To inform my audience how to write an effective job résumé.

To inform my audience about what makes an airplane fly.

As these examples suggest, there are two kinds of informative speeches about processes. One kind explains a process so listeners will *understand* it better. Your goal in this kind of speech is to have your audience know the steps of the process and how they relate to one another. If your specific purpose is "To inform my audience how an atomic bomb works," you will explain the basic steps in making a bomb and how they result in an atomic explosion. You will not instruct your listeners how they can *make* an atomic bomb.

A second kind of speech explains a process so listeners will be better able to *perform* the process themselves. Your goal in this kind of speech is to have the audience learn a particular skill. Suppose your specific purpose is "To inform my audience how to take pictures like a professional photographer." You will present the basic techniques of professional photography and show your listeners how they can utilize those techniques. You want the audience to be able to *use* the techniques as a result of your speech.

Both kinds of speeches about processes may require visual aids. At the very least, you should prepare a chart outlining the steps or techniques of your process. In some cases you will need to demonstrate the steps or techniques by performing them in front of your audience. One student did sleight-of-hand magic tricks to show the techniques behind them. Another acted out the basic methods of mime. Yet another executed elementary karate maneuvers. In each case, the demonstration not only clarified the speaker's process but captivated the audience as well. (If you are using visual aids of any kind, be sure to review Chapter 12 before your speech.)

When informing about a process, you will usually arrange your speech in *chronological* order, explaining the process step by step from beginning to end. For example:

Specific Purpose: To inform my audience of the basic steps in the classic Japanese tea ceremony.

Central Idea: There are five major steps in the Japanese tea ceremony.

Main Points: I.   First, the guests approach the teahouse, taking time on the way to purify their hands.
II. Second, the guests enter the teahouse, admire the hanging scroll and the vase with a flower arrangement, and seat themselves.
III. Third, the tea master prepares a bowl of tea for each guest, following the prescribed ritual.
IV. Fourth, each guest in turn takes exactly three-and-a-half sips of tea.
V.   Fifth, the guests admire the tea implements, admire the interior of the teahouse, and depart.

Sometimes, rather than leading your audience through a process step by step, you will focus on the major principles or techniques involved in performing the process. Then you will organize your speech in *topical* order. Each main point will deal with a separate principle or technique. For example:

Specific Purpose: To inform my audience of the common methods used by stage magicians to perform their tricks.

Central Idea: Stage magicians use two common methods to perform their tricks—mechanical devices and sleight of hand.

Main Points: I.   Many magic tricks rely on mechanical devices that may require little skill by the magician.
II. Other magic tricks depend on the magician's skill in fooling people by sleight-of-hand manipulation.

Concise organization is especially important in speeches about processes. You must make sure each step in the process is clear and easy to follow. If your process has more than four or five steps, group the steps into units so as to limit the number of main points. Otherwise, you will have too many main points for listeners to grasp and recall. For example, in a speech explaining how to set up a home aquarium, a student presented the following main points:

    I.   First you must choose the size of your tank.
   II.   Then you must determine the shape of your tank.
  III.   You must also decide how much you can afford to pay for a tank.
  IV.   Once you have the tank, you need a filter system.
   V.   A heater is also absolutely necessary.
  VI.   You must also get an air pump.
 VII.   Once this is done, you need to choose gravel for the tank.
VIII.   You will also need plants.
  IX.   Other decorations will round out the effects of your aquarium.
   X.   Now you are ready to add the fish.
  XI.   Fresh-water fish are the most common.
 XII.   Salt-water fish are more expensive and require special care.

Not surprisingly, this was too much for the audience to follow. The speaker should have organized the points something like this:

   I.   The first step in establishing a home aquarium is choosing a tank.
      A.   The size of the tank is important.
      B.   The shape of the tank is important.
      C.   The cost of the tank is important.

  II.   The second step in establishing a home aquarium is equipping the tank.
      A.   You will need a filter system.
      B.   You will need a heater.
      C.   You will need an air pump.
      D.   You will need gravel.
      E.   You will need plants.
      F.   You may also want other decorations.

 III.   The third step in establishing a home aquarium is adding the fish.
      A.   Fresh-water fish are the most common for home aquariums.
      B.   Salt-water fish are more expensive and require special care.

As you can see, the subpoints cover the same territory as that originally covered by the twelve main points. But three main points are much easier to understand and remember than twelve.

Speeches About Events

The *Random House Dictionary* defines an event as "anything that happens or is regarded as happening." By this definition, the following are examples of suitable subjects for informative speeches about events:

lightning	job interviews
Halloween	cosmetic surgery
sleep disorders	San Francisco earthquake
civil rights movement	gum disease
slips of the tongue	final exams
television viewing	assassination of Abraham Lincoln

As usual, you will need to narrow your focus and pick a specific purpose you can accomplish in a short speech. Here are examples of good specific purpose statements for informative speeches about events:

To inform my audience about the major types of cosmetic surgery.

To inform my audience about the impact of television viewing on children.

To inform my audience of the warning signs and prevention of gum disease.

To inform my audience what happened the night Abraham Lincoln was assassinated.

To inform my audience of the major kinds of sleep disorders.

As you can see, there are many ways to discuss events. If your specific purpose is to recount the history of an event, you will organize your speech in *chronological* order, relating the incidents one after another, in the order they occurred. For example:

Specific Purpose: To inform my audience about the history of Halloween observances.

Central Idea: Halloween has been celebrated in the late autumn for at least two thousand years.

Main Points: I.   The ancient Druids lit huge bonfires on the night we call Halloween to ward off evil spirits evoked by Saman, lord of the dead.

II.   When the Romans conquered the Druids, they added elements of their harvest festival to the ritual.

III.   After the Christian church established the feast of All Hallow's Day on November 1, the preceding dark night came to be known as All Hallow's Eve, or Halloween.

IV.   Modern observances of Halloween combine the focus on ghosts and evil spirits with harvest symbols such as pumpkins and apples.

Instead of recounting the history of an event, you might take a more analytical approach and explain its causes and/or effects. In such a case, you will organize your speech in *causal* order. Let's say your purpose is "To inform my audience why so many lives were lost when the 'unsinkable' ocean liner *Titanic* sank." Working from cause to effect, your outline might look like this:

Specific Purpose:	To inform my audience why so many lives were lost when the "unsinkable" ocean liner *Titanic* sank.
Central Idea:	Inability to remove the passengers and crew from the doomed *Titanic* caused the death of more than two-thirds of those on board.

Main Points:

I.   There were two major causes for the great loss of life when the *Titanic* went down.

    A.   The *Titanic* carried insufficient lifeboats for the number of people on board.

    B.   On the ship *Californian,* which was nearby, the radio operator had shut down the radio and gone to sleep.

II.   The effects of these two situations were disastrous.

    A.   When all usable lifeboats had been filled, more than 1,500 people remained on board the *Titanic.*

    B.   The *Californian,* unaware of the distress signal, steamed on while the *Titanic* went to the bottom.

There are other ways to deal with an event besides telling what happened or why it happened. Indeed, you can approach an event from almost any angle or combination of angles—features, origins, implications, benefits, future developments, and so forth. In such cases, you will put your speech together in *topical* order. And you should make sure your main points subdivide the subject logically and consistently. For instance:

Specific Purpose:	To inform my audience about the four traditional events in women's gymnastics.
Central Idea:	The four traditional events in women's gymnastics are floor exercise, vault, balance beam, and uneven parallel bars.

Main Points:

I.   The floor exercise combines dancing, acrobatics, and tumbling.

II.   The vault features explosive strength and dramatic midair maneuvers.

III.   The balance beam requires precise routines and perfect coordination.

IV.   The uneven parallel bars demand great strength, flexibility, and agility.

Speeches About Concepts

Concepts include beliefs, theories, ideas, principles, and the like. They are more abstract than objects, processes, or events. The following are some examples of subjects for speeches about concepts:

transcendentalism	philosophies of education
concepts of science	principles of psychology
film theory	constitutionalism
romanticism	historical interpretations
principles of feminism	theories of poetry

Taking a few of these general subjects, here are some good specific purpose statements for speeches about concepts:

To inform my audience about the basic beliefs of transcendentalism.

To inform my audience about the different philosophies of education in Japan and the United States.

To inform my audience about the theory of birth order as a factor in psychological development.

To inform my audience about the constitutional beliefs of the Founding Fathers.

To inform my audience about the *auteur* theory in film making.

Speeches about concepts are usually organized in *topical* order. One common approach is to enumerate the main features or aspects of your concept.

Specific Purpose: To inform my audience of the basic principles of Confucianism.

Central Idea: The Confucian ethic centers on the supreme virtue known as *jen,* which has two major aspects.

Main Points: I.   The first major aspect of *jen* is *chung,* or faithfulness to oneself and others.
II.   The second major aspect of *jen* is *shu,* or altruism, usually stated as the golden rule: Do unto others as you would have others do unto you.

A more complex approach is to define the concept you are dealing with, identify its major elements, and illustrate it with specific examples. For instance:

Specific Purpose: To inform my audience of the basic principles of nonviolent resistance.

Central Idea: Nonviolent resistance is a philosophy of protest that has been used successfully in at least two major mass movements of the twentieth century.

Main Points: I. Nonviolent resistance is defined as "the refusal to use violence in response to oppressive authority."

II. There are three major elements of nonviolent resistance: maintaining the purity of means and ends; refusing to inflict violence on one's enemies; and using suffering as a powerful social force.

III. The best modern examples of nonviolent resistance are Gandhi's movement against British colonial rule in India and the American civil rights movement of the late 1950s and early 1960s.

Yet another approach is to explain competing schools of thought about the same subject. For example:

Specific Purpose: To inform my audience of the three major theories to account for the extinction of dinosaurs.

Central Idea: The three major theories accounting for the extinction of dinosaurs stress a natural change in climate, the emergence of mammals, and the collision of the earth with a giant asteroid.

Main Points: I. One theory says dinosaurs became extinct because natural changes in the earth's climate made it too cold for them to survive.

II. A second theory claims dinosaurs became extinct because they could not compete with mammals for food.

III. A third theory holds dinosaurs became extinct due to the collision of the earth with a giant asteroid.

As you can see from these examples, speeches about concepts are often more complex than other kinds of informative speeches. Concepts are abstract and can be very hard to explain to someone who is learning about them for the first time. When explaining concepts, pay special attention to avoiding technical language, to defining terms clearly, and to using examples and comparisons to illustrate the concepts and make them understandable to your listeners.

The lines dividing speeches about objects, processes, events, and concepts are not absolute. Some subjects could fit into more than one category, depending on how you develop the speech. You could treat the Declaration of Independence as an object—by explaining its history and its role in the American Revolution. Or you could deal with the meaning of the Declaration, in which case you would be speaking about a concept—an idea bound up with freedom and democracy. To take another example, a speech about the destruction of the ancient city of Pompeii by the eruption of Mount Vesuvius would probably deal with its subject as an event, but a speech on what causes volcanoes to erupt would most likely treat its subject as a process. The important step is to decide how you will handle your subject—as an object, a process, an event, or a concept. Once you do that, you can develop the speech accordingly.

One final word about organizing your informative speech: Regardless of which method of organization you use, be sure to give your listeners plenty of help in sorting out facts and ideas during the speech. One way is by using enough transitions, internal previews, internal summaries, and signposts (see pages 158–162). Another way is to follow the old maxim: "Tell 'em what you're going to say; say it; then tell 'em what you've said." In other words, preview the main points of your speech in the introduction, and summarize them in the conclusion. This will make your speech not only easier to understand but also easier to remember.

GUIDELINES FOR INFORMATIVE SPEAKING

Actually, all the previous chapters of this book relate to the principles of informative speaking. Choosing a topic and specific purpose, analyzing the audience, gathering materials, choosing supporting details, organizing the speech, using words to communicate meaning, delivering the speech—all of these must be done effectively if your informative speech is to be a success. Here we shall emphasize five points to help you avoid the mistakes that plague many informative speakers.

Don't Overestimate What the Audience Knows

In a speech about witches, a student said, "The Salem witchcraft trials were the most notorious outburst of mass hysteria over witches in American history." Then she went on to other matters, leaving her listeners to puzzle over what the Salem witchcraft trials were, when they happened, and what kind of hysteria took place.

The speaker assumed the audience already knew these things. But her classmates were not experts on witchcraft or American history. Even those who had heard of the Salem witchcraft trials had just a hazy notion of them. Only the speaker knew the trials took place in 1692 in Salem, Massachusetts, where more than 100 people were imprisoned, and 19 hanged, for practicing witchcraft.

As many speakers have discovered, it is very easy to overestimate the audience's stock of information. "You just can't assume that people know what any boob knows, or that they still remember what has once been explained to them."[2] Most Americans know remarkably little even about something as basic as the structure of the U.S. political system. Polls have shown that less than half the population knows how many United States senators their state sends to Washington, D.C., while only about one-third know the term of office for members of the House of Representatives. In one survey, only 23 percent of Americans could name any provision of the Bill of Rights.[3] In another, 64 percent of the people surveyed agreed with the totally erroneous statement that the Constitution establishes English as the national language and requires that it be used in public schools.[4]

A number of studies have shown that many college students are not much more knowledgeable. In one study, questionnaires were distributed among 1,657 students enrolled in introductory public speaking at the University of Wisconsin from 1986 to 1988. The results were astounding. Only 36 percent could name both U.S. senators from their state, while fewer than 20 percent could identify the Chief Justice of the United States. Although 97 percent knew who Mick Jagger is, barely 35 percent could name the U.S. Secretary of State.

Many of the students in this survey were also ill-informed about basic historical, cultural, and scientific facts. A meager 37 percent knew where the Magna Charta was signed (England), while fewer than 30 percent could say who uttered the immortal words "Give me liberty, or give me death" (Patrick Henry) or what country the United States fought in the War of 1812 (England). Only 32 percent could identify where the Andes Mountains are located, and 58 percent mistakenly thought India borders on the Mediterranean Sea. Perhaps most amazing, 8 percent could not state who Adolf Hitler was!

None of this means the students were stupid. Rather, it points up the fact that today's educational system does not always expose students to the storehouse of facts their elders take for granted. In preparing your speeches, you will do well to adapt the news reporters' code: "Never *over*estimate the information of your audience; never *under*estimate the intelligence of your audience."

In most classroom informative speeches, your listeners will be only vaguely knowledgeable (at best) about your topic. Therefore, you must lead them step by step, without any shortcuts. You cannot *assume* they will know what you mean. Rather, you must *be sure* to explain everything so thoroughly they cannot help but understand. As you work on your speech, always consider whether it will be clear to someone who is hearing about the topic for the first time.

Suppose you are talking about the protective tariff. Although many of your classmates might have heard of the protective tariff, you cannot assume they have a firm grasp of it. So you should start by telling them what it is. How will you tell them? Here's one way:

A protective tariff is a form of customs duty. It is a tax on imported goods, but it differs from other taxes in that its primary purpose is not financial but economic— not to increase a nation's revenue but to protect its domestic industry from foreign competition.

To someone who knows a lot about business and commerce this is perfectly clear. But someone who does not will probably get lost along the way. The tone of the statement is that a of a speaker reviewing information already familiar to the audience—not of a speaker introducing new information.

Speeches to inform are given in a wide range of situations. Here Akio Morita, Chief Executive Officer of Sony Corporation, addresses a meeting of the American Electronics Association. (© Robert A. Isaacs/ Photo Researchers)

Here, in contrast, is another explanation of protective tariffs:

What is a protective tariff? Let me explain with an example.

Suppose you make shoes. So does someone in Taiwan. But he can sell his shoes here cheaper than you can. As a result, you are going bankrupt.

So you appeal to the government for help. The government sets up a tariff to protect you from being ruined by the cheap foreign shoes. This means that the government puts a tariff—a tax—on every shoe that comes into the United States for sale from Taiwan. If the tariff is high enough, the shoes from Taiwan will now be more expensive than yours.

Your business has been protected by the tariff. Hence the name, protective tariff.[5]

This statement is clear and simple. Its tone is that of a teacher unraveling a new subject.[6]

Is it too simple? Will your classmates feel you are talking down to them? Almost certainly not. Many students hesitate to speak simply because they are afraid they will sound simple-minded. They think they need big words and complicated sentences to sound intelligent. But nothing could be further from the truth. The test of a good speaker is to communicate even the most complex ideas clearly and simply. Anyone can go to a book and find a learned-sounding definition of a protective tariff like the first one above. But to say in plain English what a protective tariff is—that takes hard work and creative thinking.

Also, remember that readers can study a printed passage again and again until they extract its meaning, but listeners don't have that luxury. They must understand what you say in the time it takes you to say it. The more you assume they know about the topic, the greater your chances of being misunderstood.

If you have circulated a questionnaire among your listeners before the speech, you should have a good idea of their knowledge about the topic. If not, you will usually do better to aim for the low end of the knowledge spectrum. Some experts recommend preparing a speech as if the audience had never heard of the subject. That may be a bit extreme, but it is one way to make sure you define every special term, clarify every idea, illustrate every concept, and support every conclusion.[7] You cannot go wrong by following the advice of Abraham Lincoln (who was anything but simple-minded): "Speak so that the most lowly can understand you, and the rest will have no difficulty."

Relate the Subject Directly to the Audience

The English dramatist Oscar Wilde arrived at his club after the disastrous opening-night performance of his new play.
"Oscar, how did your play go?" asked a friend.
"Oh," Wilde quipped, "the play was a great success, but the audience was a failure."

Speakers have been known to give much the same answer in saving face after a dismal informative speech. "Oh," they say, "the speech was fine, but the audience just wasn't interested." And they are at least partly right—the audience *wasn't* interested. Then was the speech fine? Not by any objective standard. A speech is measured by its impact on a particular audience. There is no such thing as a fine speech that puts people to sleep. It is the speaker's job to get listeners interested—and to keep them interested.

Informative speakers have one big hurdle to overcome. They must recognize that what is fascinating to them may not be fascinating to everybody. A mathematician, for example, might be truly enthralled by a perfect equation, but most people wouldn't want to hear about it. Once you have chosen a topic that could possibly be interesting to your listeners, you should take special steps to relate it to them. You should tie it in with their interests and concerns. Start in the introduction. Instead of saying:

I want to talk to you about the government's cutbacks in money for student loans.

You could say:

> Last week I lost my student loan. Next week you may lose yours—if you haven't already. What will you do when that happens? How will you get through college?

Get your audience involved right at the beginning. Let them know why your message is important to them. Don't assume they will figure it out for themselves. Don't leave it to chance. Tell them. (If you are having trouble with this, recheck the sample introduction on pages 178–179.)

Don't stop with the introduction. Whenever you can, put your listeners into the body of the speech. After all, nothing interests people more than themselves. Don't just rattle off statistics and concepts as if you were reciting a shopping list. Find ways to talk about your topic in terms of your listeners. Bring your material home to them. Get it as close to them as possible.

Here's an example. Let's say you are explaining how people can discover whether they are "secret southpaws"—that is, people who are naturally left-handed but who have grown up preferring the right hand because they were taught to use it as a child. You have plenty of facts and could recite them like this:[8]

> According to *Science* magazine, half of all people who are naturally left-handed assume they are right-handed because that is the hand they use to eat, to write, and to play sports. But how can it be determined whether one is a natural southpaw? According to Abram Blau, author of *The Master Hand*, there are a number of simple tests. For one thing, most natural left-handers can write spontaneously backwards or upside down with the left hand. For another, when left-handers clasp their hands in front of themselves, they usually place the left thumb on top. In contrast, when left-handers grab a broom, they normally place their left hand below the right. Finally, when using the right hand, natural left-handers will draw a circle clockwise, while natural right-handers will draw it counterclockwise. People who give a left-handed response on three or more of these tests may well be secret southpaws.

This is fascinating information, but it is not made fascinating to the audience. Let's try again:

> Just because *you* use *your* right hand to eat, to write, and to play sports, *you* may assume *you* are naturally right-handed. But, says *Science* magazine, half of all people who are naturally left-handed grow up using their right hands. How can *you* tell if *you* are a natural lefty? Dr. Abram Blau, author of *The Master Hand*, gives some tests *you* can try.
>
> First, on a sheet of paper see if *you* can write backwards or upside-down with *your* left hand. If *you* are left-handed, *you* can probably do this spontaneously, without practice or training. Second, clasp *your* hands in front of *you*; whichever thumb *you* place on top usually indicates *your* dominant hand. Third, grab hold of a broomstick. Odds are *you* will place *your* dominant hand on the bottom. Finally, draw a circle on a piece of paper with *your* right hand. If *you* draw it counterclockwise, *you* are probably

a natural right-hander. But if *you* draw it clockwise, *you* are very likely a natural lefty.

If *you* test left-handed on three of these tests, there is a good chance *you* are a secret southpaw.

Look at all the "you's" and "your's." The facts are the same, but now they are pointed directly at the audience. This is the kind of thing that gets listeners to sit up and pay attention.

Don't Be Too Technical

What does it mean to say an informative speech is too technical? It may mean the subject matter is too specialized for the audience. Any subject can be popularized—but only up to a point. The important thing for a speaker to know is what can be explained to an ordinary audience and what cannot.

Say your subject is stereo amplifiers. It's no trick to demonstrate how to operate an amplifier (how to turn it on and off, adjust the volume, set the tone and balance controls). It's also relatively easy to explain what an amplifier does (it boosts the sound received from a radio, record player, or tape deck). But to give a full scientific account of how an amplifier works—that is another matter. It cannot be done in any reasonable time unless the audience knows the principles of audio technology. You would be better off not even trying. The material is just too technical to be understood by a general audience.

Even when the subject matter is not too technical, the language used to explain it may be. Every activity has its jargon. This is true of baseball (portsider, roundtripper, senior circuit); of genetics (allele, nucleotide, cytoplasm); of cooking (blanch, julienne, roux); of music (sonata form, allegro, diminished seventh). If you are talking to a group of specialists, you can use technical words and be understood. But you must do all you can to avoid technical words when informing a general audience such as your speech class.

You may find this hard to do at first. Many people are so addicted to the lingo of their subject that they have trouble escaping it. As you get more practice, though, you will become more and more adept at expressing your ideas in everyday, nontechnical language.

Here, for instance, are two statements explaining the disorder of autism in children. The first is in psychiatric jargon and would have little impact on ordinary listeners:

Autism is a severe communication and behavioral disorder occurring in infants and characterized by ritualistic response to environmental stimuli. Symptoms include an inability to utilize language meaningfully and an inability to process information about the environment. Half of all autistic children are totally mute; those who have limited capacity for verbalization tend to repeat mechanically any aural stimuli to which they are exposed. Other common symptoms are a vacant, withdrawn facial expression, fascination with mechanical objects, and resistance to environmental alteration.

The second statement is perfectly understandable. It shows how technical information can be made clear to the average person:

> The parents of an autistic child may find him to be both their greatest problem and their greatest love. I say "him" because four out of five autistic children are male. The problem usually shows up before the child turns three. It may last for years, or it may last for the entire life of the child. Autism always brings heartbreak to the family of the victim. We can only guess what horrors it brings to the victim himself.
>
> Imagine this: You are the parent of a beautiful little boy. He may not speak at all, ever; half of all autistic children don't. If he does speak, he may just croon the same word over and over in a singsong voice, perhaps a word you've said to him a minute or so earlier. Much of his time is spent in rocking his body, back and forth, back and forth, endlessly. He lives almost entirely in his own world, inside his own head. But that doesn't mean he's not aware of what's going on around him. Beware of changing something in his room or moving his toys around! He may become frantic and fly into a tantrum.

Much better, isn't it? The only technical word in the whole passage is "autism." The language is straightforward, the ideas easy to grasp. This is what you should strive for in your informative speeches.

Avoid Abstractions

"My task," said the novelist Joseph Conrad, "is, before all, to make you see." And make the reader see is just what Conrad did. Witness this passage, in which Conrad describes the aftermath of an explosion on shipboard:

> The first person I saw was Mahon, with eyes like saucers, his mouth open, and the long white hair standing straight on end round his head like a silver halo. He was just about to go down when the sight of the main deck stirring, heaving up, and changing into splinters before his eyes, petrified him on the top step. I stared at him in unbelief, and he stared at me with a queer kind of shocked curiosity. I did not know that I had no hair, no eyebrows, no eyelashes, that my young mustache was burnt off, that my face was black, one cheek laid open, my nose cut, and my chin bleeding.[9]

A speech is not a novel. Still, too many abstractions are tedious—whether in a novel or in a speech. Many informative speeches would be vastly improved by the novelist's bent for color, specificity, and detail.

One way to avoid abstractions is through *description.* When we think of description, we usually think of external events, such as the explosion described by Conrad. But description is also used to communicate internal feelings. Here is how one student, himself a hemophiliac, tried to convey to his audience what it means to suffer a hemophiliac hemorrhage in a joint like the knee, elbow, or ankle:

Medical authorities agree that a hemophiliac joint hemorrhage is one of the most excruciating pains known to mankind.

That sounds awful. What is the pain like?

To concentrate a large amount of blood into a small, compact area causes a pressure that words can never hope to describe.

Now we know what a hemophiliac joint hemorrhage is. We also know that words can never fully describe the pain.

And how well I remember the endless pounding, squeezing pain. When you seemingly drown in your own perspiration, when your teeth ache from incessant clenching, when your tongue floats in your mouth and bombs explode back of your eyeballs; when darkness and light fuse into one hue of gray; when day becomes night and night becomes day—time stands still—and all that matters is that ugly pain.[10]

We have been warned that words cannot capture the pain, yet the speaker does a good job of trying. The vivid description lends reality to the speech and draws the audience further in.

Another way to escape abstractions is with *comparisons* that put your subject in concrete, familiar terms. Do you want to convey the vastness of space and the enormous distance between stars? You could say this:

Although the stars look close together when viewed from earth, they are actually trillions of miles apart.

True, but "trillions of miles" is so remote from our experience that we cannot fathom its meaning. Now suppose you add this:

To give you an idea how vast the distance between stars is, if there were just three bees in the whole United States, the air would be more congested with bees than space is with stars.[11]

Now you have made the abstract specific and given us a bright new slant on things.

Like comparison, *contrast* can put an abstract idea into concrete terms. Suppose you want to make the point that teachers are underpaid. You could say "The average salary of a teacher is only $24,000." The word "only" suggests that you consider $24,000 low, but low in contrast to what? One speaker offered this contrast:

The average salary of a teacher is $24,000. The average salary of a plumber is $44,000. We expect teachers to fix the leaks in our educational system, but we pay them less than we would a plumber to fix a leaky sink.[12]

Now an abstract fact has been put into meaningful perspective. See if you can do something similar in your informative speech.

Personalize Your Ideas

Listeners want to be entertained as they are being enlightened.[13] Nothing takes the edge off an informative speech more than an unbroken string of facts and figures. And nothing enlivens a speech more than personal illustrations. Remember, people are interested in people. They react to stories, not statistics. Whenever possible, you should try to *personalize* your ideas and dramatize them in human terms.

Let's say you are talking about the effects of electromagnetic radiation—the kind of radiation emitted by such everyday items as microwave ovens, CB radios, automatic garage door openers, and video display terminals. You would surely say that sustained exposure to electromagnetic radiation has been linked to headaches, dizziness, fatigue, loss of judgment, sterility, cataracts, and leukemia. You would also note that these health problems have been caused by electromagnetic radiation at one-tenth of a milliwatt, and that a number of consumer products emit radiation at levels 50 to 100 times as high.

But these are only numbers. If you really want to get your audience involved, you will weave in some examples of people who have been harmed by electromagnetic radiation. You might do as one student did and tell the story of Becky Krimson, who worked for the Citizens National Bank in Chicago:

Throughout her three-year period of employment there, Becky often complained of headaches, dizziness, fatigue, and loss of hair. Her boss said she occasionally suffered partial memory loss, while her co-workers frequently complained about Becky's emotional instability. Upon a visit to her doctor she was given some pills, told to take a few days' rest, and sent home. At the time Becky did not know that the video display terminal she worked with at the bank was zapping her with radiation, and that rest and pills could not cure her symptoms.[14]

One speaker, discussing the differences between primary school education in Japan and the United States, found an ingenious way to personalize his subject. He created a "fictional, yet typical, Japanese child—Ruriko," and led his audience through a day in Ruriko's life. Here is an excerpt:

Ruriko awakens at 6:30 a.m. By 7:30 she has put on her neat, plaid-skirted school uniform, eaten her breakfast of rice and fish, picked up the beautifully arranged box lunch made by her mother, and departed for her school in central Yokohama. Ruriko is ten years old.

Classes continue, with only a break for lunch, until early afternoon. Then Ruriko's mother picks her up and takes her to a gymnastics lesson. (Tomorrow it will be a music lesson, the next day calligraphy, the day after that swimming.) As soon as the lesson is over, Ruriko and her mother jump on the train and hurry to the next scheduled appointment. It is time for *juko*, the special "cram school" many Japanese children attend to improve their chances of gaining admission to private school. For three hours, at *juko*, Ruriko is tutored in science and math.

Ruriko and her mother board the train again and return home, where they enjoy a hasty supper. Then Ruriko settles down to her homework. Around 11:00 p.m. her mother brings her a snack of noodles and tea to keep up her energy for study. Shortly after 1:00 a.m. Ruriko goes to bed. Another day in the life of an ambitious Japanese schoolchild has ended.

This speaker could simply have listed facts about the Japanese system of primary education as though he were reciting from an encyclopedia. Instead he chose a better method—inventing "Ruriko"—to bring the topic to life. No matter what your subject, you can almost always find a way to express it in personal terms.

SAMPLE SPEECH WITH COMMENTARY

The following classroom speech provides an excellent example of how to apply the guidelines for informative speaking discussed in this chapter.[15] As you study the speech, notice how the speaker takes what could be a rather dry and technical topic and makes it dramatic. Pay special attention to how crisply the speech is organized, how the speaker adapts the topic directly to her audience, how she clarifies her ideas with concrete language and vivid description, and how she uses examples to personalize the speech and bring it alive.

THE HEIMLICH MANEUVER

Beginning with a story—real or imaginary—is a fine way to capture attention and interest. The story in this speech works particularly well for two reasons. First, it is vivid, dramatic, and realistic in its details. Second, it relates the topic directly to the audience and gets them involved in the speech.

Imagine this scene. You are sitting with a friend at dinner. You tell a joke and your friend bursts out laughing. Then, suddenly, he isn't laughing any more, or making any sound at all. His eyes seem about to pop out of his head; his face turns pale and then blue. Finally, he collapses over his plate. You rush to his side, trying to figure out what is wrong. Could it be a heart attack? Then you realize what has happened. Your friend has choked on a piece of food that "went down the wrong way." You start to pound him on the back, try to help in any way you can. But it is too late. Five minutes have passed, and your friend is dead.

Because the opening story is hypothetical, the speaker must show it is not far-

This story is imaginary, but it could be real. Incidents like this one happen every day—in restaurants, in the home,

fetched. She does this with statistics that prove choking to be a major cause of accidental death in the United States. Notice that she also reveals the source of her statistics and translates "95 percent" into a specific number of lives that could be saved by using the Heimlich maneuver.

In this paragraph the speaker establishes her credibility and reveals the specific purpose of her speech.

Here the speaker states her central idea and previews the two main points to be discussed in the body. An explicit preview statement at the end of the introduction is especially important in speaking to inform.

Now the speaker moves into her first main point.

The story about the medical convention dramatizes the importance of being able to recognize when a person is choking. It also highlights Dr. Heimlich's achievement in identifying the symptoms of choking and devising a method to save the victims. By using brief stories such as this, the speaker personalizes her ideas, which makes them more interesting and easier to recall. This speech is a fine model of how to work human interest factors into an informative speech.

The speaker does a good job of emphasizing the key symptom of a choking victim—the inability to produce vocal sound.

in dormitory cafeterias. According to a report from the National Safety Council, choking causes 3,900 deaths per year, which makes choking the sixth leading cause of accidental death in the United States. This statistic is even more tragic because 95 percent of these deaths could be prevented—more than 3,700 lives could be saved each year—if someone near the choking victim knew of a simple technique called the Heimlich maneuver.

The Heimlich maneuver was developed by Dr. Henry Heimlich, a professor of clinical sciences at Xavier University in Cincinnati, and it is so easy to learn that even a child can perform it. I learned the maneuver from my mother, who is a nurse, and I have read several articles about it. Today I would like to teach it to you.

The effectiveness of the Heimlich maneuver depends on two factors—knowing the symptoms of a choking victim, and knowing how to perform the maneuver to save the victim. First I will explain the symptoms. Then I will demonstrate the maneuver.

If you are to use the Heimlich maneuver, you must be able to recognize when a person has a piece of food or some other object caught in the windpipe. You may be surprised to know that until Dr. Heimlich offered a clear list of symptoms, not even doctors were sure how to diagnose a choking victim. There is a famous story of a medical convention in Washington, D.C., at which a large group of doctors had gathered for a dinner meeting. All at once a member of the group began to choke on a piece of food. A hundred doctors sat by helplessly while the man choked to death, because the doctors didn't know what was wrong and didn't know what to do.

Fortunately, Dr. Heimlich has since provided a reliable list of symptoms. First, the choking victim is unable to breathe or to speak. Then, because not enough oxygen is reaching the brain, the victim becomes pale, turns blue, and falls unconscious. Of these symptoms, the most important is the victim's inability to speak. There are other conditions that might cause someone to have difficulty breathing and to pass out—a heart attack, for example. But when a conscious person cannot speak—or make any utterance whatever—it is usually because something is lodged in the air passage. In most cases, blockage of the airway is so complete that the choking victim is not able to make any sound at all.

This brief paragraph underscores the urgency of being able to recognize a choking victim and of being able to act quickly to save his or her life. The last sentence is especially effective, because it relates "four or five minutes" to the audience's immediate experience.

This paragraph begins with a transition into the second main point. Rather than assuming that listeners will know the principle behind the Heimlich maneuver, the speaker explains the principle briefly but clearly.

The speaker previews the three positions in which the Heimlich maneuver can be performed. An internal preview is a very easy and effective way to help listeners keep track of your ideas.

The speaker's explanation of how to perform the Heimlich maneuver is very clear. Demonstrating the maneuver on a volunteer allows the audience to *see* exactly how the maneuver is executed. The speaker had arranged for a volunteer from the class well ahead of time, and the volunteer participated in the speaker's final practice session. That way, the volunteer knew exactly what to expect, and the speaker could get the timing of her demonstration just right.

Even though the speaker demonstrates the Heimlich maneuver, she also explains it verbally, step by step. Remember, a visual aid is usually no more effective than the clarity of the explanation that accompanies it.

Another important aspect of the speaker's explanation is its personal tone. Rather than talking about how an abstract "someone" might perform the Heimlich maneuver, the speaker talks in terms of "you." This strengthens the

It is important that you, as an observer, learn to recognize these symptoms and to act quickly. There is no time to waste. Within about four minutes the victim will suffer permanent brain damage. Within about five minutes the victim will be dead. Four to five minutes—that is just a minute or so longer than the amount of time that has passed since I began this speech.

Now that you know how to recognize when a person has something caught in the air passage, you are ready to apply the Heimlich maneuver. When applied properly, it is the most effective way to save the life of a choking victim. The principle behind the maneuver is quite simple. Even when a foreign object is lodged in the windpipe, there is still enough air left in the lungs to dislodge the object if the air is forced upward suddenly. The purpose of the Heimlich maneuver is to create a strong enough burst of air from the lungs to free whatever is stuck in the windpipe.

You can apply the maneuver in any of three positions— while a victim is standing, sitting, or lying on the floor. Let me demonstrate with each position.

If possible, hold the victim up in a standing position to perform the Heimlich maneuver. This is the most effective way to dislodge whatever is caught in the air passage. Stand behind the victim and put both your arms around his waist. Let his head, arms, and upper torso hang forward. Make a fist with one hand and place it thumb side in against the victim's abdomen—slightly above the navel but below the rib cage. Then cover the fist with your other hand and press into the abdomen with a quick upward thrust, bending your arms at the elbows. [Here the speaker gently demonstrated the procedure on a volunteer.] Repeat this action as many times as necessary until the food pops out.

If the victim is sitting down and you cannot get him up, kneel behind him, put your arms around both him and the chair, and perform the maneuver in the same way. [Demonstration by the speaker.] Again, continue the upward thrusts until the food pops out.

If the victim is already prostrate and you cannot get him up, you may have to perform the Heimlich maneuver with the victim lying down. In this event, lay the person flat on his back, with his face turned upward (not to the side). Kneel straddling the victim. Do not try to perform the

speaker's rapport with the audience and helps keep the audience interested.

The conclusion is short and to the point. By referring to the introduction, the speaker again relates the topic directly to the audience, cues listeners that the speech is nearing an end, and enhances the unity of the entire speech. The final sentences reinforce the central idea and summarize the main points of the speech.

maneuver from the side, because you could rupture the victim's liver or spleen. Place the heel of one hand against the choking victim's abdomen, above the navel but below the ribs. Put your other hand on top of the first one and press into the victim's abdomen with a quick upward thrust. [Demonstration by the speaker.]

As you can see, the Heimlich maneuver is easy to learn and easy to perform. Thousands of people, from children to senior citizens, have saved lives by using it. So if you are ever in a situation like the one I described at the start of this speech, remember what you have heard today: If your dinner companion suddenly can neither breathe nor speak, he or she has a foreign object stuck in the air passage. By applying the Heimlich maneuver, you can expel the object and save your companion's life.

SUMMARY

Speaking to inform occurs in a wide range of everyday situations. Yet it is a difficult task that requires more skill than you might think. Improving your ability to convey knowledge effectively will be most valuable to you throughout your life.

Informative speeches may be grouped into four categories—speeches about objects, speeches about processes, speeches about events, and speeches about concepts. These categories are not absolute, but they are helpful in analyzing and organizing informative speeches.

Objects, as defined here, include places, structures, animals, even people. Speeches about objects usually are organized in chronological, spatial, or topical order. A process is a series of actions that work together to produce a final result. Speeches about processes explain how something is made, how something is done, or how something works. Clear organization is especially important in speeches about processes, because listeners must be able to follow each step in the process. The most common types of organization for speeches about processes are chronological and topical.

An event is anything that happens or is regarded as happening. You can approach an event from almost any angle. You might explain its origins, causes, effects, implications, major features, and so on. Usually speeches about events are arranged in chronological, causal, or topical order. Concepts include ideas, theories, values, principles, and beliefs. Speeches about concepts are often more complex than other kinds of informative speeches, and they typically follow a topical pattern of organization.

No matter what the subject of your informative speech, be careful not to overestimate what your audience knows about it. In most classroom speeches your listeners will be no more than slightly familiar with your topic. Therefore, you cannot assume they will know what you mean. Explain everything so thoroughly they cannot help but understand. Avoid being too technical. Make sure your ideas and your language are fully comprehensible to someone who has no specialized knowledge about the topic.

Equally important, recognize that what is fascinating to you may not be fascinating to everybody. It is your job to make your informative speech interesting and meaningful to your audience. Find ways to talk about the topic in terms of your listeners. Avoid too many abstractions. Use description, comparison, and contrast to make your audience *see* what you are talking about. Finally, try to personalize your ideas. No matter what your subject, you can almost always find a way to dramatize it in human terms.

REVIEW QUESTIONS

After reading this chapter, you should be able to answer the following questions:

1. What are the four types of informative speeches discussed in the chapter? Give an example of a good specific purpose statement for each type.

2. Why must informative speakers be careful not to overestimate what the audience knows about the topic? What can you do to make sure your ideas don't pass over the heads of your listeners?

3. What should you do as an informative speaker to relate your topic directly to the audience?

4. What two things should you watch out for in making sure your speech is not overly technical?

5. What are three methods you can use to avoid abstractions in your informative speech?

6. What does it mean to say that informative speakers should personalize their ideas?

APPLICATION EXERCISES

1. Below is a list of subjects for informative speeches. Your task is two-fold: (1) Select four of the topics and prepare a specific purpose statement for an informative speech about each of the four. Make sure that your four specific purpose statements include at least one that deals with its topic as an object, one that deals with its topic as a process, one that deals with its topic as an event, and one that deals with its topic as a concept; (2) Explain what method of organization you would most likely use in structuring a speech about each of your specific purpose statements.

Statue of Liberty	karate
hurricanes	socialism
music	the stock market
baseball	Egyptian pyramids
Tournament of Roses parade	diamonds
astrology	beer

2. Analyze the speech in the Appendix by Jeffrey Moran ("Nothing to Sneeze At," pages 402–405). Identify the specific purpose, central idea, main points, and method of organization. Evaluate the speech in light of the guidelines for informative speaking discussed in this chapter.

NOTES

[1] The category system used here is based on James H. Byrns, *Speak for Yourself: An Introduction to Public Speaking* (New York: Random House, 1981), Chaps. 10–15.

[2] William Zinsser, *On Writing Well,* 3rd ed. (New York: Harper & Row, 1985), p. 134.

[3] Fred I. Greenstein and Frank B. Feigert, *The American Party System and the American People,* 3rd ed. (Englewood Cliffs, N.J.: Prentice-Hall, 1985), pp. 13–15.

[4] *Wisconsin State Journal,* February 15, 1987.

[5] Adapted from Rudolf Flesch, *The Art of Readable Writing* (New York: Harper & Brothers, 1949), p. 82.

[6] William L. Rivers, *Writing: Craft and Art* (Englewood Cliffs, N.J.: Prentice-Hall, 1975), p. 101.

[7] James J. Welsh, *The Speech Writing Guide* (New York: Wiley, 1968), p. 51.

[8] Adapted from a speech by Kenda Creasy Dean.

[9] Joseph Conrad, "Youth: A Narrative," in *Typhoon and Other Tales of the Sea* (New York: Dodd, Mead, 1963), p. 256.

[10] Ralph Zimmerman, "Mingled Blood," in *Winning Orations, 1956* (Evanston, Ill.: Interstate Oratorical Association, 1956), p. 54.

[11] George Will, "Meet Halley's Comet," *Newsweek* (August 3, 1981), p. 80.

[12] Adapted from Darrell A. Disrud, "The Flood of Incompetency," in *Winning Orations, 1981* (Mankato, Minn.: Interstate Oratorical Association, 1981), p. 79.

[13] James Humes, *Roles Speakers Play* (New York: Harper & Row, 1976), p. 25.

[14] Elighie Wilson, "Before It's Too Late," in *Winning Orations, 1979* (Mankato, Minn.: Interstate Oratorical Association, 1979), p. 19.

[15] Reprinted with permission of Kelly Marti.

CHAPTER 14

Speaking To Persuade

Susan Meeker began that particular school day by having a slight disagreement with her roommate. "Kathy, please," she implored, "can't you *try* to keep your side of the room a little neater? You *know* some people from my French class are coming in tonight to study. It embarrasses me for them to see all that mess." Susan's roommate promised she'd make more of an effort, and Susan went off to breakfast.

Her first stop before classes was an appointment with her English professor. "The reason I wanted to see you," she began, "is . . . well . . . I know I shouldn't ask for special favors . . . but I don't think I can meet the deadline for my term paper. That same week I have a French exam and have to give a speech in my public speaking class. I really want to do a good job on the paper, and I know I will if you only give me three extra days." The professor hemmed and hawed. Then he said, "Okay. You've turned in all your other assignments on time. Just this once."

With a sigh of relief, Susan went off to her morning classes. At noon she was racing across campus when a friend stopped her. "Want to get some lunch?" he asked. "Oh, I can't," replied Susan. "It's my turn to stand at the table and get signatures on the petition against higher dorm fees. I'll see you later, though."

During the afternoon Susan had a free period, and she used the time to make a quick trip to a sportswear shop off campus. After haggling with two clerks, she got to see the store manager. "Look," she said, "I *know* swimsuits are not supposed to be returnable. But this one has a big tear in the back. I didn't notice it until I got the suit back to my room. There's no way to fix it, and I can't wear it this way. So I've thrown away $30." Finally, the store manager relented, and Susan got a new suit.

In the evening, Susan's classmates came by to work together on a difficult French translation. She noticed that one of them had a terrible cough. "Larry," she asked, "what's the matter with you?" "Oh, it's nothing," he replied, "Just the end of a cold that goes on and on." "It sounds awful," said Susan. "You know, it could be bronchitis or even pneumonia. Why don't you see a doctor to be on the safe side?" After a bit of resistance, Larry agreed to stop at the health center the next day.

If you asked Susan how she spent her day, she might say, "I went to classes, I worked the petition table, I returned a swimsuit, I studied with some friends." In fact, she spent a large part of her day *persuading*—persuading people to do things that they were reluctant to do or that had not occurred to them. Most of us do a certain amount of persuading every day, although we may not realize it or call it that. Public speaking to persuade is essentially an extension of this. It involves trying to convert a whole group, not just an individual, to your point of view on a particular subject.

Although persuasion has been studied for the past 2,000 years, it is still the subject of lively debate among scholars. There are a number of respected theories about how persuasion works, a variety of scientific models of the persuasive process, even a wide range of competing definitions of what persuasion is.[1]

For our purpose it is enough to know that when you speak to persuade, you act as an advocate. Your job is to change listeners' minds—to get them to agree with you and, perhaps, to act on that belief. Your goal may be to defend an idea, to refute an opponent, to sell a program, or to inspire people to action.

Because persuasive speakers must communicate information clearly and concisely, you will need all the skills you used in speaking to inform. But you will also need new skills—skills that take you from conveying information to affecting your listeners' beliefs or actions.

Of all the aspects of public speaking, persuasion is the most complex and the most difficult. Your objective is more ambitious than in speaking to inform, and audience analysis and adaptation become much more demanding. In some persuasive speeches you will deal with controversial topics that touch on your listeners' most basic attitudes and values. This will increase your listeners' resistance to persuasion and make your task that much more challenging.

It is much easier, for example, to explain the history of capital punishment than to persuade an audience either that capital punishment should be abolished or that it should be reinstituted in every state. In the persuasive speech you must contend not only with your audience's knowledge of capital punishment but also with their attitudes toward crime and justice, their beliefs about whether capital punishment deters people from committing violent crimes, and their values about the taking of human life. Lines of argument that work with one part of the audience may fail with—or even upset—another part. What seems perfectly logical to some listeners may seem wildly irrational to others. No matter how expert you are on the topic, no matter how skillfully you prepare the speech, no matter how captivating your delivery—some listeners will not agree with you.

But this does not mean persuasion is impossible. It does mean you should enter a persuasive speaking situation with a realistic sense of what you can accomplish. You cannot expect a group of die-hard Democrats to become Republicans, or a steak-lover to turn vegetarian, as a result of one speech. If listeners are not strongly committed one way or another on your topic, you can realistically hope your speech will move at least some of them toward your side. If listeners *are* strongly opposed to your viewpoint, you can consider your speech a success if it leads even a few to reexamine their views.

As with other kinds of public speaking, you are more likely to be effective in persuasion if you approach it systematically and with a clear understanding of the methods available to you. This chapter explores the basic skills of persuasive speaking. We will begin by looking at three major kinds of persuasive speeches. Then we will deal with special features of audience analysis and adaptation in persuasive speaking. Finally, we will investigate the methods of persuasion.

TYPES OF PERSUASIVE SPEECHES: ANALYSIS AND ORGANIZATION

A persuasive speech always occurs in a situation where two or more points of view exist. The speaker believes in reincarnation, but many listeners do not. The speaker considers euthanasia to be murder, but some in the audience think it is justified in certain circumstances. The speaker wants everyone in the audience to sign up immediately to work for the United Way, but most listeners are inclined to procrastinate and will do it "someday." The different points of view may be completely opposed or they may simply be different in degree. Whichever the case, there must be a disagreement, or else there would be no need for persuasion.

Persuasive speeches may center on a question of *fact,* a question of *value,* or a question of *policy.* Determining the kind of question in dispute is the first step in persuasive speaking, for it will affect both the content and the organization of your speech.

Speeches on Questions of Fact

What major college football team has won the most games since 1975? Who was President of the United States during World War I? How far is it from New York to Moscow? These questions of fact can be answered absolutely. You can look up the answers in a reference book, and no reasonable person would dispute them. The answers are either right or wrong.

But many questions of fact cannot be answered absolutely. There *is* a true answer, but we don't have enough information to know it. Some questions like this involve prediction: Will the economy be better or worse next year? Who will win the Super Bowl this season? Will a major earthquake hit California before the year 2000?

Other questions deal with issues on which the facts are murky or inconclusive: Is there intelligent life on other planets? Did the legendary city of Atlantis ever really exist? Did Napoleon die of natural causes, or was he poisoned? What is the leading cause of heart disease? No one has the final answers to these questions, but that doesn't stop people from speculating about them or from trying to convince others that they have the best available answers.

In some ways, a persuasive speech on a question of fact is similar to an informative speech. But the two types of speeches take place in different kinds of situations and for different purposes. The situation for an informative speech is *nonpartisan.* The speaker acts as a lecturer or a teacher. The aim is to give information as impartially as possible, not to argue for a particular point of view. On the other hand, the situation for a persuasive speech on a question of fact is *partisan.* The speaker acts as an advocate. His or her aim is not to be impartial but to present one view of the facts as persuasively as possible. The speaker may mention competing views of the facts, but only to refute them.

As an example of this, we might consider the Bermuda Triangle—an area of ocean off the coast of Florida where more than fifty ships and airplanes have vanished, often under seemingly mysterious circumstances. Even though government agencies, insurance companies, scientists, and other researchers have spent thousands of hours studying the Bermuda Triangle, they still do not know exactly what phenomenon caused all those ships and planes to disappear. But a number of facts *are* known: Ocean currents in the Bermuda Triangle are swift and unpredictable. The Bermuda Triangle is one of two places in the world where the compass needle points to true north rather than magnetic north. Weather conditions in the Bermuda Triangle can turn violent with little or no warning. Many experienced pilots and sailors have reported bizarre happenings in the Bermuda Triangle. The informative speaker would merely recite these facts. The persuasive speaker, however, would draw a conclusion from them and try to convert listeners to one specific explanation of the strange events in the Bermuda Triangle.

If there were no possibility of dispute on questions of fact, there would be no need for courtroom trials. In a criminal trial there is usually at least one known fact—a crime has been committed. But did the defendant commit the crime? And if so, for what reason? The prosecuting attorney will try to persuade the jury that the defendant is guilty. The defense attorney will try to persuade them that the defendant is innocent. It will be up to the jury to decide which view of the facts is more persuasive.

Persuasive speeches on questions of fact are usually organized *topically*. Suppose, for example, you want to convince your classmates that a major earthquake will hit California within the next fifteen years. Each main point will present a *reason* why someone should agree with you:

Specific Purpose:	To persuade my audience that a major earthquake will hit California in the next fifteen years.
Central Idea:	There are three good reasons to believe that a major earthquake will hit California in the next fifteen years.
Main Points:	I. California is long overdue for a major earthquake. II. Many geological signs indicate that a major earthquake may happen soon. III. Experts agree that a major earthquake could hit California any day.

Or suppose you try to persuade your classmates that IQ tests discriminate against racial and ethnic minorities. Your specific purpose, central idea, and main points might be:

Specific Purpose:	To persuade my audience that IQ tests discriminate against racial and ethnic minorities.
Central Idea:	The vocabulary, the questions, and the situation of IQ tests all work to lower the scores of children from ethnic and racial minorities.
Main Points:	I. The vocabulary used in IQ tests is often unfamiliar to children from racial and ethnic minorities. II. The questions asked in IQ tests are usually based on white, middle-class values and experiences. III. The testing situation for IQ tests may also hinder the performance of minority children.

Occasionally you might arrange a persuasive speech on a question of fact *spatially*. For example:

Specific Purpose:	To persuade my audience that poaching of wild animals has become a serious international problem.
Central Idea:	Poaching—or illegal hunting of wildlife—is threatening the survival of animal species throughout the world.
Main Points:	I. In Africa poaching has claimed thousands of leopards, cheetahs, rhinoceroses, and elephants.
	II. In Asia poaching has all but eliminated Bengal tigers, snow leopards, and musk deer.
	III. In South America poaching has driven jaguars and swamp deer to the brink of extinction.
	IV. In North America poaching has drastically reduced the number of bald eagles, grizzly bears, timber wolves, and giant otters.

Notice that in all these examples the speaker's purpose is limited to persuading the audience to accept a particular view of the facts. Sometimes, however, the dispute that gives rise to a persuasive speech will go beyond a question of fact and will turn on a question of value.

Speeches on Questions of Value

Who was the greatest baseball pitcher of all time? Are animal-to-human organ transplants morally justifiable? What are the ethical responsibilities of journalists? Such questions involve matters of fact, but they also demand *value judgments*—judgments based on a person's own beliefs about what is right or wrong, good or bad, moral or immoral, ethical or unethical, proper or improper.

Take the issue of brain death. It can be discussed at a purely factual level by asking such questions as "How long can a person showing no brain activity be sustained on life-support systems?" Or "How much does it cost to maintain such a person in a hospital or nursing home for one month?" These are factual questions. The answers you reach are independent of your beliefs about the morality of terminating life support. But suppose you ask "Is it morally justifiable to remove life-support systems from a living body?" Or "Is it acceptable to burden a family with the cost of maintaining life support when there is no hope for the patient's recovery?" Now you are dealing with questions of value. How you answer will depend not only on your factual knowledge about brain death but also on your moral values.

This does not mean questions of value are totally subjective, totally matters of personal opinion or whim. When speaking about questions of value you must *justify* your opinion. Suppose you claim that bicycle riding is the ideal form of land transportation. The first step in justifying your claim is to define what you mean by an "ideal" form of land transportation. Do you mean a mode of transportation that gets people where they want to go as fast as possible? That is relatively inexpensive? That is fun? Nonpolluting? Beneficial for the user? In other words, you must first establish your *standards* for an "ideal form of land transportation." Then you can show how bicycle riding measures up against those standards. If you were giving a speech on this subject, your specific purpose, central idea, and main points might be:

Specific Purpose:	To persuade my audience that bicycle riding is the ideal form of land transportation.
Central Idea:	Bicycle riding is the ideal form of land transportation because it is faster than walking or running, does not exploit animals or other people, is nonpolluting, and promotes the health of the rider.

Main Points:	I. An ideal form of land transportation should meet four major standards.
	A. It should be faster than walking or running.
	B. It should not exploit animals or other people.
	C. It should be nonpolluting.
	D. It should be beneficial for the person who uses it.
	II. Bicycle riding meets all these standards for an ideal form of land transportation.
	A. Bicycle riding is faster than walking or running.
	B. Bicycle riding does not exploit the labor of animals or other people.
	C. Bicycle riding is not a source of air, land, water, or noise pollution.
	D. Bicycle riding is extremely beneficial for the health of the rider.

When you speak on a question of value, you do not always have to devote a separate main point to setting forth the standards for your value judgment. But you must make sure to justify your judgment against *some* identifiable standards. In the following example, notice how the speaker judges capital punishment against specific moral and legal standards:

Specific Purpose:	To persuade my audience that capital punishment is morally and legally wrong.
Central Idea:	Capital punishment violates both the Bible and the U.S. Constitution.

Main Points:	I. Capital punishment violates the Biblical commandment "Thou shalt not kill."
	II. Capital punishment violates the constitutional ban on "cruel and unusual punishment."

As you can see, speeches on questions of value may have strong implications for our actions. A person who is persuaded that capital punishment is morally and legally wrong is more likely to support legislation abolishing the death penalty. But speeches on questions of value do not argue directly for or against particular courses of action. They do not urge listeners to *do* anything. Once you go beyond arguing right or wrong to arguing that something should or should not be done, you move from a question of value to a question of policy.

Speeches on Questions of Policy

Questions of policy arise daily in almost everything we do. At home we debate whether or not to buy a new stereo, what to do during spring vacation, which television program to watch at 8 o'clock. At work we discuss whether to go on strike, what strategy to use in selling a product, how to increase productivity. As citizens we ponder whether to vote for or against a political candidate, what to do about surrogate motherhood, how to improve the quality of public education.

All these are questions of policy, because they deal with specific courses of action. Questions of policy inevitably involve questions of fact. (How can we decide whether to vote for a candidate unless we know the facts about his or her stand on the issues?) They may also involve questions of value. (The policy you favor on surrogate motherhood will be affected by whether you think surrogate motherhood is moral or immoral.) But questions of policy *always* go beyond questions of fact or value to consider whether something should or should not be done.

When put formally, questions of policy usually contain the word *should*, as in these examples:

Should workers be permitted to choose between contributing to Social Security or to a private pension plan?

What steps should our school take to deal with vandalism on campus?

How should the United States deal with the growing problem of teenage pregnancies?

What should the United States and other countries do to curb the continuing depletion of the ozone layer?

What actions should be taken to limit the spread of pornography?

If you speak on a question of policy, your goal may be to evoke either passive agreement or immediate action from your listeners. *Passive agreement* means your audience agrees with you that a certain policy is desirable, but it will not necessarily do anything to enact the policy. Suppose, for example, you want to persuade people that the United States should abolish the electoral college and elect the President by direct popular vote. If you seek passive agreement, you will try to get your audience to concur that the President should be chosen directly by the people rather than by the electoral college. But you will not urge the audience to take any action right now to help change presidential election procedures.

When your goal is *immediate action,* you want to do more than get your listeners to nod their heads in agreement. You want to motivate them to action. Beyond convincing them that your cause is sound, you will try to rouse them to take action right away—to sign a petition for abolishing the electoral college, to campaign for better food in the dorms, to boycott movies that degrade women, to work for a political candidate, to contribute to a fund drive, to donate blood to the Red Cross, and so forth.

Some experts say you should seek action from your audience whenever possible. Although it is easier to gain passive agreement than to elicit action, the listener is not making much of a commitment by thinking, "Sure, I agree with you." Within a day or two that same listener may forget entirely about your speech—and about his or her agreement with it. Action, however, reinforces belief. If you can persuade a listener to take some kind of action— even if it is no more than signing a petition, putting a bumper sticker on the car, or attending a meeting to learn about the sorority system—you have gained a more serious commitment. Once a listener acts in behalf of a speaker's position, no matter if the action is minor, he or she is more likely to remain committed to the speaker's position and to take future action in support of it.[2]

When you call for action in a persuasive speech, you should make your recommendations as specific as possible. Don't just urge listeners to "do something." Tell them exactly what to do and how to do it. If you want them to donate blood to the Red Cross, tell them where to go, how to get there, what will happen after they arrive, and how long the whole procedure will take. After the speech give everyone a brochure from the Red Cross to reinforce your message. Remember, the more specific your instructions, the more likely your call to action will succeed.[3]

Basic Issues of Policy Speeches   Regardless of whether your aim is to elicit passive agreement or inspire immediate action, you will face three basic issues whenever you discuss a question of policy—need, plan, and practicality.

There is no point in arguing for a policy unless you can show a *need* for it:

Is there a need for more student parking on campus?

Is there a need to control the use of illegal drugs in the workplace?

Is there a need for businesses to provide maternity leaves for women employees?

Your first step is to convince listeners there is a problem with things as they are. No doubt you have heard the old saying, "If it ain't broke, don't fix it." People are not inclined to adopt a new policy unless they are convinced the old one is not working. This is why the burden of proof always rests with the speaker who advocates change. If you are speaking in favor of a new policy, you must prove to your listeners' satisfaction that there is a serious problem with existing policy, that the problem will only get worse with time, and that action must be taken now to solve the problem. (Of course, you may be defending present policy, in which case you will argue that there is *no* need to change—that things are already working as well as can be expected.)

The second basic issue is *plan*. What is your solution to the problem?

What can we do to get more student parking on campus?

What specific measures should be taken to control the use of illegal drugs in the workplace?

How long should maternity leaves be, and should women receive salaries while on leave?

Answering such questions is particularly important if you call for a new policy. It's easy to complain about problems; the real challenge is to develop solutions. In most classroom speeches you will not have time to describe your plan in detail, but you should at least identify its major features. If you advocate maternity leaves for women employees, you might follow the lead of some proponents and urge that businesses be required to give a new mother 18 weeks of unpaid leave. Or you might propose a more ambitious plan, in which women would be granted 6 weeks paid leave after the birth of a child. Or you could even call for a system such as that in West Germany, where women employees can take up to 40 weeks of maternity leave, with full pay for 18 of those weeks. But whatever your plan, be sure to explain any aspects of it that might seriously affect your audience's willingness to accept it.

The third basic issue is *practicality*. Will the new policy work? Will it solve the problem? Or will it create new and more serious problems?

You could certainly provide more student parking by building a multilevel parking ramp on campus, but the cost would be astronomical.

Requiring regular drug testing for workers in sensitive jobs might help reduce the use of illegal drugs in the workplace, but errors in the tests could lead to some people being unfairly branded as drug users.

Maternity leaves for women employees would surely help ease the burden on working mothers, but it might lead businesses to reduce the number of jobs open to women.

These are significant concerns. Whenever you advocate a new policy, you must be prepared to show it is workable. No matter how serious a problem may be, listeners usually want some assurance that a speaker's plan will actually solve the problem.[4] One way to provide this assurance is by citing expert testimony in support of your policy. An even better way is to show that a plan similar to yours has been successfully implemented elsewhere. For example, if you support a law requiring drug testing for workers in sensitive jobs, you might point to the experience of the U.S. Navy, whose testing program has proved to be reliable and has cut the rate of drug use by 67 percent.

If you oppose a shift in policy, one of your major arguments will be that the change is impractical—that it will create many more problems than it can solve. Opponents of maternity leaves for women employees, for instance, say that such leaves would cost billions of dollars each year and would force businesses to cut back other benefits for both women and men. If listeners accept these arguments, they will likely decide that a policy requiring businesses to grant maternity leaves should not be adopted.[5]

How much of your speech should you devote to need, to plan, and to practicality? The answer depends on your topic and your audience. If your audience is not aware of any need to control the use of illegal drugs in the workplace, you will have to give much of your time to need before covering plan and practicality. But if your listeners already know about the lack of on-campus parking for students, you can remind them quickly of need, then devote most of your speech to plan and practicality.

Or suppose you advocate the passage of tougher antipornography laws. Most people agree that the spread of hard-core pornography is a problem, but many fear that a crackdown on pornographers may ultimately threaten the First Amendment right to free speech for all citizens. Therefore, you should devote a large part of your speech to practicality—to demonstrating that pornography can be curbed without placing undue restrictions on freedom of expression.

Organizing Policy Speeches   Students usually find the policy speech easy to organize. If you advocate a change in policy, your main points often fall naturally into *problem-solution* order. In the first main point you show the extent and seriousness of the problem. In the second main point you explain your solution and show its practicality. For example:

Specific Purpose: To persuade my audience that America should act now to protect the quality of its drinking water.

Central Idea: Impure drinking water is a serious national problem that requires action by citizens and government alike.

Main Points:

I.   Impure drinking water has become a serious national problem.
    A.   Many American communities now have a drinking water problem that threatens public health.
    B.   The problem is becoming more severe with every passing day.

II.   Solving the problem requires action by citizens and government alike.
    A.   The first step is citizen awareness of the problem.
    B.   The second step is establishing and enforcing tough water-quality standards.

You can use the problem-solution format just as easily to organize a speech opposing a change in policy. In such a speech your job is to defend the current system and to attack your opponents' proposed policy. Thus in the first main point you might argue that there is *not* a need for change. In the second main point you might show that even if there were a serious problem, the suggested new policy would *not* solve it and would create serious problems of its own. For example:

Specific Purpose: To persuade my audience that the government should not pass laws limiting the amount of money spent in political campaigns.

Central Idea: Limiting the amount of money spent in political campaigns is neither necessary nor practical.

Main Points: I.   Campaign spending limits are not necessary.
        A.   The amount of money spent by a candidate is not the decisive factor in most elections.
        B.   Almost all of the rise in campaign spending since 1978 is due to either inflation or the high cost of television advertising.
    II.   Besides being unnecessary, campaign spending limits are highly impractical.
        A.   National campaign spending limits cannot adjust to the diverse needs of candidates in different parts of the country.
        B.   Campaign spending limits hurt a challenger's odds of unseating an incumbent office-holder.

For a variation on problem-solution order, you might arrange your speech in *problem-cause-solution* order. This produces a speech with three main points—the first identifying a problem, the second analyzing the causes of the problem, and the third presenting a solution to the problem. For instance:

Specific Purpose: To persuade my audience that the industrialized nations should take firm action to control acid rain.

Central Idea: Acid rain has become an international problem that requires international solutions.

Main Points: I.   The problem of acid rain has now spread throughout the United States and into many other countries as well.
        A.   Recent studies show that acid rain now endangers lakes, streams, forests, and urban property in *all* parts of America—including the Far West.
        B.   Acid rain poses similar problems in other industrialized nations—including Canada, England, West Germany, and the Soviet Union.

II. There are two major causes for the spread of acid rain.
   A. The first major cause is an excess of airborne pollutants from automobiles and industrial plants.
   B. The second cause is lack of cooperation among the industrialized nations to control acid rain.
III. An effective solution must deal with both major causes of the problem.
   A. Individual nations must impose strict controls on the emission of airborne pollutants from automobiles and industrial plants.
   B. The industrialized nations must work together in maintaining strict controls on acid rain.

Some teachers prefer this method of organization because it requires a speaker to identify the causes of the problem. This in turn makes it easier to check whether the proposed solution will get at the causes of the problem rather than simply controlling its symptoms.

When your audience already agrees that a problem exists, you can devote your speech to comparing the advantages and disadvantages of competing solutions. In such a situation, you might put your speech in *comparative-advantages* order. Rather than dwelling on the problem, you would devote each main point to explaining why your solution is preferable to other proposed solutions.

Suppose you want to convince your audience that the U.S. space program should shift its emphasis from highly glamorous staffed flights such as the new space shuttle to unstaffed scientific missions that gather information about other planets and the nature of the solar system. Using comparative advantages order, you would compare unstaffed scientific missions with staffed space flights and show why the former would be a better choice. Your specific purpose, central idea, and main points might look like this:

Specific Purpose: To persuade my audience that the U.S. space program should put greater priority on unstaffed scientific missions that gather information about the planets and the solar system.

Central Idea: Unstaffed scientific missions are less costly and more beneficial than staffed space flights.

Main Points: I. Unstaffed scientific missions are far less costly than staffed space flights.
II. Unstaffed scientific missions provide many more practical benefits than staffed space flights.

If you want to motivate your listeners to action, you may prefer a specialized organizational pattern known as *Monroe's motivated sequence.* Developed in the 1930s by Alan Monroe, a professor of speech at Purdue University, the motivated sequence is based on the psychology of persuasion.[6] It has five steps:

1. *Attention.* First you gain the attention of your audience. You do this in the introduction, by using one or more of the methods described in Chapter 8—relating to the audience, showing the importance of the topic, making a startling statement, arousing curiosity or suspense, posing a question, telling a dramatic story, or using visual aids.

2. *Need.* Having captured the interest of your audience, you next make them feel a need for change. You show there is a serious problem with the existing situation. It is important to state the need clearly and to illustrate it with strong supporting materials—statistics, examples, and testimony—that relate directly to the audience's values or vital interests. By the end of this step, listeners should be so concerned about the problem that they are psychologically "primed" to hear your solution.

3. *Satisfaction.* Having aroused a sense of need, you satisfy it by providing a solution to the problem. You present your plan and show how it will work. Be sure to offer enough details about the plan to give listeners a clear understanding of it.

4. *Visualization.* Having given your plan, you intensify desire for it by visualizing its benefits. The key to this step is using vivid imagery to show your listeners how *they* will profit from your policy. Make them *see* how much better conditions will be once your plan is adopted.

5. *Action.* Once the audience is convinced your policy is beneficial, you are ready to call for action. Say exactly what you want the audience to do—and how to do it. Give them the address to write to. Tell them where they should go to join the Young Republicans. Show them how to sign up for counseling. Then conclude with a final stirring appeal that reinforces their commitment to act.

Many students prefer the motivated sequence because it is more detailed than problem-solution order. It follows the process of human thinking and leads the listener step by step to the desired action. One indication of its effectiveness is that it is widely used by people who make their living by persuasion—especially advertisers. The next time you watch television, pay close attention to the commercials. You will find that many of them follow the motivated sequence, as in this example:

Attention: We see a pleasant house. Guests are arriving for a party. The hostess is in the kitchen making last-minute preparations. Suddenly, she gasps in dismay.

Need: "These wine glasses are all spotted!" she exclaims to her husband. "And your boss here for dinner. I'm so embarrassed! Oh, how could my Spiffo have done this?" "The market was all out of Spiffo," replies her husband, "so I bought this bargain brand. You're right! These glasses don't look nearly as clean as the ones you washed yesterday in Spiffo!"

Satisfaction: Husband and wife search the cupboards frantically for enough glasses washed in Spiffo. The announcer, in voice-over, tells us, "Only Spiffo has a built-in spot remover."

Visualization: Wife proudly carries in the Spiffo-washed glasses. Husband beams as he pours wine for his boss and the other guests. Husband's boss says, "What beautiful glasses! My boy, if your work sparkles as much as these glasses do, you've got a great future ahead of you!"

Action: The audience is urged to buy Spiffo.

Try using the motivated sequence when you want to spur listeners to action. You should find it easy and effective, as did one student who used it in a speech urging classmates to work for passage of a local tenants' rights bill. Here are the highlights of his speech:

Attention: Have you ever had cockroaches running through the cupboards in your apartment? Have you sweltered in the heat because the air conditioning didn't work? Or shivered in the cold because the furnace was broken? Or waited months for the security deposit you never got back even though you left your apartment as clean as when you moved in?

Need: Throughout this city students and other apartment tenants are being victimized by unresponsive and unethical landlords. Just last year more than 200 complaints were filed with the city housing department, but no action has been taken against the landlords.

Satisfaction: These problems could be solved by passing a strong tenants' rights bill that defines the rights of tenants, specifies the obligations of landlords, and imposes strict penalties for violators.

Visualization: Such bills have worked in a number of college communities across the nation. If one were passed here, you would no longer have to worry about substandard sanitary or safety conditions in your apartment. Your landlord could not violate the terms of your lease or steal your security deposit.

Action: A tenants' rights bill has been proposed to the city council. You can help get it passed by signing the petition I will pass around after my speech. I also urge you to help by circulating petitions among your friends and by turning out to support the bill when it is debated in the city council next week. If we all work together, we can get this bill through the council.

Monroe's motivated sequence is entirely compatible with the standard method of speech outlining discussed in Chapter 9. The following outline shows how one student incorporated the sequence into a speech supporting restrictions on cigarette smoking in enclosed public areas. In its full form, the student's outline included supporting materials for all the subpoints in the body of his speech.

INTRODUCTION

Attention: I. What simple action could cut indoor air pollution by 90 percent, reduce the rate of respiratory diseases, and save Americans billions of dollars a year?

II. All this could be achieved by a law restricting cigarette smoking in enclosed public areas.

III. Today I would like to explain the need for such a law and encourage you to support it.

BODY

Need: I. The need to restrict smoking in enclosed public areas can no longer be denied.
   A. According to the U.S. Surgeon General, cigarette smoking is unquestionably a major health hazard for nonsmokers as well as for smokers.
   B. The National Research Council reports that smoking in public areas costs the whole society—nonsmokers as well as smokers—billions of dollars a year in medical, cleaning, and insurance bills.

Satisfaction: II. These problems could be greatly reduced by a law restricting smoking in all enclosed public areas.
   A. The law would include schools, office buildings, stores, industrial facilities, restaurants, banks, hospitals, hotel lobbies, airports, bus stations, and train depots.
   B. Violators would receive a $70 fine for the first offense, and a $100 fine for each additional offense.

Visualization: III. Similar bills have worked in other communities and can work here.
   A. More than 1,200 cities in 42 states now have laws restricting smoking in enclosed public areas.
   B. If we had such a law here, you could enjoy shopping, going out for dinner, attending school, and the like in a smoke-free environment.

CONCLUSION

Action: I. So I urge you to support such a bill by signing the petition I am passing around, to be sent to our city council and state legislature,

II.   The evidence is clear about the harmful effects of cigarette smoke on smokers and nonsmokers alike; it is now time to act.

THE TARGET AUDIENCE

Whether you are speaking on a question of fact, value, or policy, you must tailor your message to your audience if you hope to be persuasive. You must adjust to their knowledge and interests, their values and attitudes, their goals and beliefs. In Chapter 4 we considered the general principles of audience analysis. Now we should take that analysis one step further and apply it to the *target audience.*

No matter what the subject of your speech, you will seldom be able to persuade all your listeners. Some will be so opposed to your views that you will have absolutely no chance of changing their minds. Others will already agree with you, so there is no need to persuade them. Like most audiences, yours will probably contain some listeners who are hostile to your position, some who favor it, some who are undecided, and some who just don't care. You would like to make your speech equally appealing to everyone, but this is rarely possible. Most often you will have in mind a particular *part* of the whole audience that you want to reach with your speech. That part is called the target audience.

Concentrating on a target audience does not mean you should ignore or insult the rest of your listeners. But no matter how noble your intentions or how hard you try, you can't persuade all the people all the time. It only makes sense, then, to decide which portion of the audience you *most* want to reach.

Again advertising gives us an effective model. Successful commercials are aimed at particular segments of the market, and their appeals are picked to fit the target audience. Banks have found that modern-looking advertisements don't draw as many deposits as old-fashioned ones, because older people have more money to deposit. Soft drink commercials, on the other hand, are meant to hook young people. So they feature teen-agers, play their kind of music, and echo their values. Beer commercials? They focus on men who portray the strong, masculine, hearty qualities of male blue-collar workers. Why? Because blue-collar men drink the most beer.[7]

For your classroom speeches, you don't have the sophisticated market-research capability of a large advertising agency. But as we saw in Chapter 4, you can use observation, interviews, and questionnaires to find out where your classmates stand on your speech topic. This is your equivalent of market research. From it you can identify your target audience.

Here is how one student, Kim Lee Chung, determined her target audience for a policy speech urging her classmates to get involved in intramural athletics:

There are 20 students in my audience. From my questionnaires I know that 4 of the 20 are already active in intramurals. They don't need my speech. I also know that 4 have no desire whatsoever to participate in intramurals. They are probably not going to change their minds regardless of what I say. The other 12 students do not participate in intramurals but feel they are in worse physical shape since coming to college and express an interest in learning about intramural athletics. They are my target audience.

Not only did Kim pinpoint her target audience, she also knew from her questionnaires the issues she would have to discuss to be convincing:

Of the 12 students in my target audience, 9 give "lack of time" as the main reason for not participating in intramural recreation. They feel they are too busy with work, studies, or other activities to get involved with intramurals. The other 3 give "lack of athletic ability" as their main reason for staying out of intramurals. The questionnaires also reveal that 7 of the 12 students in my target audience don't know very much about the intramural program and the activities it offers.

With all this information, Kim was able to put together a first-rate speech. What made her speech successful, however, was not just that she did a good job of audience analysis. Knowing your target audience does not guarantee a good speech. The key is how well you *use* what you know in preparing the speech. Once you know where your target audience stands, you must tailor the speech to fit their values and concerns—aim at the target, so to speak.

Most important, you must answer your listeners' objections to your proposal. You cannot convert skeptical listeners unless you deal directly with the reasons for their skepticism.[8] As you prepare your persuasive speech, put yourself in the place of your target audience and imagine how they will respond. For this to work, you must be as tough on your speech as your audience will be. Every place they will raise a question, answer it. Every place they will have an objection, refute it. Every place they will see a hole in your argument, fill it. Leave nothing to chance.

Here is Kim's analysis of how she could do this in her speech. Notice how carefully she answers her target audience's reasons for not engaging in intramurals:

I want to persuade my target audience to try participating in intramural athletics. But I can't do that by talking in general terms. First I must reinforce my target audience's feeling that they need more exercise. Then I will show how the intramural program can meet that need. Since quite a few people don't know much about the program, I'll have to explain exactly what it is and the kinds of sports it includes. To convince people they have time for intramurals, I will point out that the program is designed for the busy student. Games are only once a week and last 45 minutes to an hour. Students can pick the day of the week they want to play and are not obligated to make every game. Finally, to convince the nonathletes, I will state that the sports are divided into beginning, intermediate, and advanced skill levels. People can play even though they don't know much about a sport or don't consider themselves very athletic.

Kim spent her time talking *specifically* about the issues important to her target audience. As a result, she was able to convince several of her classmates to sign up for intramurals.

A speaker will not always be this successful. Persuasion is a complex business. The situation, the speaker's delivery, outside interference, audience resistance—all can upset even the most carefully plotted speech. But if you know your target audience and adapt your message directly to their concerns, you have a much better chance of achieving your purpose.

METHODS OF PERSUASION

What makes a speaker persuasive? Why do listeners accept one speaker's views and reject those of another speaker? People have been trying to answer these questions since the days of the ancient Greeks.[9] Although many answers have been given, we can say that listeners will accept a speaker's ideas for one or more of four reasons:

Because they perceive the speaker as having high *credibility*

Because they are won over by the speaker's *evidence*

Because they are convinced by the speaker's *reasoning*

Because their *emotions* are touched by the speaker's ideas or language

Let us look at each in turn.

Building Credibility

Here are two sets of imaginary statements. Which one of each pair would you be more likely to believe?

"The American automobile industry will meet the challenge of foreign competition and become even stronger in the 1990s." (Lee Iacocca)

"The American automobile industry cannot compete with foreign imports and will only get weaker in the 1990s." (Bill Cosby)

"Television situation comedies are entering a new and more sophisticated stage." (Bill Cosby)

"Television situation comedies are no longer an important form of entertainment." (Lee Iacocca)

Most likely you chose the first in each pair of statements. If so, you were probably influenced by your perception of the speaker. You are more likely to respect the judgment of Iacocca, President of Chrysler Corporation, when he speaks about the automobile industry, and to respect the judgment of Cosby, well-known comedian and star of a hit television series, when he speaks about situation comedy. Some teachers call this factor *source credibility*. Others refer to it as *ethos*, the name given by Aristotle.

Over the years researchers have given much time to studying credibility and its effect on speechmaking. They have discovered that many things affect a speaker's credibility, including sociability, dynamism, physical attractiveness, and similarity of experience between speaker and audience. Above all, though, a speaker's credibility is affected by two factors:

> *Competence*—how an audience regards a speaker's intelligence and knowledge of the subject.

> *Character*—how an audience regards a speaker's sincerity, trustworthiness, and concern for the well-being of the audience.[10]

The more favorably listeners view a speaker's competence and character, the more likely they are to accept what the speaker says. No doubt you are familiar with this effect from your own experience. Suppose you take a course in economics. The course is taught by a distinguished professor who has published widely in all the prestigious journals, who sits on a major international commission, and who has won several awards for outstanding research. In class, you hang on this professor's every word. One day the professor is absent; a colleague of his from the Economics Department—fully qualified but not so well known—comes to lecture in the professor's place. Possibly the fill-in instructor gives the same lecture the distinguished professor would have given, but you do not pay nearly as close attention. The other instructor does not have as high credibility as the professor.

It is important to remember that credibility is an attitude. It exists not in the speaker but in the minds of the audience. A speaker may have high credibility for one audience and low credibility for another. A speaker may also have high credibility on one topic and low credibility on another. Looking back to our imaginary statements, most people would more readily believe Bill Cosby speaking about television situation comedies than Bill Cosby speaking about the American automobile industry.

Finally, we can distinguish three types of credibility:

> *Initial credibility*—the credibility of the speaker before he or she starts to speak.

> *Derived credibility*—the credibility of the speaker produced by everything he or she says and does during the speech itself.

> *Terminal credibility*—the credibility of the speaker at the end of the speech.[11]

All three are dynamic. High initial credibility is a great advantage for any speaker, but it can be destroyed during a speech, resulting in low terminal credibility. The reverse can also occur. A speaker with low initial credibility may enhance his or her credibility during the speech and end up with high terminal credibility, as in the following example:

Lawrence Wood, the public relations officer for a commuter railroad, was scheduled to address a local citizens' group. His topic was "The Future of Our Railroad." As it happened, this particular railroad had an unusually poor service record. The trains were always late—sometimes by an hour or more. They were equipped with outmoded engines, which seemed to catch fire at least once a week. Both air conditioning and heating had long since stopped working, so the passengers froze in the winter and sweltered in the summer. In the face of all this, Lawerence stood up to address an audience composed mainly of commuters.

As you might expect, Lawrence had low initial credibility. No one believed the railroad would ever again do anything right. But Lawrence knew this and was prepared. He came armed with facts to prove that steps were being taken to improve the railroad's service. The operating manager had been fired and a replacement brought in. New equipment had been ordered, to be delivered within six months. Maintenance standards had been upgraded. All through his speech Lawrence took the approach, "We know we have failed you, and we know why. We are working hard to correct it." By the time he had finished, much of the audience was on his side. He had achieved high terminal credibility.

In classroom speeches, you will not face the same problems with credibility as do controversial public figures. Nonetheless, credibility is important in *every* speaking situation, no matter who the participants are or where it takes place. In every speech you give you will have some degree of initial credibility, which will always be strengthened or weakened by your message and how you deliver it. And your terminal credibility from one speech will affect your initial credibility for the next one. If your classmates see you as sincere and competent, they will be much more receptive to your ideas.

How can you enhance your credibility in your speeches? At one level, the answer is frustratingly general. Since everything you say and do in a speech will affect your credibility, you should say and do *everything* in a way that will make you appear capable and trustworthy. Good organization will improve your credibility. So will appropriate, clear, vivid language. So will fluent, dynamic delivery. So will strong evidence and cogent reasoning. In other words—give a brilliant speech and you will achieve high credibility!

The advice is sound but not all that helpful. There are, however, some specific, proven ways you can boost your credibility while speaking. One is to advertise your competence.[12] Did you investigate the topic thoroughly? Then say so. Do you have experience that gives you special knowledge or insight? Again, say so.

Here is how two students revealed their qualifications. The first stressed his study and research:

I never knew much about UFOs until I did a research project on them in my high school science class. Since then, I have read quite a bit about them, including the latest reports of the highly respected Center for UFO Studies in Evanston, Illinois. As a result, I have decided that the evidence strongly suggests that Earth has been—and continues to be—visited by spaceships from other planets.

The second student emphasized her background and personal experience:

Most of us have no idea what it means to be poor and hungry. But before returning to school last year, I spent eight years as a volunteer at local assistance centers. During those years I worked in every part of the city and with every kind of person, from struggling welfare mothers to hardened street people. I cannot begin to tell you everything I have seen—how poverty destroys people's souls and how hunger drives them to desperation. But on the basis of what I *can* tell you, I hope you will agree with me that government help for the poor and the needy must be increased.

In both of these cases, the speakers greatly increased their persuasiveness by establishing their credibility.

Another way to bolster your credibility is to show common ground with the audience. You do not persuade listeners by assaulting their values and rejecting their opinions. This only antagonizes people. It puts them on the defensive and makes them resist your ideas. As the old saying goes, "You catch more flies with honey than with vinegar." The same is true of persuasion. Show respect for your listeners. You can make your speech more appealing by identifying your ideas with those of your audience—by showing how your point of view is consistent with what they believe.[13]

Creating common ground is especially important at the start of a persuasive speech. Begin by identifying with your listeners. Show that you share their values, attitudes, and experiences. Get them nodding their heads in agreement, and they will be much more receptive to your ultimate proposal. Here is how a businessman from Massachusetts, hoping to sell his product to an audience of people in Colorado, began his persuasive speech:

I have never been in Colorado before, but I really looked forward to making this trip. A lot of my ancestors left Massachusetts and came to Colorado nearly 150 years ago. Sometimes I have wondered why they did it. They came in covered wagons, carrying all their possessions, and many of them died on the journey. The ones who got through raised their houses and raised their families. Now that I've seen Colorado, I understand why they tried so hard!

The audience laughed and applauded, and the speaker was off to a good start.

This method of establishing common ground is used often in speeches outside the classroom. Now look at a different approach, used in a classroom speech favoring a tuition increase at the speaker's school—a very unpopular point of view with her classmates. She began by saying:

As we all know, there are many differences among the people in this class. But regardless of our age, major, background, or goals, we all have one thing in common—we are all concerned about the quality of education at this school. And that quality is clearly in danger. Because of budget reductions, faculty salaries have fallen below those at comparable schools, library purchases have been cut back, and more and more students are being crowded out of classes they need to take. Whether we like it or not, we have a problem—a problem that affects each of us. Today I would like to discuss this problem and whether it can be solved by an increase in tuition.

By stressing common perceptions of the problem, the student hoped to get off on the right foot with her audience. Once that was done, she moved gradually to her more controversial ideas.

Speaking techniques aside, the most important way to strengthen your credibility is to speak with genuine conviction. President Harry Truman once said that in speaking, "sincerity, honesty, and a straightforward manner are more important than special talent or polish." If you wish to convince others, you must first convince yourself. If you want people to believe and care about your ideas, you must believe and care about them yourself. Let the audience know you are in earnest—that your speech is not just a classroom exercise. Your spirit, your enthusiasm, your conviction will carry over to your listeners.

Using Evidence

Evidence consists of supporting materials—examples, statistics, testimony—used to prove or disprove something. As we saw in Chapter 6, most people are skeptical. They are suspicious of unsupported generalizations. They want speakers to justify their claims. If you hope to be persuasive, you must support your views with evidence. Whenever you say something that is open to question, you should give evidence to prove you are right.

Evidence is particularly important in classroom speeches because few students are recognized as experts on their speech topics. Research has shown that speakers with very high initial credibility do not need to use as much evidence as do speakers with lower credibility. For most speakers, though, strong evidence is absolutely necessary. It can enhance your credibility, increase both the immediate and the long-term persuasiveness of your message, and help "inoculate" listeners against counterpersuasion.[14]

Evidence is also crucial whenever your target audience opposes your point of view. In such a situation listeners will not only be skeptical of your ideas; they will challenge them at every step of the speech. They will mentally argue with you—asking questions, raising objections, and creating counter-arguments to "answer" what you say.[15] The success of your speech will depend partly on how well you anticipate these internal responses and give evidence to refute them.

You may want to review Chapter 6, which shows how to use supporting materials. The following example illustrates how they work as evidence in a persuasive speech.

Let's say one of your classmates is talking about the harmful effects of excessive exposure to the sun. Instead of just telling you what she thinks, the speaker offers strong evidence to prove her point. As you read the example, notice how the speaker carries on a mental dialogue with her listeners. At each juncture she imagines what they might be thinking, anticipates their questions and objections, and then gives evidence to answer the questions and resolve the objections. She begins this way:

> Many college students are sun worshippers. They believe that having a nice, rich suntan is glamorous and healthy. Well, it may be glamorous, but it certainly is not healthy. In fact, it can have very dangerous consequences.

How do you react? If you already know about the dangers of sun tanning, you probably nod your head in agreement. But what if you don't know? Or don't agree? If you enjoy sunbathing and like having a deep, dark tan, you probably don't *want* to hear anything bad about it. Certainly you will not be convinced by the general statement that exposure to the sun can have "very dangerous consequences." Mentally you say to the speaker, "How do you know? Can you prove it?" or even, "Don't be ridiculous!" Anticipating just such a response, the speaker gives evidence to prove her point:

> According to Dr. Isaac Willis, professor of dermatology at Morehouse School of Medicine, "Tanning is unhealthy in all respects." Although its immediate effects may be no worse than a painful sunburn, in the long run tanning permanently damages the skin, causing it to wrinkle, sag, and age prematurely.

"That's unfortunate," you may think. "But I don't mind getting a few wrinkles twenty years from now if I can have a great-looking tan today." Keeping one step ahead of you, the speaker continues:

> The damage, however, is more than cosmetic. The same ultraviolet rays that dry and shrivel your skin can also cause cancer. As a result of our quest for the perfect tan, says the American Cancer Society, more than 500,000 Americans will get skin cancer this year.

"I didn't know that," you say to yourself. "But is skin cancer all that serious? Can't it be cured?" The speaker answers:

> There are three types of skin cancer. Although two of them can usually be removed with minor surgery if they are caught soon enough, both are deadly if they are left untreated. Moreover, both tend to recur, and both leave the skin with blotches and blemishes. The third type of skin cancer—malignant melanoma—is far more dangerous. It spreads rapidly and is often fatal. Taken together, all three types killed 5,800 Americans last year. That's a steep price to pay for a suntan.

"Still," you wonder, "I don't spend all that much time in the sun. Do I really have to worry?" The speaker tells you:

> What's especially frightening is that you do not have to be a fanatical sun worshipper to wither your skin or even to get cancer. According to *Newsweek*, researchers now believe that malignant melanoma, the deadliest type of skin cancer, can be caused by one or more serious, blistering sunburns as early in life as childhood or adolescence. In other words, as dermatologist Fred Urbach of Temple University warns, even one day of excessive exposure to the sun can produce permanent damage.

This is impressive evidence. Is there anything else?

> One last point. Although skin cancer usually hits people over the age of forty, the Skin Cancer Foundation says the disease is becoming more common among people of college age. I know this at firsthand, because last year I had surgery for skin cancer. The surgery was successful, but the fear and worry remain. I never thought it would happen to me, but it did. I hope it never happens to you, but it can—unless you treat the sun with the respect it deserves.

Now are you convinced? Chances are you will at least think about the possible ill effects of sunbathing the next time you are ready to take off for the pool or beach. Maybe you will spend less time in the sun; perhaps you will use a sunscreen to protect your skin. You may even reassess your whole attitude toward sun tanning. Why? Because the speaker did not just spout her opinions as if they were common knowledge, but instead supported each of her claims with evidence. You should try to do the same in your persuasive speeches.

Any of the supporting materials discussed in Chapter 6—examples, statistics, testimony—can work as evidence in a persuasive speech. No matter what kind of evidence you use, it will be more persuasive if you state it in specific rather than general terms.[16] In the speech about sun tanning, for instance, the speaker did not say "Lots of people get skin cancer each year." That would have left the audience wondering how many "lots" amounts to. By saying "more than 500,000 Americans will get skin cancer this year," the speaker made her point much more effectively. She also enhanced her credibility by showing she had a firm grasp of the facts.

Evidence is also more likely to be persuasive if it is new to the audience.[17] You will gain little by citing facts and figures that are already well known to your listeners. If those facts and figures have not persuaded your listeners before, they will not do so now. You must go beyond what the audience already knows and present striking new evidence that will get them to say, "Hmmm, I didn't know *that.* Maybe I should rethink the issue." Finding such evidence is not always easy. It usually requires hard digging and resourceful research, but the rewards can be well worth the effort.

When using evidence, you should also follow the guidelines explained in Chapter 6. Make sure your examples are vivid, relevant, and representative. Use statistics fairly, and explain them in terms that are meaningful to the audience. When offering testimony, be sure your sources are qualified and objective, and double check to see that you quote or paraphrase them accurately.

Reasoning

The story is told about Hack Wilson, a hard-hitting outfielder for the Brooklyn Dodgers baseball team in the 1930s.[18] Wilson was a great player, but he had a fondness for the good life. His drinking exploits were legendary. He was known to spend the entire night on the town, stagger into the team's hotel at the break of dawn, grab a couple of hours' sleep, and get to the ballpark just in time for the afternoon game.

This greatly distressed Max Carey, Wilson's manager. At the next team meeting, Carey spent much time explaining the evils of drink. To prove his point, he stood beside a table on which he had placed two glasses and a plate of live angleworms. One glass was filled with water, the other with gin—Wilson's favorite beverage. With a flourish Carey dropped a worm into the glass of water. It wriggled happily. Next Carey plunged the same worm into the gin. It promptly stiffened and expired.

A murmur ran through the room, and some players were obviously impressed. But not Wilson. He didn't even seem interested. Carey waited a little, hoping for some delayed reaction from his wayward slugger. When none came, he prodded, "Do you follow my reasoning, Wilson?" "Sure, skipper," answered Wilson. "It proves that if you drink gin you'll never get worms!"

What does this story prove? No matter how strong your evidence, you will not be very persuasive unless listeners grasp your reasoning. You should know, therefore, how to reason clearly and persuasively.

Many people think of reasoning as an esoteric subject of interest only to philosophers, but in fact we all use reasoning every day in practical life. Reasoning is simply the process of drawing a conclusion based on evidence. Sometimes we reason well—as when we conclude that ice particles forming on the trees may mean the roads will be slippery. Other times we reason less effectively—as when we conclude that spilling salt will bring bad luck. Most superstitions are actually no more than instances of faulty reasoning.

As we saw in Chapter 1 (pages 13–15), reasoning is an important component of critical thinking, and it permeates all areas of our lives. For example, we are bombarded daily with persuasive messages ranging from television commercials to political appeals. Sometimes the reasoning in those messages is sound, but often it is faulty—as when we are told that drinking Pepsi will make us more youthful or that using an IBM personal computer will turn the drudgery of writing a term paper into an effortless pleasure. Unless you know how to reason clearly, you may be easy prey for unscrupulous advertisers and glib politicians.

Reasoning in public speaking is basically an extension of reasoning in other aspects of life. As a public speaker you have two major concerns with respect to reasoning. First, you must make sure your own reasoning is sound. Second, you must try to get listeners to agree with your reasoning. Let us look, then, at the basic methods of reasoning and how to use them in your speeches.

Deductive Reasoning   We are all familiar with tests that include problems in logic of this kind:

a.   All men are mortal.
b.   Socrates is a man.
c.   Therefore, Socrates is mortal.

This is the classic deductive syllogism. You reason from a general premise (All men are mortal) to a minor premise (Socrates is a man) to a specific conclusion (Therefore, Socrates is mortal).

Although public speakers seldom reason this formally, they often rely on informal deductive reasoning when trying to persuade an audience. Take the simple claim, "If you want to get better grades, you should study harder." Put into syllogistic form, the claim would look like this:

a.   People who study harder usually get better grades.
b.   You want to get better grades.
c.   Therefore, you should study harder.

This, too, is a deductive syllogism, moving from the general to the specific. You progress from a general premise (People who study harder usually get better grades) to a minor premise (You want to get better grades) to a specific conclusion (Therefore, you should study harder).

Once a speaker's claims are put in this form, they can be evaluated by asking two questions: (1) Are the premises true? (2) Does the conclusion follow logically from the premises? In this case, the answer to both questions is yes. The speaker's conclusion—"If you want to get better grades, you should study harder"—certainly seems reasonable.

But suppose the speaker says:

a.   People who drink coffee usually get better grades.
b.   You want to get better grades.
c.   Therefore, you should drink coffee.

No careful listener would accept this reasoning because the general premise is very doubtful. There is no evidence that people who drink coffee usually get better grades than people who don't. Besides, even if by some coincidence coffee drinkers do get better grades than non-coffee drinkers, there is no basis for concluding that they do so *because* they drink coffee.

In the preceding case the reasoning is flawed by a false premise. But sometimes both premises can be true and the conclusion can *still* be wrong, as in the following example:

a.   Every engineering major is required to take calculus.
b.   Monica is required to take calculus.
c.   Therefore, Monica is an engineering major.

Here the reasoning overlooks the fact that even though all engineering majors are required to take calculus, other majors—math, computer science, physics, statistics—also require calculus. That Monica has to take calculus does not prove she *is* an engineering major, only that she *could be* an engineering major. A sound progression of deductive reasoning would run like this:

a.   Only engineering majors are required to take calculus.
b.   Monica is required to take calculus.
c.   Therefore, Monica is an engineering major.

When you use deductive reasoning in a speech, pay special attention to your general premise. Will listeners accept it without evidence? If not, give evidence to support it before proceeding to your minor premise. You may also need to support your minor premise with evidence. When both premises are soundly based, your audience will be much more likely to accept your conclusion.

Suppose, for example, you plan to speak about excessive salt in the American diet. You begin by formulating a specific purpose:

Specific Purpose: To persuade my audience to limit their consumption of fast foods, canned goods, and frozen foods because of their excessive salt content.

Next, you decide to structure your speech along the lines of a deductive syllogism. The syllogism looks like this:

a.   Excessive consumption of salt is dangerously unhealthy.
b.   Fast foods, canned goods, and frozen foods contain excessive amounts of salt.
c.   Therefore, we should limit our consumption of fast foods, canned goods, and frozen foods.

Now that you have the syllogism, you need to make it work. First, you should support the general premise: Excessive consumption of salt is dangerously unhealthy. You cite medical evidence and research studies. Part of your speech might go like this:

High salt intake has been linked with hypertension, or high blood pressure, which is a major cause of heart disease, kidney disease, and stroke. In northern Japan, where the typical diet contains enormous amounts of sodium, hypertension is the major cause of death. But among people who eat very little salt, such as the preliterate tribes of New Guinea, hypertension and hypertension-related deaths are virtually unknown.

Having supported your general premise, you now go on to bolster your minor premise: Fast foods, canned goods, and frozen foods contain excessive amounts of salt. Your evidence includes the following:

The human body needs only 230 milligrams of sodium per day to function efficiently. But many fast foods, canned goods, and frozen foods deliver several times that amount in a single serving. One McDonald's Big Mac has 1,510 milligrams of sodium—nearly seven times the daily requirement. One serving of canned tomato soup has 1,050 milligrams of sodium—nearly five times the daily requirement. One frozen turkey dinner has 2,567 milligrams of sodium—*eleven* times the daily requirement. No wonder we have a salt overload!

Now you have lined up your ammunition very effectively. You have supported your general premise and your minor premise. You can feel confident in going on to your conclusion:

Therefore, we should limit our consumption of fast foods, canned goods, and frozen foods.

And you can expect your audience to take you seriously. When used properly, deductive reasoning is highly persuasive.

Inductive Reasoning   Inductive reasoning—also called generalization or reasoning from specific instances—is the opposite of deduction. It moves *from the specific to the general*. When you reason inductively, you progress from a number of particular facts to a general conclusion. For example:

Fact 1: My philosophy course last term was boring.

Fact 2: My roommate's philosophy course was boring.

Fact 3: My brother's philosophy course was boring.

Conclusion: Philosophy courses are boring.

As this example suggests, we use inductive reasoning daily, although we probably don't realize it. Think for a moment about all the generalizations that arise in conversation: Used-car salesmen are crooks. Professors are bookish. Texas women are pretty. Sigma Chi's are good students. Physical education courses are easy. Republicans are conservative. Where do such generalizations come from? They come from induction—from observing particular used-car salesmen, professors, Republicans, and so on, and then concluding that what is true in the particular cases is true in general.[19]

The same thing happens in public speaking. The speaker who concludes that nuclear power is unsafe because there have been mishaps at several nuclear power plants is reasoning inductively. So is the speaker who argues that violence on television causes violence in society because several people have enacted in real life crimes they have seen dramatized on television. And so is the speaker who maintains that home birthing with a midwife is dangerous because there are recorded cases of newborns dying under this type of care.

Such conclusions are never foolproof. No matter how many specific instances you give (and you can give only a few in a speech), it is always possible that an exception exists. Throughout the ages people observed countless numbers of white swans in Europe without seeing any of a different color. It seemed an undeniable fact that all swans were white. Then in the nineteenth century, black swans were discovered in Australia![20]

When reasoning inductively, you should follow a few basic guidelines. First, avoid generalizing too hastily. Beware of the tendency to jump to conclusions on the basis of insufficient evidence. Make sure your sample of specific instances is large enough to justify your conclusion. Also, make sure the instances you present are fair, unbiased, and representative. (Are three philosophy courses *enough* to conclude that philosophy courses are boring? Are the three courses *typical* of most philosophy courses?)

Second, be careful of your wording. If your evidence does not justify a sweeping conclusion, qualify your argument. For example, suppose you are talking about the crisis in American medicine brought on by the dramatic increase in malpractice insurance premiums. You document the problem by providing a number of specific instances. Then you draw your conclusion. You might say:

As we have seen, average rates for malpractice insurance have risen by 100 percent in the past five years. We have also seen that the high cost of malpractice insurance is forcing some doctors to leave medicine altogether, while others now refuse to perform high-risk procedures that might result in malpractice suits. It certainly seems fair, then, to conclude that the rising cost of malpractice insurance is threatening the quality of medical care available to many Americans.

This is not as dramatic as saying, "The cost of malpractice insurance is destroying the American medical system," but it is more accurate and will be more persuasive to careful listeners.

Third, reinforce your argument with statistics or testimony. Since you can never give enough specific instances in a speech to make your conclusion irrefutable, you should supplement them with testimony or statistics demonstrating that the instances are in fact representative. If you were talking about violence against teachers in the public schools, you could say:

Assaults against teachers by students have reached epidemic proportions. A Los Angeles teacher had her hair set on fire by students angry over low grades. A New York teacher required hospitalization after being beaten by a gang. A Chicago teacher resigned after being terrorized with midnight phone calls and threats against his family.

The specific examples help make the conclusion persuasive, but a listener could easily dismiss them as sensational and atypical. To prevent this from happening, you might go on to say something like:

Although these examples are dramatic, they are representative of what is happening across the country. The National Education Association reports that some 65,000 teachers were attacked by students last year. Nor is this violence confined to inner-city schools. According to *U.S. News and World Report*, violence against teachers is turning up in the affluent suburban schools as well. Some schools have become so dangerous that psychologists say many teachers suffer from ''combat fatigue,'' with neuroses similar to those of soldiers coming out of war zones.

With this backup material, not even a skeptical listener could reject your examples as isolated.

When you reason inductively in a speech, you can either state your conclusion and then give specific instances, or you can give specific instances and then draw your conclusion. Look back for a moment at the example about malpractice insurance. In that example the speaker first gives three facts and then draws a conclusion (''It certainly seems fair, then, to conclude that the rising cost of malpractice insurance is threatening the quality of medical care available to many Americans''). Now look again at the example just given about assaults against teachers. In this example the conclusion—''Assaults against teachers by students have reached epidemic proportions''—is stated first, followed by three specific instances. It doesn't matter which order you use, as long as your facts really do support your conclusion.

Causal Reasoning   There is a patch of ice on the sidewalk. You slip, fall, and break your arm. You reason as follows: *''Because* that patch of ice was there, I fell and broke my arm.'' This is an example of causal reasoning, in which someone tries to establish the relationship between causes and effects. In this example the causal reasoning is pretty straightforward. You can test it in reverse: ''If the patch of ice *hadn't* been there, I wouldn't have fallen and broken my arm.''

As with induction and deduction, we use causal reasoning daily. Something happens and we ask what caused it to happen. We want to know the causes of political unrest in Latin America, of the football team's latest defeat, of our roommate's peculiar habits. We also wonder about effects. We speculate about the consequences of American military aid in Nicaragua, of the star quarterback's leg injury, of telling our roommate that a change is needed.

When using causal reasoning, be sure to avoid the fallacy of false cause. This fallacy is often known by its Latin name, *post hoc, ergo propter hoc,* which means, ''after this, therefore because of this.'' In other words, just because one event happens after another does not mean that the first is the cause of the second. The closeness in time of the two events may be entirely coincidental. If a black cat crosses your path and five minutes later you fall and break your arm, you needn't blame it on the poor cat.

A student in speech class once argued that the popularity of such television programs as ''Dallas'' and ''Dynasty'' was caused by the influx of large numbers of women into the work force. Her reasoning? During the late 1970s millions of American women found work outside the home. Shortly afterward ''Dallas'' and ''Dynasty'' hit the top of the Nielsen ratings. The speaker concluded that because so many women were no longer at home to watch daytime soap operas, they looked for a similar type of entertainment in the evening, resulting in the success of ''Dallas'' and ''Dynasty.'' The student's classmates were not persuaded. They maintained that "Dallas" and "Dynasty" would have been popular escapist drama no matter when they appeared, and that, moreover, large numbers of men also watch the shows.

A second pitfall to avoid when using causal reasoning is assuming that events have only one cause. We all tend to oversimplify events by attributing them to single, isolated causes. In fact, though, most events have several causes. What, for example, causes the election of a presidential candidate? Unhappiness with the incumbent? A good media campaign? Economic conditions? Desire for a change? World affairs? Support of the party regulars? A clever make-up job for a television debate? A solid, intelligent party platform? *All* of these factors—and others—affect the outcome of a presidential election. When you use causal reasoning, be wary of the temptation to attribute complex events to single causes.

A third common error in causal reasoning is to confuse major causes with minor causes. Although any event usually has multiple causes, not all of those causes are equally important. Suppose you argue that the firing on Fort Sumter by Confederate troops on April 12, 1861, *caused* the Civil War. A careful listener would challenge you by saying, "The attack on Fort Sumter may have *triggered* the start of the Civil War, but it was not enough by itself to cause the war. The *major* causes of the Civil War go much deeper and include the agitation against slavery by Northern abolitionists, the desire of Southern leaders to save slavery at any cost, the economic tensions between North and South, the secession of the deep South after Abraham Lincoln's election as President, and the determination of Lincoln to maintain the Union despite the risk of war." Whenever you discuss causes and effects, take care to separate the different causes and decide which are most important.

You cannot escape causal reasoning. All of us use it daily, and you are almost certain to use it when speaking to persuade—especially if you deal with a question of fact or policy.

Analogical Reasoning   What do these statements have in common:

If you're good at racquetball, you'll be great at Ping-Pong.

The Japanese make reliable, high-quality cars for reasonable prices. There is no reason why Americans cannot do the same.

Both statements use reasoning from analogy. By comparing two similar cases, they infer that what is true for one must be true for the other. The first speaker reasons that because a person is good at playing racquetball, he or she should be good at playing Ping-Pong. The second speaker reasons that because Japan makes good, reasonably priced cars, the United States should be able to as well.

Is the reasoning valid? The answer depends on whether the two cases being compared are essentially alike. Is playing racquetball the same as playing Ping-Pong? Not really. To be sure, both involve hitting the ball with a racquet or a paddle. But racquetball uses a stringed racquet and a rubber ball. Ping-Pong uses a solid paddle and a smaller, lighter, celluloid ball. Racquetball is played by hitting the ball against the walls or ceiling of an enclosed court. Ping-Pong is played by hitting the ball back and forth over a net stretched across a table. Skill at one is no guarantee of skill at the other. The analogy is not valid.

What about the second analogy? That depends on how much alike the Japanese and American auto industries are. Are labor costs roughly the same in both countries? Are workers equally productive in both? Do auto makers in the two countries pay comparable prices for raw materials? Do they both have up-to-date, high-technology factories? Do they both benefit from government assistance? In other words, are the same factors that allow Japanese firms to make reliable, high-quality cars for reasonable prices also present in the United States? If so, the analogy is valid. If not, the analogy is invalid.

Reasoning from analogy is used most often in speeches on questions of policy. When arguing for a new policy, you should find out whether a similar policy has been tried somewhere else. You may be able to claim that your policy will work because it has worked in like circumstances elsewhere. Here is how one student used reasoning from analogy to support her claim that controlling handguns will reduce violent crime in the United States:

> Will my policy work? The experience of foreign countries suggests it will. In England, guns are tightly regulated; even the police are unarmed, and the murder rate is trivial by American standards. In Japan, the ownership of weapons is severely restricted and handguns are completely prohibited. Japan is an almost gun-free country, and its crime rate is even lower than England's. On the basis of these comparisons, we can conclude that restricting the ownership of guns will control the crime and murder rates in America.

By the same token, if you argue against a change in policy, you should check whether the proposed policy—or something like it—has been implemented elsewhere. Here, too, you may be able to support your case by reasoning from analogy—as did one student who opposed gun control:

> Advocates of gun control point to foreign countries to prove their case. They often cite England, which has strict gun-control laws and little violent crime. But the key to low personal violence in England—and other foreign countries—is not gun-control laws but the generally peaceful character of the people. For example, Switzerland has a militia system; 600,000 assault rifles each with two magazines of ammunition are sitting at this moment in Swiss homes. Yet Switzerland's murder rate is only 15 percent of ours. In other words, cultural factors are much more important than gun control when it comes to violent crime.

As these examples illustrate, argument from analogy can be used on both sides of an issue. You are more likely to persuade your audience if the analogy truly shows a parallel situation.[21]

Appealing to Emotions

Emotional appeals—sometimes called *motivational appeals*—are intended to make listeners feel sad, angry, guilty, afraid, happy, proud, sympathetic, or nostalgic. These are often appropriate reactions when the question is one of value or policy. Few people are moved to change their attitudes or take action when they are complacent or bored. As George Campbell wrote in his *Philosophy of Rhetoric,* "When persuasion is the end, passion also must be engaged."[22]

Here is how one speaker used emotional appeal when a strict recital of facts might not have been so effective. The subject was illegal trapping of wild animals. The audience was a group of citizens and the Village Board in a semirural town. The speaker was a representative of the humane society. Here is what she might have said, stripping the topic of emotional content:

Trapping of wild animals on town property is not only illegal. It is also dangerous. The traps are left untended, and they do not discriminate. On several occasions domestic animals have been caught in traps set for raccoons, squirrels, and beavers.

What she actually said went something like this:

Tina was found dead last week—her neck broken by the jaws of a steel trap. I didn't know Tina, and most of you didn't either. But Mr. and Mrs. John Williamson knew her, and so did their children, Tony and Vanessa. Tina had been a beloved member of their family for ten years. She was a Samoyed—a handsome, intelligent dog, pure white with soft, dark eyes. When she died she was only 200 yards from her back door. Tina had gone out to play that morning as usual, but this time she found something *un*usual—an odd-shaped box with delicious-smelling food inside. She put her head inside the box to get at the food. When she did, the trap closed and Tina was killed.

Unless we crack down on illegal trapping within town property, this tragedy will be repeated. The next time it might be *your* family dog. Or your pet cat. Or your child.

People who listen to a speech like that will not soon forget it. They may well be moved to take action, as the speaker intends them to. The first speech, however, is not nearly so compelling. Listeners may well nod their heads, think to themselves "good idea"—and then forget about it.

If you want to move listeners to act on a question of policy, emotional appeals are not only legitimate but perhaps necessary. If you want listeners to do something as a result of your speech, you must arouse their feelings. You must appeal to their hearts as well as their heads.

There is one type of persuasive speech in which emotional appeal is *not* appropriate—the speech on a question of fact. Here you must deal only in specific information and logic. For example, did Edward Kennedy try to cover up the facts in the drowning of Mary Jo Kopechne at Chappaquiddick Island? If you say "No, because I admire Kennedy," or "Yes, because I have always disliked Kennedy," then you are guilty of applying emotional criteria to a

While good reasoning and
sound evidence are vital to
persuasion, emotional appeals
often make a speaker's ideas
come alive for an audience.
(Patricia Ann Schwab/Stock, Boston)

purely factual question. The events at Chappaquiddick Island are matters of
fact and should be discussed on factual and logical grounds.

Even when trying to move listeners to action, you should never substitute
emotional appeals for evidence and reasoning. You should *always* build your
persuasive speech on a firm foundation of facts and logic. This is important
for ethical reasons. But it is also important for practical reasons. Unless you
prove your case, careful listeners will not be stirred by your emotional appeals.
You need to build a good case based on reason *and* kindle the emotions of
your audience.[23]

How do you decide which emotional response you want to tap in your
listeners? The answer depends on your topic, your audience, and your specific
purpose. There are no formulas for using emotional appeals effectively. Below
is a list of some of the emotions evoked most often by public speakers.
Following each emotion are a few examples of subjects that might stir that
emotion:

fear—of nuclear war, of serious illness, of unsafe aviation standards, of
natural disasters

compassion—for the handicapped, for battered wives, for neglected animals, for starving children in Third World countries

pride—in one's country, in one's school, in one's family, in one's personal
accomplishments

anger—at the actions of political terrorists, at members of Congress who abuse the public trust, at landlords who exploit student tenants, at vandals and rapists

shame—about not helping people less fortunate than ourselves, about not considering the rights of others, about not doing one's best

reverence—for an admired person, for traditions and institutions, for one's deity

Obviously the list is not complete. There are many other emotions and many other subjects that might stir them. However, this brief sample should give you an idea of the kinds of emotional appeals you might use to enhance the message of your persuasive speech.

As we saw in Chapter 10, one way to generate emotional appeal is to use emotion-laden words. If you want to move your listeners, use moving language. Here, for instance, is part of the conclusion from a student speech about politics in Iran:

> So what have we seen in our look at life in Iran under the present regime? We have seen civil liberties completely squashed by religious fanaticism and political dictatorship. We have seen mob violence, brutal torture, even murder become everyday events. We have seen a vicious reign of terror that respects neither dignity nor freedom nor human life.

The underlined words and phrases have strong emotional power. By using them, the speaker hopes to produce an emotional response.

There can be a problem with this, however. Packing too many emotionally charged words into one part of a speech can call attention to itself and undermine its impact. When a sudden barrage of passionate language is inconsistent with the rest of the speech, it may strike the audience as ludicrous or extravagant—obviously not the desired effect.

A better technique is to let your emotional appeal grow naturally out of the content of your whole speech. Remember, the emotion rests in your audience, not in your words. Even the coldest facts can touch off an emotional response if they strike the right chords in a listener. The following is part of a speech advocating support of the foster care program for children. The language is not very emotional, but the story affected the audience more powerfully than any string of passionate words could have:

> If you still have any doubts about the merit of the Foster Care program, listen to the story of Louis. It is a true story.
>
> Louis doesn't know who his father was. When Louis was just five years old, his mother abandoned him and his older sister Charlotte. Charlotte wasn't lucky. She landed in a public institution. By the age of sixteen she had been arrested several times for drug use and streetwalking.
>
> Louis *was* lucky. He was taken in as a foster child by a family in a pleasant

suburban community. There were already three children in the family, but the parents had enough money—and more than enough love—to share with another child. Louis was treated as a full-fledged member of the family. The parents took him to Sunday school, encouraged him to make friends, sat up night after night helping him with his homework. Mostly, they showed they cared.

Louis is 23 now. He has a job with a construction company that builds architectural modules. His employers are so pleased with his work they have offered to pay for him to take engineering courses in night school. He is very proud. Recently, Louis came "home" to his foster parents for Thanksgiving. There was a full house, much food, and many toasts. Finally, Louis stood up. He said, "Nobody here has more to be thankful for than I have." Then he turned to his foster parents. "I've always called you Aunt Ann and Uncle David. Now I want to say, *thanks,* Mom and Dad!"

So you see, foster care *can* make a difference. Just ask Louis.

The content of this story is so moving that adorning it with emotional language would only weaken its impact.

The strongest source of emotional power is the conviction and sincerity of the speaker. All of your emotion-laden words and examples are but empty trappings unless *you* feel the emotion yourself. And if you do, your emotion will communicate itself to the audience through everything you say and do— not only through your words, but also through your tone of voice, rate of speech, gestures, and facial expressions.

SAMPLE SPEECH WITH COMMENTARY

The following persuasive speech was presented in a public speaking class at the University of Wisconsin–Madison.[24] It deals with a question of policy and is a good example of how student speakers can try to persuade their classmates to take immediate action.

As you read the speech, notice how the speaker blends his personal experience with well-chosen statistics to create a powerful persuasive appeal. Notice also how clear and uncluttered the speech is. There are few wasted words, and the ideas progress cleanly and crisply. Finally, notice how the speaker relates the topic directly to his audience at every stage of the speech.

COMMENTARY	SPEECH

SEATBELTS: A HABIT THAT COULD SAVE YOUR LIFE

The opening sentences get the audience's initial attention and arouse its curiosity to learn why the speaker has been on crutches for so long.	As you may have noticed, I was on crutches for two months this semester. I had already been on crutches for three months before that, and last year I was on them for seven months. You see, I've had hip surgery three times in the last year and a half.

By telling a dramatic story based on his personal experience, the speaker draws his audience into the speech. The story is particularly effective because of its specific details about the speaker's injuries and how close he came to dying. In contrast, imagine if the speaker had merely said, "A year and a half ago I was in a serious automobile accident." This would not have had nearly the same impact. Nor would it have done as much to establish the speaker's credibility.

When the speaker said he will have a "piece of metal this long" in his hip for the rest of his life, he held his hands fourteen inches apart to indicate the length of the piece.

Moving smoothly out of his opening story, the speaker reveals the topic of his speech and relates it directly to his audience.

The final sentence of this paragraph establishes the speaker's good will. Although the sentence may seem "corny," it had a strong emotional impact when delivered in class.

Here the speaker ends his introduction by previewing the main points to be covered in the body of his speech. While the introduction is longer than usual, it is extremely effective in preparing the audience to accept the persuasive appeals that will follow.

The speaker leads into his first main point with a question. This is a good technique, for it invites a subliminal answer that gets the audience more involved with the speech. The statistics in this paragraph are presented clearly and come from highly credible sources.

It all started when I experienced my first serious car accident. I swerved off the road to avoid a head-on collision with another car. My car rolled over and struck a large tree. I was not wearing a seatbelt. In the process of being thrown back and forth across the car, I chipped a tooth, cut the back of my head, broke my hip, and cracked three ribs, which resulted in a punctured lung and massive internal bleeding. When they got me to the hospital, my blood pressure was down from a normal 120-over-70 to 50-over-30 as a result of all the internal and external bleeding and as a result of shock. The doctors waited more than twenty-four hours to do surgery to repair my hip because they didn't think I was going to survive all of my other injuries.

Somehow I survived, and now a year and half later I am finally walking normally, though I will be walking around for the rest of my life with a piece of metal this long in my hip, and I'm not allowed to do any athletic activities that require running.

All that pain and suffering could have been avoided if only I had been in the habit of wearing a seatbelt. But I wasn't in that habit, and I know from my class survey that 40 percent of you do not usually wear a seatbelt, and 75 percent of you do not always wear one. Yet the National Highway Traffic Safety Administration tells us that each person stands a one-in-three chance of being in a serious car accident at some time in his or her life. So we can possibly predict that one-third of you will be in a serious accident at some point. And it may sound corny, but I mean it, so I'm going to say it—I don't want what happened to me to happen to any of you.

So I want to talk to you about wearing seatbelts. First I'm going to tell you to what extent you will be protected by wearing a seatbelt. Then I'm going to look at some of the reasons why people don't wear seatbelts and point out the problems with those reasons. And after I've given you the evidence, I am going to ask you all to make a habit of wearing seatbelts.

So first, to what extent will you be protected by wearing a seatbelt? Well, the Wisconsin Department of Transportation says if you are in an accident and are not wearing a seatbelt, you are four times more likely to be killed than if you are wearing one. Furthermore, consider this—there are 35,000 deaths each year in the United States as a result of traffic accidents. The National Highway Traffic Safety Administration, the National Child Passenger

Safety Association, and the Wisconsin Department of Transportation all estimate that traffic deaths would decrease from 35,000 to around 17,000 annually if everyone wore seatbelts.

So our most knowledgeable and reliable sources of information on seatbelts have all come to the same conclusion—that we would cut traffic deaths in half if everyone wore seatbelts, and that we would save 18,000 lives each year. Now let me put that number into perspective—18,000 people, or the equivalent of more than half the undergraduates on this campus, are needlessly killed every year because they do not wear seatbelts.

But why is this true? What does a seatbelt do to protect you? Well, in a head-on collision, which is usually the worst type, your body will be thrown forward into the steering wheel, into the dashboard, or through the windshield with incredible force. Imagine falling headfirst from the top of a three-story building. The force with which you would land on the ground is equal to the force with which you would be thrown forward in only a 30 mile-per-hour collision. But a seatbelt will absorb that force and prevent you from slamming into the interior of the car.

In my own experience there is little doubt that a seatbelt would have minimized my injuries. I looked at pictures of the car after my accident. The car was totaled, and it was an ugly mess, but the two front seats and the entire driving compartment were completely intact. I have to believe that if I had been strapped into that seat, I would have walked away from my accident with minor bruises. But remember I used the word "if"—if I had worn a safety belt.

So the evidence is strongly in favor of wearing seatbelts. That brings me to the next question—why don't people wear seatbelts?

People often say that in an accident they would rather be thrown free of the car, or at least be able to get out of the car in case of fire or submersion in water. Well, according to the Wisconsin Department of Transportation, accidents involving fire and submersion make up less than one out of every 200 auto accidents. Furthermore, you are actually more likely to be able to get out of the car if you are wearing a seatbelt, because you are more likely to be conscious and not seriously injured. And with regard to being thrown free of the car, the Wisconsin Department of Transportation says you are 25 times more likely to be killed if you are thrown

---

The speaker does an excellent job here of reemphasizing figures from the previous paragraph and translating them into terms that relate directly to his listeners. As we saw in Chapter 6, this is something you should try to do whenever you use statistics in a speech.

Now the speaker explains why a seatbelt is so valuable in helping to prevent injuries. Notice how clearly he compares the force of a 30 mile-per-hour collision to falling headfirst from a three-story building. Also notice how he uses the words "you" and "your" here (and throughout the speech) to keep his audience personally involved.

By drawing upon his own experience, the speaker reinforces his point about the value of wearing a seatbelt. The impact of the last sentence was enhanced considerably by the speaker's use of pauses, vocal variety, and strong eye contact to communicate directly with his listeners.

A transition bridging the first and second main points helps the audience keep track of where the speaker is in the speech.

This and the next paragraph are extremely important, for they answer the audience's two major objections to wearing seatbelts. Had the speaker ignored these objections, his speech would have been much less effective. Here he uses compelling statistics to show that the fear of being trapped in a burning or sinking car is not a valid reason for refusing to wear seatbelts. Like many other statistics in the speech, these come from the Wisconsin Department of Transportation. While this would not have been the best source for a speaker in another state, it was an excellent source for this speech, which was presented to a class at the University of Wisconsin. If you were giving a speech on the same topic in a different state, you would be well advised to use figures from transportation officials in that state.

The signpost ("The other major reason why people don't wear seatbelts") keeps the movement of thought clear and easy to follow. The speaker's reasoning in this paragraph was reinforced by his delivery, in which he used his hands to represent the two sides of the scale. As in other parts of the speech, the speaker addresses his listeners directly as "you." In addition to increasing audience involvement, this gives the speech a strong conversational quality. The speaker comes across as talking *with* the audience, not *at* them.

Now the speaker moves to his third main point, which is a call to action. He begins by restating key statistics from earlier in the speech. This is an excellent technique. Rather than overwhelming listeners with a barrage of figures, the speaker uses a few well-chosen statistics to drive home his message.

After the evidence of the previous paragraph, the first sentence of this paragraph acquires special force. Here, as elsewhere, the speaker's appeal is enhanced by his clear, direct language.

The speaker begins his conclusion by referring to the accident he discussed in the introduction and by reinforcing his central idea. His evident sincerity here and throughout the speech did much to enhance his credibility and persuasiveness.

This last paragraph ends the speech on a strong emotional note. The final sentence states how lucky the speaker was to survive his accident, but it also implies that members of the audience might not be so lucky if they fail to wear seatbelts.

out of the car, because you can be thrown onto hard pavement, thrown into stationary objects, or struck by other cars. Clearly you are safer being strapped in than being thrown around.

The other major reason why people don't wear seatbelts is that seatbelts are uncomfortable and restrict movement. Now, if this is your reason for not wearing a seatbelt, let me ask you to do something right now. Imagine in your mind a two-sided scale. On one side of the scale, put the value that you place on being completely comfortable while driving. And on the other side of the scale, put the value that you place on your life and your health. Which side is heavier? If your life and your health mean more to you than a little bit of extra comfort while driving, then it only makes sense to wear a seatbelt.

So I'm here today to ask all of you to make a habit of wearing seatbelts. The statistics are simple—chances are that about one-third of you will be in a serious auto accident at some time in your life. It could happen fifty years from now, and it could happen tomorrow. And if you are in an accident, you are four times more likely to be killed if you are not wearing a seatbelt than if you are wearing one.

So if you think you are safer not wearing a seatbelt, you're betting against heavy odds. And if you still won't wear a seatbelt, because a seatbelt is uncomfortable and inconvenient, then you're placing your momentary comfort ahead of your life and your health. So tell yourself that you are going to make a habit of wearing seatbelts. Then do it.

There is nothing I can do about my accident now, and I don't plan to go around for the rest of my life kicking myself because I didn't wear a seatbelt that day. What's important is that I learned something from the experience. I've made a habit of wearing seatbelts when I ride in a car, and I'm hoping that each of you will do the same if you haven't already.

I will never be able to play basketball or go downhill skiing again, but at least I'm here and at least I can walk. I was a lot luckier than 35,000 other Americans that year.

SUMMARY

When you speak to persuade, you act as an advocate. Your job is to sell a program, to defend an idea, to refute an opponent, or to inspire people to action. Persuasive speeches may center on questions of fact, questions of value, or questions of policy.

Some questions of fact can be answered absolutely. Others cannot—either because the facts are murky or because there is not enough information available to us. In giving a persuasive speech about a question of fact, your role is akin to that of a lawyer in a courtroom trial. You will try to get your listeners to accept your view of the facts.

Questions of value go beyond the immediate facts to involve a person's beliefs about what is right or wrong, good or bad, moral or immoral, ethical or unethical. Although questions of value have strong implications for our actions, speeches on questions of value do not argue directly for or against particular courses of action.

Once you go beyond arguing right or wrong to urging that something should or should not be done, you move to a question of policy. When you speak on a question of policy, your goal may be to evoke passive agreement or to spark immediate action. In either case, you will face three basic issues—need, plan, and practicality. How much of your speech you devote to each issue will depend on your topic and your audience. In most circumstances you will arrange your speech in problem-solution order, in comparative-advantages order, or in a more specialized order called Monroe's motivated sequence.

Whether you speak on a question of fact, value, or policy, you must adapt to your target audience—that part of the whole audience you most want to reach with your message. If your listeners are persuaded, it will be for one or more of four reasons—because they perceive you as having high credibility; because they are won over by your evidence; because they are convinced by your reasoning; because they are moved by your emotional appeals.

Your credibility will be affected primarily by how the audience views your competence and character. Although credibility is partly a matter of reputation, you can take some specific steps in your speech to build your credibility. Let listeners know why you are competent to speak on the topic. Establish common ground with your listeners. Above all, speak with genuine conviction. Your spirit and enthusiasm will carry over to your listeners.

If you hope to be persuasive, you must also support your views with evidence—examples, statistics, and testimony used to prove or disprove something. Whenever you say something that is open to question, give evidence to show that you are right. As you prepare the speech, try at each point to imagine how your audience will react. Anticipate their doubts and answer them with evidence.

No matter how strong your evidence, you will not be very persuasive unless listeners agree with your reasoning. In deductive reasoning, you reason from a general premise to a specific conclusion. Inductive reasoning is the reverse; you reason from a number of particular facts to a general conclusion. In causal reasoning you try to establish the relationship between causes and effects. When you use analogical reasoning, you compare two similar cases and infer that what is true for one is also true for the other.

Finally, you may persuade your listeners by appealing to their emotions—fear, anger, pride, pity, sorrow, and so forth. Although emotional appeals are not appropriate on questions of fact, they are often essential when you want to move listeners to act on a question of policy. You should never substitute emotional appeals for evidence and reasoning. But if you want listeners to do something as a result of your speech, you may need to appeal to their hearts as well as to their heads.

REVIEW QUESTIONS

After reading this chapter, you should be able to answer the following questions:

1. What are questions of fact? Give an example of a specific purpose statement for a persuasive speech on a question of fact.

2. What are questions of value? Give an example of a specific purpose statement for a persuasive speech on a question of value.

3. What are questions of policy? Give an example of a specific purpose statement for a persuasive speech on a question of policy.

4. What are the three basic issues you must deal with when discussing a question of policy? What methods of organization are used most often in speeches on questions of policy?

5. What is the target audience?

6. What is credibility? How can you build your credibility by what you say in your speech?

7. What is evidence? Why do persuasive speakers need to use evidence?

8. What is deductive reasoning? What are the two questions to ask in evaluating deductive reasoning?

9. What is inductive reasoning? What guidelines should you follow when using inductive reasoning?

10. What is causal reasoning? What three errors must you be sure to avoid when using causal reasoning?

11. What is analogical reasoning? How do you judge the validity of an analogy?

12. What is the role of emotional appeals in persuasive speaking?

APPLICATION EXERCISES

1. Below are four specific purpose statements for persuasive speeches. In each case explain whether the speech associated with it concerns a question of fact, a question of value, or a question of policy. Then, rewrite the specific purpose statement to make it appropriate for a speech about one of the other two kinds of questions. For instance, if the original purpose statement is about a question of policy, write a new specific purpose statement that deals with the same topic as either a question of fact or a question of value.

EXAMPLE:

Original statement: To persuade my audience that violence on television is a major cause of violent behavior in society. (*question of fact*)

Rewritten statement: To persuade my audience that further reforms should be enacted to reduce the amount of violence on television programs designed for children. (*question of policy*)

   a. To persuade my audience that colleges have a moral obligation to ensure that all scholarship athletes receive their degrees.

   b. To persuade my audience that all government programs should be cut equally to help reduce the federal budget deficit.

   c. To persuade my audience that lie-detector tests are inherently unreliable.

   d. To persuade my audience to protest against the proposed cutback in funding for evening courses.

2. Identify the kind of reasoning used in each of the following statements. What weaknesses, if any, can you find in the reasoning of each?

   a. Of course the contemporary women's movement was caused by Betty Friedan's *The Feminine Mystique.* Friedan's book was published in 1963, and the women's movement got underway shortly thereafter.

   b. Instant replays have been used successfully by the National Football League for the past several seasons to double-check close calls by the referees. Surely, then, instant replays can also be used successfully in sports such as baseball and basketball.

   c. People who eat an average of 2 ounces of fish daily have a much lower rate of heart disease than do people who eat little or no fish. All of us want to avoid heart disease. Therefore, we should increase the amount of fish in our diets to an average of 2 ounces a day.

   d. Chernobyl and Three Mile Island are two well-known instances of accidents at nuclear power plants. We can see, therefore, that nuclear power plants are too dangerous to rely on for America's future energy needs.

3. Analyze the speech in the Appendix by Sheila Mir ("Drinking and Boating: A Deadly Combination," pages 406–408). Because this is a speech on a question of policy, pay special attention to how the speaker deals with the three basic issues of need, plan, and practicality. Does the speaker present a convincing case that a serious problem exists? Does she offer a clear plan to solve the problems? Does she demonstrate that the plan is practical?

NOTES

[1] This diversity is clearly reflected in the latest books on persuasion. See, for example, Herbert W. Simons, *Persuasion: Understanding, Practice and Analysis* (New York: Random House, 1986): Stephen W. Littlejohn and David M. Jabusch, *Persuasive Transactions* (Glenview Ill.: Scott, Foresman, 1987); Erwin P. Bettinghaus and Michael J. Cody, *Persuasive Communication*, 4th ed. (New York: Holt, Rinehart and Winston, 1987).

[2] For a review of research on this aspect of persuasion, see James P. Dillard, John E. Hunter, and Michael Burgoon, "Meta-Analysis of Foot-in-the-Door and Door-in-the-Face," *Human Communication Research,* 10 (1984), 461–488. A more popular treatment of the same topic is in Robert B. Cialdini, *Influence: How and Why People Agree to Things* (New York: William Morrow, 1984), pp. 66–114.

[3] Howard Leventhal, Robert Singer, and Susan Jones, "Effects of Fear and Specificity of Recommendation upon Attitudes and Behavior," *Journal of Personality and Social Psychology,* 2 (1965), 20–29. But also see, in comparison, Franklin J. Boster and Paul Mongeau, "Fear-Arousing Persuasive Messages," in Robert N. Bostrom and Bruce H. Westley (eds.), *Communication Yearbook 8* (Beverly Hills, Calif.: Sage, 1984), pp. 351–352.

[4] K. H. Beck and A. Frankel, "A Conceptualization of Threat Communications and Protective Health Behavior," *Social Psychology Quarterly*, 3 (1981), 204–217.

[5] For more detail on strategies to deal with the issues of need, plan, and practicality, see Ruth Anne Clark, *Persuasive Messages* (New York: Harper & Row, 1984), pp. 119–185.

[6] Douglas Ehninger, Bruce E. Gronbeck, Ray E. McKerrow, and Alan H. Monroe, *Principles and Types of Speech Communication,* 10th ed. (Glenview, Ill.: Scott, Foresman, 1986), pp. 151–172.

[7] Alec Benn, *The 27 Most Common Mistakes in Advertising* (New York: American Management Association, 1978), pp. 84–85.

[8] See the classic study by Carl I. Hovland, Arthur A. Lumsdaine, and Fred D. Sheffield, "The Effects of Presenting 'One Side' versus 'Both Sides' in Changing Opinions on a Controversial Subject," in *Experiments on Mass Communication* (Princeton, N.J.: Princeton University Press, 1949), pp. 201–227.

[9] See, for example, Mary John Smith, *Persuasion and Human Action: A Review and Critique of Social Influence Theories* (Belmont, Calif.: Wadsworth, 1982); Gerald R. Miller, Michael Burgoon, and Judee K. Burgoon, "The Functions of Human Communication in Changing Attitudes and Gaining Compliance," in Carroll C. Arnold and John Waite Bowers (eds.), *Handbook of Rhetorical and Communication Theory* (Boston: Allyn and Bacon, 1984), pp. 400–474.

[10] Two of the many useful reviews of research on the factors of credibility are James C. McCroskey and Thomas J. Young, "Ethos and Credibility: The Construct and

Its Measurement After Three Decades," *Central States Speech Journal*, 32 (1981), 24–35; Richard E. Petty and John T. Cacioppo, *Attitudes and Persuasion: Classic and Contemporary Approaches* (Dubuque, Iowa: W. C. Brown, 1981), pp. 61–69, 235–237.

[11] James C. McCroskey, *An Introduction to Rhetorical Communication,* 4th ed. (Englewood Cliffs, N.J.: Prentice-Hall, 1982), pp. 62–79.

[12] For the effectiveness of this method, see Lawrence R. Wheeless, "Effects of Explicit Credibility Statements by a More Credible and a Less Credible Source," *Southern Speech Communication Journal,* 39 (1973), 33–39.

[13] See Walter Weiss, "Opinion Congruence with a Negative Source on One Issue as a Factor Influencing Agreement on Another Issue," *Journal of Abnormal and Social Psychology,* 54 (1975), 180–186.

[14] The many studies on evidence and persuasion include Dale Hample, "Predicting Belief and Belief Change Using a Cognitive Theory of Argument and Evidence," *Communication Monographs*, 46 (1979), 142–151; Rodney A. Reynolds and Michael Burgoon, "Belief Processing, Reasoning, and Evidence," in Robert N. Bostrom (ed.), *Communication Yearbook 7* (Beverly Hills, Calif.: Sage, 1983), pp. 83–104.

[15] See, for example, Richard M. Perloff and Timothy C. Brock, " 'And Thinking Makes It So': Cognitive Responses in Persuasion," in Michael E. Roloff and Gerald R. Miller (eds.), *Persuasion: New Directions in Theory and Research* (Beverly Hills, Calif.: Sage, 1980), pp. 67–90.

[16] John A. Kline, "Interaction of Evidence and Readers' Intelligence on the Effects of Short Messages," *Quarterly Journal of Speech,* 55 (1969), 407–413. For a lively exchange on other factors affecting listeners' reception of evidence, see James B. Stiff, "Cognitive Processing of Persuasive Message Cues: A Meta-Analytic Review of the Effects of Supporting Information on Attitudes," *Communication Monographs*, 53 (1986), 75–89; Richard E. Petty, Jeff A. Kasmer, Curt P. Haugtvedt, and John T. Cacioppo, "Source and Message Factors in Persuasion: A Reply to Stiff's Critique of the Elaboration Likelihood Model," *Communication Monographs*, 54 (1987), 233–249.

[17] Donald Dean Morley, "Subjective Message Constructs: A Theory of Persuasion," *Communication Monographs*, 54 (1987), 183–203.

[18] Adapted from James C. Humes, *A Speaker's Treasury of Anecdotes About the Famous* (New York: Harper & Row, 1978), p. 131.

[19] Lionel Ruby, *The Art of Making Sense* (Philadelphia: Lippincott, 1954), p. 261.

[20] *Ibid.*, p. 261.

[21] For more detail on the basic methods of reasoning, see Stephen Toulmin, Richard Rieke, and Allan Janik, *An Introduction to Reasoning,* 2nd ed. (New York: Macmillan, 1984); Howard Kahane, *Logic and Contemporary Rhetoric: The Use of Reason in Everyday Life*, 4th ed. (Belmont, Calif.: Wadsworth, 1984).

[22] George Campbell, *The Philosophy of Rhetoric,* ed. Lloyd F. Bitzer (Carbondale, Ill.: Southern Illinois University Press, 1988), p. 77. For a survey of different views about the role of emotional appeal in speechmaking, see Lester Thonssen, A. Craig Baird, and Waldo W. Braden, *Speech Criticism,* 2nd ed. (New York: Ronald Press, 1970), pp. 419–444.

[23] Research on fear appeals, for example, suggests that messages devoted exclusively to arousing fear in the audience are less effective than messages that balance emotional appeal with rational appeal. See Petty and Cacioppo, *Attitudes and Persuasion*, pp. 72–73.

[24] Reprinted with permission of Andrew Kinney. This speech is also available on the videotape supplement to *The Art of Public Speaking*, 3rd ed.

CHAPTER 15

Speaking On Special Occasions

SPEECHES OF INTRODUCTION

SPEECHES OF PRESENTATION

SPEECHES OF ACCEPTANCE

COMMEMORATIVE SPEECHES

AFTER-DINNER SPEECHES

Special occasions are the punctuation marks of day-to-day life, the high points that stand out above ordinary routine. Christenings, weddings, funerals, graduations, award ceremonies, inaugurals, retirement dinners—all these are occasions, and they are very special to the people who take part in them. Nearly always they are occasions for speechmaking. The best man proposes a toast to the bride and groom; the sales manager presents an award to the sales representative of the year; the President delivers an inaugural address; the basketball coach gives a speech honoring the team's most valuable player; a close friend delivers a moving eulogy to the deceased. These speeches help to give the occasion its "specialness." They are part of the ceremonial aura that marks the event.

Speeches for special occasions are different from the speeches we have considered so far in this book. They may convey information, but that is not their primary purpose. Neither is their primary purpose to persuade. Rather, they aim to fit the special needs of a special occasion. In this chapter we look at the most common special occasions and the kinds of speeches appropriate for each.

SPEECHES OF INTRODUCTION

"Ladies and gentlemen, the President of the United States." If you are ever in a situation in which you have to introduce the President, you will need no more than the nine words that begin this paragraph. The President is so well known that any further remarks would be inappropriate and almost foolish.

Most of the time, however, a speech of introduction will be neither this brief nor this ritualized. If you are introducing any other speaker, you will need to accomplish three purposes in your introduction:

Build enthusiasm for the upcoming speaker.

Build enthusiasm for the speaker's topic.

Establish a welcoming climate that will boost the speaker's credibility.

A good speech of introduction can be a delight to hear and can do much to ease the task of the main speaker. The basic message of such a speech should be "Here is a speaker you will enjoy, and this is why."[1] Usually you will say something about the speaker and about the topic—in that order. Following are some guidelines for speeches of introduction. Most of the points apply also to the other types of special-occasion speeches discussed in this chapter.

Be Brief   During World War I, Lord Balfour, Britain's Foreign Secretary, was to be the main speaker at a rally in the United States. But the speaker who was supposed to introduce Lord Balfour gave a 45-minute oration on the causes of the war. Then, almost as an afterthought, he said, "Now Lord Balfour will give his address." Lord Balfour rose and said, "I'm supposed to give my address in the brief time remaining. Here it is: 10 Carleton Gardens, London, England."[2]

Every speaker—and audience—who has ever sat through a long-winded introduction knows how dreary it can be. The audience is thinking, "Oh, for heaven's sake, get *on* with it." For the speaker, it is even more troublesome. He or she is psyched up. The adrenaline is pumping. But as the introducer drones on, the feeling of readiness begins to drain away. By the time the introducer finally sits down, the speaker may well have lost much of his or her creative energy.

The purpose of a speech of introduction is to focus attention on the main speaker, not on the person making the introduction. Under normal circumstances, a speech of introduction will be no more than two to three minutes long, and it may be shorter if the speaker is already well known to the audience.

Make Sure Your Introduction Is Completely Accurate   Many an introducer has embarrassed himself or herself, as well as the main speaker, by garbling basic facts about the speaker. Always check with the speaker ahead of time to make sure your introduction is accurate in every respect.

Above all, get the speaker's name right. This may seem obvious, but it needs repeating. Remember that nothing is more important than a person's name. When you get a name wrong, you strip that person of identity and importance. If the speaker's name is at all difficult—especially if it involves a foreign pronunciation—practice saying it well in advance. However, don't practice so much that you frighten yourself about getting it wrong. This was the plight of an announcer whose gaffe is now a classic: "Ladies and gentlemen, the President of the United States—Hoobert Heever!"

Adapt Your Remarks to the Occasion   In preparing your introduction, you may be constrained by the nature of the occasion. Formal occasions require formal speeches of introduction. If you were presenting a guest speaker at an informal business meeting, you might be much more casual than if you were presenting the same speaker to the same audience at a formal banquet.

Adapt Your Introduction to the Main Speaker   No matter how well it is received by the audience, a speech of introduction that leaves the main speaker feeling uncomfortable has failed in part of its purpose. How can you make a main speaker uncomfortable? One way is to praise the person overmuch—and especially to praise him or her for speaking skills. Never say, "Our speaker will keep you on the edge of your seat from beginning to end!" This is like prefacing a joke with the line, "Here is the funniest joke you've ever heard." You create a set of expectations that are almost impossible to fulfill.

Another way to create discomfort is by revealing embarrassing details of the speaker's personal life or by making humorous remarks that are in poor taste from the speaker's point of view. An introducer may think this kind of remark is funny: "Why, I've known Anita Connelly since she was ten years old and so fat that everybody in the class called her Blimpo!" To the speaker, however, the remark will probably not be a bit funny and may be painful.

Adapt Your Remarks to the Audience Just as you adapt other speeches to particular audiences, so you need to adapt the speech of introduction to the audience you are facing. Your aim is to make *this* audience want to hear *this* speaker on *this* subject.[3] If the speaker is not well known to the audience, you will need to establish his or her credibility by recounting some of the speaker's main achievements and explaining why he or she is qualified to speak on the topic at hand. But if the speaker is already personally known to the audience, it would be absurd to present him or her as if the audience had never heard of the person.

Also, you will want to tell each audience what *it* wants to hear—to give the kind of information that is interesting and accessible to the members of that audience. If you were introducing the same speaker to two different groups, some of the information in the speeches of introduction might be the same, but it would be slanted differently. Suppose, for example, the police commissioner of a certain city is going to address two groups—an audience of elementary-school children and the members of the City Council. The introduction to the school children might go something like this:

> Children, we have a very important guest with us today. He is the number-one policeman in our city, the head of all the other police officers. Besides knowing a lot about crime right here at home, the police commissioner has also spent time working with Interpol—a special group of police officers who deal with crimes around the world. Today he is going to talk about how all of us can help to prevent crime. Let's give a big round of applause and listen carefully to Police Commissioner Patrick McCarter.

But the introduction to the City Council would be along these lines:

> Members of the City Council and distinguished guests: It is my privilege to introduce to you today the police commissioner, who will address us on the subject of measures to counteract crime in our community. Most of you know that the commissioner has a distinguished record as head of our police force for more than ten years. However, you may not know that he also holds a doctorate in criminology and studied abroad for a year with Interpol—the international police force.
>
> One of the commissioner's favorite projects has been the Neighborhood Watch Program—in which citizens are encouraged to keep an eye on their neighbors' houses and report any suspicious activity to the police. When the commissioner first proposed this idea, he was accused of "reinventing the busybody." The *Morning Herald* ran an editorial headlined "First Busybody of the City," in which it pictured townspeople lurking behind their curtains and jotting down the license plate numbers of their neighbors' relatives.
>
> Well, the "First Busybody" has gotten the last laugh. Since the program was inaugurated a year ago, burglaries and vandalism in parts of our city have decreased by 30 percent! Today the commissioner is going to tell us more about how the program works and how it can be expanded to other areas of the community. I am sure we will all be interested to hear what he has to say. Please welcome Police Commissioner Patrick McCarter.

Try to Create a Sense of Anticipation and Drama   You may have noticed one detail shared by the two speeches introducing the police commissioner: In both cases the speaker's name was saved for last. This is a convention in speeches of introduction. While there may occasionally be good reason to break the convention, usually you will avoid mentioning the speaker's name until the final moment—even when the audience knows exactly whom you are discussing. By doing this you build a sense of drama, and the speaker's name comes as the climax of your introduction.

Often you will find yourself in the situation of introducing someone who is fairly well known to the audience—a classmate, a colleague at a business meeting, a neighbor in a community group. Then you should try to be creative and cast the speaker in a new light. Try to increase the audience's eagerness to hear the speaker. Talk to the speaker beforehand and see if you can learn some interesting facts that are not generally known—especially facts that relate to the speaker's topic. If possible, interview some of the speaker's close friends or family.

Above all, if you expect to be creative and dramatic, be sure you practice your speech of introduction thoroughly. Even though it is short, there is no excuse for not working out the delivery as fully as possible. You should be able to deliver the speech extemporaneously, with sincerity and enthusiasm.

SPEECHES OF PRESENTATION

Speeches of presentation are given when someone is receiving publicly a gift or an award. Usually such speeches are relatively brief. They may be no more than a mere announcement ("And the winner is . . .") or be up to four or five minutes in length.

As with other kinds of speeches, speeches of presentation need to be adapted to the audience and to the occasion. The main theme of a speech of presentation is to acknowledge the achievements of the recipient. You need to tell the audience why the recipient is receiving the award. Point out his or her contributions, achievements, and so forth. Do not deal with everything the person has ever done. Focus on achievements related to the award, and discuss these achievements in a way that will make them meaningful to the audience.

Depending on the audience and the occasion, you may also need to discuss two other matters in a speech of presentation. First, if the audience is not familiar with the award and why it is being given, you should explain briefly—or at least allude to—the purpose of the award. Second, if the award was won in a public competition and the audience knows who the losers are, you might take a moment to praise the losers as well.

Below is a sample speech of presentation. It was delivered by Gregory Peck in presenting the Jean Hersholt Humanitarian Award to Danny Kaye at the 1982 Academy Awards ceremony in Los Angeles. Because the Hersholt Award is a special honor bestowed by the Academy's board of governors, there

Speeches of presentation and acceptance, like other kinds of speeches, must be adapted to the audience and the situation. (Bob Daemmrick/Stock, Boston)

are no public competitors for the award. Thus Peck did not need to say anything in recognition of the "losers." His speech focused on Kaye's contributions to UNICEF and to symphony orchestras as the reasons for bestowal of the award.[4]

PRESENTING THE JEAN HERSHOLT HUMANITARIAN AWARD

Gregory Peck

It's a long trip from Brooklyn to Buckingham Palace, and it's a far piece from Beverly Hills to an obscure village in Bangladesh. Danny Kaye has made both journeys, sustained by his remarkable gifts, his grace, and his intelligence. He has been a star of the first magnitude since his remarkable talent exploded on the Broadway stage in *Lady in the Dark* in 1941, and one who has had a high sense of priority: His wife, Sylvia, and daughter, Dena, have always come first in his life—and then, in no special order, his work, the world's children, and great music.

For UNICEF (United Nations International Children's Emergency Fund), he continues to travel the world, bringing joy and hope to children on all the continents, and initiating programs to save them from hunger and give them a better chance in life. He has been doing this for years, with no pay and without fanfare. No trumpets. No headlines. His reward, the laughter of children.

As forbearing and skillful as he is with children, so he is with symphony orchestras, groups of seventy or eighty highly disciplined artists. He cannot read music, yet he has conducted major orchestras all over the world with musicianship that is sensitive, completely serious, and, at times, likely to veer off alarmingly into the hilarious. Danny's irrepressible *joie de vivre* makes his concerts joyous occasions for musicians and audiences alike. Bach and Mozart have no better friend. Nor have the orchestras and their pension funds. Nor have we.

And thus, for his prodigious labors for the children of the world, for the wondrous people who make music, the Board of Governors proudly gives the Jean Hersholt Humanitarian Award to a ''Citizen of the World'' who does honor to our profession— Mr. Danny Kaye.

SPEECHES OF ACCEPTANCE

The purpose of an acceptance speech is to give thanks for a gift or an award. When giving such a speech, you should thank the people who are bestowing the award, and you should recognize the people who helped you gain it.

The acceptance speech that follows is the companion piece to the speech of presentation by Gregory Peck. It was delivered by Danny Kaye in accepting the Jean Hersholt Humanitarian Award at the 1982 Academy Awards ceremony, and it exemplifies the three major traits of a good acceptance speech—brevity, humility, and graciousness.[5]

ACCEPTING THE JEAN HERSHOLT HUMANITARIAN AWARD

Danny Kaye

I am terribly excited to be given this great honor. And I'm so delighted that I find myself, as we say, trembling. If I were any more delighted, I think I'd be in an institution.

However, I feel a little bit guilty about all the praise that Greg lavished on me. It was really no hardship at all. Really. I am crazy about children. I am crazy about conducting, and I am crazy about flying.

I am definitely not crazy about disease or famine or neglect. But, then, neither are any of you. And we, all of us in our profession, share a long and wonderful tradition of doing something about it—of giving of our time and our talent wherever and whenever needed—without prejudice, without stint. That's one of the reasons that I am so very proud of our profession and so proud to be one of you.

I share this award with you, with all of you, and I give thanks to the memory of Dag Hammarskjold and Maurice Pate, with whom I started to work for UNICEF about twenty-eight years ago. And to Gene Ormandy, who put a baton in my hand, my little nervous hand, and made me an offer I couldn't refuse—to stand in front of a symphony orchestra and conduct. Wow! That's the greatest feeling of neurotic power in the world. You ought to try it!

My special thanks to the Board of Governors. I love this and I love you. Thank you.

COMMEMORATIVE SPEECHES

Commemorative speeches are essentially speeches of praise or celebration. Eulogies, Fourth of July speeches, testimonial addresses, and dedications are examples of commemorative speeches. Your aim in such speeches is to pay tribute to a person, a group of people, an institution, or an idea.

As in an informative speech, you probably will have to give the audience information about your subject. After all, the audience must know *why* your subject is praiseworthy. They will need to know something about the history of the institution or the life of the person being praised. As in other speeches, you may draw on examples, testimony, even statistics to illustrate the achievements of your subject.

Your fundamental purpose in a commemorative speech, however, is not just to inform your listeners but to *inspire* them—to arouse and heighten their appreciation of or admiration for the person, institution, or idea you are praising. If you are paying tribute to a person, for example, you should not compose a biography that simply recounts the details of the person's life. Rather, you should create a speech that goes beyond biography—that penetrates to the *essence* of your subject and generates in your audience a deep sense of respect.

When speaking to commemorate, you do not exhort like the advocate or explain like the lecturer. You want to express feelings, to stir sentiments—joy and hope when a new building is dedicated or a new President is inaugurated; anticipation and good wishes at a commencement celebration; lament and consolation at a funeral or memorial service; admiration and respect at a testimonial dinner. In some ways, a commemorative speech is like an impressionist painting—"a picture with warm colors and texture capturing a mood or a moment."[6]

But while the painter works with brush and colors, the commemorative speaker works with language. Of all the kinds of speeches, perhaps none depends more on the creative and subtle use of language than does the speech to commemorate. Some of the most memorable speeches in history—including Abraham Lincoln's Gettysburg Address—have been commemorative. We remember such speeches—we continue to find them meaningful and inspiring—largely because of their eloquent use of language.

One of the most eloquent speakers in our recent history was Adlai Stevenson. Shortly after the death of Winston Churchill in 1965, Stevenson was chosen to deliver a eulogy at a memorial service in Washington's National Cathedral. Below are two versions of Stevenson's opening lines. The first is what he *might* have said, stripping the text of its warm emotional content and poignant language:

The reason for our gathering today is to mourn the death of a great man, Winston Churchill, who has just died. Churchill was a powerful speaker, and he used his speaking ability for many political and social purposes. All of us will miss hearing him speak, and we will miss the man as well.

Here is what Stevenson *actually* said:

Today we meet in sadness to mourn one of the world's greatest citizens. Sir Winston Churchill is dead. The voice that led nations, raised armies, inspired victories and blew fresh courage into the hearts of men is silenced. We shall hear no longer the remembered eloquence and wit, the old courage and defiance, the robust serenity of indomitable faith. Our world is thus poorer, our political dialogue is diminished and the sources of public inspiration run more thinly for all of us. There is a lonesome place against the sky.

The final sentence—"There is a lonesome place against the sky"—is especially effective. It reinforces Churchill's towering stature in the world of public affairs and captures perfectly the irreplaceable loss caused by his death.

When speaking to commemorate, you will deal for the most part with intangibles. Your success will depend on your ability to put into language the thoughts and emotions appropriate to the occasion. It is easy—too easy—to fall back on clichés and trite sentiments. Your challenge will be to use language imaginatively so as to invest the occasion with dignity, meaning, and honest emotion.

Confronted with the evocative words of a Lincoln or a Stevenson, you may decide the speech of commemoration is far beyond your abilities. But other students have delivered excellent commemorative speeches—not immortal, perhaps, but nevertheless dignified and moving. The following speech was given by Kim Lacina, a student at the University of Wisconsin in a public speaking class. The assignment was to give a brief speech paying tribute to a person, an institution, or an idea. Kim spoke about her grandfather.[7]

MY GRANDFATHER

Kim Lacina

Every day people are born and people die. Human beings come into this world and leave it—most without their names being immortalized in any history books. Millions of people have lived and worked and loved and died without making any great claims to fame or fortune.

But they aren't forgotten—not by their friends, not by their families. And some of these people, some very special people, are not forgotten even by those who hardly knew them. My grandfather was one of these very special people.

What made him so special? Why is he remembered not only by friends and family but even by casual acquaintances? Very simply, because he was the essence of love. More than that, he was the essence of what I think of as "active" love. Just as his heart was not empty, his words were not empty.

He didn't just speak of compassion. During the Great Depression he took homeless people off the street into his home when they needed a place to sleep. He gave them food when they needed something to eat. And though he wasn't a rich man by any means, he gave them money when they had none. Those people off the street will remember the man who had enough love in his heart to share with them all that he had.

He didn't just speak of tolerance. During the 1960s, when his peers were condemning those "long-haired hippies," I can remember riding in the car with my grandfather, picking up dozens and dozens of those "long-haired hippies" who were hitchhiking, and going miles out of our way to give them a ride somewhere. Those men and women will remember the man who had enough love in his heart to bridge the gap between his world and theirs and to practice the spirit of brotherhood.

And he didn't just speak of courage. He proved his courage time and time again. He proved it to a little girl who was trapped in the basement of a burning building. He pulled her out of the flames and gave her back her life. And that little girl, now a grown woman, will remember the man who had enough love in his heart to risk his life for a person he didn't even know.

He also proved his courage, in a more personal way, to his family. In 1966 he was told he had leukemia and only a year to live. He immediately started chemotherapy treatment, and I don't know which is worse—the effects of the disease or the effects of those treatments. In the ensuing year we saw his hair fall out, we saw his skin turn a pasty shade of gray, and we saw him lose so much weight that he seemed to shrivel up into half the size he had been. We didn't want to see him go out that way.

And we didn't. He fought that disease with all his strength and all his courage. And despite the pain he endured, he never complained. I think about him when I catch myself complaining about my "tons of homework" or a "terrible headache," and suddenly that homework or that headache doesn't seem so terrible after all.

He lived through that first year, and he lived through eight more. And that disease never stopped him from working, and it never stopped him from caring. All through those years of suffering, he continued to show compassion and tolerance and courage.

He died in 1975. And though he left this world without ever making the pages of a history book, he still left the world a great deal. He left to the people who knew him a spirit to exemplify life—a spirit of unconditional, selfless, and truly inspiring love.

AFTER-DINNER SPEECHES

After-dinner speeches may be harder to define than any other kind of speech. While the custom of saying a few words of tribute or celebration following a meal is probably as old as civilization itself, after-dinner speeches as a formal type of speech developed in England during the early nineteenth century.[8] By the 1880s they had become so popular on this side of the Atlantic that one observer called them "the style of oratory most cultivated" in the United States.[9] At that time they were delivered, literally, after dinner. By the 1920s, however, with the growing popularity of noon meetings for groups such as the

Lions and Kiwanis clubs, "after-dinner" speeches could be heard after lunch as well. Because so many organizations now have breakfast gatherings, you are as likely to hear an "after-dinner" speech today at eight o'clock in the morning as at eight o'clock in the evening.

After-dinner speeches are best thought of as a kind of speech to entertain. Whether presented after breakfast, lunch, or dinner—in a formal dining room or at an outdoor barbecue—they usually have a lighter touch than a speech to inform or to persuade. This will obviously have some impact on your choice of topic. AIDS, child abuse, drunk driving, cancer, toxic waste, nuclear war—all are important, but audiences do not expect to hear about such weighty matters in the relaxed atmosphere of the typical after-dinner speech. For the most part, though, any topic suitable for an informative or persuasive speech can be appropriate for an after-dinner speech, as long as you approach it in a lighthearted manner.

Suppose, for example, that your subject is nutrition. If you were giving an informative speech on this topic, your specific purpose might be "To inform my audience of the four basic nutrients in the human diet." If you were presenting a persuasive speech, your specific purpose might be "To persuade my audience that they should reduce their consumption of red meat in favor of more fish, vegetables, and grains." But if you were giving an after-dinner speech on the topic of nutrition, your specific purpose might be "To entertain my audience by showing them the ridiculous extremes some people go to in following special diets."

Or to take another example, say your subject is meteorology. If you were making an informative speech, your specific purpose might be "To inform my audience of the different methods used by meteorologists to predict the weather." If you were giving a persuasive speech on the same topic, your specific purpose might be "To persuade my audience that the federal government should not reduce the budget for weather-related research." If you were giving an after-dinner speech, however, your specific purpose might be "To entertain my audience by showing them how preposterous it is to talk about the 'typical' weather in our state."

As these examples suggest, after-dinner speeches should not be technical or argumentative. They may contain information that is new to the audience, and they may even have a persuasive impact, but their supporting materials should be chosen primarily for their entertainment value. Audiences for after-dinner speeches are seldom in a mood to follow a close train of reasoning, a complicated set of statistics, or a series of abstract concepts. Rather, they are looking for a good-natured speech that stimulates the imagination by approaching the topic in a novel way, treating it lightly, even whimsically.

This is not to say after-dinner speeches should be rambling or totally frivolous. Like all other speeches, they require careful preparation and organization. They should have a central theme, and they should strive to make a thoughtful point about that theme—whether it be about an aspect of human nature (such as vanity or the desire for immortality), of college life (such as final exams or finding a decent apartment), of sports (such as the similarities between modern football and the ancient Roman gladiators), of family life (such as the perils of summer vacations or the experience of being a father for the first time), of work (such as putting up with the boss or dealing with weird customers), of travel (such as poor service by the airlines or dealing with unusual customs abroad), or even of current events (such as how we choose presidential candidates or jitters over the stock market).

As you might imagine, humor can be an important part of after-dinner speeches. Some of America's finest after-dinner speakers have been humorists such as Mark Twain and Will Rogers, Art Buchwald and Andy Rooney. This does not mean, however, that you need to be a stand-up comic to be a successful after-dinner speaker. The purpose of humor in an after-dinner speech is more to provoke smiles or chuckles than to convulse the audience with a series of one-liners. Nor is humor used merely to make the audience laugh. In the best after-dinner speeches, humor grows naturally out of the speech materials and helps the speaker make his or her point by providing special insight into the topic.

Tickling an audience's funnybone, however, can be difficult even for accomplished public speakers. If you don't feel confident working for a laugh, don't worry. Humor can contribute to a successful after-dinner speech, but it is not essential. Indeed, the best approach is usually not to work specifically for laughs. If you deal with the topic creatively, select supporting materials that are interesting in their own right, and use the resources of language to create sharp imagery, vivid descriptions, colorful details, and clever phrasing, you should do just fine.

All of these traits are represented in the following after-dinner speech. It was given by Julie Daggett, a student at the University of Wisconsin, to her public speaking class.[10]

THE HORROR OF IT ALL

Julie Daggett

They never did find his head or hands. I crouched in the corner, peering through my fingers as he moaned and wailed in an endless search for his missing appendages. I was terrified—but not as terrified as poor Bette Davis. They put her in the nuthouse. I simply turned on the light and ran to the safety of my father's lap. As I perched, shuddering, he said the phrase I was to hear over and over through the coming years, "It's okay, it's only a movie." It did not end for me there, however. The movie *Hush, Hush, Sweet Charlotte* was just the beginning of my love/hate relationship with horror movies.

My scaredy-cat tendencies actually began at a very early age. As a young child, I insisted the hall light be kept on when I went to bed—no measly night-light would do for a hard-core chicken. My parents would come upstairs after the news and tell each other to "turn off the l-i-g-h-t." I could be heard miles away screaming, "NO! I know what that spells!" After *The Ghost and Mr. Chicken* with Don Knotts, my bedtime ritual went something like this—look under the bed, look in the closet, turn off the light, and leap into the sack. As time passed, however, this childish nonsense began to subside. I was growing up.

But then it happened. Theater owners offered up *The Exorcist*, a temptation I could not resist. That delicious, horrible feeling of being terrified was renewed. I was hooked. I stayed pretty sane, though, until I read the book, at which time I discovered I was possessed by the Devil. I had six of the ten symptoms, including headaches, nausea, and loss of sleep. It may not have been Satan himself, but there was definitely a demon lurking somewhere.

Over the next several years, the movie industry fed my passion for terror—and my paranoia. The movie *Halloween* ended any possibility of parking on a deserted road after a date. I was not going to fog up the windows making myself a sitting duck for any escaped mental patient. The *Friday the 13th* series put a stop to any thought of camping overnight in the wilderness, while *Night of the Living Dead* put a dent in my car. I was in such a panic to get out of the dark parking lot after viewing this old classic that I slammed into a pole, causing $300 damage to my trusty Chevy.

My fright-flick fanaticism was taking a toll on my everyday life. I began to notice that guys who took me to these movies didn't often ask me out again—apparently my squirming and screaming in the theater embarrassed them a bit. Some people just don't know how to really get into a movie. I no longer took babysitting jobs because I was afraid to be alone in a strange house. I wouldn't do laundry at night because that meant I had to go down to the basement.

My fears weren't even limited to being alone. One Friday night I was home watching HBO with my Mom. Let me explain that our house is situated in the dead center of a very isolated woods. As a kid I remember thinking it would be an ideal place for escaped convicts to hide out and hold hostages. Anyway, there we were, munching away on junk food, when suddenly the lights went out. Keep in mind that this was a calm summer evening—no rain, no lightning, not even any wind. There was only one explanation—we had a madman in the basement. In my alarm I turned to the woman who had protected me all my life. My Mom looked at me and said the only thing she could say, ''Grab the potato chips.'' Chips and keys in tow, we bolted for the car. But this was not to be the end of our ordeal—no electricity, no electric garage door opener. I looked at my Mom and said the only thing I could say, ''Ram it!'' Bravely, Mom kept her head. She crept out of the security of the locked car to manually open the garage door and drive us, in our pajamas, to safety. It was then that I knew I was out of control. It was then that I decided to go cold turkey—no more horror films.

It's been two years now, and I can finally look back at these escapades and laugh. It's been two years now, and I pride myself on the fact that I live alone. The only thing that keeps me awake nights these days is writing speeches. I'm not going to end up in the nuthouse like Bette Davis. But I'm not going to get too overconfident, either. Remember all those unsuspecting kids in *Halloween*? They were just out having a good time when, WHAM—and the rest is history.

SUMMARY

Special occasions include weddings, funerals, dedications, award ceremonies, retirement dinners, and the like. Nearly always they are occasions for speechmaking. In this chapter we have considered speeches of introduction, speeches of presentation, speeches of acceptance, commemorative speeches, and after-dinner speeches.

When you make a speech of introduction, your job is to build enthusiasm for the main speaker and to establish a welcoming climate that will boost his or her credibility and confidence. Keep your remarks brief, make certain they are completely accurate, and adapt them to the audience, the occasion, and the main speaker.

Speeches of presentation are given when someone is receiving publicly a gift or an award. The main theme of such a speech is to acknowledge the achievements of the recipient. You need to tell the audience why the recipient is receiving the award.

The purpose of an acceptance speech is to give thanks for a gift or an award. When delivering such a speech, you should thank the people who are bestowing the award and recognize the contributions of people who helped you gain it. Be brief, humble, and gracious.

Commemorative speeches are essentially speeches of praise or celebration. They include Fourth of July speeches, eulogies, testimonial addresses, and the like. Your aim in such a speech is to pay tribute to a person, a group of people, an institution, or an idea. When making a commemorative speech you want to inspire your audience—to arouse and heighten their appreciation of and admiration for the subject. You will deal for the most part with intangibles, and your success will depend on how well you put into language the thoughts and feelings appropriate to the occasion.

After-dinner speeches are best thought of as a kind of speech to entertain, and they usually have a lighter touch than informative or persuasive speeches. Neither technical nor argumentative in nature, they seek to stimulate the imagination by approaching the topic in a novel or unexpected way. Although humor can be an important part of after-dinner speeches, it is not essential. If you do use humor, it should grow naturally out of the speech materials and provide insight into the topic.

REVIEW QUESTIONS

After reading this chapter, you should be able to answer the following questions:

1. What are the three purposes of a speech of introduction? What guidelines should you follow in preparing such a speech?

2. What is the main theme of a speech of presentation? Depending on the audience and occasion, what two other themes might you include in such a speech?

3. What are the three major traits of a good acceptance speech?

4. What is the fundamental purpose of a commemorative speech? Why does

a successful commemorative speech depend so much on the creative and subtle use of language?

5. What is the primary difference between an after-dinner speech and a speech to inform or to persuade? What is the role of humor in after-dinner speaking?

APPLICATION EXERCISES

1. Attend a speech on campus. Pay special attention to the speech introducing the main speaker. How well does it fit the guidelines discussed in this chapter?

2. Observe several speeches of presentation and acceptance—at a campus awards ceremony or on a television program such as the Academy Awards, Grammy Awards, Emmy Awards, or Tony Awards. Which speeches do you find most effective? Least effective? Why?

3. Analyze the commemorative speech by Kim Lacina ("My Grandfather," pages 355–356). Assess the speech in light of the criteria for commemorative speaking presented in the chapter.

NOTES

1 William Norwood Brigance, *Speech: Its Techniques and Disciplines in a Free Society,* 2nd ed. (New York: Appleton-Century-Crofts, 1961), p. 505.
2 James C. Humes, *Roles Speakers Play* (New York: Harper & Row, 1976), p. 8.
3 Ralph N. Schmidt, *How to Speak with Confidence* (New York: Fell, 1965), p. 165.
4 Reprinted with permission of Gregory Peck and the Academy of Motion Picture Arts and Sciences. Copyright 1982 by the Academy of Motion Picture Arts and Sciences.
5 Reprinted with permission of Danny Kaye and the Academy of Motion Picture Arts and Sciences. Copyright 1982 by the Academy of Motion Picture Arts and Sciences.
6 Humes, *Roles Speakers Play,* pp. 33–34, 36.
7 Reprinted with permission of Kim Lacina.
8 Chauncey M. Depew, *My Memories of Eighty Years* (New York: Scribner's 1924), p. 378.
9 Barnet Baskerville, *The People's Voice: The Orator in American Society* (Lexington, Ky.: University Press of Kentucky, 1979), p. 112.
10 Reprinted with permission of Julie Daggett.

Speaking In Small Groups

Human beings have a natural tendency to form groups. We form groups to produce and raise children (families), to pool our learning resources (schools), to protect our rights as workers (unions), to share in our worship (churches and temples). Each of these different groups has a purpose. In some instances the group will disband once the purpose has been served, as in a school class. Other groups are permanent for the lives of the members. Whichever the case, the group answers a need. It performs some function better than could individual people acting on their own.

No doubt you belong to a number of *informal groups*. You get together with a "group" of your friends, you were born into a family "group," and so forth. Participants in informal groups do not necessarily work on specific tasks or have any particular objectives in mind. Rather, they maintain the group for the sake of the relationships established by being associated with the group—the support of friends, the love of one's family, having fun with others.

By contrast, *formal groups* are created to undertake specific tasks. Examples of formal groups include students cooperating on a class project, city council members working out a budget, business associates planning a sales strategy, faculty members deciding on next year's curriculum. In this chapter we concentrate on a particular kind of formal group known as the *small group*.

WHAT IS A SMALL GROUP?

Traits of a Small Group

We can identify four traits of a small group, as it is defined by most communication theorists.

First, a small group has a minimum of three members. (A group of two persons is called a dyad, and it operates quite differently from a group of three or more.)[1] There is some difference of opinion about the maximum number of people who constitute a small group. Some experts set the maximum at eight, others go as high as twelve. For our purposes, we will consider a small group to consist of between three and twelve people. The important point is that the group must be small enough to allow free discussion among all members. In small-group communication, all participants are potentially speakers *and* listeners. A manageable number of people permits everyone to shift easily between speaking and listening.[2]

Second, the members of a small group are interdependent. What one member does affects all the other members. You do not give up your individuality when you become part of a small group, but you do assume responsibilities that go beyond your own personal ideas and goals. You are involved in a cooperative venture. If you participate fully and contribute to the group, you will help it be successful. But if you shirk your responsibilities, you will undermine the efforts of everyone else in the group. Everything you do as a member of the group will have some impact—either positive or negative—on the rest of the group.

Third, members of a small group influence one another through communication. They exchange ideas, knowledge, and beliefs with one another. At times they inform their fellow members. At other times they seek to persuade them. As a participant in a group, you might influence your colleagues by giving them important information, by encouraging them to speak, by persuading them to change their minds, by leading them into a new channel of discussion, even by getting them to end a meeting of the group. All other members of the group in turn have the chance to influence you in the same ways through effective communication.[3]

Fourth, members of a small group assemble for a specific purpose. They are not just a band of three to twelve people who happen to end up in the same room. Several shoppers milling around the clothing section of a department store are not a small group, even if they speak to one another or comment about high prices and poor service. But if those same shoppers decided to meet together and prepare a formal complaint to the store manager about high prices and poor service, they would then constitute a small group. They would have assembled for a specific purpose.

Kinds of Small Groups

There are four major kinds of small groups—experiential groups, learning groups, information-gathering groups, and problem-solving groups.

Experiential groups are usually composed of persons who come together to develop personal insights, overcome personality problems, or grow as individuals from the advice and feedback of others.[4] Examples of experiential groups include marriage encounter groups, drug rehabilitation groups, management training groups, and microtherapy groups. Such groups typically perform one of two functions. They may help people cope with personal crises by offering the support and understanding of other group members. Or they may help people become aware of how and why they act as they do in certain situations, so they can change their behavior in positive ways.

The purpose of *learning groups* is to help members learn about a subject by sharing their knowledge and insights. A seminar is one kind of learning group, as is the study session you hold with a group of friends to prepare for an examination. Another kind of learning group is the business, church, or community "roundtable," in which several people gather informally to share knowledge on a topic.

The main objective of an *information-gathering group* is to come up with adequate information about a topic. Suppose, for example, the state highway department plans to build a new road. The department might appoint a committee to gather information about the environmental impact of the proposed route, about the cost of building the road over certain types of terrain, and about the amount of time needed to complete the project. The purpose of the information-gathering group is not to make a decision but to provide information so others can make an intelligent decision.

Problem-solving groups are formed to solve a particular problem. They exist in virtually every area of life. Business groups consider ways of increasing sales. Church groups discuss how to raise funds and provide for the needy. Groups of mothers work on establishing day-care centers. The President's cabinet debates a foreign policy move. A ski club evaluates proposals for the next outing. You will almost certainly be a member of a problem-solving group sometime in your life. Because the problem-solving group is so pervasive, we will concentrate on it in this chapter.

BENEFITS OF SMALL GROUPS

Even though small groups are everywhere, you may be skeptical about them. There's an old saying that "a camel is a horse designed by a committee." If you have ever been part of a committee that seemed to get nothing done, you may be inclined to say, "Oh, let one person decide and get it over with." The problem in such cases, however, is not that there is a committee, but that the committee is not functioning effectively. If all members of a problem-solving group work well together, they can almost always deal with the problem better than a single person can.[5] There are good reasons for this.

First, groups have more resources than do individuals. Several people working together can gather more information, offer more viewpoints, and—through division of labor—get more work done.

Second, effective groups have a built-in error-correcting mechanism. An error in judgment or information by one member is likely to be noticed and corrected by another member. Here is what can happen when a single person tries to undertake a complex task:

The president of a small company decided to remodel the office space on his management floor. He assigned his youngest vice president, Chris Morrow, to make a plan for remodeling the offices and to carry through on the plan.

Chris was very pleased with his plan. He thought he had taken everyone's needs into account, and he had arranged for most of the remodeling work to be done over a long weekend, so no one's work would be disrupted. On the Monday morning after the move, Chris settled back in his office waiting for congratulations to pour in.

Instead, a crowd of angry people stormed into his office. "There's no telephone jack in my room," said the advertising manager, "and the telephone company says they can't put one in for three weeks. How can I do business without a telephone?" Right behind him was the president's administrative assistant. "Do you realize," she said, "how far I have to walk to get to the president's office? It's only 15 feet from my room, but with that partition you put in I have to walk halfway around the building!" The research manager said, "What am I supposed to do with my library? You didn't leave any space for my library! All the books are packed up in boxes, and there's no place to put them."

Next came the head of the duplicating department, who said, "I suppose you know you're not going to get any copies made. You've put all the copy machines in an inside office, with no window. Don't you know there's a city ordinance that copying machines have to be in a windowed space?'' Angriest of all was another vice president. "For Pete's sake,'' she said, "why didn't you *ask* me? The same things happened the *last* time the offices were moved around. I could have told you to watch out for the phone jacks and the copy machines.''

Wearily, Chris went back to his blueprint, making plans to rearrange the offices again.

What went wrong? Chris did not have enough resources on his own to make a successful office plan. If a group, instead of a single person, had been assigned to remodel the offices, the problems might have been averted. One person could have taken charge of space needs, another of traffic paths, a third of telephones and other equipment, and so forth. The final plan would have taken *all* factors into account.

We have said that small groups often make better decisions than individuals. But the word "often" should be stressed here. To make sound decisions, groups need effective leadership. We turn, therefore, to a discussion of leadership in small groups.

LEADERSHIP IN SMALL GROUPS

Have you ever watched a group of children squabbling on a playground? Or a group of politicians squabbling in a committee? In both situations—and many others—one wants to ask, "Who's in charge here?" The implication is that somebody *ought* to be in charge—that somebody ought to be exercising leadership.

Broadly conceived, leadership is the ability to influence members in such a way as to achieve the goals of the group.[6] Here are some ways in which leadership is exercised:

When a member arranges the time and place of a group meeting

When a member helps the group decide exactly what agenda it will follow in its meetings

When a member argues for a certain position and convinces the rest of the group to accept it

When a member keeps the group from getting sidetracked on irrelevant issues

When a member resolves a difference of opinion between two other members of the group

When a member encourages a less vocal person to express his or her ideas about the group's task

When a member summarizes what the group has accomplished in a given meeting

Kinds of Leadership

There are at least four kinds of leadership that may occur in a small group.

Sometimes there is *no specific leader.* In such a situation, members of effective groups tend to have equal influence. When a need for leadership arises, any of the members can—and one of them probably will—provide the necessary leadership. A typical instance might be a class project, in which you and several classmates are working together. From time to time each of you will help the group move toward its goal by suggesting when and where to meet, by outlining the strengths and weaknesses of a certain viewpoint, by resolving disagreements among other members, and so forth.

In some circumstances a group may have an *implied leader.* For example, if a business meeting includes one vice president and a number of subordinates, the vice president becomes the implied leader. The same is true if one member of the group is a specialist in the topic at hand and the others are not. Members will likely defer to the person with the highest rank or greatest expertise, and that person will become the group's implied leader.

Even when a group starts out leaderless, there may be an *emergent leader.* This is a person who, by ability or by force of personality or just by talking the most, takes a leadership role.[7] The emergence of a leader may or may not be desirable. If the group is stalemated or has dissolved into bickering or making jokes, an emergent leader can put the group back on track. There is a danger, however, that the emergent leader may be not the most effective leader but merely the most assertive personality. Ideally, each member of the group should be prepared to assume a leadership role when necessary.

Finally, there may be a *designated leader*—a person elected or appointed as leader when the group is formed. A group that meets for only one session should almost always have a designated leader, who takes care of the procedural tasks and serves as spokesperson for the group.[8] Likewise, a formal committee will usually have a designated chairperson. The chair can perform leadership functions or delegate them, but he or she remains in charge of the group.

A group may or may not need a specific leader, but it always needs leader*ship.* When all members of the group are skilled communicators, they can take turns at providing leadership even if the group has a designated or implied leader. As you develop your group communication skills, you should be prepared to assume a leadership role whenever necessary.

Functions of Leadership

An effective leader helps the group reach its goals by fulfilling three overlapping sets of needs—procedural needs, task needs, and maintenance needs.

Procedural needs can be thought of as the "housekeeping" requirements of the group. They include:

Deciding when and where the group will meet

Reserving the room, checking the number of chairs, making sure the heat or air conditioning is turned on

Setting the agenda of each meeting

Starting the meeting

Taking notes during the meeting

Preparing and distributing any written handouts needed for the meeting

Summarizing the group's progress at the end of the meeting

If there is a designated leader, he or she can attend to these needs or assign one or more group members to do so. Otherwise, members of the group must devise ways to split the procedural responsibilities.

Task needs go beyond procedural needs and are substantive actions necessary to help the group complete the particular task it is working on. They include:

Analyzing the issues facing the group

Distributing the work load among the members

Collecting information

Soliciting the views of other members

Keeping the group from going off on a tangent

Playing devil's advocate for unpopular ideas

Formulating criteria for judging the most effective solution

Helping the group reach consensus on its final recommendations

Most members will help the group satisfy its task needs. Leadership becomes necessary when some task needs are not being fulfilled adequately, as in this example:

A group of students had undertaken to solve the parking problems on their campus. The group had held several meetings, and most of its task needs had been met. Members had done a good job polling students for their opinions, discussing alternative solutions with the administration, and considering the relative merits of each solution. However, one member of the group, Rachel, noticed that two items had not been given enough attention. No one had investigated potential sources of money for new parking facilities, and no one had studied the environmental impact of constructing additional parking spaces. Therefore, Rachel briefly took a leadership role to perform a task need for the group. She pointed out that these two areas had been neglected and recommended that the group explore them further.

The effective leader—whether permanent or temporary—has a realistic notion of the group's task needs and of how to meet them.[9]

Maintenance needs involve interpersonal relations in the group. They include such factors as:

How well members get along with one another

How willing members are to contribute to the group

Whether members are supportive of one another

Whether members feel satisfied with the group's accomplishments

Whether members feel good about their roles in the group

If interpersonal problems dominate discussion, the group will have a difficult time working together and reaching a decision. This is one of the more important areas calling for effective leadership. A leader can do much to create and sustain supportive communication in the group. By helping group members handle conflict, by working out differences of opinion, by reducing interpersonal tension, by encouraging participation from all members, by being alert to personal feelings, and by promoting solidarity within the group, a leader can make a tremendous contribution toward helping the group achieve its goals.[10]

RESPONSIBILITIES IN A SMALL GROUP

Every member of a small group must assume certain responsibilities, which can be divided into five major categories: (1) commit yourself to the goals of your group, (2) fulfill individual assignments, (3) avoid interpersonal conflicts, (4) encourage full participation, and (5) keep the discussion on track. Some of these responsibilities involve leadership roles, but all five are so important that each participant should take them as personal obligations, regardless of the group's leadership. Let us look more closely at each of these responsibilities.

Commit Yourself to the Goals of Your Group

For a group to succeed, members must align their personal goals with the group's goal. This sounds obvious, but it is not always easy. When you are working with other students on a class project, the group goal—and most likely the goal of each member—is to get a good grade, which should ensure a positive attitude toward the group. There is a strong incentive for members to cooperate, work closely together, and commit themselves to completing the task.

Problems arise when one or more members have personal goals that conflict with the group's goal. Here is the kind of situation that can occur:

Irene Messner is a member of her church's committee to buy new equipment for the parish house kitchen. Because the budget is very tight, the committee's goal is to get the best equipment for the lowest price. But unknown to the other members of the group, Irene's son-in-law is a salesman for a distributor of rather high-priced kitchen appliances. Privately, Irene has reasoned that if she can sway the committee toward that company, her son-in-law will get a large commission. Irene does not mention this fact to the group. Instead, she argues that *quality*—not price—should be the determining factor in the purchase. The group process breaks down because Irene will not surrender her private goal.

This is an extreme example, but there can be more subtle kinds of private goals, as in the following case:

Fred and Valerie are part of a group, and Fred would like to be on closer terms with Valerie. In order to impress her, he may agree with everything she says, regardless of whether he really shares her views. Fred's expressed views are consequently not his actual views. In short, Fred has a *hidden agenda* in the group meeting. The group's agenda is to solve the problem, but Fred's agenda is to get a date with Valerie.

Group members may have all sorts of hidden agendas. One may be experiencing personal problems—lowered grades, a breakup with a friend, trouble at home, or just a bad day. Another may have a commitment to some different group, whose goals conflict with those of the present group. A third may want to take charge of the group for reasons of personal power, regardless of the group's task.

Remember that what one member of a group does affects all the other members. You should not try to advance your own interests or boost your own ego at the expense of the group and its goals. Beware of hidden agendas—whether yours or someone else's—and participate with a positive spirit. If a group is to work effectively, all members must commit themselves to the goals of the group and cooperate to achieve them.

Fulfill Individual Assignments

As mentioned earlier, one of the advantages of the group process is that it divides the work load among several people. Work assignments might involve gathering information, making arrangements for a meeting, researching a particular aspect of the group's topic, taking notes at a meeting, and so forth. Unless every member fulfills his or her assignments, the group's entire project may fail—as in the following example:

One student group decided that as a class project they would bring Easter baskets to the patients in the children's ward of a local hospital. After the project had been approved, assignments were given out. Bob would coordinate with the hospital authorities, Marilyn would handle fund-raising for the needed supplies. Peter would supervise the egg-decorating team. Sharon would be responsible for buying baskets and chocolate bunnies. Phil would arrange for transportation to the hospital.

Everybody completed their assignments except Phil, who was busy writing a term paper. He asked a friend to pick up a bus schedule and assumed everything would be fine. On Easter morning the group assembled at the bus stop, loaded down with baskets for the children. And they waited and waited. After an hour Phil called the bus company, only to discover that the buses did not run on holidays. By the time Phil had made other arrangements to get to the hospital, visiting hours were over, and the group could not get in.

No matter what other assignments they may have, *all* members of a group have one very critical assignment—listening. If you tune out the person who is speaking, or if you concentrate entirely on what *you* plan to say next, the group is not going to make very much progress. Effective listening is vital to small-group communication. First, it helps you understand what is happening in the group. And unlike a public speaking situation, you can stop the speaker and ask for clarification on any point about which you are confused. Second, listening helps you evaluate the merits of the speaker's position in relation to your own. Third, listening provides support for the speaker and helps establish a positive climate for discussion.[11] In group discussion, as in other kinds of situations, listening is crucial to effective communication.

Avoid Interpersonal Conflicts

If groups were made up of robots, there would be no problem with interpersonal conflicts. But groups are made up of people—people with likes and dislikes and animosities and prejudices and very different personalities. It is vital to the group process that disagreements be kept on a task level, rather than on a personal level. Suppose you disagree with another member's idea. Disagreement on the personal level could sound like this: "That's the stupidest idea I ever heard of! Do you realize how much money it would cost to do that?" But on the task level disagreement is aimed at the *idea,* not the person: "Potentially that's a very good solution, but I'm not sure we have enough money to accomplish it."

When disagreements are allowed to become personal, some members may start to see the group as a kind of debating society. Rather than focusing on the task, they may spend their time getting even with other participants, defending themselves, trying to score points, and jumping on people's ideas. Other members—especially those who are shy or soft-spoken—may recoil from the verbal combat and withdraw from active participation in the group's deliberations.

No matter what the group, personal antagonism leaves a bad taste in everyone's mouth and harms the performance of the group. It is essential that someone take a leadership role and bring the discussion back to the relevant issues. Let's say your group is considering the practicality of adding a vegetarian section to the dormitory cafeteria. The discussion might go like this:

JOAN: It seems to me a waste of time, money, and space to make a special section for vegetarians. There are plenty of vegetables on the menu now. Anyone who doesn't want to eat the meat doesn't have to.

TOM: You're not getting the point. Vegetarian menus have to be *balanced* with enough vegetable protein. It's not enough to say, ''Don't eat the meat.'' We need a special section where the menus are planned for a nutritious vegetarian diet.

JOAN: Oh, for pity's sake, you food freaks are all alike. You think you've got the true faith and all the rest of us are sinners just because we eat a hamburger now and then.

TOM: If you want to kill innocent animals to eat, that's none of my business. Go ahead, ruin your health, load yourself up with cholesterol. I don't care. But don't stand in the way of people who really care about their bodies.

LEADER: Just a minute. Before we go on with this part of the discussion, don't we have some figures on how many students would actually use the vegetarian section? Lisa, I think that was your department. What did you find out?

None of this is to say that members of a group should never disagree. In fact, a serious problem occurs when members get along so well and are so concerned about maintaining the harmony of the group that they will not disagree with one another about anything. Whenever one member makes a suggestion, everybody else thinks it's a wonderful idea. When this happens, the group misses the benefit of having a group in the first place. There is no chance to reach the best decision by exploring an array of perspectives, opinions, and information. A group that is concerned above all with dodging disagreement will not be any more effective than one that dissolves into personal quarreling.

The point, then, is not that groups should avoid disagreement but that they should keep it at the task level and not allow it to degenerate into personal feuding. There is usually little achievement—and even less feeling of satisfaction—when a group becomes consumed with personal bickering and antagonism.

Encourage Full Participation

If a group is to work effectively, all members must contribute fully and share their ideas with one another. Every member of a group should take responsibility for encouraging other members to participate. You can do this, first of all, by listening attentively. Listening provides support for the speaker. After all, how would you like to speak in a group where everybody else appeared to be bored or distracted?

If there are one or two quiet members in the group, you can draw them into the discussion by asking their opinions and showing your interest in their ideas and information. For instance, you can say something like, "We haven't heard from Sue in a while, and she has some personal experience in this matter. Sue, can you tell the others what you told me about this plan?"

Another way to encourage participation is to help build a supportive environment. When a member speaks, you can say, "That's an interesting idea." Or, "I never knew that. Can you tell us more about it?" Conversely, try to avoid negative comments that will squelch a speaker before he or she has finished—comments like "Oh, no, that never works" or "What a dumb idea." Supportive comments create good will among group members and make everyone feel free to discuss their ideas without ridicule or embarrassment.

If you are shy or afraid your ideas will be taken too critically, you may be unwilling to participate at first. To overcome your diffidence, try to remember that your contribution is necessary to the group. This is why you are there. At the very least, you can help provide a supportive environment for discussion by listening, reacting, and encouraging the free exchange of ideas.

Keep the Discussion on Track

In some groups the discussion proceeds like a stream-of-consciousness exercise. Here is a hypothetical example, in which a town planning board is considering installing a new traffic light at a busy intersection:

JOE: You know, we're going to have trouble getting cars to come to a full stop even if we do put in a traffic light.

KAREN: Tell me about it! I came through there yesterday and hit my brakes and the car just kept going. Maybe I need the brakes adjusted, though.

MAX: Get ready to pay through the nose. I had a brake job on my car last week, and it was nearly twice as much as last time.

PETER: That's nothing. Have you looked at lawnmowers lately? And if you think lawnmowers are high . . .

KIM: Who mows lawns? I had my yard planted with ground cover and put gravel over the rest. It's . . .

LEADER: Excuse me, folks, but weren't we talking about the *traffic light*?

It is the responsibility of every member to keep the discussion on track and to intervene if the group wanders too far afield. There is nothing wrong with a little casual conversation to break the tension or provide a brief respite from work, but it shouldn't be allowed to get out of hand. When working in a problem-solving group, make sure the group's ultimate goal is always in the forefront. Do your best to see that discussion proceeds in an orderly fashion from one point to the next and that the group does not get bogged down in side issues.

On the other hand, you need to guard against the tendency to progress to a solution too quickly, without thoroughly exploring the problem. This concern can be especially serious when members of a group are tired or discouraged. If you feel your group is taking the easy way out and jumping at an easy solution, try to make the other members aware of your concern. By suggesting that they talk about the problem in more detail, you may bring out vital information or ideas. One classroom group found out the perils of making a snap decision:

The group's first job was to decide what they should do for a class project. Near the beginning of their first meeting, someone suggested that they observe an established small group—the city council of their community—to see how the group worked. Everyone thought it was a splendid idea, and the class group wrapped up their session, congratulating themselves on having disposed of the problem so quickly.

But what looked at first like a great idea proved to have some crucial drawbacks. First, it turned out that the city council would not meet again until after the group's class project was due. Second, the city council had twenty people on it—not really an appropriate number to study as a small group. Finally, city council meetings were not always open to the public. The quick solution turned out to be no solution at all.

Fortunately, there are systematic ways to keep the discussion on track and to avoid hasty group decisions. If your group follows a tested method of decision making, it will have a much better chance of reaching a satisfactory decision. We turn, therefore, to the most common decision-making technique for small groups—the reflective-thinking method.[12]

THE REFLECTIVE-THINKING METHOD

The reflective-thinking method is derived from the writings of the famous American philosopher John Dewey. It offers a logical, step-by-step process for discussion in problem-solving groups. The method consists of five steps: (1) defining the problem, (2) analyzing the problem, (3) establishing criteria for solving the problem, (4) generating potential solutions, and (5) selecting the best solution. By following these steps your group will make its work much easier.

Let us take a closer look at the reflective-thinking method. As we do so, we shall illustrate each step by following a single group through the entire process.

Define the Problem

Before a problem-solving group can make progress, it must know exactly what problem it is trying to solve. Defining the problem may seem easy, but it is not always so. In a sense, defining the problem for group discussion is akin to settling on a specific purpose for a speech. Unless it is done properly, everything that follows will suffer.

The best way to define the problem is to phrase it as a question of policy. We discussed questions of policy in Chapter 14 (see pages 308–311). Here it is enough to note that questions of policy inquire about the necessity and/or practicality of specific courses of action. Questions of policy typically include the word "should." For example:

What steps should the city take to deal with the shortage of parking spaces downtown?

What should be the policy of the United States with respect to nuclear arms control?

What measures should our school take to deal with declining enrollment?

In phrasing the question for discussion, your group should follow several guidelines.[13] First, make sure the question is as clear and specific as possible. For example:

Ineffective: What should be done about the federal budget deficit?

More Effective: What should the United States government do to balance the federal budget by 1995?

Second, phrase the question to allow a wide variety of answers. Be especially wary of questions that can be answered with a simple yes or no. For example:

Ineffective: Should the city build more bicycle paths?

More Effective: What steps should the city take to improve services for bicycle riders?

Third, avoid biased or slanted questions. For example:

Ineffective: How can we keep the campus bookstore from ripping off students?

More Effective: What changes, if any, should be made in the pricing policies of the campus bookstore?

Fourth, make sure you pose a single question. For example:

Ineffective:	What revisions should the college consider in its admissions requirements and in its graduation requirements?
More Effective:	What revisions should the college consider in its admissions requirements?
More Effective:	What revisions should the college consider in its graduation requirements?

To clarify this first step of the reflective-thinking method, let's see how our model problem-solving group defined the problem:

As a class project, the group set out to discuss the problem of sharply rising costs for attending college. Following the reflective-thinking method, they began by defining the problem. After several false starts they phrased the problem this way: "What steps should our school take to reduce student costs for attending college?"

Analyze the Problem

After the problem has been defined, the group begins to analyze it. Too often, groups (like individuals) start mapping out solutions before they have a firm grasp of what is wrong. This is like a doctor prescribing treatment before fully diagnosing the patient's ailment. If your group investigates the problem as thoroughly as possible, you will be in a much better position to devise a workable solution.

In analyzing the problem, pay particular attention to two questions. First, how severe is the problem? Investigate the scope of the problem. Determine how many people it affects. Assess what might happen if the problem is not resolved. Second, what are the causes of the problem? Check into the history of the problem. Learn what factors contributed to it. Ascertain its major causes.

As you might imagine, analyzing the problem requires research. Effective group decisions depend on having the best information available. You can get this information in the same way you gather materials for a speech. Sometimes you can rely on your own knowledge and experience. More often, you need to get information from other sources—by writing away for it, by interviewing someone with expertise on the topic, or by working in the library (see Chapter 5). When meeting with your group, make sure you have done the research assigned to you, so you can offer complete and unbiased information.

Let's return now to our sample group and see how they analyzed the problem of rapidly escalating student costs for attending college:

The group talked first about the severity of the problem. Tuition and fees had risen dramatically, as had outlays for books and incidentals. One member offered statistics to show that the cost of attending college had doubled in the past ten years.

Other members noted that the problem was affecting not only students. Merchants within the college community were being hurt because students had less money to spend on such items as records, entertainment, and clothes. The institution itself was affected, since rising costs were driving away students who might otherwise have applied.

To determine the causes of the problem, the group researched articles in the library about the rise in student costs for attending college across the nation. They also interviewed an economics professor and the head of the student aid program on campus. After studying the matter thoroughly, the group identified several major causes, including administrative costs, faculty salaries, the rising price of textbooks, and increased living expenses.

Establish Criteria for Solutions

If you planned to buy a car, how would you proceed? You would probably not just walk into a dealer's showroom and buy whatever appealed to you on the spur of the moment. You would most likely decide ahead of time what kind of car you wanted, what options it should have, and how much money you could afford to spend. That is, you would establish *criteria* to guide you in deciding exactly which car to buy.

You should do much the same thing in group discussion. Once your group has analyzed the problem, you should not jump immediately to proposing solutions. Instead, you should take time to establish criteria—standards—for responsible solutions. You should work out (and write down) exactly what your solutions must achieve and any factors that might limit your choice of solutions. If, for example, a committee is authorized to spend a maximum of $1,000 on a club's annual banquet, one of the criteria for the committee's decision will be that the banquet cost no more than $1,000.

A common failing of problem-solving groups is that they start to discuss solutions before agreeing on criteria for the solutions. When this happens, a group runs into trouble. Some people will propose solutions based on one set of criteria, while others will propose solutions based on different criteria. You can avoid such conflicts by making sure the group sets up criteria before proposing solutions.

To give a better idea of how this stage of the reflective-thinking method works, let's look at the cost-cutting group we have been following:

After some discussion, the group established these criteria for possible solutions: (1) The solution should significantly reduce students' costs. (2) The solution should come into force at the start of the next school year. (3) The solution should not hurt the prestige of the college. (4) The cost of the solution should be minimal and should be paid by the administration. (5) The human resources needed to implement the solution should come from administrative personnel already working on the school's staff. (6) The solution should involve only actions the college had authority to control—not matters controlled by outside individuals or agencies.

Generate Potential Solutions

Once your group has the criteria firmly in mind, you are ready to discuss solutions. Your goal at this stage is to come up with the widest possible range of potential solutions—not to judge the solutions. That comes later. At this stage you are only suggesting possibilities. One member of the group should be responsible for writing down all the solutions proposed at this time.

Many groups find the technique of *brainstorming* helpful in this stage. Brainstorming allows a group to generate a variety of solutions without prematurely evaluating them. In Chapter 3 we discussed how brainstorming can work for an individual in choosing a speech topic. Here brainstorming is expanded to the whole group. Usually it begins when one member of the group proposes a solution, and then each of the other members in turn proposes a different solution. The process continues until the group cannot think of any more solutions. The member who is responsible for writing down the solutions should be alert to similar ideas and combine them wherever possible to reduce the total number.

Brainstorming has two advantages. First, it encourages creativity by enabling members to "piggyback" their ideas onto the ideas of other members. For example, if one person says, "We could establish food co-ops," another person might add, "Yes, and we could establish clothing co-ops too." The person who is recording the solutions would then write down "Establish food and/or clothing co-ops." The second advantage of brainstorming is that it encourages equal participation. A round-robin discussion makes it unlikely that one or two members will dominate or that quiet members will hold back. Since the goal is to generate a lot of ideas—no matter how far-fetched—no one need fear that his or her ideas will be hooted down. Let's see how our cost-cutting group handled this stage:

> By brainstorming, the group came up with the following possible solutions: (1) Reduce the number of required books for each course. (2) Cut some of the "fat" from the administrative staff. (3) Make all professors teach more courses. (4) Approach landlords about stabilizing rent and utility costs. (5) Establish food and clothing co-ops. (6) Increase financial aid. (7) Decrease the amount of money available for faculty research. (8) Boycott businesses around the campus where price mark-ups are highest. (9) Increase out-of-state tuition. (10) Decrease dormitory expenses. (11) Organize fund-raising programs with the student union. (12) Redirect some money from construction of new buildings into student aid. This was a good yield from a brainstorming session—twelve solid suggestions.

Select the Best Solution

After all potential solutions have been listed, it is time to evaluate them and choose the best solution or solutions. The best way to proceed is to take a particular solution, discuss it with regard to the criteria established earlier in the group's deliberations, then move on to the next solution, and so on. This orderly process ensures that all potential solutions receive equal consideration.

As each potential solution is discussed, the group should make every effort to reach *consensus*. A consensus decision is one that all members accept, even though the decision may not be ideal in the eyes of every member. In other words, consensus may range from full approval of a decision to "Well, I can live with it." Because it usually results in superior decisions, as well as in high unity within the group, consensus is the ideal of group decision making. It comes about when members have been so cooperative that they reach a common decision through reasoning, honest exchange of ideas, and the full examination of issues.[14]

Like most ideals, consensus can be difficult to achieve. If there are different viewpoints, members of the group will often try to find the easiest way to resolve the differences. Sometimes a member will call for a vote, which is very agreeable to those holding a majority opinion—since they will win—but not so pleasant for those in the minority. Resorting to a vote does resolve the immediate conflict, but it may not result in the best solution. Moreover, it weakens unity in the group by fostering factions and perhaps by creating bitterness among the members who lose on the vote. A group should vote only when it has failed in every other attempt to find a solution agreeable to all members.

In our culture, compromise is a highly valued form of decision making. If we can find a compromise between two parties with different opinions, we think we have reached the best possible solution. Often, however, we have not. Compromise in a group creates a lose/lose situation. Everyone has to make concessions, so no one is completely satisfied. Some groups are far too willing to reach compromise solutions instead of trying for consensus. But doing the extra work needed to reach consensus is usually well worth the effort. Such a situation occurred at a fraternity meeting:

The fraternity council was trying to decide what kind of band they wanted for the next social event. Half the members wanted a country/western band, and the other half wanted a rock band. Neither side was willing to give in. As a result, one member proposed that the group hire a local band that could play both types of music. On the face of it this seemed like a good compromise, but there was one drawback. The band in question didn't play either type of music very well. For the sake of compromise, the fraternity would get bad country/western music and bad rock.

Then another person had a flash of inspiration. For roughly the same amount of money the fraternity could hire a first-rate rhythm-and-blues band. To everyone's surprise it developed that both camps liked rhythm and blues and would be happy with this solution. The council voted unanimously to hire the blues band.

Of course, circumstances do arise in which it is virtually impossible to reach consensus. For example, in labor-management negotiations involving pay increases, consensus may not be possible because of limited resources. Labor cannot get all it wants because management does not have the money; and management cannot get all the concessions it wants because the workers will strike. In cases like this, compromise is necessary. When a group cannot reach consensus, compromise is certainly better than stalemate. But whenever possible, consensus is much more desirable.

What kind of final decision did our model cost-cutting group reach? Let's see:

The cost-cutting group had twelve possible solutions to evaluate. Three were rejected because they violated the group's criterion that an acceptable solution must involve only actions controlled directly by the college: Redirecting building money to student aid could be done only by the state legislature. Approaching landlords about stabilizing rent and boycotting campus businesses were also outside the jurisdiction of college administrators.

Three more solutions were rejected because they were economically impractical: Increasing financial aid would hurt many students, because the funds would have to come from student fees. Raising out-of-state tuition would drive away 10 percent of the college's out-of-state students. And decreasing dorm costs would make it impossible to provide minimally acceptable services.

The proposal to reduce funds for faculty research was also rejected, since most research money comes from government, corporations, and foundations. Besides, research was recognized as a primary means of maintaining the college's prestige. Finally, the suggestion to reduce administrative "fat" was rejected as too costly, because a group would have to be established to audit all administrative duties.

After refining the remaining suggestions, the group finally reached consensus on a solution that included the following provisions: (1) A student should not have to spend more than $50 on required books for any single course. (2) The university should authorize the student union to organize food, book, and clothing co-ops. (3) The student union should conduct five fund-raising projects each academic year. (4) Each professor should teach one more class a year.

Once consensus has been reached on a solution or solutions to the problem, the group is ready to present its findings.

PRESENTING THE RECOMMENDATIONS OF THE GROUP

The work of a problem-solving group does not end with the last stage of the reflective-thinking process. Once a group has agreed on its recommendations, it usually needs to present them to somebody. A business group might report to the president of the company or to the board of directors. A special committee of the city council will report to the full council. A presidential commission will report to the President and to the nation at large. A classroom group reports to the instructor and the rest of the class. The purpose of such reports is to present the group's recommendations clearly and convincingly.

Sometimes a group will prepare a formal written report. Often, however, the written report is supplemented with—or replaced by—an oral report, a symposium, or a panel discussion.

Oral Report

An oral report is much the same in content as a written report. If the group has a designated leader, he or she will probably deliver the report. Otherwise, the group will have to select one person for the job.

If you are picked to present your group's report, you should approach it as you would any other speech. Your task is to explain the purpose, procedures, and recommendations of your group. As with any speech, your report should have three main sections. The introduction will state the purpose of the report and preview its main points. The body will spell out the problem addressed by your group, the criteria set for a solution, and the solution being recommended. The conclusion will summarize the main points and in some cases urge that the group's recommendation be adopted.

Also, as with any speech, you should adapt your report to the audience. Use supporting materials to clarify and strengthen your ideas, and consider whether using visual aids will enhance your message. Make sure your language is accurate, clear, vivid, and appropriate. Rehearse the report so you can deliver it fluently and decisively. Afterward, you—and possibly other members of the group—may be called on to answer questions from the audience.

Symposium

A symposium consists of a moderator and several speakers seated together in front of an audience. If the group presenting the symposium has a designated leader, he or she will typically be the moderator. The moderator's job is to introduce the topic and the speakers. Each speaker in turn delivers a prepared speech on a different aspect of the topic. After the speeches, there may be a question-and-answer session with the audience.

The symposium is often used for group reports in speech classes. One way to organize it is to have each member of the group present a brief talk sketching the group's work and decisions during one stage of the reflective-thinking process. Another way is to have each speaker deal with a major issue relating to the discussion topic. A group dealing with capital punishment, for example, might have one speaker present the group's conclusion on the issue of whether capital punishment is an effective deterrent to crime, another speaker present the group's position on the morality of capital punishment, and so forth.

No matter what kind of symposium your group presents, all the speeches should be carefully planned. They should also be coordinated with one another to make sure the symposium reports on all important aspects of the group's project.

Panel Discussion

A panel discussion is essentially a conversation in front of an audience.[15] The panel should have a moderator, who introduces the topic and the panelists. Once the discussion is under way, the moderator may interject questions and comments as needed to focus the discussion. The panelists speak briefly, informally, and impromptu. They talk to each other, but loudly enough for the audience to be able to hear. As with a symposium, a panel discussion may be followed by a question-and-answer session with the audience.

Because of its spontaneity, a panel discussion can be exciting for participants and audience alike. But unfortunately, that spontaneity inhibits systematic presentation of a group's recommendations. Thus the panel discussion is seldom used by problem-solving groups, although it can work well for information-gathering groups.

If you are a participant in a panel discussion, beware of the common fallacy that no serious preparation is required. Although you will speak impromptu, you need to study the topic ahead of time, analyze the major issues, and map out the points you want to be sure to make during the discussion. An effective panel discussion also requires planning by the moderator and panelists to decide what issues will be discussed and in what order. Finally, all panelists must be willing to share talking time. One purpose of a panel is to have all participants voice their ideas, not to have one or two members monopolize the discussion.

Whatever method your group uses to present its findings, you can benefit from the public speaking guidelines given throughout this book. The techniques of effective speech need refinement for different situations, but the principles remain the same whether you are one person addressing an audience, part of a small group of people working to solve a problem, or a participant in a symposium or a panel discussion.

SUMMARY

A small group consists of three to twelve persons assembled to achieve a specific goal. All members of the group are potentially speakers and listeners. They are interdependent and influence each other through communication. Four major kinds of small groups are experiential groups, learning groups, information-gathering groups, and problem-solving groups. In this chapter we have focused mostly on problem-solving groups.

When small groups have effective leadership, they usually make better decisions than do individuals by themselves. Most groups have a designated leader, an implied leader, or an emergent leader. Some groups do not have any specific leader, in which case all members of the group must assume leadership responsibilities. An effective leader helps a group reach its goals by fulfilling procedural needs, task needs, and maintenance needs. As you develop your skills in group communication, you should be prepared to assume a leadership role whenever necessary.

Apart from leadership, all members of a group have five basic responsibilities. You should commit yourself to the goals of your group, fulfill your individual assignments, avoid interpersonal conflict within the group, encourage full participation by all members, and help keep the group on track. Meeting these responsibilities is vital if your group is to be successful.

Your group will also be more successful if it follows the reflective-thinking method, which offers a logical, step-by-step process for decision making in problem-solving groups. The method consists of five steps: (1) Defining the problem as clearly and specifically as possible; (2) Analyzing the problem to determine its severity and causes; (3) Establishing criteria to guide the group in evaluating solutions; (4) Generating a wide range of potential solutions; (5) Selecting the best solution or solutions.

Once your group has agreed on its recommendations, it usually has to present them to somebody. Sometimes this will require a written report. Often, however, it will involve some kind of oral presentation—a report by one member of the group, a symposium, or a panel discussion. Whichever kind of oral presentation your group gives will call for the skills of effective speechmaking explained throughout this book.

REVIEW QUESTIONS

After reading this chapter, you should be able to answer the following questions:

1. What are the four major traits of a small group?

2. What are the differences among experiential groups, learning groups, information-gathering groups, and problem-solving groups?

3. Why do small groups often make better decisions than do individuals?

4. What are the four kinds of leadership that may occur in a small group? Explain the three kinds of needs fulfilled by leadership in a small group.

5. What are the five major responsibilities of every participant in a small group?

6. What are the stages of the reflective-thinking method? Explain the major tasks of a group at each stage.

7. What are three methods for presenting orally the recommendations of a problem-solving group?

APPLICATION EXERCISES

1. Identify the flaw (or flaws) in each of the following questions for a problem-solving group discussion. Rewrite each question so it conforms with the criteria discussed in the chapter for effective discussion questions.

    a. Should all students be required to take two years of a foreign language to graduate from college?
    b. What should be done to prevent the outrageously cruel and inhumane treatment of animals in laboratory experiments?
    c. What should be done about violent crime?
    d. What should our state government do to control the cost of welfare and to combat unemployment?
    e. Should the federal government institute a system of national health insurance?

2. If possible, arrange to observe a problem-solving small group in action. You might attend a meeting of your city council, the school board, the zoning commission, a local business, a church committee. To what extent does the discussion measure up to the criteria of effective discussion presented in this chapter? What kind of leadership does the group have, and how well does the leader (or leaders) fulfill the group's procedural needs, task needs, and maintenance needs? How do the other members meet their responsibilities? What aspects of the meeting are handled most effectively? Which are handled least effectively?

3. Identify a relatively important decision you have made in the last year or two. Try to reconstruct how you reached that decision. Now suppose you could remake the decision following the reflective-thinking method. Map out exactly what you would do at each stage of the method. Do you still reach the same decision? If not, do you believe the reflective-thinking method would have led you to a better decision in the first place?

4. Attend a symposium or panel discussion on campus. Prepare a brief analysis of the proceedings. First, study the role of the moderator. How does he or she introduce the topic and participants? What role does the moderator play thereafter? Does he or she help guide and focus the panel discussion? Does he or she summarize and conclude the proceedings at the end?

    Second, observe the participants. Are the speeches in the symposium well prepared and presented? Which speaker (or speakers) do you find most effective? Least effective? Why? Do participants in the panel discussion share talking time? Does their discussion appear well planned to cover major aspects of the topic? Which panelist (or panelists) do you find most effective? Least effective? Why?

NOTES

1 A. Paul Hare, *Handbook of Small Group Research,* 2nd ed. (New York: Free Press, 1976), pp. 226–227.

2 Edward A. Mabry and Richard E. Barnes, *The Dynamics of Small Group Communication* (Englewood Cliffs, N.J.: Prentice-Hall, 1980), pp. 5–7.

3 For a concise review of scholarship on this aspect of small groups, see Dennis S. Gouran and B. Aubrey Fisher, "The Functions of Human Communication in the Formation, Maintenance, and Performance of Small Groups," in Carroll C. Arnold and John Waite Bowers (eds.), *Handbook of Rhetorical and Communication Theory* (Boston: Allyn and Bacon, 1984), pp. 622–658.

4 John K. Brilhart, *Effective Group Discussion,* 5th ed. (Dubuque, Iowa: Brown, 1986), p. 12.

5 For an interesting recent debate on the value of groups, see Christian J. Buys, "Humans Would Do Better Without Groups," *Personality and Social Psychology Bulletin,* 4 (1978), 123–125; Lynn R. Anderson, "Groups Would Do Better Without Humans," *Personality and Social Psychology Bulletin,* 4 (1978), 557–558; Leigh S. Shaffer, "On the Current Confusion of Group-Related Behavior and Collective Behavior: A Reaction to Buys," *Personality and Social Psychology Bulletin,* 4 (1978), 564–567.

6 Marvin E. Shaw, *Group Dynamics: The Psychology of Small Group Behavior,* 3rd ed. (New York: McGraw-Hill, 1981), pp. 316–319.

7 B. Aubrey Fisher, *Small Group Decision Making: Communication and the Group Process,* 2nd ed. (New York: McGraw-Hill, 1980), pp. 207–221.

8 Brilhart, *Effective Group Discussion,* p. 222.

9 Thomas M. Scheidel and Laura Crowell, *Discussing and Deciding: A Desk Book for Group Leaders and Members* (New York: Macmillan, 1979), pp. 111–251, provides an excellent step-by-step guide to meeting the procedural and task needs of a small group.

10 See John F. Cragan and David W. Wright, *Communication in Small Group Discussions: A Case Study Approach* (St. Paul, Minn.: West, 1980), pp. 153–179.

11 Scheidel and Crowell, *Discussing and Deciding,* pp. 73–74.

12 For other decision-making techniques see Cragan and Wright, *Communication in Small Group Discussions,* pp. 226–243.

13 Gerald M. Phillips, Douglas J. Pedersen, and Julia T. Wood, *Group Discussion: A Practical Guide to Participation and Leadership* (Boston: Houghton Mifflin, 1979), pp. 150–155.

14 Fisher, *Small Group Decision Making,* pp. 129–130; Phillips, Pedersen, and Wood, *Group Discussion,* pp. 11, 49.

15 Loren Reid, *Speaking Well,* 4th ed. (New York: McGraw-Hill, 1982), p. 360.

APPENDIX

Speeches for Analysis and Discussion

A REEL DOCTOR'S ADVICE
TO SOME REAL DOCTORS

Alan Alda

An actor giving a commencement speech at a medical school? Many people must have asked themselves this question when it was announced that Alan Alda would address the 210th graduating class of New York's Columbia College of Physicians and Surgeons in May 1979.

Of course, Alda is not just any actor. He is known to millions as Army surgeon Captain Hawkeye Pierce in the classic television series *M*A*S*H*. He has won Emmy awards as an actor, writer, and director. Public opinion polls have shown him to be among America's most respected public figures. *Time* magazine once called him ''perhaps America's favorite doctor.''

Still, the idea of an actor offering advice to doctors is so unusual that Alda begins his speech by asking, ''Why get someone who only *pretends* to be a doctor when you could get a real one?'' Note how skillfully Alda answers this question, builds his credibility, and establishes common ground with his audience *before* offering them advice. Also note how Alda uses humor both to lighten his speech and to reinforce its message. Finally, to get a fuller sense of the speech's impact, try to ''hear'' Alda delivering it.

Alda's speech was greeted enthusiastically by his listeners and received much favorable comment in the press. It is reprinted here with permission from the Columbia College of Physicians and Surgeons.

1   Ever since it was announced that a nondoctor, in fact an actor, had been invited to give the commencement address at one of the most prestigious medical schools in the country, people have been wondering—why get someone who only *pretends* to be a doctor when you could get a real one?

2   Some people have suggested that this school had done everything it could to show you how to *be* doctors and in a moment of desperation had brought in someone who could show you how to act like one.

3   It's certainly true that I'm not a doctor. I have a long list of nonqualifications. In the first place I'm not a great fan of blood. I don't mind people having it, I just don't enjoy seeing them wear it. I have yet to see a real operation because the mere smell of a hospital reminds me of a previous appointment. And my knowledge of anatomy resides in the clear understanding that the hip bone is connected to the leg bone.

4   I am not a doctor. But you have asked me, and all in all, I think you made a wonderful choice.

5   I say that because I probably first came to the attention of this graduating class through a character on television that I've played and helped write for the past seven years—a surgeon called Hawkeye Pierce. He's a remarkable person, this Hawkeye, and if you have chosen somehow to associate his character with your own graduation from medical school, then I find that

very heartening. Because I think it means that you are reaching out toward a very human kind of doctoring—and a very real kind of doctor.

6 We didn't make him up. He really lived as several doctors who struggled to preserve life 25 years ago during the Korean War. In fact, it's because he's based on real doctors that there is something especially engaging about him.

7 He has a sense of humor, and yet he's serious. He's impertinent, and yet he has feeling. He's human enough to make mistakes, and yet he hates death enough to push himself past his own limits to save lives. In many ways he's the doctor patients want to have and doctors want to be.

8 But he's not an idealization. Finding himself in a war, he's sometimes angry, sometimes cynical, sometimes a little nuts. He's not a magician who can come up with an instant cure for a rare disease without sweating and ruining his make-up. He knows he might fail. Not a god, he walks gingerly on the edge of disaster—alive to his own mortality.

9 If this image of that very human, very caring doctor is attractive to you—if it's ever touched you for a moment as something to reach for in your own life—then I'm here to cheer you on. Do it. Go for it. Be skilled, be learned, be aware of the dignity of your calling—but please, don't ever lose sight of your own simple humanity.

10 Unfortunately, that may not be so easy. You're entering a special place in our society. People will be awed by your expertise. You'll be placed in a position of privilege. You'll live well. People will defer to you, call you by your title—and it may be hard to remember that the word "doctor" is not actually your first name.

11 I know what this is like to some extent because in some ways you and I *are* alike. We both study the human being. And we both try to offer relief—you through medicine, I through laughter; we both try to reduce suffering. We've both learned difficult disciplines that have taken years to master, and we've both dedicated ourselves to years of hard work. And we both charge a lot.

12 We live in a society that has decided to reward my profession and yours, when we succeed in them, very highly. It can sometimes be easy to forget that the cab driver also works 14 or 15 hours a day and is also drained of energy when he's through. It's easy to think that because our society grants us privilege we're entitled to it.

13 Privilege feels good, but it can be intoxicating. As good doctors, I hope you'll be able to keep yourselves free of toxins.

14 It's no wonder, though, that people will hold you in awe. I know I do.

15 You've spent years in a grueling effort to know the structure and process of human life. I can't imagine a more difficult task. It has required the understanding of complexities within complexities, and there has been more pressure placed on you in four years than most people would be willing to take in a lifetime. I stand here in utter amazement at what you've accomplished. And I congratulate you.

16 I only ask one thing of you: Possess your skills, but don't be possessed by them.

17   Certainly your training has encouraged you to see the human side of your work, and you've examined the doctor-patient relationship. But still, the enormity of your task has required you to focus to such an extent on technique and data that you may not have had time enough to face your feelings along the way.

18   You've had to toughen yourself to death. From your first autopsy, when you may have been sick, or cried, or just been numb, you've had to inure yourself to death in order to be useful to the living. But I hope in the process you haven't done too good a job of burying that part of you that hurts and is afraid.

19   I know what it's like to be absorbed in technique. When I write for *M*A*S*H* I'm always writing about people in crisis with what I hope is compassion and feeling. And yet one day I found myself talking to someone who was in a real crisis and real pain—and I remember thinking, "This would make a *great* story."

20   Both of these things—becoming set apart and becoming your skill— can make it tough to be a compassionate person.

21   All right, that's my diagnosis of the problem. Here's my prescription.

22   I'd like to suggest to you, just in case you haven't done it lately, that this would be a very good time to give some thought to exactly what your values are, and then to figure out how you're going to live by them. Knowing what you care about and then devoting yourself to it is just about the only way you can pick your way through the minefield of existence and come out in one piece.

23   It can be a startling experience when you try to rank your values, though. Just ask yourself what's the most important thing in the world to you. Your work? Your family? Your money? Your country? Getting to heaven? Sex? Alcohol? What? (I don't need a show of hands on this!)

24   Then, when you get the answer to that, ask yourself how much time you actually spend on your number-one value—and how much time you spend on what you thought was number five, or number ten. What in fact is the thing you value most?

25   It may not be easy to decide. We live in a time that seems to be split about its values. In fact it seems to be schizophrenic.

26   For instance, if you pick up a magazine like *Psychology Today,* you're liable to see an article like "White Collar Crime: It's More Widespread Than You Think." Then in the back of the magazine they'll print an advertisement that says, "We'll write your doctoral thesis for 25 bucks." You see how values are eroding? I mean a doctoral thesis ought to go for at least a C-note.

27   The question is, *where* are their values? *What* do they value? Unfortunately, the people we look to for leadership seem to be providing it by negative example.

28   All across the country this month commencement speakers are saying to graduating classes, "We look to you for tomorrow's leaders." That's because today's leaders are all in jail.

29   Maybe we can afford to let politicians operate in a moral vacuum, but we can't afford to let doctors operate under those conditions.

30   You know how we're feeling these days, as the power and fuel monopoly has its way with us. Well, you people graduating today are entering a very select group. You have a monopoly on medical care. Please be careful not to abuse this power that you have over the rest of us.

31   You need to know what you care about most and what you care about least. And you need to know now. You will be making life-and-death decisions, and you will often be making them under stress and with great speed. The time to make your tender choices is not in the heat of the moment.

32   When you're making your list, let me urge you to put people first. And I include in that not just people, but that which exists *between* people.

33   I suggest to you that what makes people know they're alive—and in some cases keeps them alive—is not merely the interaction of the parts of their bodies, but the interaction of their selves with other selves. Not just people, but what goes on between people.

34   Let me challenge you. With all your study, you can name all the bones in my body. You can read my x-rays like a telegram. But can you read my involuntary muscles? Can you see the fear and uncertainty in my face?

35   If I tell you where it hurts, can you hear in my voice where I ache? I show you my body, but I bring you my person. Can you see me through your reading glasses?

36   Will you tell me what you're doing, and in words I can understand? Will you tell me when you don't know what to do? Can you face your own fear, your own uncertainty? When in doubt, can you call in help?

37   These are things to consider even if you don't deal directly with patients. If you're in research, administration, if you write—no matter what you do—eventually there is always going to be a patient at the other end of your decisions.

38   Now, of course, everyone is for this in principle. Who's against people? But it gets harder when you get specific.

39   Will you be the kind of doctor who cares more about the *case* than the *person?* ("Nurse, call the gastric ulcer and have him come in at three." "How's the fractured femur in Room 208?") You'll know you're in trouble if you find yourself wishing they would mail you their liver in a plain brown envelope.

40   Where does money come on your list? Will it be the sole standard against which you reckon your success? How much will it guide you in relating to your patients? Do patients in a clinic need less of your attention than private patients? Are they, for instance, less in need of having things explained to them?

41   Where will your family come on your list? How many days and nights, weeks and months, will you separate yourself from them, buried in your work, before you realize that you've removed yourself from an important part of your life?

42 And if you're a male doctor, how will you relate to women? Women as patients, as nurses, as fellow doctors—and later as students. Will you be able to respect your patient's right to know and make decisions about her own body? Will you see nurses as colleagues—or as handmaidens? And if the day comes when you are teaching, what can young women medical students expect from you?

43 Questionnaires filled out by women at 41 medical schools around the country have revealed a distressing pattern. The women were often either ignored in class or simply not taken seriously as students. They were told that they were only there to find a husband and that they were taking the places of men who would then have to go out and become chiropractors. (Logic is not the strong point of sexism.)

44 They were often told that women just didn't belong in medicine. And at times they were told this by the very professors who were grading them. They would be shown slides of *Playboy* nudes during anatomy lectures—to the accompaniment of catcalls and wisecracks from male students. And in place of discussions about their work, they would often hear a discussion of their appearance. These are reports from 41 different medical schools.

45 I'm dwelling on this because it seems to me that the male-female relationship is still the most personal and intense test of humane behavior. It is a crucible for decency.

46 I hope you men will work to grant the same dignity to your female colleagues that you yourselves enjoy.

47 And if you're a female doctor, I hope you'll be aware that you didn't get where you are all by yourself. You've had to work hard, of course. But you're sitting where you are right now in part because way back in 1848, in Seneca Falls, women you never knew began insisting you had a right to sit there. Just as they helped a generation they would never see, I urge you to work for the day when your daughters and their daughters will be called not "A woman doctor," or "My doctor, who's a woman," but simply "My doctor."

48 It may seem strange to rank the things you care about. But when you think about it, there isn't an area of your work that won't be affected by what you decide to place a high value on and what you decide doesn't count.

49 Decide now.

50 Well, that's my prescription. I've given you kind of a big pill to swallow, but I think it'll make you feel better. And if not—well, look, I'm only human.

51 I congratulate you, and please let me thank you for taking on the enormous responsibility that you have—and for having the strength to have made it to this day. I don't know how you've managed to learn it all.

52 But there is one more thing you can learn about the body that only a nondoctor would tell you—and I hope you'll always remember this: The head bone is connected to the heart bone—and don't let them come apart.

WARNING: HOUSEHOLD CHEMICALS
Susan Zaeske

Drano, Eazy-Off, Lysol, Endust. Every day millions of Americans use these and similar products to clean their homes. Yet few people realize such products contain powerful, potentially toxic chemicals that can damage lung tissue, blister skin, induce blindness, and even cause death. The following speech seeks to explain the dangers of household chemicals. According to the speaker, Susan Zaeske, a student at the University of Wisconsin, consumers should handle household chemicals with great care and, whenever possible, explore safe, practical alternatives to the more hazardous home cleaners.

As you read the speech, study how the speaker uses statistics, examples, and testimony. Does she convince you that household chemicals can be dangerous? Does she present a workable solution to the problem? How could she have made the speech more effective?

This speech is printed with permission from Susan Zaeske and has been edited slightly for publication. It is also available on the videotape supplement that accompanies this edition of *The Art of Public Speaking*.

1   In Portland, Maine, Halloween pranksters splattered eggs on the windows of a 68-year-old woman's house. In the morning, she decided to clean the windows using a combination of household ammonia and chlorine bleach. And the combination worked well. When she took the pail inside, however, she was overcome by toxic fumes. The woman's niece tried to revive her, but she, too, was overcome. Both women died.

2   This tragic incident, far from hypothetical, illustrates a threat that we face intimately every day—household chemicals. According to Lance Wallace, from the Harvard School of Public Health, "Your home may be more of a toxic waste hazard than Love Canal or a chemical company nearby."

3   I found this statement very surprising because I thought, like many of you, that the government regulates household chemicals. That's not true. The truth is that there is no law requiring the testing of a household product before it hits the market. The Food and Drug Administration merely requires that manufacturers clearly label their products and that they designate chemicals which have been called harmful. The result, as one scientist stated in *The Household Pollutants Guide*, is that "The consumer becomes a test animal in the laboratory of the home."

4   Let's take a cleaning tour through your house or apartment and discover some of the chemicals that may harm you in your home. Before we start, we'll stop at the supply cabinet to get the products we need. Then we'll clean the bathroom and the kitchen, where we will encounter caustic chemicals. Then we'll move into the living room, where we will encounter solvents. And finally we'll clean the bedroom, where we will get a dose of aerosols. When

we're finished with the dirty work, I'll share with you some solutions to make your cleaning routine safer and cheaper.

5   The first stop in our cleaning tour is to get supplies. According to James Woods, senior scientist at Honeywell Corporation, if you're like most Americans, your home contains forty-five aerosol cans, each with fifteen different chemical compounds. Add to this two dozen nonaerosol containers, a few insect killers, paint thinners, and ink. In all, Woods says, there are more than 50,000 chemicals in the average home.

6   Now that you have the products you need, we'll start with our cleaning tour. Like it or not, most of us have had to clean the bathroom. Not only is this task unpleasant, it may also be dangerous because the majority of chemicals that you use to clean your bathroom are caustic.

7   Well, the drain is clogged, but don't despair—you're armed with Crystal Drano. Hopefully, you won't be harmed like the more than 10,000 people who are harmed in this country every year using drain cleaners or toilet cleaners. According to *Consumer Reports* magazine, when they tested products in May of last year, one individual who was doing the testing suffered lingering throat irritation when he inhaled Drano and other products like it, even though he followed the manufacturers' instructions exactly. Another product that was tested, Instant Plumber, which is simply diluted sulfuric acid, ate through its container and destroyed its instructions. *Consumer Reports* warns that when chemicals fail, consumers are often tempted to clean the drain by using a plunger. But this is dangerous because the caustic chemicals can splash in your face and burn your skin or blind you.

8   You have finished with the bathroom, and now you head for the kitchen to do the worst task imaginable—cleaning the oven. I had to do the same after a dinner party I had on New Year's Eve. And although I was extremely careful—using protective gloves and glasses, and opting for brush-on Eazy-Off rather than the aerosol spray—some of the substance managed to splash on my face, close to my eye, painfully burning my skin. And I am not alone, because the Center for Science in the Public Interest warns that 3,000 people are harmed every year using oven cleaners. Aerosol oven cleaners are even worse because they disperse droplets of the caustic chemical which may land on your skin or be inhaled into your lungs. Lung tissue doesn't regenerate like skin tissue, so you could suffer long-term harm.

9   Now that we know the dangers of household caustics, let's move to the living room, where we will encounter solvents. Since advertising tells us that homes must be dust-free, you grab the Endust and begin dustbusting. Well, this product is a solvent. Solvents puts oils and waxes into solution so that after application they evaporate, leaving a protective coating on your furniture. Solvents such as Endust contain petroleum distillates, which can cause skin irritation; naptha, which can induce cardiac arrest; and oil of cedarwood, a nervous stimulant. In fact, the Center for Science in the Public Interest reports that in high concentrations oil of cedarwood has been used to induce abortions.

10   Your final task is to clean the bedroom. You walk to your roommate's side of the room and a pungent oder emanates from the hamper. You grab the Lysol to disinfect a pile of mildewy socks. Well, if you've ever used Lysol, you may guess that it is dangerous. Lysol contains creosol, which has been found to be the tumor-promoting agent in tobacco smoke. As long ago as 1975, the Mitre Corporation reported that absorbing enough creosol through the skin has been found to cause digestive disturbances, nervous disorders with faintness, mental changes, and skin eruptions.

11   Now, you may be saying to yourself, the danger of household chemicals is exaggerated. If I eat five pounds of almonds every day, I'll get arsenic poisoning. After all, none of us sniffs Lysol or sprays it on our skin, or actually drinks Drano. But the point is that *Consumer Reports, The Household Pollutants Guide*, and *Science News* have all shown that these products can be dangerous even when you follow the manufacturers' instructions.

12   Well, the house is clean, so you're ready to go. You step outside onto the street, away from your house or apartment, which has now become a toxic waste dump, and glance at a chemical company nearby. Ironically, according to Lance Wallace, the Harvard scientist I quoted earlier, the air outside is probably safer than that in your house.

13   It doesn't have to be this way, though. There are solutions you can take to make household chemicals—and your cleaning routine—much safer. Of course, you could get a self-cleaning oven and a maid. But for us more practical folks, Albert Fritsch from the Center for Science in the Public Interest states, "Only an alert and informed citizenry can bring about the proper sharing of responsibility for the safe use of chemicals."

14   As we saw earlier, the government does not test household products, so you must take the initiative to make your house safe. Ask yourself, do I really need specialized cleaners, or will a few simple chemicals do? I think you'll agree that many household special cleaners are unnecessary. I can suggest a few alternatives you can use instead of household cleaners, and after my speech I will give you a fact sheet that outlines how you can make some of these alternatives.

15   For example, never again will I use Eazy-Off to clean the oven. Instead, I will place one-fourth cup of household ammonia in the oven overnight to loosen the debris. Then in the morning, I will scrub the oven with baking soda. Baking soda can also be used instead of abrasive scouring powders like Ajax. It's less dangerous for your eyes and your skin, it works just as well, and it feels better on the wallet, too. Look at the fact sheet, and you'll find ways to make glass cleaners, furniture polish, air fresheners, and more.

16   But if you don't want to use these alternatives, at least use common sense. The Food and Drug Administration has published several pamphlets which will tell you how to use chemicals more safely in your home. Some of their recommendations are that you should have proper ventilation when you're using chemicals; always read the label; wear protective gloves, glasses, and sometimes face masks; keep dangerous products away from children; and

don't pour chemicals down the drain. Avoid wearing soft contact lenses while you're cleaning because they can absorb chemical fumes and hold them close to your eyes until the contacts are removed. Also be especially careful in combining chemicals. In fact, avoid it completely because such chemicals as bleach and ammonia can emit toxic gases when they are combined.

17   We've seen, then, that although household products are not tested by the government, they are dangerous. The threat is not an outside force, something abstract, but the "friendly" products you invite into your home. I urge you to use simple, inexpensive alternative products, and to use common sense. Careless use of household chemicals is one case in which cleanliness may put you next to godliness before your time.

18   The woman in Portland, Maine, was no doubt frightened by the spooks that lurked in the night. But ironically it was not the spooks that killed her, but the supposedly friendly chemicals she invited into her home.

DAVID—AND A LOT OF OTHER NEAT PEOPLE

Kathy Weisensel

Many people have misconceptions about the nature of mental retardation. In the following speech, Kathy Weisensel seeks to correct some of those misconceptions. Kathy's audience was her public speaking class at the University of Wisconsin–Madison.

As you read the speech, study its organization and use of supporting materials. Can you identify the introduction, body, and conclusion? Can you pick out the main points and subpoints in the body? Do you have a better understanding of mental retardation than you had before reading the speech? To what extent are you influenced by the speaker's personal involvement with the topic?

The text of this speech is taken from Wil A. Linkugel, R. R. Allen, and Richard L. Johannesen (eds.), *Contemporary American Speeches*, 5th ed. (Dubuque, Iowa: Kendall/ Hunt, 1982). It is reprinted here with permission from Kathy Weisensel.

1   There is a problem which is shared by millions of people in the United States. It knows no barrier to age, sex, or social class. Yet, it is a problem that for years was hidden in society's darkest closet. Only recently has the closet door begun to open. That problem is mental retardation.

2   One out of 33 persons is born mentally retarded. It is the most widespread, permanent handicap among children. It is among the least understood handicaps of adults. In Wisconsin alone, there are 120,000 retarded people.

3   My involvement with mental retardation has been lifelong and deeply personal. For you see, David, my older brother, is mentally retarded.

4 As our family adjusted to David's problem, we became aware of a number of misconceptions which cloud the public's vision. Among these misconceptions are that mentally retarded people are mentally ill and therefore dangerous; that mentally retarded people are ineducable; and that mentally retarded people are incapable of leading happy and productive lives. Since these misconceptions are socially harmful and painful to the retarded and their families, it is important that they be corrected.

5 How do you correct the notion that retarded people are somewhat crazy and therefore not really to be trusted? It may be helpful to start with a definition. According to Dr. E. Milo Pritchett, "Mental retardation is a condition of impaired, incomplete, or inadequate mental development. Mental retardation is NOT mental illness. Mental illness is a breakdown of mental functions which were once normal. Specialized care and treatment may restore the person to normalcy. Retardation is a condition for which there is no cure."

6 But let's extend that definition with a series of contrasts. Mental retardation is always permanent; mental illness is usually temporary. Mental retardation is subnormal intelligence; mental illness is distorted intelligence. Mental retardation involves deficient cognitive abilities; mental illness involves emotional impairment of cognitive abilities. Mental retardation is manifested early; mental illness may occur anytime in life. The mentally retarded person is behaviorally stable; it is the mentally ill person who is given to erratic behavior. The extremely mentally retarded person is submissive and mute; the extremely mentally ill person may be violent and criminally dangerous.

7 Thus retarded people are retarded, and no more. We need no longer place them in pens with the criminally insane, as was the custom in medieval societies.

8 OK, the skeptic says, so what if they aren't mentally ill—they're still ineducable. Those who favor this misconception have, in the words of Dorly D. Wang, formerly of Woods School in Pennsylvania, "one-dimensional views of the retarded." They fail to "distinguish degrees of retardation" and tend to perceive "all the retarded with one image"—and that image is of the intellectual vegetable, more appropriately planted in a cell or ward than in the school classroom.

9 But retarded people are not all alike. Most psychologists identify three subgroups of mentally retarded people: the educable, the trainable, and the custodial.

10 The educable mentally retarded have IQ's ranging from 75 to 50. In the nation's schools, they are placed in a curriculum with a special classroom base, but are encouraged to enter the curricular mainstream whenever it is possible. Most of these students share with normal students instruction in home economics, physical education, shop, and music.

11 The trainable mentally retarded's I.Q. is usually 50 to 30. In the schools, these students are not found in any normal class. Rather, they work exclusively in special classrooms under the direction of teachers who understand their needs. In these classes they learn self-care, and they train for social

and economic usefulness. Three percent of the present school population is made up of the educable and trainable mentally retarded.

12 The custodial mentally retarded have IQ's below 30. They are usually confined to institutions such as Central Colony, just across Lake Mendota from this university. These people experience little mental development. Few exceed the intellectual acuity of a normal three-year-old.

13 Thus the mentally retarded are not a faceless, hopeless mass. While not all of them may profit from schooling, many will. Careful and loving teachers will eventually be rewarded by what one teacher of the retarded has called "the smile of recognition."

14 But to say that the mentally retarded person is not mentally ill and is not ineducable is not enough. It does not destroy the myth that one must be of average mentality to be socially productive and happy. In a society characterized by speed, change, competition, and progress, it is difficult for us so-called "normals" to understand that retarded people can live happily and productively in a life pattern alien to our own.

15 Bernard Posner, Deputy Executive Secretary of the President's Committee on Employment of the Handicapped, has captured society's dilemma in coming to grips with the mentally handicapped. He commented:

> Ours are norms in which change is a way of life. In the United States, we change jobs every five years and homes every seven years. We say that to stand still is to regress. Where do the retarded fit in, those without the capacity for constant change?
>
> Ours are norms of competition. We compete in school, at play, at love, at work. Where do the retarded fit in, those who can go to school, can play, can love, can work, but who cannot always come out on top in competition?
>
> Ours are norms of discontent. Life becomes a series of stepping-stones leading who knows where? Each of life's situations is not to be enjoyed for itself, but is to be tolerated because it leads elsewhere. Where do the retarded fit in, those who can be happy with a stay-put existence?

16 But retarded people do fit in and do lead useful and rewarding lives. A few years ago, I worked with a girl who is educably mentally retarded. Mary went to my high school and attended two normal classes—home economics and physical education. She had a driving desire to become a waitress. Her determination was evident as I tutored her in addition, subtraction, making change, and figuring sales tax. She is working today in a small restaurant—happy and self-supporting.

17 My brother David is another example. Under Wisconsin law he was entitled to school until age 21, and he spent all those years in a separate special class. There he learned the basic skills of reading, writing, and mathematics. After graduation he was employed by the Madison Opportunity Center, a

sheltered workshop for the retarded. He leaves home each morning on a special bus and returns each evening after eight hours of simple assembly-line work. While he is by no means self-supporting and independent, he loves his work, and he is a happy man and a neat person with whom to share a family.

18 As a final example, I give you Jeff, age 14. He is custodially mentally retarded at Central Colony. In the three years that I have worked with him, I have found him to be incredibly happy and content in his "permanent childhood." He enjoys toys, writing letters of the alphabet, and watching "Sesame Street." This last summer he was especially proud to be selected as a jumper in the Special Olympics. To tell you the truth, he was chosen because he was one of the few kids in the ward who could get both feet off the floor at the same time. But Jeff doesn't know that the competition wasn't keen, and he's proud and happy.

19 While misconceptions are slow to pass away, they must surely die. Our nation's retarded are not mentally ill, totally ineducable, or incapable of happy and productive lives.

20 I know, in a deeply personal way, the pain that these misconceptions inspire. But I also know that the world is changing. I have a deep faith that you and others of our generation will reject the senseless and destructive stereotypes of the past. As Bernard Posner has said:

> The young people of the world seem to be forging a new set of values. It appears to be a value system of recognizing the intrinsic worth of all humans, retarded or not, . . . a value system of acceptance: of accepting life as it is, and people as they are.

21 Thank you for your acceptance.

I HAVE A DREAM
Martin Luther King, Jr.

Martin Luther King's "I Have a Dream" speech is widely regarded as a masterpiece. It was delivered August 28, 1963, to some 200,000 people who had come to Washington, D.C., to participate in a peaceful demonstration to further the cause of equal rights for black Americans. King spoke from the steps of the Lincoln Memorial, in the "symbolic shadow" of Abraham Lincoln, and the crowd filled the vast area between the Memorial and the Washington Monument. In addition, millions of Americans watched the speech on television or listened to it on the radio.

Like most ceremonial addresses, "I Have a Dream" is relatively short. Although it took King only sixteen minutes to deliver the speech, he prepared it more carefully than any other speech in his career to that time. His purpose was to set forth as succinctly and as eloquently as possible the guiding principles of the civil rights movement, and to reinforce the commitment of his listeners to those principles.

One of the most interesting features of this speech is King's use of language to make the abstract principles of liberty and equality clear and compelling. Throughout, King relies on familiar, concrete words that create sharp, vivid images. He uses many more metaphors than do most speakers, but they are appropriate to the occasion and help to dramatize King's ideas. Finally, King makes extensive use of repetition and parallelism to reinforce his message and to enhance the momentum of the speech.

If you have heard a tape recording of "I Have a Dream," you know its impact was heightened by King's delivery. In his rich baritone voice, marked by the fervor of the crusader and modulated by the cadences of the Southern Baptist preacher, King gained the total involvement of his audience. As William Robert Miller says, "The crowd more than listened, it participated, and before King had reached his last phrase, a torrent of applause was already welling up."

The text of this speech was taken from a tape recording and is reprinted here with the permission of Joan Daves. Copyright 1963 by Martin Luther King, Jr.

1   I am happy to join with you today in what will go down in history as the greatest demonstration for freedom in the history of our nation.

2   Five score years ago, a great American, in whose symbolic shadow we stand today, signed the Emancipation Proclamation. This momentous decree came as a great beacon light of hope to millions of Negro slaves, who had been seared in the flames of withering injustice. It came as a joyous daybreak to end the long night of their captivity.

3   But one hundred years later, the Negro still is not free. One hundred years later, the life of the Negro is still sadly crippled by the manacles of segregation and the chains of discrimination. One hundred years later, the Negro lives on a lonely island of poverty in the midst of a vast ocean of material prosperity. One hundred years later, the Negro is still languished in the corners of American society and finds himself an exile in his own land. And so we've come here today to dramatize a shameful condition.

4   In a sense we've come to our nation's Capitol to cash a check. When the architects of our republic wrote the magnificent words of the Constitution and the Declaration of Independence, they were signing a promissory note to which every American was to fall heir. This note was a promise that all men— yes, black men as well as white men—would be guaranteed the unalienable rights of life, liberty, and the pursuit of happiness.

5   It is obvious today that America has defaulted on this promissory note insofar as her citizens of color are concerned. Instead of honoring this sacred obligation, America has given the Negro people a bad check—a check which has come back marked "insufficient funds."

6   But we refuse to believe that the bank of justice is bankrupt. We refuse to believe that there are insufficient funds in the great vaults of opportunity of this nation. And so we've come to cash this check—a check that will give us upon demand the riches of freedom and the security of justice.

7   We have also come to this hallowed spot to remind America of the

fierce urgency of now. This is no time to engage in the luxury of cooling off or to take the tranquillizing drug of gradualism. Now is the time to make real the promises of democracy. Now is the time to rise from the dark and desolate valley of segregation to the sunlit path of racial justice. Now is the time to lift our nation from the quicksands of racial injustice to the solid rock of brotherhood. Now is the time to make justice a reality for all of God's children.

8   It would be fatal for the nation to overlook the urgency of the moment. This sweltering summer of the Negro's legitimate discontent will not pass until there is an invigorating autumn of freedom and equality. Nineteen sixty-three is not an end, but a beginning. Those who hope that the Negro needed to blow off steam and will now be content will have a rude awakening if the nation returns to business as usual. There will be neither rest nor tranquillity in America until the Negro is granted his citizenship rights. The whirlwinds of revolt will continue to shake the foundations of our nation until the bright day of justice emerges.

9   But there is something that I must say to my people, who stand on the warm threshold which leads into the palace of justice. In the process of gaining our rightful place, we must not be guilty of wrongful deeds. Let us not seek to satisfy our thirst for freedom by drinking from the cup of bitterness and hatred.

10   We must forever conduct our struggle on the high plane of dignity and discipline. We must not allow our creative protest to degenerate into physical violence. Again and again we must rise to the majestic heights of meeting physical force with soul force.

11   The marvelous new militancy which has engulfed the Negro community must not lead us to a distrust of all white people. For many of our white brothers, as evidenced by their presence here today, have come to realize that their destiny is tied up with our destiny. They have come to realize that their freedom is inextricably bound to our freedom. We cannot walk alone.

12   As we walk, we must make the pledge that we shall always march ahead. We cannot turn back. There are those who are asking the devotees of civil rights, "When will you be satisfied?" We can never be satisfied as long as the Negro is the victim of the unspeakable horrors of police brutality. We can never be satisfied as long as our bodies, heavy with the fatigue of travel, cannot gain lodging in the motels of the highways and the hotels of the cities. We cannot be satisfied as long as a Negro in Mississippi cannot vote and a Negro in New York believes he has nothing for which to vote. No, no, we are not satisfied, and we will not be satisfied until justice rolls down like waters, and righteousness like a mighty stream.

13   I am not unmindful that some of you have come here out of great trials and tribulations. Some of you have come fresh from narrow jail cells. Some of you have come from areas where your quest for freedom left you battered by the storms of persecution and staggered by the winds of police brutality. You have been the veterans of creative suffering. Continue to work with the faith that unearned suffering is redemptive.

14   Go back to Mississippi, go back to Alabama, go back to South Carolina,

go back to Georgia, go back to Louisiana, go back to the slums and ghettos of our Northern cities, knowing that somehow this situation can and will be changed. Let us not wallow in the valley of despair.

15   I say to you today, my friends, so even though we face the difficulties of today and tomorrow, I still have a dream. It is a dream deeply rooted in the American dream.

16   I have a dream that one day this nation will rise up and live out the true meaning of its creed, "We hold these truths to be self-evident, that all men are created equal."

17   I have a dream that one day on the red hills of Georgia the sons of former slaves and the sons of former slaveowners will be able to sit down together at the table of brotherhood.

18   I have a dream that one day even the state of Mississippi, a state sweltering with the heat of injustice, sweltering with the heat of oppression, will be transformed into an oasis of freedom and justice.

19   I have a dream that my four little children will one day live in a nation where they will not be judged by the color of their skin but by the content of their character. I have a dream today.

20   I have a dream that one day, down in Alabama, with its vicious racists, with its governor having his lips dripping with the words of interposition and nullification, one day right there in Alabama little black boys and black girls will be able to join hands with little white boys and white girls as sisters and brothers. I have a dream today.

21   I have a dream that one day every valley shall be exalted, every hill and mountain shall be made low, the rough places will be made plane and the crooked places will be made straight, and the glory of the Lord shall be revealed, and all flesh shall see it together.

22   This is our hope. This is the faith that I go back to the South with. With this faith we will be able to hew out of the mountain of despair a stone of hope. With this faith we will be able to transform the jangling discords of our nation into a beautiful symphony of brotherhood. With this faith we will be able to work together, to pray together, to struggle together, to go to jail together, to stand up for freedom together, knowing that we will be free one day.

23   This will be the day—this will be the day when all of God's children will be able to sing with new meaning, "My country 'tis of thee, sweet land of liberty, of thee I sing. Land where my fathers died, land of the pilgrim's pride, from every mountainside, let freedom ring." And if America is to be a great nation, this must become true.

24   So let freedom ring from the prodigious hilltops of New Hampshire. Let freedom ring from the mighty mountains of New York. Let freedom ring from the heightening Alleghenies of Pennsylvania!

25   Let freedom ring from the snowcapped Rockies of Colorado! Let freedom ring from the curvaceous slopes of California!

26   But not only that. Let freedom ring from Stone Mountain of Georgia!

27   Let freedom ring from Lookout Mountain of Tennessee!

28 Let freedom ring from every hill and molehill of Mississippi. From every mountainside, let freedom ring.

29 And when this happens, when we allow freedom ring—when we let it ring from every village and every hamlet, from every state and every city—we will be able to speed up that day when all of God's children, black men and white men, Jews and Gentiles, Protestants and Catholics, will be able to join hands and sing in the words of the old Negro spiritual, "Free at last! Free at last! Thank God almighty, we are free at last!"

NOTHING TO SNEEZE AT

Jeffrey Moran

Did you know that the ancient Greeks and Romans considered sneezing a favorable sign from the gods? That the custom of saying "Bless you" after a person sneezes began as a response to the bubonic plague during the Middle Ages? That scientists in India are investigating ways to artificially induce healthy sneezes? That stifling a sneeze can cause nosebleeds, popped blood vessels, even blindness?

These are just a few of the interesting facts presented in the following informative speech. As you read the speech, study how the speaker blends historical and scientific materials to produce an entertaining, yet highly instructive, look at sneezing. Also study how the speaker applies the principles of effective informative speaking discussed in Chapter 13.

This speech was delivered in a public speaking class at the University of Wisconsin. Printed here with permission of Jeffrey Moran, it is also available on the videotape of sample speeches that accompanies this edition of *The Art of Public Speaking*.

1 You feel it welling up inside you, this delicate tingling, as if your every nerve were firing at once. You want to grope for the newspaper, your homework—anything—but you no longer control your body.

2 These seconds of helpless anticipation seem like an eternity, but then the spell is broken. You crash forward, your muscles contracting like a fist, and you can't even see that people are running away from you because something has forced your eyes shut.

3 And then it's over. You relax. Your head is clear, your body under control.

4 I'm talking, of course, about sneezing. I come from a long line of sneezers. My father sneezed, and his father and his father's father before him were all men for whom a blast from the nose was every bit as bracing as a plunge into the snow following a sauna.

5 This involuntary reflex known as the sneeze is not one of the burning mysteries of our time, but I'd like to tell you about some superstitions that

have sprung up around sneezing and also let you know what's actually happening when you sneeze. Finally, in the interests of social harmony, I'll tell you how to sneeze safely and politely.

6   Sneezing is old. Citizens of the Roman Empire sneezed, but they were only following the tradition of the ancient Greeks, among them Aristotle, who considered the sneeze a favorable omen.

7   A sneeze worked wonders for Xenophon, the Greek historian and general. According to the *Concise Dictionary of Ancient History*, in 400 B.C. Xenophon, while still a mere foot-soldier, marched with the Greek army deep into hostile Persia, where the enemy slew all the Greek leaders and threatened to do the same to the confused troops when nightfall postponed the slaughter.

8   The desperate Greeks spent the night debating who should lead them in battle the next day. Xenophon rose to give a dramatic oration exhorting the men to follow him to liberty or to death. He spoke for an hour in the flickering firelight until a soldier to his right seconded his conclusion with a sneeze. Thinking this sneeze a favorable sign from the gods, the Greeks made Xenophon general, and when the sun rose the next morning, they marched to safety 10,000 strong behind their new leader.

9   Sneezing is seldom this dramatic, but many cultures echo the Greeks in their praise of the nose's most conspicuous function. Indeed, the *Encyclopedia of Occult Sciences, Superstitions, and Folklore* devotes eleven tightly spaced, oversized pages to the subject. For example, a Zulu who has just sneezed proclaims, "I am now blessed; the ancestral spirit is with me. It has come to me. Let me salute it, for it is he who causes me to sneeze."

10   Sneezing in India provokes a shorter, but no less salutary, response. If you were walking down the dusty streets of Karim Nagar, for instance, and you sneezed, bystanders would shout, "Live!" and you, as a polite tourist, must reply, "Live with you!" Most Indians consider sneezing healthy, if not supernatural; it is the inability to sneeze that is cause for alarm. *Science* magazine reports Indian scientists have labeled this malady "asneezia" and are currently researching ways to artificially induce the healthy sneeze.

11   In the West, despite the cheerful, almost compulsive blessing we give anyone experiencing spontaneous nasal expulsion, the sneeze has long been regarded with suspicion. Some people, my grandmother among them, believe we say "Bless you" because the heart skips a beat when you sneeze. It's true your eyes must close when you sneeze, but the heartbeat remains steady. I used to think we say "Bless you" because of the superstition that when you sneeze the soul exits through your nostrils. If no one blesses you, evil beings with a penchant for nasal drip will snatch your spiritual essence. Natives of Motlan and Mota in the South Pacific believe this, but our European blessing has a grimmer origin.

12   The Black Death of 590 A.D. left one half of Europe's population dead. The bubonic plague responsible for this holocaust didn't kill its victims without warning. Instead, it signified its presence by rosy rashes, swelling, and, as any medical student can tell you, telltale fits of sneezing. Since death so frequently followed sneezing, people began to say, "Bless you"—a final blessing.

13   However differently a sneeze is reacted to throughout the world, its cause is generally the same: nasal irritation. Pollens from grass, trees, house dust, and a dozen other sources are basically harmless, but when they irritate the nose your body responds as if they were rampaging predators. In a case of mistaken identity and overkill, you inhale sharply and exhale with explosive force—up to 104 miles per hour.

14   Pollen is not the only culprit, though. The nose mistakes strong odors, sudden chills, and even bright lights for more dangerous parasites, and it tries to defend itself by banishing the intruders with a sneeze.

15   In addition to its physical causes, the *New York Times* reports a sneeze can also be brought on by psychological and emotional factors. If a man lunged at you with a knife, fear might make you sneeze. Once he left, your anguish and frustration over losing your valuables could cause you to sneeze again. If you decide to chase the criminal, bring along some tissues—the excitement could give you another sneezing fit.

16   In each of these cases, sneezing is assisting the nose in reaching equilibrium. Strong emotions can cause your nasal membranes to shrink or expand, and a sneeze brings you back to normal quickly and forcefully.

17   Occasionally, someone is blessed with an overly active equilibriating mechanism. In 1966 June Clark had a fit in which she sneezed every twelve seconds for 174 days. Before she finally stopped, doctors had tried tranquilizers, narcotics, x-rays, muscle relaxants, shock treatment, and even hypnosis, which almost worked until she sneezed and broke the trance.

18   Sneezing will probably never give you the trouble it gave June Clark, but the odds are that sooner or later you'll have to sneeze in a social setting. This can be especially uncomfortable given that no one carries a handkerchief any more—at least not in my social circle. Nevertheless, when you're in a crowded room, don't try to stifle or abort your sneeze in the interests of social propriety—you don't want to stop a force going over 100 miles per hour. With the air pressure that builds up from a stifled sneeze, people have been known to get nosebleeds, pop blood vessels, or even go blind.

19   Instead, open your mouth while you sneeze so your nose doesn't take all your force. Most important, cover your nose. Jane Brody writes in the *New York Times* that "An unimpeded sneeze sends two to five thousand bacteria-filled droplets into the air." With a single sneeze, any one of us could raise this room's bacterial count for the next forty-five minutes. Understandably, every etiquette theorist from Lord Chesterfield and Amy Vanderbilt to Eleanor Roosevelt and Miss Manners advocates being a quick draw with a handkerchief. Failing this, hold the hankie over your nose after the sneeze—it shows good faith.

20   Whatever the cause and whichever country you're sneezing in, with practice and luck you'll be able to cover your sneeze quickly and effectively. Then you can sit back and relax, waiting for someone to bless you, wish you *gesundheit*, or, if you're in the right place at the right time, appoint you to high military command.

DRINKING AND BOATING:
A DEADLY COMBINATION

Sheila Mir

"There is nothing—absolutely nothing—half so much worth doing as simply messing about in boats." So wrote Scottish author Kenneth Grahame in his classic children's book, *The Wind In the Willows*. Unfortunately, boating accidents have become the second leading cause of transportation-related deaths in the United States. In the following speech, Sheila Mir, a student at the University of Wisconsin, argues that drinking and boating pose a serious problem that can no longer be ignored. The solution, Sheila argues, lies in a combination of mandatory boat safety education and tougher laws to curb drinking and boating.

Because this speech deals with a question of policy, be sure to assess how the speaker defines the problem and what she offers as a solution. How well does she relate the topic to her listeners? Do you find her evidence clear and compelling? What does she do to build her credibility? Does she appeal to the emotions of her audience? What could she have done to make the speech more effective?

This speech was presented in an introductory public speaking class at the University of Wisconsin—Madison. It is printed here with the permission of Sheila Mir.

1   The proud owner of a splashy new sixteen-foot speedboat cruised up to a waterfront nightclub on Lake Pontchartrain in Louisiana for a drink, where he met a couple and invited them for a spin around the lake. The passengers will never forget the ride; the driver will never remember. He died when his boat smashed into the seawall. Investigators of the accident concluded that alcohol was the cause.

2   Drinking and boating is a deadly combination—a deadly combination that may affect you. Last summer I spent many afternoons on the lakes and beaches here in Madison, and I couldn't believe the number of drunk boat drivers I saw. As I researched this speech, I became more and more convinced that it is inconsistent for our society to be so obsessed with drinking and driving in automobiles and yet so willing to view boating and drinking as "recreational."

3   Today I would like to discuss this issue with you. First, I will show you that drinking and boating is a serious problem. Second, I'll explore the causes of this problem. And third, I will propose a solution. Let's start with the problem.

4   Recreational boating and alcohol-related accidents is a larger and more serious problem than we realize. The kind of tragedy I told you about in my introduction is repeated time and again each year in every part of the country. Just last summer, five people were killed in a collision between two speedboats on Fox Lake in Illinois. Alcohol was the cause. In another state, two men and a woman were heading home at 9 P.M. after consuming a considerable amount of beer. They didn't have the lights of their small boat turned on, and they

collided with a much larger, lighted boat. The two men were killed instantly and the woman's body was found floating in the water the next day. Alcohol, again, was the cause.

5   Statistics show that these are not atypical examples. The National Safety Council reports that over 1,200 Americans died while pleasure boating last year. According to the United States Department of Transportation, that ranks boating second only to car crashes among transportation fatalities. Here in Wisconsin, a study by the State Center for Health Statistics found that there were 813 boating accidents between 1981 and 1985. These accidents killed 133 people, or an average of 27 per year. The United States Coast Guard estimates that half of the boating accidents in the U.S. are alcohol-related, while the National Transportation Safety Board concludes that alcohol may be a factor in 80 percent of boating fatalities.

6   Why is this such a problem? Why do we have so many alcohol-related boating accidents? The two main causes are a lack of education and inconsistency in the laws.

7   By a lack of education I refer to the fact that people don't understand that alcohol affects their bodies faster when they drink on water than when they drink at home or in a bar. The reason for this is a phenomenon known as "boater's hypnosis." According to a report by the National Transportation Safety Board, boater's hypnosis develops after four hours or more, when you are exposed to sun, wind, glare, noise, and vibration while on the water. It significantly slows your reactions—much as alcohol does. When you add alcohol, it greatly intensifies the effect of boater's hypnosis.

8   According to William Gossard, a national safety board official in Washington, D.C., car drivers are considered legally drunk with a blood-alcohol concentration of .10 percent or greater. But because of boater's hypnosis, on water a level as low as .035 percent can affect a person's ability to operate a boat. In other words, if you feel yourself losing control after drinking three cans of beer on land, you will feel yourself losing control after drinking one can of beer on water.

9   In addition to a lack of education about boater's hypnosis, the problem of drinking and boating is caused by two glaring legal inconsistencies. The first has to do with the blood-alcohol concentration level. In Wisconsin, as in most states, you are not supposed to operate a motorboat with a blood-alcohol concentration of .10 percent or more. This is the same blood-alcohol concentration used to determine drunkenness while driving a car. So the law says, in essence, that you are capable of driving a boat safely until you have reached a blood-alcohol concentration of .10 percent. Yet as I stated earlier, due to boater's hypnosis, your ability to operate a boat can be impaired at a level as low as .035 percent. In reality, a boater may be drunk long before the police can pronounce him or her as legally drunk.

10   The second inconsistency in the laws is that it is legal to drink while driving a boat. We all know it is illegal to drink while driving a car. Why should it be legal to drink while driving a boat—especially since alcohol affects the body faster on water than on land? Just because lakes and rivers don't contain

stop signs, speed limits, and center lines, it should not be legal to drink and drive on the water. After all, as *Newsweek* explains, some power boats have top speeds of up to 90 miles per hour and, unlike cars, no boat has brakes.

11   As you can see, the combination of booze and boats is a serious problem—serious because there is a lack of education about boater's hypnosis and because there are inconsistencies in our laws about drinking and boating. So what can we do? How can we solve the problem?

12   First, there should be mandatory boat safety education. In Wisconsin, children between the ages of ten and twelve are required to take a boat safety class if they want to operate a boat. If someone is convicted of driving drunk on the water, they too must take a boat safety class. But according to former state conservation warden Robert Arends, these are the only people who have to take a boat safety class. In Arends' view, however, all boaters should have to take a safety class. And I agree. It would make boaters aware of safety procedures and hazards, and it would give special attention to such topics as boater's hypnosis and the dangers of drinking while on the water.

13   Second, we need some changes in our laws. To begin with, since alcohol affects the body faster on water than on land, the blood-alcohol concentration allowed for boaters should be lowered. No one should be allowed to operate a motorboat with a blood-alcohol concentration of greater than .035 percent. In addition, it should be illegal to drink while driving a boat just as it is illegal to drink while driving a car. According to Captain Frank Wood of the Maryland Department of Water Safety, this would go a long way toward reducing the problem of drunken boat drivers.

14   Educating everyone and changing the laws will help solve this serious problem. But one factor is missing from our solution. That factor is you! You can make a difference in safer boating here in Wisconsin. You can write to either State Senator Fred Risser or State Assemblyman Spencer Black at the State Capitol, as I have. Let them know you want the laws changed so we can have safer waters here in Wisconsin. Then go one step further. If you are involved in any type of water sports, take a boat safety class. If you drive a motorboat, please don't drink—for your safety as well as for the safety of others.

15   According to State Senator Lynn Adelman, the drunken boater is the "single biggest problem in boating safety today. Even when he does not kill or maim, the drunken boater detracts from everyone else's enjoyment of public waters." As I've tried to show you today, drinking and boating is a deadly combination from Louisiana to Wisconsin and everywhere in between.

16   You are now aware of this problem, of its causes, and of a solution. Show that you are concerned, not only by writing to the State Capitol but also in your actions. And this summer, when the sun is just a little too hot and you feel like cooling off in the lake for a while, remember to be careful. Because just when you thought it was safe to go back in the water, it may not be!

INDEX

Abstract words, 216–217, 290–292
Acceptance, speeches of, 353
Accuracy, in language, 211–213
Action, appeal to, in conclusion of speech, 184, 313–317
After-dinner speeches, 356–359
Alinsky, Saul, 72
Alliteration, 223, 225
Analogy, 332–333
Anecdotes. *See* Examples, extended
Anthony, Susan B., 4
Antithesis, 223
Appearance (image) of speaker, 32, 34, 243
Aristotle, 320
Aronson, Eliot, 123
Articulation, 241
ASI (*American Statistics Index*), 108
Atlases and gazetteers, 104–105
Attention-getting devices, 169–174, 313–317. *See also* Audience, attentiveness of
Audience
    adaptation to, 17, 53, 57–58, 66–87, 284–293, 303, 317–319, 323–326, 334–337, 350
    affected by physical setting, 77
    age of, 73
    attentiveness of, 19, 71–72, 78, 169–174, 287–289, 313–317. *See also* Attention-getting devices
    classmates as, 70–71
    cultural background of, 75–76
    demographic analysis of, 72–76
    disposition of, 78–81, 303
        toward occasion, 80
        toward topic, 78–79
        toward speaker, 79–80
    economic class of, 76
    educational level of, 76
    ethnicity of, 75–76

group membership of, 76
impact of physical setting on, 77
interviewing the, 81
occupations of, 76
overestimating, 284–287
psychology of, 71–72
questionnaires for, 81–85
racial background of, 75–76
relating subject to, 17, 53, 57–58, 68–71, 85–86, 284–293, 303, 317–319, 323–326, 334–337, 350
religious background of, 74–75
sex (gender) of, 73–74
size of, 76–77
target, 317–319
Audience-centeredness, 17, 68–70

Balfour, Lord, 348
Bar graph, 261–262
Beliefs, personal, as speech topics, 48–49
Bibliography, 109–110, 193
Biographical aids, 103–104
Biography Index, 104
Birdwhistell, Ray, 243
Blackman, Veda, 122–123
Bodily action, 244
    as visual aid, 263–264
Body of speech
    connectives used in, 158–162
    and main points, 147–157, 274–284, 304–317
    in outline, labeling, 191
    and supporting materials, 118–140, 157–158, 323–326
Brainstorming, 49–51, 379
Breathing, deep, as antidote to nervousness, 12
Bush, George, 225

Card catalogue, 100–101
Campbell, George, 334
Carson, Johnny, 232
Central idea
    in conclusion of speech, 182–184

in introduction of speech, 177
phrasing of, 58–62
in preparation outline, 190–191
Channel, speech communication process and, 16–17
Charts, as visual aids, 262
Cher, 243
Churchill, Winston, 4, 215, 221–222, 236, 354–355
Clarity, in language, 213–218
Clutter, 217–218
Commemorative speeches, 354–356
Common ground, establishing, 322–323
Communication, nonverbal, 242–246
Communication process, speech, 15–20
Comparison and contrast, 291
Computer-assisted research, 106–108
Concentration, listening and, 29–30, 33–34
Concepts as speech topics, 281–284
Conclusion of speech, 179–185
    delivery in, 180–182
    functions of, 180–184
    in outline, labeling, 191
    sample, 185
    tips for preparing, 185
Concrete words, 216–217, 219
Confidence, development of, 9–13
Connectives
    in body of speech, 158–163
    internal previews, 159–160
    internal summaries, 160–161
    signposts, 161–162
    transitions, 160
Connotative meaning, 210–211
Conrad, Joseph, 290
Conversation, compared with public speaking
    differences, 7–9
    similarities, 5–7

ABOUT THE AUTHOR

Stephen Lucas teaches public speaking, rhetorical criticism, and American public address in the Department of Communication Arts at the University of Wisconsin–Madison. He received his bachelor's degree from the University of California, Santa Barbara, and his master's and doctorate degrees from Penn State University.

Professor Lucas has been recognized for his work as both a scholar and a teacher. His previous book, *Portents of Rebellion: Rhetoric and Revolution in Philadelphia, 1765–1776,* won the Speech Communication Association's Golden Anniversary Award in 1977 and was nominated for a Pulitzer Prize. In 1988, he received the Chancellor's Award for Excellence in Teaching at the University of Wisconsin–Madison.